*A History of False Hope*

# A HISTORY
# OF FALSE HOPE

*Investigative Commissions in Palestine*

Lori Allen

STANFORD UNIVERSITY PRESS
Stanford, California

STANFORD UNIVERSITY PRESS
Stanford, California

Printed in the United States of America on acid-free, archival-quality paper

Library of Congress Control Number: 2020944202

Cover design: Kevin Barrett Kane

Cover image: February 1956 map of UN Partition Plan for Palestine,
adopted November 29, 1947, with boundary of previous UNSCOP
partition plan added.

Typeset by Newgen in 10.25/15 Adobe Caslon Pro

*For Yezid*

What's the use
of something
as unstable
and diffuse as hope—
the almost-twin
of making-do,
the isotope
of going on:
what isn't in
the envelope
just before
it isn't:
the always tabled
righting of the present.
      Kay Ryan, "Hope"

# Contents

# Acknowledgments

This book is the product of a tremendous amount of collective effort, jointly considered ideas, and unflagging support from many. I am grateful to my various interlocutors who I met in Palestine and elsewhere, who took the time to talk to me about their experiences with commissions and other things. My friends in ʿAida and al-ʿAzza Refugee Camps, the al-ʿAzza family, and many others, especially in the West Bank, remain an inspiration.

Ajantha Subramanian's whip-smart readings of multiple iterations of this book's parts have been invaluable. Ajantha and Vince Brown remain a steady source of all that is good in a friendship, and that makes talking about books and titles fun. Amahl Bishara, Lara Deeb, and Jessica Winegar remain my longtime, draft-reading anthropological interlocutors, whose suggestions have made this work better. Along with Esra Ozyurek, a recent and reassuring pair of eyes co-opted into the collective writing process that this book has been, they have gently reminded me of what anthropology can be good for, and have inspired me by being such good anthropologists. For the ongoing support of this and all my projects, I'd especially like to thank Toby Kelly and Ilana Feldman, who consistently go above and beyond, for reading and considering this book from title to endnotes. I am also very grateful to Darryl Li, who, with his unique combination of legal knowledge and anthropological insight, pointed his laser-beam brain at the manuscript, sympathetically illuminating its flaws and tracing paths for improvement.

Seth Anziska's eager reading and wholehearted positive responses to my early chapters gave me the assurances I needed to stretch my toes across disciplinary boundaries, for which I am sincerely grateful. Helpful comments from other historians offering their expert reviews, suggestions, and challenges came from Charles Anderson, Andrew Arsan, Joel Beinin, Ellen Fleischman, Awad Halabi, Jens Hennssen, Ussama Makdisi, Mezna Qato, and Natasha Wheatley. I am appreciatively indebted.

Enthusiastic responses from Ayşe Parla gave me some much-needed inspiration at just the right time. Critical defense of my historical informants from Paru Raman and Jean Comaroff helpfully pushed me to crystallize my points. Many thanks to Alia Mossallam, whose appreciation of the literary and reading suggestion helped unstick my conclusion. Also thanks to Omar Dajani and Tor Krever for their patient readings and suggestions. I'm so lucky to know so many smart and generous people.

For conversations, citations, suggestions, inspirations, music, and drink, I thank new friends made at the Institute for Advanced Study—especially Ayşe Parla, Fadi Bardawil, Karen Engle, Vanja Hamzić, Andrew Dilts, Reuben Jonathan Miller, and Peter Redfield—whose insights and creativity scooted this project along in important ways. For the opportunity to have a magical year in the Princeton woods, I am eternally grateful to Didier Fassin, Bernard Harcourt, and Joan Scott. I count myself so fortunate for having had the chance to get to know them and learn from them. Also at the IAS I extend my sincerest thanks for sorting all that needed sorting to Linda Cooper, Laura McCune, and Donne Petito. Also in Princeton, providing encouragement, sustenance, and fun with moving teeth, thanks are due to Lara Harb, Fulvio Domini, and Dalia Domini, whose happy friendship I value to the moon and back. For their sustaining friendship and writing retreat connections, my warmest thanks to Dimitris Livanios, Anna Mastrogianni, George Mehrabian, and Natasa Terlexi. Knowing that Jessica Clark, Dan Cook, Helen Pope, and Sarah Zimmerman are always only a call away keeps me going.

For the kind attention, challenging questions, and PowerPoint assistance from my Red Square/Stokey audience of Seth Anziska, Tareq Baconi, Neve Gordon, and Catherine Rottenberg, I extend my warmest thanks. It has been a treat to have such smart and fun neighbors who also cook so well. Thanks are also due to Steve, Howard, Paul, Michael, Ikenna, and the whole team at Red Square for all their organizational support and expertise.

For her many reference suggestions, conversational walks, and ongoing solidarity, my thanks to Haneen Naamneh. Hanan Elmasu, Adam Hanieh, and Rafeef Ziadeh also offered morale-boosting sustenance throughout this project. I am thankful to them and to Cathy Cook for all the people and ideas they have introduced me to that enriched this project and my life enormously. Conversations, teas, and documents that Cecil and Zelfa Hourani and Walid Khalidi shared with me are much appreciated.

To all my colleagues in the Department of Anthropology at SOAS, I am grateful for their solidarity and their patience with my various stints away working on this epic project. I extend to all of them my thanks for listening to and reading various bits of this book. Special thanks to Richard Fardon, David Mosse, and Ed Simpson for their comments on a very long chapter draft.

Feedback from audiences and participants at various universities have helped me think harder about my ideas and have encouraged me to express them with greater nuance. I am indebted to the anthropologists, historians, legal scholars, and others who engaged with this work at Cambridge University, Johns Hopkins University, the Hagop Kevorkian Center for Near Eastern Studies at New York University, the Program in Near Eastern Studies at Princeton University, Queen Mary University Department of Law, the American Studies Institute at Seoul National University, Stanford University, University College London, UCLA Center for Near Eastern Studies, University of Illinois-Chicago, Oslo University Centre for Islamic and Middle East Studies, Scripps College, Harvard University, and Karim Makdisi and the Issam Fares Institute at the American University of Beirut. I would particularly like to thank Aslı Bâli at UCLA for her challenging questions and inviting me to hear them in such a beautiful location.

This book would never have been completed without the tremendous work of several research assistants. Doaa Nakhala has been there every step of the way. I declare without exaggeration that her abilities as a researcher, her determination, her organization, and her Arabic skills made much of what's in this book possible. Also indispensible was the research and assistance of Jordan Allen, Taroob Boulos, Kyle Craig, James Eastwood, Vittoria

Federici, Matt De Maio, Fuad Musallam, Daniela Rodriguez, Yasmine Saab, and Amy Thompson. Thank you.

The project was my first foray into archival research, and throughout it I was reminded again of how generous and kind librarians tend to be as a genus and what remarkable institutions libraries are, as public spaces open for searching and thinking, where people help you and take your puzzles on as their own. Special thanks go to the indefatigable librarians at the Institute for Advanced Study, especially Kirstie Venanzi, Karen Downing, Marcia Tucker, and Cecilia Kornish. At the UN library in New York, Susan Kurtas and her colleagues were superstars. Also thanks are due to the folks at the British Library, St. Antony's Middle East Centre Library, and staff at the many other libraries housing archives and other materials across the United States, Palestine, and Israel. I hope these librarians enjoyed some of the same glee I did with every document they helped me find.

I am very grateful for the generous financial support that made it possible for me to access all these libraries, pay these research assistants, and have time to write this book. Fellowships and grants from the Arts and Humanities Research Council (RG65583), the British Academy (MD150027), CRASSH and the Faculty of Asian and Middle Eastern Studies at Cambridge University, the Institute for Advanced Study in Princeton, Issam Fares Institute for Public Policy and International Affairs at the American University of Beirut, the Harvard Academy for International and Area Studies, the Leverhulme Trust (RF-2017-706), the Newton Trust, SOAS University of London, and Thriplow Charitable Trust provided crucial resources. None of these institutions or interlocutors is responsible for the insufficiencies and mistakes of this monograph.

I am so glad I've had another chance to work with people at Stanford University Press, especially Kate Wahl, whose famed efficiency and professionalism have made this process so smooth and enjoyable. Thanks also to Jessica Ling for her careful editorial attention.

I am also grateful for my family, for their support that comes in so many ways. Thanks to Jeff, Jari, Dana, Tom, Vicki, Michele, Terry, Jim, Tim, Janice, Abby, Joey, Lisa, Ben, Delaney, Scott, Drew, Mercedes, Jessica, Chris, Elijah, Jordan, Cooper, Parker, Christina, Nick, and Henry. I'm thankful, too, for the memory of Dave Benyo, someone who helped me think harder about what

I'm doing and why when he asked if I was getting an advance for this book. And for the memory of my father, Joe Allen, who reminded me what "PhD" stands for. The wisdom of some of his insights has become clearer with time. I am especially grateful to my mom, Betty Allen, for her gentle and unpressured interest in the progress of this book and her forever full-hearted support of me in general.

For welcoming me into her extended clan, and for the inspiration that her life offers, I extend my warm appreciation to Rosemary Sayigh. And the same to the rest of the family for their hospitality, friendship, and amazing food.

And finally, I wish to express how happy and thankful I am to have had Yezid Sayigh at my side throughout this long, long project. We've had innumerable conversations about every aspect of this book, and he's rooted for me and for it from the beginning, reminding me to stay true to my own ideas and not worry too much about the rest. I remain grateful for his smart readings, his last-minute edits, his patience, his love, and all the fun he brings to every day of our joint escapade.

# Abbreviations

| | |
|---|---|
| AACI | Anglo-American Committee of Inquiry |
| AHC | Arab Higher Committee |
| CEIRP | United Nations Committee on the Exercise of the Inalienable Rights of the Palestinian People |
| IAAA | Institute of Arab American Affairs |
| ICC | International Criminal Court |
| NAM | Non-Aligned Movement |
| NSU | Negotiations Support Unit |
| PA | Palestinian Authority |
| PLO | Palestinian Liberation Organization |
| UNCCP | United Nations Conciliation Commission for Palestine |
| UNGA | United Nations General Assembly |
| UNHRC | United Nations Human Rights Council |
| UNRWA | United Nations Relief and Works Agency for Palestine Refugees in the Near East |
| UNSC | United Nations Security Council |
| UNSCIIP | United Nations Special Committee to Investigate Israeli Practices Affecting the Human Rights of the Population of the Occupied Territories |
| UNSCOP | United Nations Special Committee on Palestine |

# Major Commissions on Palestine

| | |
|---|---|
| 1919 | King-Crane Commission |
| 1920 | Palin Commission |
| 1921 | Haycraft Commission of Enquiry |
| 1926 | Bertram-Young Commission |
| 1929–30 | Shaw Commission |
| 1930 | Hope-Simpson Commission |
| 1936 | Peel Commission |
| 1938 | Woodhead Commission |
| 1945–46 | Anglo-American Committee of Inquiry |
| 1947 | UN Special Committee on Palestine (UNSCOP) |
| 1968–present | United Nations Special Committee to Investigate Israeli Practices Affecting the Israeli Military Occupation of Human Rights of the Population of the Occupied Territories (UNSCIIP) |
| 1982 | MacBride Commission |
| 2000–01 | United Nations High Commission for Human Rights Inquiry Commission for the Palestinian Territories |
| 2001 | Sharm el-Sheik Fact-Finding Committee |
| 2002 | UN Fact-Finding Team on Jenin Refugee Camp Massacre |
| 2008 | High-Level Fact-Finding Mission to Beit Hanoun |

*A History of False Hope*

# International Law as a Way of Being

IN MAY 2018, the United Nations Human Rights Council (UNHRC) voted to send an "independent, international commission of inquiry" to investigate violent events in the Gaza Strip that occurred around the Palestinians' Great March of Return. To mark the seventieth anniversary of the Palestinian "Nakba," or "catastrophe," thousands of Palestinians had been demonstrating around the border between the Gaza Strip and Israel, demanding the right of return to their homes in historic Palestine, from which they had been expelled when Israel was established in 1948. Israeli forces shot and killed sixty protestors and injured thousands in the days before the UNHRC voted to establish the inquiry.[1]

The moral-juridical premise of that 2018 fact-finding commission was articulated by the High Commissioner for Human Rights, Prince Zeid Ra'ad Zeid al-Hussein of Jordan. The commission was established, he said, in "the hope [that] the truth regarding these matters will lead to justice," and that "those responsible for violations must in the end be held accountable."[2] Like most other recent investigative forays in Palestine, the relationship between facts, the truth about a set of events, accountability, justice, and political change was asserted, but the lines connecting them were left vague. The implicit theory of change embedded in fact-finding activities like this UN inquiry rests on a humanitarian ethos that posits a direct connection between revelation and action, justice and accountability. The actual activities

of investigative commissions, however, reveal the more circuitous meander-
ings of morality and political action as they are channeled through the liberal
legal logic of global governance.

The case of Palestine is a particularly clarifying lens onto these dynamics. Through a historical anthropology and ethnographic study, this book
analyzes Palestinians' engagement with commissions of inquiry that have
investigated Palestine over the past one hundred years. It demonstrates how
commissions have shaped Palestinian politics and the conflict with Zionism and Israel in many ways, foremost among which has been through their
activation of international law as a primary medium and ideology of politics.

Tens of commissions have visited Palestine over the past century. Many
were formed during periods of crisis to address an increase in violence between Palestinians and Zionists (and then Israelis after 1948). Palestine,
which was a part of the Ottoman Empire until its demise after World War I,
had become the focus of Jewish nationalists seeking to make the Holy Land
their political home. With colonialist methods and ideologies, Jews from
Europe began to settle in Palestine, just as a distinctly Palestinian national
identity was also crystallizing.[3] The question of who deserved sovereignty
over the land produced disputes carried out in every form—from diplomacy
and lobbying to civil disobedience and armed attacks. Under the auspices of
the League of Nations, the British gained control over Palestine and formalized their commitment to making it a Jewish national home even while the
league's charter committed Britain and other mandatory powers to leading
their charges into self-rule. Arab frustration at this situation of declining
self-representation and autonomy, as well as worry about the Zionists' de-
signs on their country, led to periodic violent interchange among the Arabs,
Zionists, and British. Most of these periods of intensified conflict resulted in
Great Britain sending investigative commissions.

The British were famous for their use of commissions across their empire,
but they receded from the scene when Israel became an independent state
that covered most of historic Palestine in 1948.[4] At that point, the Americans
and especially the United Nations became the most active dispatchers of
investigations. The stated aim of these missions usually has been to gather
facts, examine them in light of international law, and seek a path to peace.
Based on voluntary and public consultation, and drawing on legal language

and approximating legal standards of evidence, commissions function in the realm of dialogue and civility, operating on the premise that international law can be a means to resolving the conflict. Palestinian participants have faithfully adopted these parameters and tried to explain why they deserve an independent nation-state, how their case is supported by international law, and why their deprivation of the right to sovereignty is among the root causes of the violence.

Usually consisting of academics, lawyers, military, and other experts, investigative commissions are favored by governments the world over as a mechanism for looking like they're producing policy on the firm basis of fact. Just as often, the reports that commissions issue—sometimes bureaucratic and boring, often full of legalese and reiterations of existing policy dressed up as innovation—become a means of expressing concern while kicking a touchy political issue into the long grass. A typical, and typically unsuccessful, diplomatic device of conflict resolution and policy production, commissions investigating the problem of Palestine have never formulated the political decisions that were put into practice, never led to the implementation of international law, and certainly never come close to resolving the conflict. And yet they have been repeatedly set up and sent—by Britain, the United States, the United Nations, and other state coalitions—to investigate and make recommendations. Despite their apparent lack of political efficacy, and despite being labeled by critics as a political smoke screen, investigative commissions have been for decades a consistent feature of international engagement with Palestine.

Pushing beyond the easy recognition of the cynical political use of commissions, this book asks questions about their broader social and ideological effects as they spread liberalism's ideals through international law's institutions.

Commissions establish a liberal communicative space that explicitly prioritizes what Habermas calls "communicative rationality," which Palestinians have also prioritized in their interactions with investigators.[5] The impact of commissions has not come from their reasonably deliberated recommendations, however. More significant has been the way that commissions have shaped the form, content, and tenor of political discourse about Palestine, determining the nature of authorized conversation between Palestinians and

Western powers. Although they establish legal frameworks of interaction, commissions stage affective performances, providing a venue from which to make judgments about Palestinian political worthiness. They shield the actually subjective and affectively charged nature of those judgments with the claimed objectivity of international legal referents.

## International Law as Tradition

Briefly stated, my argument is that international investigative commissions are a mechanism by which an increasing range of Palestinians have become entangled with international law and its liberal sensibilities. The legal approach has become part of a Palestinian political tradition—and all that "tradition" implies: of habit, depth of belief, or even blind faith. Talal Asad's deployment of the concept of tradition "to address . . . the use of inherited language and . . . the acquisition of embodied abilities by repetition" is useful for thinking about law in Palestinian politics, for the attention it draws to law "as a mode of being."[6] In particular, it is international humanitarian and human rights law—not its doctrine or rules, but its habitus—that has become part of the Palestinian political "mode of being."

This embroilment in international law on the part of everyone from political representatives, technocrats, and lawyers to NGO activists, fishermen, and farmers has narrowed political vision and action for Palestine. It has also provided "the international community" with a means to justify and enable practical refusal of Palestinian claims to independence. International law, as uniquely activated through investigative commissions, is an arena in which liberalism has functioned as an ideology of rule—in different ways, both for the rulers and the ruled. In this study, "international law" does not solely refer to the international legal canon, its rules and regulations or doctrine. Rather, it denotes a discourse and institutional network purporting to embody the international legal system's ideals. Human rights law and particularly the laws of war and occupation are the most significant legal elements, but this study's specific focus is on the social dynamics and political contexts shaped by this globally resonant set of norms and agreements.

Fundamentally, international law is "a social (and especially interpretative) process" that bears within it a set of moral precepts and visions of political order.[7] The protection of civilians during war, the regulation of military occupation, and physical security are among the themes covered in the laws of war and in human rights law that are most relevant for this study. They bespeak certain beliefs about the values by which societies should be organized, the right way for governments to treat people, and the basic conditions of life that humans deserve even during the mayhem of war and existence under foreign military rule. The ways that political opponents argue about these values are also arguments about the meaning of social life and humanity.

Many believe these principles and the international legal system they justify to be necessarily benevolent, an "uncontested self-evident good."[8] It is only through considering the historical details of how this system has functioned in people's lives that we may reconsider this taken-for-granted beneficence. We can also identify the moments in which this self-evident doxa—that which is taken for granted—is challenged by heterodox notions and practices—such as transnational solidarity or grassroots violence, for example. We can then see anew and pose questions of the mechanisms that are activated to reimpose the orthodoxy of international humanitarian law.[9] International legal ideals and actors are closely linked to (but are not totally subsumed by) the ideology of liberal internationalism and the rule of law, which legal scholars promote as *the* means to foster civilizational order.[10] Through their activation of international law, commissions have propagated liberal legalism as a useable norm of political practice among Palestinians and others seeking a means to end the conflict. Liberal legalism has at its core the idea that law is a distinct sphere of action that runs on the basis of objective rules, which can yield predictable and fair results when applied in a juridical process. Although commissions are not formally legal proceedings, they are legalistic and take liberal legalism as a fundamental premise.[11] Commissions make spectacles of legalized dramas and, in so doing, publicize legally codified moral notions, but always couch these performances within a liberal legal framework.

All of this does not happen solely on a philosophical, notional, or ethical plane, of course. The physical expression of power through force is the core category and concern of these legal regulations and the arguments over them. International humanitarian and human rights law seeks to define and regulate what is the correct, acceptable deployment of violence against different categories of human. This is also why international law is significant, even if its implementation is erratic. What's in the balance for many Palestinians—whether as third-class citizens of Israel or residents of Jerusalem, as subjects of military occupation in the West Bank and Gaza Strip, or as refugees in Lebanon legally banned from working in thirty-nine professions—is finding some normative force that can influence and restrain the nonrepresentative governments that control their lives.[12]

## An Alternative History of Liberalism

*A History of False Hope* traces the life of international law in Palestine to explain how some Palestinians have found in liberalism an ideology and political methodology through which to speak to that nebulous audience, "the international community," and mobilize solidarity around their fight for independence and human rights.[13] Although liberalism and international law are not coterminous, many values that are claimed as liberalism's core stand as the justification and goal of international law. Also claiming to promote those values are commissions, which provoke a beehive of activity—discursive, material, and ideological—across a wide international geography on the part of often self-consciously globalist actors. Commissions have summoned experts and witnesses to analyze, pontificate, and represent; they have motivated organizational and lobbying activity with a carbon footprint to shatter the ozone; and they have produced reams of reports that circulate extensively through international media, yielding a cacophony of argument and debate attracting widespread attention. Around every commission new publics are drawn, as these investigations shine a spotlight on the Palestine conflict as an international problem and concern.

In charting the social worlds that have congealed around each commission, this book offers a history of Palestine that chronicles how some Palestinians have understood international law, the hopes that many have invested in it, the disappointments they have experienced, the cynicism triggered by international law's unfulfilled promises, and the renewed optimisms provoked by international legal innovations. It illuminates the ways in which legal liberalism as manifest in the workings of investigative commissions has shaped politics across a century of Palestinian history. Perhaps surprising to some, this history reveals a consistent investment in liberal principles and institutions, which runs counter to narratives of Palestinian nationalism that focus solely on armed struggle.

*A History of False Hope* is also an alternative history of liberalism and international law that places actors from the Global South in the same analytical field—and on the same liberal plane—as the Euro-Americans who typically populate histories of international law. In so doing, it presents a historical ethnography of lived liberalism that throws the limits, blind spots, and contradictions of liberal internationalism into relief. Most basically, the book provides more evidence that the humanitarian imagination and human rights system are never politically neutral. But it seeks to go beyond this obvious fact to probe a different set of puzzles regarding the hegemonic power of liberal internationalism and international law in politics. Although international law has been thoroughly criticized for its role in maintaining the dominant status of already powerful states, this study shifts the focus to ask why people nonetheless engage with international law, specifically humanitarian and human rights law. By attending to the many dimensions of international law and liberalism—ideological, political, institutional, social, affective, moral, and symbolic—the book seeks to explain how international law accrued hegemonic force and became part of Palestinian common sense.

Commissions put on display the liberal aims of international law, bringing political opponents together in a shared framework of social and intellectual interaction that is posited as a level playing field—but never is. Commissions are established with explicit and implicit terms of reference that bespeak core liberal principles: self-determination and the consent of the governed, the laws and ethical precepts of human rights and humanitarianism, citizenship and equality before the law, tolerance for minorities and religious freedom, aspirations and expectations for capitalist economic development, belief in moral and political progress, and faith in the resolution of conflict and establishment of political order through reasoned discourse. Although they are not the only forums activating international law, investigative commissions offer a particularly clarifying view of a terrain where fundamental political questions of freedom, justice, political order, and the law are debated. Although framed in different ways and prompted by different events, the stated goal of these commissions has been to resolve the conflict between Palestinians and Zionists through international law, an aim as yet unrealized (to put it mildly). Yet what is far more emblematic of the work of these commissions across a century is the continuously shifting criteria of sovereignty that they advance. As is the persistent inability of Palestinians to fulfill them. This sustained pattern of promise, evaluation, and denial begs a question about international legal liberalism: is its real purpose the maintenance of Palestinian unfreedom?

## The Historical Narrative and its Characters

Palestinian politics as strained through the filter of international law is the primary focus of this study, but imperialists, colonialists, self-proclaimed freedom fighters, and liberal do-gooders of all stripes and from all over are part of the picture, too. Some of the characters who appear in these pages include Akram Zu'aytir and 'Izzat Darwaza, Palestinian nationalist firebrands and memoirists; William Yale, an employee of the Standard Oil Company and the embodiment of Orientalist hubris; Sir John Singleton, an irritable Tory High Court judge; Syrian rebel Fawzi Qawuqji; Joe Hutcheson, a Bible-quoting Texas judge; Angie Brooks, the Liberian president of the twenty-fourth session of the UN General Assembly; an unnamed housewife who gave anonymous testimony about being deported from the West Bank; George Mitchell, a US senator; Omar Dajani, a Palestinian-American legal scholar; Christine Chinkin, a British legal scholar; Hina Jilani, a human rights activist and an advocate of the Supreme Court of Pakistan; Mousa al-Silawi, an elderly Palestinian man who lived through Israel's bombardment of the al-Maqadma Mosque in Gaza; and Richard Goldstone, a former South African Constitutional Court judge and former chief prosecutor of the UN International Criminal Tribunal for Rwanda and the former Yugoslavia. In tracking the wide and diverse range of people who have represented Palestine before the commissions, this study shows how international law has saturated Palestinian political society throughout its modern history. Although liberal elites are some of the main characters populating these pages, commissions have attracted a diversity of Palestinians into their dramas.

I begin the story in the period after World War I, when a doctrine of liberal internationalism had consolidated and "was embraced by the architects of a new world order."[14] Liberal internationalism is an ideological and institutional complex propounding liberal values as the way to deal with "the central conundrums of international politics, including the nature and causes of war, the role and character of ethics and law, and the preconditions necessary for securing peace."[15] That the liberal international order would mean dispossession and disorder for many soon became clear to those living in what we now call the Global South.

As transformations in the institutions of liberal internationalism have multiplied, eventually fusing into a self-defining regime of "global governance" in the 1990s, the array of methods by which law has been put into practice in order to manage international relations has increased.[16] The Permanent Mandates Commission (PMC) at the heart of the League of Nations' oversight regime was a first foray into maintaining the liberal international order after World War I. "Very much an imperialists' club," the PMC was made up of colonial officials, diplomats and lawyers, liberal academics, and peace campaigners, who together "*performed* impartiality" as they assessed how well Europeans were governing the backward nations they were meant to be tutoring into civilization.[17] They heard often from Arab representatives who thought the Europeans were not doing a very good job at all.

Representatives of Palestinians, who insisted that the Europeans should not be there in the first place, were particularly active in demanding their independence from British rule. Although the British took over the governance of Palestine and other parts of the Middle East after the fall of the Ottoman Empire, the popular understanding was that this was, and should be, only temporary, as Arabs transitioned into defining and governing their own independent states. The 1919 King-Crane Commission asking Arabs what kind of government they wanted and the Arabs' initial rejection of the 1936–1937 Peel Commission that considered the partition of Palestine between the Zionists and the Arabs were early examples of how liberal internationalism could function differently within and outside of the international legal frame. These commissions stirred up activities both within and outside the liberal framework, provoking the consolidation of nationalist identities and transnational Arab solidarities. While Arab engagement with the King-Crane Commission showed how high were the hopes many Palestinians had in the new international legal order (Chapter 1), the anticolonial rebellion that propelled their boycott of the Peel Commission (Chapter 2) provides one answer to those who object to my critiques of international law with "Well, what else could Palestinians do?"

The Anglo-American Committee of Inquiry of 1945–1946, which examined the position of Jews in relation to the question of Palestine after World War II, was formed during another transitional phase as the British Empire lost global influence and the United States became more interested in the Middle East. This period is marked by a shift toward the politics of humanitarianism in which sympathy for the suffering of Jews after the Holocaust became a requirement of the good liberal. Palestinians who continued to insist on the democratic principle of majority rule were caught in an unresolvable bind (Chapter 3).

When the British withdrew from Palestine, the political hot potato that was Palestine was tossed about, leaving the newly formed United Nations to pick up where the League of Nations left off. The proposed partitioning of Palestine and establishment of the state of Israel in 1948 was its first major diplomatic endeavor.[18] A complex institution, the United Nations evolved into multiple bodies, some of which serve the hundreds of thousands of Palestinian refugees and their offspring who were exiled from their homes in the wake of the war in 1948.[19] The United Nations General Assembly (UNGA) has been a significant meeting place in which the political aspirations and crises of Palestine (and elsewhere) have been put up for international discussion. The UNGA was originally conceived of by the Great Powers as nothing more than a place for "small nations to blow off steam," as US President Franklin Roosevelt once admitted.[20] But the assembly saw its membership and activities increase and diversify over time, changing its demography and interests as the wave of decolonization occurred in the 1950s and 1960s and more states from the Global South joined the United Nations, making it an arena from which anti-colonial and anti-racist ideals could be propagated and publicized. It eventually transformed into an overseer of the human rights regime.[21] Soon after Israel's military occupation of the West Bank, Gaza Strip, and East Jerusalem in 1967, the UNGA established the United Nations Special Committee to Investigate Israeli Practices Affecting the Human Rights of the Population of the Occupied Territories (UNSCIIP), which has conducted an annual investigation and issued a yearly report ever since. The approaches of UNSCIIP over this period reflect transformations in the epistemological bases of international law, from the production of proof and demands for corroboration to requests for proclamations of hope and expressions of Palestinian suffering. The early years of UNSCIIP illustrate how the synergy of the UN and "The Question of Palestine" developed, but also demonstrate how the language and forums of international law became a mode of politically impotent solidarity (Chapter 4).

The United States has been a major player throughout this history. Although it has been a significant base for Zionist activity and Israel's biggest supporter, it also claimed the mantle of peace-broker, an ill-fitting cloak now tattered and soiled.[22] As part of its involvement in peacemaking, the United States spearheaded the Mitchell Committee in 2000, which, along with the European Union, Norway, and Turkey, examined the causes of the second *intifada* (uprising) against Israeli occupation in the occupied Palestinian territory. It generated telling debate over the political significance of international law (Chapter 5).

Since 2000, several other UN entities have emerged as central to Palestinian politics. The Human Rights Council is a major forum in which the UN addresses human rights and humanitarian crises, and has become the body most active in forming investigative commissions. Although the UN has sent many commissions to Palestine, the Goldstone Mission has been by far the most controversial. Launched in the wake of Israel's assault on Hamas in the Gaza Strip in December 2008–January 2009 ("Operation Cast Lead"), it highlighted the category of international crime in discussions of Israel's treatment of Palestinians and, with this anti-impunity turn, reignited Palestinian hope in international law (Chapter 6). The International Court of Justice and most recently the International Criminal Court (ICC) have become major international legal institutions in which the trend toward anti-impunity in international relations is most visible. Palestinians have sought to mobilize all of these bodies and commissions in their arguments for an end to Israel's military occupation and in their pursuit of national independence.

Many other commissions have been involved in Palestine, including: earlier investigations sent by Great Britain during the mandate; the UN Special Committee on Palestine (UNSCOP) that delivered a decision to partition the country and awarded the greater part of the country to the Zionists;

the MacBride Commission, an ad hoc investigation of Israel's actions during its invasion of Lebanon; and many other UN commissions, including the most recent one (at the time of this writing), the United Nations Commission of Inquiry on the 2018 Protests in the Occupied Palestinian Territory, which concluded in March 2019.[23] (See List of Major Commissions on page xix.) Although each was instigated by unique historical circumstances and followed its own dynamic, they all offer more evidence of how commissions function as a modality of political arbitration. Each illustrates how international law has been a terrain of struggle in the conflict over Palestine and a defining force in its international management. The specific commissions that are the focus of this book provide a good sample of the diversity of kinds of international investigative engagements and how Palestinians have responded. Together they trace a historical arc that demonstrates the depth of international legal involvement in Palestine, exemplifying both the continuities and changes within. Although international law has remained a baseline of Palestinian engagement with the international community, what commission investigators have focused on has shifted, from seeking out public opinion to sympathetic stories of suffering, just as they have demanded different qualities from the Palestinians, whether it be nationalist enthusiasm, sympathy for the Jewish plight, or willingness to compromise.

By foregrounding investigative commissions as a lens for viewing a realm of legal and political action over time, this book throws into relief the operations of liberalism through international humanitarian and human rights law on "the problem of Palestine." It reveals more general dynamics too, as these are the same paradigms that have constituted the material, discursive, and even moral terrain of political engagement for people struggling for their rights and freedoms elsewhere, from Syria to the Democratic Republic of Congo.[24] The history and analysis presented here illuminates shifts in the zeitgeist of global governmentality through which conflict throughout the Global South has been managed. Whereas the definition of sovereignty and its criteria have always undergirded these dynamics, what kinds of behavior are required from what specific kinds of subjects, and the criteria by which those behaviors and subjects are judged, have transformed continuously across this history.

The case of Palestine is especially illuminating of what has been stable and what has shifted, both because of the UN's originary and persistent presence in the conflict, and because of the predominant role of international law in the conflict's management and representation.[25] Although distinct dimensions of international law and the global governance regime have been studied in relation to Palestine, the reasons for Palestinians' fluctuating but tenacious engagement with liberal legalism have not been adequately considered. Given the recursive disappointment caused by commissions, it is a puzzle that so many people have gotten so excited about each fact-finding excursion, that so much din is stirred by these investigative reports, and especially, that Palestinians have invested so much hopeful effort in them. *A History of False Hope* analyzes the reasons for this hope and traces the effects of this engagement.

## An Audience in "the International Community"

Palestinians' history is one that has always been international and transnational, and their politics have always engaged "the international community" as a primary addressee—the scare quotes indicating the ambiguity of what the term signifies. As an important forum through which Palestinians and their advocates have sought these transnational engagements, commissions have continuously reanimated the idea of "the international community." Commissions portray the international community as a responsible, responsive, and caring moral-political entity organizing the international order according to principles of law, fairness, rights, and humanitarianism. It is variously embodied in the United Nations, other state groups, civil society organizations, individuals, and vaguely conceived world audiences. Analyzing Palestinian engagement with investigative commissions is a way to understand the exigencies of international law and liberal internationalism, a way to understand how the myth of an actually existing international community materializes at different moments.

The institutions and ideals of international law have been described as the "ideological framework to defend a liberal internationalist project," which hints at the mutually constitutive relationship of international law and liberalism.[26] A raft of writings in the tradition of critical legal studies has made the case for law's role in liberal imperialism specifically, leaving Florian Hoffman to contend that there "is little, if anything, to add to this grand ideology critique of international law."[27] But such a straightforward functionalist notion of ideology and a singular wrist-flicking, veil-lifting critique forecloses more interesting questions to be asked about the dynamics of this relationship. International law has been more than "Europe's distinctively successful solution to universal problems of order." It has involved a far wider range of people and projects in its ambit, sparking hopeful activity among the globe's marginalized.[28] It is a realm in which subaltern subjects, functionaries of imperialism, middle-class bureaucrats, nationalist aspirants, and internationalist visionaries have all engaged, asserting their own interpretations of what is universal and what counts as order. *A History of False Hope* posits a framework—at once historical and anthropological—for understanding this imbrication to address the multiple temporal, geographic, and ideological scales at which international law and liberalism have functioned in tandem.

## Liberalism as Habitus

Liberalism, in my usage, is more socially complex than what it is often conceived to be, especially in the work of intellectual historians and political theorists who have dominated the recent surge in debate over liberalism in empire. Liberalism is usually approached through the study of texts as a political ideology, a model for governance, and an economic system. Instead, I consider liberalism to be something that reaches deeper to function as an ethical system, a habitus, an *embodied* ideology, and a discourse, a producer of certain kinds of subjects with a particular emotional range.[29] Within the framework of liberalism, specific behaviors are required, modes of speech and social interactions are judged, and pronouncements are made according to particular but shifting criteria. The acceptable liberal subject must evince, among other stances, a reasoned, rational, tolerant way of being. The acceptable liberal subject must be—depending on the moment—sufficiently nationalist and patriotic, but not too much so; they must be industrious, not insistent or tedious, willing to compromise and forgive, professional and polite, and sincerely sympathetic.

Crucially, this habitus carries a moral valence. The "right" comportment, speech, and mode of social interaction is that which evidences a good liberal

subject. I have talked to the people involved in commissions and read the archives for what they can tell us about the policing of what is correct behavior,
of who is the correct liberal. Transcripts of commissioners' interviews and
Palestinians' testimonies reveal the tug-of-war between those unashamed
of their imperial arrogance and affronted by the uppity eloquence of their
presumed inferiors on the one hand, and on the other, those Palestinians
and others unwilling to let colonialist logic shrouded in the claims of the
civilizing mission go unchallenged. In the memoirs and diaries of Palestinian
nationalists and their Western adjudicators, we see what each side was looking for in the other and how they tried to perform their correct or superior
stance—for each other and the watching world. The exchange of argument
and articulation of aspirations in the lively Arabic press throughout the first
half of the nineteenth century also shows the internal disputes among Palestinians and their representatives about how best to make their case to their
international interlocutors.

In all the sources I could find—letters and personal papers, private diaries, national archives, interview transcripts and ethnographic interviews,
scholarly publications, reminiscences, the press and online media, official
commission records and their reports—there is evidence of Palestinians engaging in canny readings of the performative demands of the powerful. But
we also see them enacting their liberal-legal mode of being through professional and moral discourse that they believed to be not just effective, but the
correct way of going about things. Across all of these sources and throughout
this history, they express hopeful expectations of achieving reasoned and reasonable outcomes that would be determined according to liberal principles.
Although there is wariness, pessimism, refusal, and resolute disengagement
too, Palestinians' declarations of hope and energetic participation in these
commissions means that we must consider this history with an open mind,
putting aside presentist political cynicism. It requires a willingness to take
seriously the unexpected optimism, to follow carefully the pendulum swings
of enthusiasm and despair, to read this history in all its internal tensions
without downplaying the evident and persistent core of faith in liberalism's
promises.

An anthropological reading of these sources reveals dimensions of liberalism beyond the politics it formally promotes, exposing its role in the

constitution of subjects making strange bedfellows, and leading us to the venues in which the performative requirements of liberalism are put most forcefully on display. Liberalism instigates in people and institutions aspirational political desires that come with moral obligations; it comprises social identifications linked by attachments to rationality and balance. Achieving those desires and social connections requires certain emotional and embodied sensibilities, which an anthropological sensitivity to what people have said and how they have said it can capture well.

Tracing history through the lens of commissions provides a picture of the transformations that allow or induce reengagement within the liberal frame despite the disappointments. It also allows for an analysis of the sociopolitical as well as material and economic conditions that give rise to new forms of rights politics. Investigative commissions, where international law is performed, put the ideals and values of liberalism on display. The connection between liberalism and the law may be obvious, but this tells us nothing of how it works in people's daily lives and in the (re)formulations of political imaginaries at different scales. Liberalism's ideals and international law's institutions have long enticed Palestinians into their webs. It is the liberal sensibilities and faith in international law shared by Palestinians and the investigators who have listened to them that have kept them all engaged in a deeply flawed political process.

International law—a system of norms, institutions, international agreements, and purportedly universal values that was developed with the goal and pretext of managing inter-state relations—is one crucial mechanism for the instrumentalization of liberalism's promises.[30] The liberalism of international law is apparent at many different levels and at every historical moment of international law's development, whether during phases of imperialist expansion, through decolonization, or under the rubric of development.[31] From its prioritization of conditions in which capitalist relations can flourish between states to its focus on the rights-bearing individual who is at the heart of the human rights system, international law puts liberal norms into concrete practice. International law makes great promises: of equality, freedom, justice, rights, human flourishing, even human(itarian) care and sympathy. It is in the repeated articulation of those aspirational values that the attraction blossoms. In addition to such pronouncements of values that seem to many to be right, good, necessary, and universal, international humanitarian and human rights law offers the marginalized a sense of being cared about, even if they are not actually cared for. The institutions and actors of international law have become great listeners, documenters of vast atrocities, publishers of people's stories of suffering. This sympathetic listening that has become inherent to the practice of international law is also what brings so many to it, listeners and testifiers alike.

Across a hundred years, commissioners investigating Palestine usually walked away feeling like they had done a good job, although they accomplished nothing that they had set out to do—neither ending the violence nor forging a path to peace. That so many could feel so good about doing so little provides one clue about the power of commissions to seduce and sidetrack. This self-righteousness is enabled by a fetishized notion of balance as the goal of the ethical-reasonable subject and by a historically foreshortened view. During the British mandate, commissioners thought they were doing what was just by instituting balance through legal principles and by trying to ensure that neither Arab nor Jew had dominance over the other, while Zionists actually benefited from the economic and legal structures of the mandate.[32] While proclaiming their balanced stance, they obscured a history of policies and practices facilitating Jewish colonization of Palestine, blocking democratic developments and denying Palestinians' self-government.[33] And in more recent years, commission investigators—especially the liberal legal scholars among them—reported to me that they believed their work could make a difference. They thought the continual denunciation of human rights violations that commissions articulated would be heard (despite the fact that no political results would bear this out). The self-congratulatory arrogance of the imperial years was transformed into a latter-day humanitarian belief in the morality and political importance of bearing witness. As commission characters transformed from greedy colonialists to cosmopolitans full of sympathy for the downtrodden, the faith in liberal-legal methods and institutions persisted.

As "the political theory of modernity," liberalism is also a trick.[34] Assessment (by liberals) of the performances of liberal norms (by those deemed "others") has been a crucial tool for justifying the denial of liberalism's promises. Uday Mehta has identified certain "anthropological capacities" that liberal thinkers declared were lacking in non-Western peoples, making their "political·incompetence" a basis for their exclusion from liberal freedoms.[35] The colonized were denied recognition of possessing even baseline human capacities. In other formulations, this minimum was supplemented by myriad additional expectations, providing more opportunities for justifying denial of entry into civilization. Breeding and education of a certain kind was, for John Locke for example, a place to bury the "anthropological minimum . . . under a thick set of social inscriptions and signals."[36]

Less attended to in the work of intellectual historians and scholars of political thought like Mehta, however, is the fact that such appraisals happen in contexts well beyond the texts of key liberal thinkers. In meetings with ministers, across op-ed pages, and through commissioners' interrogations, assessing the liberalism of others and asserting the political and moral pre-eminence of liberal criteria becomes a core feature of political dynamics. In the contexts where commissions operate, the chance of detecting an incorrect performance or incomplete inhabitation of a liberal subjectivity is ever-present. Liberalism's system of ideals and values—its doctrine of individual and market freedom, of self-government, of the equal and inherent universal rights of the individual—describe an aspirational realm that its institutions have never achieved, and that they have never been set up to achieve for all.

Indeed, the power of liberalism comes not just from its vaunted ideas and values, but from how they can justify and promote political exclusion and repression even while the responsibility for doing so is placed on the shoulders of those excluded. Within liberalism's chain of precepts, any individual or group that does not achieve self-government and equality has somehow fallen short of embodying liberalism's ideals. They become subject to blame for their own denial of those rights and status equality. Liberalism is a tauto-logically exclusive arrangement. I am interested in the operations involved in disguising just how rigged a system it is, such that so many enroll themselves in it, despite the unlikelihood, or for some the impossibility, of gaining their rights and equality through it.

Liberalism is also an elastic concept. It is a forum of debate and practice that is always transforming, circling around some key principles regarding, at its broadest, the nature of freedom and the role of government. Liberalism encompasses "a commitment to the supreme value of freedom, equal human dignity, the rule of law, and representative democracy," as Jennifer Pitts has whittled it down to its nub.[37] Expanding slightly on this, historian Andrew Fitzmaurice includes "the desirability of liberty, rights and duties, freedom of commerce, the rule of law, and the sanctity of property," and importantly, the tendency to "dialogue about how to achieve these objectives."[38] Other key features are its "universalist commitment to the unique rational authority of liberal principles, and the meliorist philosophy" at its heart, which asserts the improvability of human social and political arrangements through the use of reason.[39] As Charles Mills notes, the variants of liberalism are united insofar as they "are supposed to be committed to the flourishing of the individual."[40] For anthropologists Gabriella Coleman and Alex Golub, the nodal point of liberalism is, with Charles Taylor, the "expressive self."[41] One of the few constants in most of the scholarship that takes liberalism as its focus is the recognition of the fact of liberalism's shifty expansiveness.[42] Flexibility is part of what gives liberalism its remarkable ideological power and, indeed, marks it as an ideology that exists as a terrain of struggle.[43] The boundaries that circumscribe the limits of any belief system, that define who is an exemplar and who is an outcast, is a feature of any ideologically weighted term or credo.

This conceptual malleability presents a number of quandaries to the analyst, only the most obvious of which is methodological: how to justify using a working definition of liberalism to then be able to explain what it is and does in the world.[44] A related question demands a justification for approaching any historical or ethnographic material, any group of people or set of political conflicts, through the lens of liberalism. Can "liberalism" offer any analytical purchase if the question of what it is has always been such a contested one?

Duncan Bell has attempted to resolve this by understanding liberalism as an "actor's category." For Bell, the liberal tradition is that which is "constituted by the sum of the arguments that have been classified as liberal, and recognized as such by other self-proclaimed liberals, across time and space."[45] But because use of the term can be rhetorical and is always ideological, narrowing the concept to explicit ascription presents a problem for critical analysis. If its ascription is by definition political, the inclusion or exclusion of groups or individuals from the category is likely to tell us about the nature of political contests rather than something fixed about what liberalism is. Although Bell's approach may reveal the hegemonic view at a given moment, it can tell us little of the process that led to the consolidation and contestations of that view.[46] Given that the label is often considered (especially by liberals) to carry positive connotations, limiting one's examination to what liberals think it refers to can obscure the darker dimensions of liberalism's history. As Charles Mills has pointed out, liberalism is usually written as a story of its ideals, not the real-life struggles around them.[47] Because liberalism is contested—not a stable category whose definition can be fixed—a more important question than "What is liberalism?" is "What are the historical and cultural dynamics that shape liberalism as a terrain of contestation?"

A related problem in the study of liberalism is the overwhelming focus on canonical figures such as Alexis de Tocqueville, John Stuart Mill, and Edmund Burke whose writings become the basis for scholarly accounts of shifting theoretical positions and arguments within liberalism.[48] Most scholarship in this vein is narrowly confined to textual exegesis and offers little sense of the social mechanics by which the views espoused in such core liberal writings were influential in the world. This tendency is carried through in the equally rich corpus of scholarship on the history of international law, where the focus is on (mostly Western) legal scholars and their writings.[49] Again, it is Duncan Bell who has stretched the boundaries of analysis in a different direction, criticizing studies of liberalism for being too focused on canonical thinkers and calling for a more "extensive archive of intellectual production." But this salutary effort remains hidebound within a mentalist or discursive frame.[50] By considering only those thinkers, canonical or not, who were considered by self-declared liberals to be liberal, the circle remains tight, limiting the domain of analysis, first, to the interpretation of discourse, and second, to that produced by those already declared part of the liberal club. This textual focus in some ways reflects liberalism's own discourse-centricity that takes ideas, ideals, and their rational discussion as the apotheosis of politics. Left mostly unconsidered, then, is the much bigger, messier social world in which liberalism has taken root, shaped characters, and left legacies of action and identity far beyond the production of a tradition of European thought.

There has been an increasing range of scholarship seeking to expand our consideration of the non-European contexts of liberalism, among which are the volumes on Arab intellectual history edited by Max Weiss and Jens Hanssen, which have helped to move the conversation "beyond the apparently symbiotic relationship between intellectual history and European traditions of liberalism."[51] With this and allied work, the meaning of liberalism in the Middle East has attracted renewed attention after a hiatus of some decades since the publication of Albert Hourani's landmark 1983 study, *Arabic Thought in the Liberal Age*, and a flurry of concern with the demise of liberalism in the region after the 1967 "naksa" that saw parts of the Middle East, including much of the rest of historic Palestine, fall to Israeli military occupation.[52] Like many, Weiss and Hanssen take liberalism "not as an ideal type but a contested ideological formation" shaped by colonial encounters.[53] This, however, means the conceptual and methodological problem remains unaddressed, leaving liberalism's meaning a matter of inference, something for the reader to determine based on the company the term keeps—"democracy, liberalism, pluralism, parliamentarianism, humanism, and universalism"—or based on who is identified as having "struggled to uphold the ideal of an inclusive, democratic state."[54]

Among political theorists and historians of political thought, the analyses of Karuna Mantena and Andrew Sartori have perhaps gone the furthest in interweaving liberal texts, their authors, and the non-European political contexts in which they took material shape.[55] In her book, *Alibis of Empire*, Mantena's gaze settles on Henry Maine, who, in his roles as imperial policy wonk and legal scholar, constituted a "main conduit between new social theory and imperial ideology and practice."[56] Through Maine, Mantena explores "the colonial exception" that rendered acceptable the suspension of liberalism's normative standards when it came to people under imperial rule.[57] In response to rebellion by "the natives" (specifically the so-called Indian Mutiny of 1857), there was a move away from trying to modernize them and toward an appreciation of their institutions as a lever through which to carry out a system of indirect rule purporting to "protect native society from traumatic impact of modernity."[58] Whereas imperial theorists such as John Stuart Mill settled on cultural difference to tie "the exercise of liberty and representative government to civilizational development," and thus circumscribe "the possibility of political liberty,"[59] for Maine, an anthropological appreciation of culture provided an alibi for imperialism, which was deemed necessary for protecting native society.[60] By considering ideas in action, Mantena's deft history shows more of the dynamism and struggles that are always part of how the justifications for and imposition of liberal imperialism change, both as a re-sult of imperial politics and in response to efforts to shake it off by its victims.

Sartori's work similarly avoids an abstracted view of liberalism and in-stead analyzes the intellectual diffusion of liberal texts and ideas, reading them in context to explain how they became compelling to the colonized in Bengal.[61] Sartori's revelation is that "colonial contexts could . . . resonate with projects of radicalizing and extending liberal commitments as easily as with circumscribing them." Crucially, he arrives at this understanding by placing more analytic weight on how "practices in indigenous society constituted the conditions for a reception of liberal ideas in social spaces in which one might not readily expect to find them."[62] His approach to investigating the liberal-ism of the colonizer and the colonized to understand their imbrication is among the most innovative and important in this field. Following Mantena and Sartori, *A History of False Hope* considers "the sociohistorical constitution of forms of liberal subjectivity" as the only way to understand how liberalism has traveled and transmogrified in ways that continually compel engagement with its perpetually unkept promises.[63]

## An Anthropology of Lived Liberalism and International Law

Tracing the development of forms of liberal subjectivity is no straightforward task, however, and this is where anthropology comes in handy. Anthropol-ogy is a field of scholarship that discerns the workings of power in subtle, sometimes mundane, but always material and embodied ways. The power of liberalism, as of any ideology, inheres in its existence as a "material force," the strength of which can only be analyzed by looking to the lived contexts in which its values are performed, become accepted and hegemonic, or rise to the level of attention to be debated and evaluated.[64] Being alive to the struggles, tensions, and changes that occur within social systems and institu-tions, anthropologists have come to understand liberalism as both a set of principles and "a cultural sensibility that, in practice, is under constant ne-gotiation and reformulation."[65] Countering claims that liberalism is a "native category of the Occident" and heritage of exclusively "Euro-American sub-jects," anthropologists have long grappled with how liberalism has traveled and taken root in diverse locales, defining peoples and their projects across the globe.[66] This scholarship is concerned with the ways in which liberal norms are lived, as they shape public discourse and political activity among everyone from journalists, conscientious objectors, and feminists to comedians and anthropologists themselves (sadly rarely the same thing).[67] My work adds commissioners and those they investigate to the list of people who have lived liberalism under a particularly bright spotlight.

*A History of False Hope* seeks to concentrate attentiveness to these dynamics of everyday liberalism as a way to understand the strength of its grip on so many who suffer from it. Although it may seem an obvious thing for anthropologists to consider the everyday inhabitations of a powerful ideology, things get easily muddled when it comes to turning liberalism itself into an object of analysis. Among anthropologists, perhaps more work has gone into deconstructing liberalism and its conceptual pretensions than has gone into understanding how liberalism maintains its power. Because the institutions and epistemics of the social sciences (including anthropology) have liberal roots, and because liberalism's claims to universalism and its ideological and geopolitical control is hegemonic, much weed-hacking must be done to clear the way for seeing beyond that which the conceptual apparatus of liberalism defines as seeable.[68] Talal Asad and many of his students have focused their talents on prying open liberalism's ideological-epistemological vault. Their critiques of "secular moderns" and their liberal presumptions have made more readily visible other interpretations of rights and the rule of law, the multiple formulations of selfhood and sensibilities that exist outside confined notions of liberal "agency," and other traditions of debate and reason, such as those that exist within Islam.[69] In this highly theoretical style of genealogical critique, however, liberalism becomes something of a foil. The more concrete details required to understand how the "secular moderns" came to be, who and where they are, and the conditions of possibility for becoming something else go missing.[70] This approach can tamp down our interest in the range of mechanisms by which liberalism has taken hold of the hearts and minds of many outside "the West" (understood as a discourse and a geography), and divert attention away from the histories by which liberal values and the institutions that propound them become embedded in any given political context. The history of investigative commissions to Palestine that I offer is one way of attending to the imbrication of liberalism with the political struggles of non-Western peoples.

Similar to most histories of liberalism, histories of international law also tend to be temporally and spatially delimited. The typical history of international law locates its beginnings in the fifteenth century, with the development of legal doctrines for regulating European and non-European state relations, and focuses on a standard set of European international legal theorists.[71] Such histories do not account for the remarkable expansion of the system into every domain of domestic and international politics.[72] Alongside the activation of the ICC, the increasing frequency with which the UN has resorted to international investigative commissions as a means of intervention in international and domestic conflicts is a prime example of this expansion in recent times.[73] Commissions are now understood to do more than simply apply international law, having become contributors to its development.[74] While mainstream legal scholarship remains hidebound by liberal presumptions and tends to accept the self-description of commissions of inquiry as being a mechanism for assuring accountability and triggering transitional justice, there is more needed to understand this proliferation.[75]

Investigative commissions have become almost a reflex reaction among distressed groups and those seeking to act on their behalf. There has been a parallel swell of academic interest in commissions of inquiry, prompting international lawyers and legal scholars to ponder at length the credibility and legal standards of commissions, while their broader implications and theoretical bases typically go unremarked. The investigation of events in Myanmar, where the Rohingya Muslim minority have been targeted in repeated pogroms for decades, exemplifies a standard sequence of events: violence against a vulnerable population reaches such proportions that the UN is summoned to investigate; a fact-finding mission quickly examines the situation in light of international law and issues a report with recommendations for steps to end the violence and uphold international law; interested parties debate the commission's neutrality and attack its report; little or nothing changes on the ground.[76] As an international legal expert on the situation of the Rohingya told me, NGOs and the UN Special Rapporteur called for a commission of inquiry into the widespread violence that the Myanmar state inflicted on this minority group even though there was no shortage of information about what was going on. It was clear to this expert that a commission of inquiry could do nothing without political will to enforce change, as is always the case. In the Rohingya context, as in Palestine, Yemen, Syria, and elsewhere, we see the "enchantment" with legal reasoning and with the "international community" at work.[77]

Victims and their advocates grasp at the hope of an authoritative accounting of the facts in an international legal framework, with the expectation or aspiration that it would be a starting point for a solution, if not a magic tool against those in power. And this despite the fact that commissions rarely offer such a launch into productive political endeavors. In authorizing lawyers, and in prioritizing solutions presented by elite experts, commissions exemplify the broader trend toward the legalization of conflict and international order creation that evacuate politics of mass participation and collective deliberation. By shoving the complex messiness of conflict into the sausage casing of legal language, commission reports may seek to present a neutral basis for negotiation, but they never can escape politicization. In addition to the sidetracking of grass-roots mobilization, the political danger of this now hegemonic approach is its elimination of meaningful political exchange. Instead, it favors legalized discourse that never addresses the hierarchies by which "political order" is defined and enforced. Beneath the progressivism of liberalism's narratives and its aspirations and claims, the actual results of commissions make their imbrication in ongoing empires more apparent.

There is already a well-developed critical historical scholarship on the role of international law in justifying and overseeing imperial rule. This critique is articulated in international legal history and in the clutch of allied streams of legal scholarship known as critical legal studies, TWAIL, NAIL, and IMAIL (Third World, new, and integrated Marxist approaches to international law).[78] As explained by Martti Koskenniemi, an influential legal scholar, these approaches stand as a corrective to an older narrative in which "the history of the law of nations was both the history of sovereign statehood and the history of universal principles that should govern states and lead into some kind of universal community beyond . . . with human rights as the crowning achievement of legal modernity."[79] Antony Anghie's has been one of the most prominent arguments in this set of conversations.[80] He explains how, from the nineteenth century onward, legal doctrine posited the difference between the West and the rest as a cultural or civilizational distinction, and in so doing wrote "uncivilized states" out of the possibility of sovereignty. Expelling the noncivilized from the "realm of international law" thereby legitimized colonial conquest as legal.[81] This parallels in many ways Uday Mehta's argument about the place of liberalism in empire.[82] Just as Mehta identified certain "anthropological capacities" that liberal thinkers declared were lacking in non-Western peoples, making their "political incompetence" a basis for their exclusion from liberalism's freedoms, critics of international law have identified the criteria of civilization and sovereignty as the means by which international law excludes the colonized and maintains their marginalization.[83] The question of how, or whether, international law can dislodge its liberal-imperial foundations to become a universally available and "meaningfully plural international normative order" likewise corresponds with debates over whether liberalism's alliance with imperial power is necessary or contingent.[84] Across these debates, the conclusions reached range from "yes," "maybe in some ways," to "no," with the assertions backed up by faith, preexisting political positions, and political aspirations as much as by evidence.

## Liberatory International Law?

Despite the insistence of so many legal scholars that international law is not just a tool of imperial domination, we still do not have a very robust account of how it functions otherwise.[85] There are many who have documented the efforts of the dominated to engage law as a "site of resistance" that functions "as a vehicle simultaneously of governmentality and of its subversion . . . of dispossession and reappropriation," but few who have indicated with confidence how effective the subversion and resistance have actually been.[86] When victories are noted, they are always complicated victories, often short-lived, and with attendant drawbacks. An example from Palestine is the International Court of Justice (ICJ) 2004 ruling on Israel's barrier (sometimes called the Separation Barrier, sometimes called the Apartheid Wall). The ruling was touted a success, inducing euphoria that the international community was finally going to push back against this tool of Israeli settler-colonialism. But it then disintegrated into dashed hopes: the ICJ's call to enforce the fourth Geneva Convention demanding that the international community not "render any aid or assistance to the Wall and the associated regime" has gone unheeded.[87] Often, a mere attempt to use the law subversively is chalked up as a victory, as when Palestinian membership in the ICC itself was described as holding Israel accountable to international law.[88] These more optimistic renderings only feed into the myth of international law's effectiveness as a protector of the weak.[89] There is a particularly vociferous and prolific contingent of legal scholars and practitioners who remain committed to international law as an important, if not the best and last, tool for achieving Palestinians' liberation from Israeli rule and its contingent abuses.[90] None of these are naive people who think law exists outside of politics; but they do see international law as a means of mobilizing solidarity and pressure that can effect political change. How that is meant to happen remains vague.

The fact that in many contexts the language of resistance and its delegitimization is itself inscribed by international law is something that should give pause to those who celebrate international law's liberatory potential.[91] There are critical questions being asked by some legal experts interested in Palestine.[92] I come back to this set of issues in the conclusion to this book and resist engaging them further until the reader has traced the permutations of liberalism's deployments across the century of Palestinians' dealings with international law and can see the full arc of changes in the valence and activation of liberal standards. Just as I contend that commissions must be analyzed from a grounded perspective in their full social and historical contexts, another premise of this book is that any assessment of liberalism or international law's liberatory potential must be grounded in an understanding of these systems' effects on people's lives and on the range of their political imagination. As in most of the scholarship on liberalism and its imperial histories, the absence of socially sensitive research into the nonelite actors and everyday dimensions of international law may be part of what has enabled the perdurance of faith in the possibility of international law as an anti-imperial tool of liberation.[93]

There has been a recent push in legal scholarship toward understanding international law as a "material project," the operations of which occur "on the mundane or 'material' plane of everyday life" beyond Europe, but questions remain about how law gains its power to enroll people into its methods and propagates its expectations.[94] Historians of international law have explained much about legal enforcement (and manipulations) of boundaries of sovereignty at the inter-state level, but have left mostly unexamined law's power to seduce and convince regular people to appeal to its mechanisms.[95] Even when they do make an effort to view international law in society, their purview remains blinkered by the institutions of law's self-definition and production; they attend more to lawyers, academies, and textbooks than to everyday discourses and actors.[96] Although Umut Özsu's call for work on international law that attends "to both its internal normative architecture and its receptivity to competing projects with extralegal moorings" is a start, the "extralegal moorings" must be conceived to include the histories of violence, traditions of conflict, and their forms of expression and memorialization that are part of how people think about justice, resolution, and rights.[97] As the Palestinian story shows, since it came to organize the end of the Ottoman Empire after World War I, international law has been to different degrees popularized, and in different ways even democratized. Its languages were made open to the masses, and its forums have become increasingly welcoming of regular people, encouraging them to come and tell "the international community" about the terrible effects of law's transgression. Although many have noted the increasing judicialization of all aspects of life as a recent phenomenon affecting everything from post-colonial politics to religion, my examination of Palestinian history shows that engagement with international law has been a consistent feature of the Zionist/Israeli-Palestinian conflict for a very long time.[98]

In sum, this book argues that the transformations in how international law is mobilized through investigative commissions is itself a crucial part of how liberalism lures, even while its guarantees remain unfulfilled. It is a study of continuity and change that calls for more historically and anthropologically grounded analyses of international law's liberal powers. A close look at commissions reveals the shifting sensibilities that underwrite the assessments of Palestinians, the differential demands made of those pleading their cases, and the ways that the "rule of cultural difference" and implicit criteria of worthiness pathologize Palestinian political subjectivity with ever changing demands. But it also reveals how each step in the evolution of international law seems to offer new opportunities for meaningful progress toward liberation and freedom. Offering these new opportunities is part of how liberalism lures.

In the League of Nations' efforts to sort ethnically homogenous and in-dependent nation-states, in the amplification of Third World demands for decolonization and an end to imperial racism through the UN General Assembly, in the human rights regime's discursive care for the victims of violence, and most recently through the activation of the ICC as the possible harbinger of accountability, new audiences offering solidarity and voices of righteous outrage and support shimmer into being.[99] Through each commission, in each historical era, we see specific demands made of Palestinians who are urged to perform an ever-shifting range of sentiments—from prop-erly contained nationalist passion to humanitarian sympathy, balance and compromise, to hope and sincere suffering. Although the continually shape-shifting criteria end up being impossible to fulfill, each permutation proffers a new opportunity for Palestinians to grasp at the carrots dangled seemingly just for them because the rules of international law demand an end to their colonial confinement. New assurances of globally dispersed democracy and new audiences that promise empathetic listening inspire hope that the latest manifestation of the international community will live up to its liberal ideals. This is part of the power of international law as ideology.

## The False Hope of Commissions

This, then, is an account, not of Palestinians' false consciousness about where their "best interests" lie, so much as it is one of false hope.[100] With the term *false hope* I mean to emphasize the active engagement of people in systems that promote expectations of the future, but do not deliver on their promises. There are those who would contend that law's significance lies in its expres-sion of "a powerful ethical vision in and of itself," in promising "order and moral answers in the midst of chaos and injustice, without being enforced," and that to focus on law's ability to regulate and enforce is to miss the point of law.[101] Indeed, it is clear that international law holds out such promises of justice and order. The lack of any real enforcement that would translate "a powerful ethical vision" into lived reality, however, is in fact critical for people living under a grueling, entrenched regime of repression. The hegemonic power of international law lies not just in its spread to all corners of political life, but also in the system's capacity to divert attention and energy from the collective work required for political change.

Although they do not always use the Marxist and Gramscian language of false consciousness, ideology, and hegemony, critical analysis of commissions from anthropological perspectives understand these investigations to be a mechanism for the authorization of particular views that validate the powerful.[102] Commissions often play a role in the creation and assertion of categories of people to be governed and the "regime of truth" that defines them, while consolidating state and national narratives to write out certain unsavory episodes of the past.[103] Adam Ashforth's book on governmental commissions in South Africa explores how commissions illuminated "ruling orders of the South African state," how they "understood the questions of sovereignty, citizenship, and territorial division," and how they worked to support structures of domination and political exclusion.[104] In a similar vein, anthropologist Ann Stoler has focused specifically on the discursive work that colonial commissions perform, arguing that their political power lies in their ability to create or cement social categories, or "designate arbitrary social facts of the world as matters of security and concerns of state."[105]

Two crucial questions are left unanswered in such critical studies of state power. One regards the historically shifting dynamics by which that power takes hold of the political imagination of those it dominates. The false hope of commissions, which breed an ambivalent faith that next time might be different and a wary optimism that international law can come to the rescue, encourages activity confined within the liberal international legal frame that never realizes its ideals on the ground. A second question ponders what happens when authorized, expert knowledge such as that produced in commission reports has no real effect on power except to name it and record it as it deepens. The fact is, for Palestinians seeking independence, the "truths" regimented by commissions—that Palestinians deserve an independent state, that they should not be randomly killed or tortured, and so on—never align with power. What the power of knowledge really is, in this case, is the power to distract.

# CHAPTER I

# *Petitioning Liberals*

## The King-Crane Commission

IN 1919, in the midst of the Paris Peace Conference that would divvy up the post-Ottoman Middle East among European powers, US President Woodrow Wilson dispatched the King-Crane Commission to Palestine and the region to assess "the state of opinion there with regard to [the post-Ottoman Middle East], and the social, racial, and economic conditions." It was intended to guide the peace conference in assigning mandates.[1] According to the commission's announcement about itself, this was "in order that President Wilson and the American people may act with full knowledge of the facts in any policy they may be called upon hereafter to adopt concerning the problems of the Near East—whether in the Peace Conference or in the League of Nations."[2]

Throughout that summer, Arabs across the region known as Greater Syria (which included Palestine) urged one another to unite to secure their country's freedom.[3] The First World War had ended, along with the Ottoman Empire, and 1919 saw "a year of travelling revolutions" across the Middle East and North Africa, as workers, villagers, and others staged demonstrations and demanded independence.[4] Wilson's promises that the postwar settlement would be guided by "the interests of the populations concerned," his reassurances that self-determination was "not a mere phrase" but "an imperative principle of actio[n],"[5] heightened the stakes of the King-Crane Commission for Arabs in the region. With the Ottoman Empire's demise,

Arabs in Palestine and elsewhere looked forward to establishing their own independent nation-states, following the logic of ethno-nationalism that was shaping this new world order. With expectations spurred by Wilson's well-publicized assurance that the "nationalities which are now under Turkish rule should be assured an undoubted security of life and an absolutely unmolested opportunity of an autonomous development," Palestinians and other Arabs understood this to mean that their own unmolested autonomous development was included.[6] They believed that religious tolerance and democratic procedures of self-governance were the ideals that would organize international life for all, and many believed that their commitment to representative democracy was shared with the Westerners deciding the fate of the peoples of the defeated empires. With its professed commitment to esteem public opinion, foster representative government, and respect the facts, the King-Crane Commission inspired optimism that imperialism in the Middle East was at an end.

## Colonial Encounters of the Closest Kinds

Critical histories of colonial encounters have largely been written as contests. We have been told that colonialism, whether in Indonesia, India, or Africa, was a conflictual dynamic that pitted the Dutch, British, colonial missionaries, and other categories of Westerners against their would-be subjects in contests of conscience, consciousness, and culture, as much as it prompted competitions of bodies in violent conflict.[7]

Anthropologists especially are inclined to tell stories of the colonial encounter that give due weight to the defiant agency of the colonized as well as to the forms of colonial knowledge that would define them as backwards.[8] The anthropological approach understands colonialism always to have been "a struggle that constantly renegotiates the balance of domination and resistance."[9] Scholars have deconstructed and critiqued the colonial constructions of caste, race, sect, and ethnicity erected to divide the colonized for the ease of colonial rule; the clashing performances set up to define respectable bodies and sexed savages; and the colonial attempts to reform the bodies, minds, and desires of non-Western peoples to further capitalism's reach.[10] What most anthropologists have noticed in these battles for sovereignty are the incongruous interpretations of key terms held by colonizer and colonized:

the multiple meanings of God and religion; the alternative notions of political leadership and divergent definitions of the legal subject; the contradictory approaches to sexual morality.

But what happens when the colonized and colonizer seem to agree? When people sharing certain values and self-understandings come together across the colonial divide to consider their shared political futures in a world that is being defined as, in fact, a shared world to be organized according to common liberal principles?

The King-Crane Commission gathered information about the Arabs' wishes for an independent polity based on democratic principles. The investigators encountered throngs of enthusiastic interlocutors who were inspired by desires for progress, a commitment to equality, and an abhorrence of sectarianism. The King-Crane Commission discovered that the Arabs had formulated their political proposals according to democratic procedures whereby consensus was reached through deliberation among contributors to a free press and through which consensual demands and proposals were presented by elected representatives. And they found that the Arabs, including people who were coming to identify themselves as Palestinian, had a clear vision for a system of governance that would include constitutional guarantees for minority rights, with special consideration for the rights of Jews as equal citizens. As one of the investigators on the commission reported favorably, his Arab interlocutors struck him as people who believed "one man is as good as another."[11]

In short, the commission found a world of liberals who thought themselves part of the "new world order" that Wilson championed. These were people who knew themselves to be members of the "program of the world's peace" that would "uphold the rule of international law and to put down autocracy and militarism."[12] The Arabs' knowledge that they deserved a political future in an independent nation-state was firm, and their expectations were high. In the Arabs' view, their interests could be fulfilled by a sovereign nation-state, an independent home for themselves, a people with a common language, culture, and history. It was only reasonable, they believed, that their shared origins and cultural and political unity, their Arab presence in a defined territory since the twelfth century, constituted proof enough of their rights to nationhood.[13]

But reason is never reason enough. Despite the promises of self-governance and equality inherent in the international legal logic being touted by Woodrow Wilson and the King-Crane Commission, the world that the Arabs encountered was operating beyond the bounds of liberal reason. It functioned according to a blend of hubris and imperialist greed. It was fueled by fantasist orientalism, by a zealous obsession with religion and Christian superiority that expressed itself in a magical belief in the ability of Westerners to know what's best for others. It was they who could understand the true intentions of fanatical Arabs, a race that was not capable of real and sincere nationalism, people who could not speak the truth or govern themselves. What the Palestinians could not know is that their model performances of liberal reason were destined to fail because the measure of self-determination was never reasonable in the first place. It was their sincere belief in this new international order organized by liberal principles, their reliance on logic and rational argument, that left them disappointed in the end.

## The Commission Brings Hope

The King-Crane Commission rolled out international law as if it were a red carpet, offering a space in which people of all kinds could enact their democratic ways, perform their solidarities, and announce their claims. The commission was the first forum in which Arabs developed a shared public hope that a liberal international order and international law would include them as equals in a nation-state of equal stature to all others of the international community. This collective hope ricocheted across the region's newspapers in the already lively transnational Arabic press, which was especially active in Palestine and infused with greater freedom after the 1908 Ottoman constitutional restoration.[14] The newspapers were inundated with observant and loquacious writers commenting on the King-Crane Commission. Although literacy was low at this time, and only the thin layer of the literate elite could publish their arguments, newspapers were being shared and read out loud in cafes, markets, and other public gatherings.[15] An observer wrote at the time: "the news of the Entente sending a commission has been spread with the rapidity of lightning in all the East."[16] *Al-Manar*'s editors (based in Cairo) urged their compatriots to unite and take an active role in the Europeans' decision about their country.[17] Between April, when the investigative commission was being formed, and August 1919 when it completed its trip in the Near East, the Syrian newspaper *al-'Asima* published one or two articles discussing the King-Crane Commission almost every week.[18] *Lisan al-Hal* and *al-Muqattam* kept pace too. The commission sparked acute interest across a variegated Arab public and became the focus of intensive political debate and activity in preparation for the Americans' investigation.

As suspenseful expectations for the King-Crane Commission's imminent arrival was building in the Arabic press, and after much to-ing and fro-ing over the commission's membership, the team of Americans set off in the summer of 1919. They visited towns and villages across Palestine, Syria, and southern parts of Anatolia. In Palestine itself, they trekked through Jaffa and Haifa, Jerusalem and Abu Dis. They heard from people hailing from Ramallah and Beit Rima, Bethlehem and Malha, Deir Dibwan and Nablus, 'Arrabe, Ya'bed and Safed, and many other towns and villages in what was then commonly known as Southern Syria. Outside of Palestine they visited Damascus, Beirut, Tripoli, Homs, Aleppo, and Adana, among other locations.[19]

What is striking about the dynamics around this commission is just how numerous and diverse were the people in Palestine who got involved. The histories of the King-Crane Commission and of Arab Palestine in this period (and later) have often been written as histories of the elite or histories of elite manipulations of the masses (reflecting what would become a standard trope of the British imperial rule).[20] Because of the constraints of historical archives, many Palestinians named in these pages, too, hail from what is traditionally recognized as "the political class." Akram Zu'aytir, 'Izzat Darwaza, Rafiq al-Tamimi, and 'Awni 'Abd al-Hadi were middle or upper class and educated. Darwaza was a politically active nationalist who was also a school director from Nablus. His achievements included cofounding the Christian Muslim Association in Nablus (of which he was also secretary) and participating in the first Arab Palestinian Conference in Jerusalem at the beginning of 1919. Before the end of the Ottoman Empire, Darwaza was a member of the Reform Party, a general secretary of the Young Arab Society (*al-Fatat*), and a part of the Decentralization Party, which called for partial autonomy for the Arab regions of the Empire. He would go on to help form the Arab Independence Party at the end of 1919.[21] In addition to these intellectuals, there were those heads of influential families who led delegations to the commission. But alongside men of high political status, the investigators also talked with spice sellers and green grocers, carpenters, priests and rabbis, factory owners and workers' associations.[22] They even heard from one delegation described as representing the opinion of "the old fashioned Moslem who does not care for politics."[23] It is clear from the range of newspaper articles and size of demonstrations greeting the commission that many were deeply invested in it. The commission brought into the open extensive discussion about the future of the region, the provenance of Palestine, and the criteria of national sovereignty. The investigators and their many interlocutors considered together the requirements of a political representative and the meaning of international law, and together they agreed on the terms of international society and cooperation.

The commissioners claimed to be on the lookout for the "broad-minded," the nonsectarian mentality that would allow true nationalism to weld the Middle Eastern states together without religious "fanaticism" or threat to Christians.[24] Arab representatives tried to demonstrate their nationalist yet tolerant mindset, and to prove to their Western investigators their political "maturity" in accordance with the evolutionary language of the day.

The Arabs had placed their faith in reasoned discourse, in representative politics, in logical argumentation. They were, after all, speaking to men who came on a mission to find the objective facts of the matter. The King-Crane Commission was yet another manifestation of the principle of "scientific knowledge for a scientific peace" that Wilson had exalted with his establishment of "The Inquiry," as the team of academic experts advising the postwar planners came to be known.[25] Invoking all the prestige and pretense to rationalism that attached to the word "scientific," Wilson and the commissioners asserted their gravitas and credibility. They made sure everyone with access to a newspaper knew that the Americans were there to hear their political views. They recorded the petitions and tallied the opinions in which most in Palestine expressed their desire for a united, independent nation to be organized constitutionally according to democratic principles, a nation in which religious minorities would be free and equal, and Jews would be included with tolerance, like other religious minorities. But the language of social science positivism belies the much livelier interactions and complicated beliefs that cross cut the King-Crane Commission's journey. As with most attempts to "scientifically" determine anything about social life, it was more belief and bias, emotion, performance, and contingency that determined the results of this investigation than any reasoned conclusion according to "objective facts."

## An Arab World of Liberals

What the commission encountered was a world already steeped in liberal activity, as nationalist campaigns were ramping up and demands for democratic political representation had been churning throughout the late decades of the Ottoman Empire. The commission's visit set in motion a new round of debate, petition drafting, and voting for representatives, as the Arabs determined what demands to present to the Americans and strategized how best to do it. These democratic procedures were elements of civic life that had become increasingly familiar throughout the Ottoman Empire from at least 1830, when experiments with representative and constitutional government had gotten under way.[26] The 1876 Ottoman constitution was another crystallizing moment in the development of liberal governance in the region.[27] The rise of Western liberal internationalism and the elaboration of its technologies of rule came at a time when Arabs were functioning with similar tools and trying out parallel institutions, with shared ideas of liberal governance circulating in their midst.[28]

Across the Arab region, new words were circulating: "autonomy, nation, homeland, personal freedom, nationality."[29] Notions of liberty, justice, consultation, public good, and accountability were prevalent as Ottoman Palestinians debated the terms of the second Ottoman constitutional revolution in 1908.[30] It was a revolution that had set in motion a plan for a representative state.[31] Among the "exercises in democracy" with which Arab publics had engaged was the 1912 Ottoman election in which Arab candidates campaigned among the people throughout the Levant, their speeches heavily covered in the press, which saw soaring rates of popularity as circulation of daily newspapers spread.[32] In the autumn of 1918, censorship was relaxed, and political activity blossomed. By the time the King-Crane Commission would appear in Palestine, nationalist Rafiq al-Tamimi would be reporting to his friend 'Awni 'Abd al-Hadi that "Palestinian public opinion has begun coagulating into a single voice" demanding total independence within a unified Syria.[33]

They were part of the liberalizing generation, "ready to play a role in the determination of their fate as a political community."[34]

Other tools of democratic self-representation and citizen engagement were also already common. Through the press and cultural associations, telegrams and petitions, public opinion came to be a more significant political force.[35] Petitioning had become a standard method of claim making among people who did so more as citizens than as imperial subjects in the Ottoman Empire. And the substance of the requests and complaints were "increasingly couched in terms of rights and constitutional responsibility."[36] Several Palestinians had already emerged as liberal reformists, and the vocabulary of citizenship, popular representation, and nationalism was commonplace by the outbreak of World War I.[37]

In their newspaper editorials, pamphlets and petitions, diaries and memoirs, Arabs expressed their clear expectations for the imminent establishment of an independent Arab state. But why would they be so hopeful? It may seem unlikely from our vantage point today that they could have believed that through their reasonable arguments to a commission they could wrest their independence from the claws of the Europeans' colonial avarice. And this especially so given the evidence of Western antagonism all around them. The French had been in Algeria from 1830 and annexed Tunisia in 1881; Britain had occupied Egypt in 1882; Italy invaded Libya in 1911; and the French would soon be putting down a Syrian revolt against them with extreme brutality, just as the British would put down a revolt in Iraq in 1920. European control had also wormed its way throughout the Ottoman Empire more subtly through the Capitulations, which were increasingly used to assert European extraterritorial jurisdiction over and privileges for non-Muslim foreigners.[38] In May 1919, French diplomat (and member of the French Colonial Party) Francois Georges-Picot was still hypocritically avowing to his Syrian audiences that France was working for the realization of Syrian independence and promising to convey their desires for independence to those at the peace conference. All the while, he was advocating Western action to counteract what he perceived to be an "Islamic movement which was under full swing in Syria."[39] Readers of Rashid al-Rida's newspaper, *al-Manar*, were being reminded of the 1916 British and French secret treaties that had divided the region into spheres of influence.[40] An observer of his countrymen,

Faysal—who declared the Arab Kingdom of Syria in 1920—explained his compatriots' "fear and horror" of the Great Powers, "whose spirit in general is inconsistent with its letter, such as entering the country under pretense of assistance and advise and subsequently making of it a colony."[41] Arabs across the Middle East had plenty of experience with Europeans' pitiless imperialism, tricky takeovers, and sugar-coated assurances. And yet, this time seemed different.

## Welcoming the Commission, Demanding Human Rights

The commission's vocal admiration of the Arabs' political organization encouraged hope that a new international arrangement that recognized their national and individual rights was coming into place.[42] Their visit to Palestine, prompting much talk and speculation about the political future, was an event that enhanced the sense of opportunity in a general atmosphere that already encouraged Arab expectations.[43] Many questions were open, and uncertainty about their fate was worrying at people's nerves, but the context itself generated excitement and widespread attention to these matters.[44] Delegations wearing their finest clothes received the commission with shouts of "America! Wilson!"[45] Littérateurs put their skills into welcoming the Americans, proclaiming to the commission: "Undoubtedly, you would be among those whose names are remembered throughout modern history, as they would be written in golden ink."[46] Great crowds came out to meet them, including many women and some children.[47] The commission thought that the women they heard from were "more determined even than the Muslim men."[48]

Many people in Palestine and across the Middle East were intent on shaping the investigators' judgments. An article in the leading Lebanese Arabic newspaper, *Lisan al-Hal*, announced that the commission was expected to arrive within days, and that its report would have "a large impact on the [Paris Peace] conference's conclusions, and in turn the future of Syria and Palestine."[49] Judging from newspaper accounts of the day, there was every expectation among the Arabs that the commission's findings would impact the peace conference and ensure an independent future of Palestine.[50]

But they knew they had to articulate their claims in the right way. Those seeking to assert their international status and achieve recognition of it knew something of how Westerners made determinations regarding other states (their own civilizational status assumed and firmly anchored in their own self-definition). This is clear from the ways Arabs argued their case, trying to stake a claim to the civilizational status that was supposed to earn them international respect and independence. Prince Faysal took one approach, invoking France's reputation as the birthplace of liberal democracy, while challenging Westerners' claims on that basis. In arguing for his right to have a voice at the peace conference, Faysal braided a narrative of Arab civilization and political liberalism into French history. He explained, "At the time of the French revolution, there came an awakening of the spirit of independence among the Arabs." Regardless of the French claims based on their economic and civilizing missions, Faysal insisted that "the Arabs had been there several thousand years before the French came there. The Arabs have rights in Syria, and he [Faysal] who had led the troops who drove out the Turks surely should have a voice."[51]

Their inherent capabilities and unity were additional pieces of evidence that Arabs used to argue their readiness for self-rule. "We have the instinctive abilities and natural intelligence, and the strength and vitality that makes us able to be independent. We are one community. There is no fighting between us and no factionalism."[52] They viewed themselves as being as "naturally gifted as any other population in the world" and certainly not inferior to the Bulgarians, Serbs, Greeks, or Romanians "in the beginnings of their independence." They objected to their designation in the League of Nations Charter as being "among the nations half-civilized who need still to be protected."[53] Palestinians asserted that their people were being educated in America and Europe; they had members of all the professions necessary for producing a functioning country, from farmer to pharmacist, mechanic to mathematician. They were liberal in its contemporary sense, valuing modernity and working for progress.[54] One delegation to the commission declared, "We have raised men who are ready with all the necessary tools for independence."[55]

The ideology of universal rights permeated their demands. "We ask for independence to live as human beings (*bashar*). This is what will guarantee us life, freedom and happiness. What will protect our dignity, and ensure that we will progress and reach our potential." They were not just superficial, fawning copycats though. They asserted their desires for progress "according to our traditions, and what our situation requires. What the spirit of the times demands. We do not wear imported clothes or [desire] to make our life a copy of others," a delegation insisted to the commissioners.[56] They had to maintain a balance between asserting their civilizational particularity that bespoke their autonomous identity and conferred national rights, and reassuring the Westerners that they functioned within a common framework of universal values. Because those values were theirs too, the anticolonial conundrum identified by Partha Chatterjee, in which Third World nationalism "simultaneously rejects and accepts the dominance, both epistemic and moral, of an alien culture," did not confront them.[57] Their epistemic and moral priorities were the same.

## International Legal Reordering

Beyond the political ferment of the late Ottoman context, also buoying Arabs' political hopes was the structural context of systemic changes in the international order and international legal tools being devised to cultivate that order. The League of Nations was a central mechanism in this context. Although the league's existence did not officially begin until January 10, 1920, the plenary assembly of the peace conference accepted a draft of the league covenant on April 28, 1919, a couple of months before the King-Crane Commission arrived in Palestine.[58] An Arabic translation of the covenant was published in what was regarded as one of the most credible newspapers, *Lisan al-Hal*, a week later.[59] The covenant announced its goal "to promote international co-operation and to achieve international peace and security . . . by the prescription of open, just and honourable relations between nations," and "by the firm establishment of the understandings of international law as the actual rule of conduct among Governments" with a Permanent Court of International Justice to ensure it.

Article 22 of the league covenant offered a mixed bag of recognition and paternalism for the people of the Middle East, however:

> Certain communities formerly belonging to the Turkish Empire have
> reached a stage of development where their existence as independent nations
> can be provisionally recognized subject to the rendering of administrative

advice and assistance by a Mandatory until such time as they are able to stand alone. The wishes of these communities must be a principal consideration in the selection of the Mandatory.[60]

Many Arab commentators refused the league's categorization of the Arabs as "peoples not yet able to stand by themselves under the strenuous conditions of the modern world." Khalil Sakakini, a Palestinian nationalist and educator, rejected the logic of mandatory "tutelage" entirely.[61] He reasoned that it was better for the Arabs to organize themselves independently "even if we committed a hundred mistakes every day." Regardless of whether the league insisted that a mandate was necessary to train them into independence, it would come to no good. "If we haven't learned independence by ourselves then no one can teach us." He presciently observed: "[Any] great teacher that enters our country will not leave without a fight."[62] Prince Faysal, described by commission members as being "liberal" and "broad-minded," thought that the European insistence on placing Greater Syria—which included present-day Palestine, Lebanon, Syria, and Jordan—under a mandatory power was the result of Arabs being "misunderstood" by Europeans.[63] The Arab representatives of this period believed in the power of "rational appeals" to win redress for their grievances and ward off the Zionists advances.[64]

Despite Article 22's articulation of the new form of tutoring colonial power, the American president's calls for the formation of this league as a "general association of nations .... under specific covenants for the purpose of affording mutual guarantees of political independence and territorial integrity to great and small states alike" stood as a reference point for the Arabs' articulation of their political vision.[65] Wilson's liberal values were widely publicized after his Fourteen Points speech before Congress in 1918 and were well known to the Arabs communicating with the King-Crane Commission.[66] In that speech Wilson had advocated liberal principles by which he thought international peace could be restored and imperialism put to an end, including the equality of nations, consent of the governed, and self-determination.[67] The European powers had been making declarations about the liberation of the Eastern peoples from the Turks, and reports of these promises circulated in Arabic newspapers.[68] It made Prince Faysal "confident that the [Great] Powers will attach more importance to the bodies and souls of the Arabic-speaking peoples than to their own material interests."[69] Petitions to the commission invoked the "noble rules . . . [of] President Wilson, the great," imploring the commission to "pay attention to us," and "in the name of humanity and justice . . . grant us our usurped freedom."[70]

Arab spokespeople continuously drew on Wilson's language of justice as a validating pillar for their political demands.[71] They believed that his pronouncements guaranteeing them absolute independence resonated with universal values. One of the Palestinian delegations to the King-Crane Commission asked that the peace conference meeting in Paris "defend the right of general humanity."[72] "Can the destiny of Palestine be determined before taking the opinion of people?" a columnist in an Arabic newspaper asked rhetorically. "We don't think so" was his rosy response.[73] Clearly not as widely known was the fact that Wilson approved the official US Department of State commentary on his speech, recognizing the "preeminent position of France in Syria and affirm[ing] that Britain was 'clearly the best mandatory for Palestine, Mesopotamia, and Arabia.'"[74] Although others in the president's circle believed him to be merely an emitter of "vague phrases and beautiful ideals," Arabs in the region seized on his statements to further their claims for independence and to raise their objections to Zionist demands for a Jewish nation, claiming the principle of self-determination for themselves, the native inhabitants of Palestine.[75]

## The Promises of International Law

It was not Wilson alone who stoked the Arabs' hopes. The very fact of the King-Crane Commission's appointment helped reassure the Arabs of Palestine and throughout the Near East that the "intellectual revolution in international legal history" that marked this new order offered them a framework in which their arguments could be heard and would be respected.[76] The league, which presented itself as constituting "a momentous first step from anarchy to order and from politics to law," was a key institution of liberal internationalism after World War I. It was the prototypical liberal regime. The story that the discipline of international law tells about itself describes 1918 as a politically progressive moment, providing a transformative break from the imperialist past, institutionalized through the League of Nations.[77] This was the instant, so the story goes, when a critique of absolute sovereignty gave way to a "modern sensibility that . . . foregrounded the interest of the international community" that would include more centrally those hitherto regarded as fixed on the "semi-periphery."[78]

International law was a language of promises. Representatives of European and American powers offered a lot of public assurances around World War I: to "the world," to humanity, to peoples and nations, and to each other.[79] Even if much of what they guaranteed was contradictory, each promise impossible to fulfill without breaking another, international law held out a horizon of possibility for those whom the system stationed at its margins. The intermediate international legal category of "semi-civilized," reserved for the Ottoman Empire among a few other states, brought the non-European and marginalized into the system, both through modes of exclusion and through means that promised partial inclusion.[80] It was the fluidity of the hierarchy and the malleability with which the criteria were deployed that encouraged those in states designated "semi-civilized" especially to engage in the competition for civilizational status. From the perspective of semi-peripheral elites, international law became an arena for engaging and confronting Western dominance.[81] The Ottoman elite of the mid-eighteenth century believed they already had a place in "the club of European states," that they had proved themselves civilized, "and that the Ottoman state had gained a legitimate right to international existence as a recognized member of the Concert of Europe."[82] The apparent room for improvement that was incorporated within the civilizational sliding scale, and the standards of civilization, created conditions in which an apparent dialogue with common terms of reference could take place.

The formalization of the hierarchy's criteria reached a new level with the imposition of different categories of mandates under the League of Nations. It institutionalized civilizational distinctions under the rubric of mandates, providing European states with the justification for their control over other people by calling it benevolent tutelage for backward nations.[83] But in those areas deemed to be almost ready for self-government, the Class A mandates that included the Levant, the European mandatory powers were meant only to provide "administrative advice and assistance."[84] That the peoples who were part of the former Ottoman Empire were designated Class A mandates—at the top of the scale of the not quite yet civilized enough—

made the path to full and equal inclusion in the society of nations look that much shorter, and scoring enough civilizational points seem that much more possible.[85] For those who did not refuse a mandate outright, acceptance of temporary assistance in technical matters to improve their progress toward sovereignty seemed a feasible move.[86]

Also encouraging faith in an international society that would be organized according to liberal terms of self-determination was the prevalence of "plebiscites"—an early form of public opinion poll.[87] The Versailles Peace Conference conducted twenty-five field investigations and consultations to feed into the discussions as the Great Powers were deciding on matters of sovereignty and self-determination after World War I. Along with boundary commissions, minorities treaties, and petition processes, plebiscites were one means through which "putative 'nations' learned to state their claims and test their powers."[88] Those seeking to ensure that international stability was achieved according to rational methods viewed plebiscites as a crucial technique of good governance.[89] And some of those seeking to have their independence recognized greeted plebiscites with enthusiasm. Algerians addressed a letter to Woodrow Wilson, "the honorable President of American Liberty," asking for an investigatory delegation to Algeria "in order to 'decide our future fate, under the aegis of the Society of Nations.'"[90] Although the Algerians did not get a commission, the Palestinians of "Greater Syria" did (figured as Syrians rather than Palestinians at this time). And they had great enthusiasm for it because, as author and president of the Bethlehem Literary Society, Youhanna Khalil Dikrat, said, the only possible outcome of an unbiased examination of the facts was their freedom.[91]

The commission came across like a living, moving embodiment of Wilsonian ideals that had representational government as a core value and promised national sovereignty to the hitherto oppressed. The commission members told their attentive public that the United States had no interests in the Near East.[92] And many believed them. Albert Lybyer, professor of history at the University of Illinois and technical advisor to Henry King and Charles Crane, recorded the prevalent view among the Arab delegations that America was not a colonizing power and "could be relied upon to withdraw from the country when her work is done, which is the case with no other power."[93] Wilson had been making a great show of distinguishing the United

States from the traditional, greedy imperial powers. His country had "no self-ish ends to serve," he announced.[94] That France and Britain were not doing a great deal to burnish their visages probably made these American efforts easier. The true belief in those principles among the dyed-in-the-wool liberals on this commission, people who "took seriously the portion of Article XXII of the Covenant of the League of Nations which said that the wishes of the inhabitants should be a principal consideration," made their opinion polling and fact finding all the more convincing.[95]

## Debating Procedures of Political Representation

The commissioners were all there to proclaim the unbiased nature of their examination, to perform a Western willingness to engage in dialogue, to hear reason, to let the people represent themselves. As representatives of the United States, "the champion of liberty and fair opportunity for all peoples," they were concerned to maintain for the commission an appearance of objectivity and wanted to make sure that anyone who had a basis for making a presentation was allowed to do so.[96] William Yale, technical advisor on the commission, recalled many years after the end of the mission that he had been in charge of ensuring that they allowed "adequate representation to all groups" "without discrimination against any."[97] Although they used the language of science and statistics to prove they did this, much of what they recorded was impressionistic. In notes on their meetings, members of the commission labeled delegates they spoke with as being "fairly representative" or "not really representative" of the city or group they came from, as being from an influential family, extremist, moderate, supposedly moderate, or insipid.[98] One Druze sheikh was simply deemed "stupid." The only note that explained how they derived this taxonomy regarded a Municipal Council delegation that was dismissed as being not really representative of the city because it had been appointed by a Turkish official.[99] The rest were assertions. It all fed into their tallies of the petitions and counting of the delegations they met. All together, they thought they had gathered a "fairly accurate analysis of present political opinion in Syria."[100] Their openness and insistence on hearing anyone who wanted to talk to them raised the commission's stakes in the eyes of those who sought to deliver their opinions and prove their facts.[101]

The Arabs did what they could to convince them that they were representative of their people, that their people wanted independence and opposed Zionism. Faysal, who "made a splendid impression as a statesman," announced himself as "political representative and defender of the rights of Syria."[102] He addressed the commission "on behalf of the Syrians . . . as a whole, . . . being authorized to represent them by official documents containing over three hundred thousand signatures." He was, he reassured the commissioners, conveying the Syrians' "true desires." Not claiming an utterly homogenous and unbelievable nationalism, Faysal explained to the commissioners that if there was any variance in how different groups may have expressed their opinions, it was only a matter of different language, diverging "only in words according to the degree of feeling, level of education, and attachment to the nationality and solidarity." But the basic desire for "Liberty and Independence" was there among all of them.[103]

While liberty and independence were indeed the generally preferred outcome, Faysal's legitimacy as representative was less clear. At the Paris Peace Conference, he filled a void left by Palestinian representatives who were forbidden from attending by the British authorities in Palestine (leaving the Zionists to lobby in full force, mostly unopposed).[104] Once the commission was headed their way, there was much debate across the region about who should represent their people in front of it and about the processes by which their representatives should be determined. As they prepared for the commission's arrival, Arabs across the region sought to determine their collective political aspirations and find a way to represent those views fairly to their investigators.[105] They were not only aiming to convince their interlocutors that their demands were the demands of the majority of their people. They were also striving to reach, and produce, an agreement that was fair and representative.

Readers of *Lisan al-Hal* wanted transparency from the Syrian Moderate Party, and they expected to have access to the influential speeches that were given at an important meeting of their party.[106] In an article penned with a tone of near panic, one unnamed writer urged their compatriots to prepare properly for the commission's visit: "We believe that the best to be done under this condition is to select a committee of wise, unbiased men, who are knowledgeable of the conditions of the country and its needs."[107]

Middle-class respectability figured heavily into how some people were judging political worthiness. The increasing political importance of intellectuals is
indicated in the suggestion of one person writing in to the same newspaper:
"As the visit of this commission approaches, we should act by forming a temporary society of justices, lawyers, teachers, authors and other thinkers. This
society is to select the members to be consulted with by the international
commission."[108]

They did more than appoint spokespeople from among the new middle
classes though. In preparation for the commissioners, Arab political party
members gathered in Damascus in June 1919 for the Syrian General Congress to prepare a unified platform to present before the investigators.[109] As
diarist Khalil Sakakini recorded at the time, individual clubs and groups had
internal meetings to decide who would take part in that congress.[110] Participants in the congress were elected according to the Turkish electoral law.[111]
The first paragraph of the platform written at the congress that would be
presented to the commission, and which was published in the Arabic press,
explains that it was written by an assembly made up of representatives from
every part of Syria, "who were granted the confidence of and delegation by"
the Muslims, Christians, and Jews of their provinces.[112]

An article in *al-'Asima* newspaper conveyed something of the urgency
that some felt in seizing the opportunity to articulate their collective wishes:

> We must join together in our demand for our future, as the international
> commission's visit to Damascus is drawing closer. For this, we require the
> convening of the Syrian conference, but when will it convene? Is it waiting
> on the Commission's arrival in order to organise itself?
>
> One group asserts that only unmitigated freedom will do. Another
> group believes that as a necessary precaution we must pick a mandate, lest
> our silence be interpreted as submission and we lose the privilege of pick-
> ing one for ourselves. The first group, which calls for absolute autonomy
> without any sort of supervision, mandate, guidance or aid, is supported by
> the majority of the population. . . .
>
> It is imperative that we unite our voices in the call for complete au-
> tonomy, as this will push the Commission and [the Paris Peace] Confer-
> ence to view our self-sufficiency and suitability for rule, as the nation that

succumbs to slavery and humiliation will never earn respect. We will not have another chance to present our wishes to a committee; we must seize the opportunity now. The fate of the region has not yet been decided, as is clear from the Commission's interactions with the people of Yafa [the Palestinian coastal city of Jaffa], and therefore this is our chance to decide it now, as Wilson remains dedicated to his fourteen points.

For these reasons, we stand by the position of the first group in requesting total independence (*istiqlal tamm*).[113]

The time for complete autonomy and national unity had come.[114]

## Representative Demonstrations

Although what is most evident in the press archives and in the commission members' notes are the missives penned by individuals hailing from the strata that historian James Gelvin has dubbed "Westernising elites," the demands they stated were restated, with some variation, by delegations in petitions, newspaper articles, and flyers throughout the areas that the King-Crane Commission visited. Many took part, demanding that their views be fairly demonstrated.[115] People worried that the commission would listen only to the elite, those privileged people who "know nothing about the meanings of life other than individualism and do not care about the collectivity." They warned in newspaper opinion articles against any monopoly on their political representation by the notables.[116] They made sure that did not happen. Crowds of hundreds gathered in the streets to greet the commission and submit their petitions, despite the British military government's official announcements discouraging such public excitement.[117] Outside of Tripoli, some one hundred men bearing swords and spears stopped the commission on its way to Homs to deliver their message of protest against the French governor who had prevented people from having their say. Atop their Arabian horses, they escorted the commission to the next roadside mounted delegation.[118] Photographs taken by commission members show that delegations included whole families. (In one picture, a commission member is shown holding a baby, like a campaigning politician.)[119] The commission was at the center of an intensely engaged transnational conversation among impassioned members of a post-Ottoman civil society.

The King-Crane Commission, as an agent of international law, opened a space of action and debate in a wide public. International law became a discursive terrain and performance space. In addition to petitions and presentations, many of which were described in the Arabic press,[120] communiqués to the commission were distributed in the bazaars. Delegations showed up bearing placards and singing anthems.[121] Banners were strung across streets, their political demands written on large sheets (until the British made people take them down).[122] The commission received missives that attempted to educate the commissioners on various points of religion, politics, and the history of the region.[123] Arts and crafts were deployed too. At an event hosted by Faysal, the commission members listened to a song ("The land is ours; we will live for it; we will die for it"), watched a marionette show of fighting and dying puppets, and were treated to a play titled *Syria Enchained* that ended with the country's liberation. Later they received a rug with the preferred map of Syria woven into it, which was to be passed on to President Wilson at the peace conference.[124]

The appeals were rational, and usually that is how they were delivered too—with calm, orderly demonstrations.[125] Political activists in Palestine had encouraged petitioners across the country to keep their presentations short and to the point.[126] This is what they thought would impress their itinerant investigators. Akram Zuʿaytir, one of the few chroniclers of the events at the time, recorded that the commission observed the mature nationalism in Palestine. Their evidence was "the agreement and unity in the presentation of the requests." Zuʿaytir believed that the "unity of the Palestinian voice and their national togetherness" impressed the commission and their compatriots. Congratulations came from all over the country to the people of Palestine for their "great success, their credible nationalism, and their strong agreement."[127]

## Opposing Zionism

Palestinian representatives cited liberal principles of representative government and presented their arguments in ways that underscored their logical nature. In one statement addressed to the Allies, "Christian and Mohammedan delegates of Southern Syria known as Palestine" protested against making a national home of the Jews in the Arabs' "native land," spelling out how the Zionist arguments were "fallacious and misleading." They hoped that the Zionist claims "might be shattered asunder through our infallible proofs." Their evidence focused on the fact of the minority presence of Jewish people in Palestine, and underscored the nonsensical nature of the Balfour Declaration that could not simultaneously avoid "prejudice[ing] the civil and religious rights of the Arabs and cause their destructions." They submitted the petition "with the full hope that these our arguments and proofs will receive due consideration and that our rights to our home will be confirmed."[128] "It is not right to ignore the fact of these strong ties" or to ignore the fact that Jews had no "historical rights" to the land. It was wrong to encourage Zionism and its "religious fundamentalism," the Palestinian groups stressed in their missives.[129] Even if Wilson missed seeing those petitions, during the peace conference he had certainly heard from Arab representatives and a couple of their Western advocates that they wanted independence, not the Jewish national home in Palestine that Balfour had promised to the Zionists. A telegram to Wilson in Paris from the King-Crane Commission, still in the midst of their travels, confirmed these positions, highlighting that the Arabs rejected the Sykes-Picot and Balfour agreements for their negation of Arab independence.[130]

The Palestinian representatives rejected the idea that Jews were a distinct national people entitled to unique political rights.[131] They had been making this point for a while, and cited "international law" as a "just witness to [their] calls" against letting "the foreigner have political rights in."[132] Those who considered themselves the enlightened intellectuals (*mutanawwirun*) also promoted a notion of modernity in which religion would be a weaker influence in the building of nations.[133] They explained that in their future state, because the native Jews, like the Christians, were a religious minority, they would be considered citizens with equal rights and duties.

In interviews with the commissioners, Palestinians made clear their distinction between interloper Zionists and the indigenous Jewish residents of Palestine. They asserted that there was strong agreement between the Muslims and Christians in Palestine. They shared an "inclination" toward justice and agreed that the Jews among the national citizens would have their rights like others. "What is incumbent upon them is incumbent upon us," a delegation told the King-Crane group.[134] The long presence of Arabs in

Palestine and their demographic majority was, for these representatives and writers, argument enough against the Jewish claim to Palestine as a national home. Jewish demands for rights to the land "based on colonization of the area from a different century" was, in their view, unreasonable, given that "by that logic this would mean that Arabs could claim Spain—or the Romans or Greeks [could] claim anywhere they were."[135] Judaism, moreover, was a religion, not a nation.[136] They had no "doubt that the civilized world will not permit that which is not reasonable," and what the Zionists were proposing was not reasonable. "It is impossible to turn the map to what it was before the Flood," they asserted.[137] In an article discussing how representatives were elected to the upcoming Syrian Congress, the author concluded, almost as an afterthought of obviousness: "As for protecting minority rights, it is obvious and does not need examination."[138]

## Minority Rights and Agreeing Political Demands

Indeed, according to ʿIzzat Darwaza, one of many Palestinian delegates at the Syrian Congress, those at the gathering agreed "without long discussion" that the future state should be based on democratic representation with the same rights and obligations conferred on all, regardless of religion. There was agreement among them that their independent government should guarantee equal citizenship, and agreement on the point regarding minority protection had been reached with no controversy.[139] Darwaza, who became secretary to the Syrian Congress, reported that opposition to Zionism was also nearly unanimous. Those gathered and polled thought that standards of international law guaranteeing national self-determination and representative government clearly supported their case for Arab, not Jewish, independence. The Zionist plan to establish a Jewish homeland in Palestine simply made no sense.[140] Obviously, any secret treaties dividing Syria among the Europeans or supporting Zionists in Palestine should be canceled, in accordance with the principles of international law that Wilson had established.[141]

The participants at this meeting ultimately set a plan for a Syrian constitution, which they wrote after studying other constitutional models.[142] But first, they completed the document containing their demands, and then elected five people from each of the three regions of Greater Syria to present it to the King-Crane Commission. When they met with the commission on July 3, the Westerners asked them about the process by which this document had come to be, probing how representative it was, how representative they were.[143] To what extent had Christian and Jewish nationals participated in this conference, they asked.[144] Many whom the commission interviewed, including representatives of different religious groups, assured them that the congress and its document reflected the breadth of Greater Syrian opinion.[145]

Representatives to the commission addressed head-on the fact that religious difference was a factor in local political dynamics. Although the generally peaceful (but not totally equal) coexistence among Jews, Muslims, and Christians was the norm in Palestine at this time, questions about the appropriate place of religion in society and politics were hot topics.[146] Sectarian bloodshed in the region had caused political crises in the not too distant past.[147] Although these debates had been going on for a while, the King-Crane Commission sparked further deliberations. Whether sectarianism should be a basis for political representation was an open question.[148] In the view of some, the commission should hear from delegates chosen on the basis of proportional representation by sect.

> We are destined to have sects lead our affairs. Thus, when the Commission consults with a committee as such, which would be considered a national committee despite its sectarian basis, it would be as if it consults with the entire people. This is because the people had formed such a committee to represent them. This would result in nothing other than the good, if God wills.[149]

They knew that minority protections were a key concern of the Western powers in this period (a fact also mentioned in the King-Crane Report).[150] This challenge for the League of Nations required finding accommodation for national minorities within states under the protection of international law.[151] Equal status for religious minorities featured centrally in how the Arab petitioners described their longed-for independent state to the commission. Faysal proclaimed that religious differences were irrelevant and that support for minority rights would be absolute, a policy based on what was right, not "merely on utilitarian grounds." Delegates in Akka (in northern

Palestine) asserted and performed their religious unity and class diversity, proving both their credentials as representatives of their people and their nationalist qualifications.[152]

Across Palestine the King-Crane Commission heard from petitioners and delegations seeking to make their wishes known. In meetings of fifteen or thirty minutes, the commission heard consistent demands across these diverse strata of the Palestinian public: the majority wanted independence in a multifaith, united Arab nation of Greater Syria (including Palestine) with a democratic government under the constitutional rule of a monarch (Prince Faysal being the choice of many).[153] Or, if they were forced to be governed by a mandatory state, they wished to be under its temporary—and they stressed that it should be temporary—tutelage. The commissioners heard this repeatedly in the statements of hundreds of delegations (a total of 442 delegations over their 42-day journey).[154] Each of the 1,863 petitions they collected (including 260 from Palestine) contained the signature, and in many cases the seal, of dozens of claimants.[155] Tens of thousands of signatures were presented in Jerusalem alone, it was said.[156] The commission's respect for "public opinion" as an element of representative governance—an important element of liberal internationalism[157]—even extended to "Muslim ladies," as the commission recorded them.[158] These were women who presented the same demands for national independence as the majority of petitioners.[159] Other women in Damascus also demanded independence, which they thought necessary to prevent their husbands from becoming "lazy."[160]

Perhaps fueled by their provisions of chocolate and instant coffee, sardines and salmon, the commission came to some preliminary conclusions just a couple of weeks into their investigation.[161] They understood that the majority did not want a mandate at all. In case there was any confusion among the commissioners, a delegation from the Lydda area of Palestine clarified matters in response to a question about their preference for a mandate for Palestine: "It makes little difference to a man condemned to die whether he be shot or hung."[162] Prince Faysal wanted technical assistance from outside powers, but he, like the Palestinian Muslim-Christian Association, wanted to pay for it "with money, not with the freedom of his people."[163] A newspaper contributor explained this position in the Arabic publication *al-'Asima*: "Our acceptance of foreign sponsorship would be an admission of our own inability to govern ourselves, and therefore deny us the opportunity at any point in the future to enjoy that right."[164] But if they were forced to be under a mandate power, the overwhelming preference was for the United States because it was believed to have no imperialist, political interests in the region.[165]

## Imperial Hangovers

Even if the Americans' statements gave the Arabs the impression that their views would be taken seriously, the Arabs faced a formidable challenge in the deeply orientalist mentality of most influential Westerners at the time. From the outset, neither France nor Britain had much interest in the commission or in the Syrians' opinions.[166] The King-Crane Commission might never even have happened had Gertrude Bell and William Westermann had their way. William Westermann was an American classicist turned Near East expert for the team advising Woodrow Wilson at the Paris peace negotiations, where other "'experts,' reporters, influence peddlers, aggrieved parties, and hangers-on" took part in "an extended merry-go-round of deliberations, dinners, and decisions."[167] In a tête-à-tête with Westermann, Bell, the British "explorer-agent," explained her opposition to the commission, still planned at that stage to be an "inter-allied" investigation. Bell said that "no Oriental ever told what he actually thought about matters, openly and in a public way."[168] It was a common orientalist position to doubt the truth of Arab words to justify Western paternalism. Howard Crosby Butler, an American archeologist who had worked in Syria, informed the commissioners in a forty-eight-page report that "it would be impossible to discover what any large number of these people desire," and even if this were possible, they wouldn't know what's best for them.[169]

Westermann, who also thought sending the commission was "an extremely foolish decision," recorded in his diary that Bell was quite sure about the Orientals, and he concurred.[170] Also among her certainties, Bell told Westermann she had "all along felt that for practical, political reasons, the French must be given the mandate over Syria." And, perhaps to be sure she was right, she advised that if a commission were to be sent, a rather narrow menu of options should be offered on a multiple-choice poll: "the question which would have to be put by the inter-allied commission would have to be . . . based on the fore-gone decision that there must be a mandatory power."[171] Judging the conclusions in advance even more definitively, Westermann opposed any commission because it could not tell them anything they did not already know.[172]

The Europeans' dillydallying over sending the commission was noticed in the Middle East "with diminishing patience."[173] Indeed, the British, who were the occupying power in Palestine at the time, were ambivalent about this investigative commission. They did not hold "free choice" in such high esteem.[174] This was, after all, the year in which the Rhodes Chair of Imperial History at King's College London and (what would later be named) the Imperial and Naval History chair were endowed "as self-conscious acts of imperial patriotism" in the empire's capital.[175] In Prime Minister Lloyd George's address at the Paris Peace Conference, he predicted that the competing nationalist claimants in Palestine were "going to grow up into two troublesome chickens; the Jew virile, brave, determined, intelligent; the Arab decadent, dishonest and producing little beyond eccentrics, influenced by the romance and silence of the desert."[176] That gives us some idea of what the Arabs were up against. The British considered Palestine to be some kind of Hobbesian barnyard, and themselves the best, order-imposing Leviathan-farmer for the job. The moral or practical rightness of self-determination for small nations was hardly a foregone conclusion for the British.[177]

According to Albert Lybyer, the fate of the investigation looked bleak until shortly before it finally set off. Its cancellation, appointment, cancellation, selection of members, and cancellation again ping-ponged from mid-April through mid-May of 1919, with "everybody opposed but Wilson, the Turks, Faisal, and Kurds."[178] But this was a new era, and Woodrow Wilson intended to "put diplomatic peacemaking on a 'rational' footing," and he finally confirmed the King-Crane Commission.[179] Like "The Inquiry," the King-Crane Commission was another means to implement Wilson's plan for a global moral commitment to peace to be achieved through rational discourse.[180] Unlike the contentious team of mostly academic "experts" on the inquiry in Paris, this commission was to consist "of men with no previous contact with Syria." The presumed objectivity conferred by ignorance, Wilson believed, would "convince the world that the [Paris Peace] Conference had tried to do all it could to find the most scientific basis possible for a settlement."[181] Although the six main members of the King-Crane

Commission did have varying levels of personal and academic familiarity with the region, they wore the scientific mantle proudly. They ordered one hundred fifty books.[182]

## William Yale's Clash of Civilizations

Alongside typological studies that grouped peoples according to the broadness of their heads or their "composite" features, the commission members were reading books that asserted that the "Moslem" system of government was theocratic, that the sultan was head of church and state, and that Islam was an all-encompassing mentality that organized every aspect of society and politics.[183] One of the authors they were reading assumed that nationality was "derived" from religion in the Ottoman Empire and understood this to be a main stumbling block in settling the "near-Eastern questions." This author averred: "The conception of a nation as a millet (religious community) is ingrained in Moslem races, and influences also races which have been subjected to or which have lived in intimate contact with Moslem civilization."[184] The problem of "ingrained" millet divisions had, according to another analyst on the commissioners' bookshelves, "fostered totally divergent civilizations" that were "fatal to the formation of nationality."[185] The commission members read descriptions of the "virile races" among the many "Mobile Semitic hordes." They read about others who were a "visible" fusion of "Semitic and Indo-European" races, who did things like "swarm," "drift," "invade," and "scatter" in their "fundamental wanderings."[186] And with this thorough study of Victorian anthropology (much of which was written by Christian missionaries), the members of this commission billed themselves as taking an organized and rational approach to discovering the opinion of the Arab people.[187] Albert Lybyer believed they were expected to "carry on a really scientific investigation."[188]

As with commissions the world over, however, some investigators were sure they understood everything there was to understand about those they were investigating without actually talking to them. For them, what they thought they knew of a culturally determined mentality that could not accommodate democratic procedure (or even truth telling) was enough.[189] Their belief that the Muslim-majority Arabs would not protect minority Christians and Jews if left to their own devices was based on assessments of the Arabs' political development and, in the view of some, presumptions about the inherent fanaticism of Muslims.[190] William Yale interpreted every political demand or attitude through the lens of a clash of civilizations. The fanatical, authoritarian Muslims wanted all power for themselves, he believed. As George Montgomery, Yale's fellow technical adviser, also contended, "Mohommedan empires grew and prospered only as long as there was loot to be looted and divided. Islam contains no nucleus of unselfishness which may hold out hope of Mohommedan reformation. . . . There is in it no heart to meet the needs of modern society."[191] A Presbyterian minister and the US ambassador in Constantinople, Montgomery believed that Islam was incompatible with the modern world and was incapable of reform. Muslims were "profoundly fanatical" and, along with Arabs generally, were excluded from "history." While Jews had a national history, Arabs did not.[192]

Like a psychologist who reads every statement of protest or denial as proof of the analysand's guilty subconscious, Yale took the Arab nationalists' objection to Article 22 of the League of Nations Charter as evidence of their fanaticism, which he knew to be "bred in the bones of all Syrians."[193] (Indeed, Palestinian educator and diarist Khaliil Sakakini said: "If it is extremist to insist on one's rights, then let's be called extremist; if it is considered rational to give in, then prefer to be crazy."[194]) Dismissing the possibility that Arab opposition to a Western mandatory government could be "simply fear that any western power assuming this responsibility would never leave the country," Yale described with certainty what the real reason for this opposition was: "the spirit of desire for Moslem domination . . . a profound anti-western feeling, the next development of which would be oppression of the native Christians and a suppression of their rights."[195] Those who believed they needed a mandatory power constituted "the more liberal group," in Yale's view. But they were in the minority, and he saw that Muslim authoritarian drive was ambitious.

Yale's fantastical orientalist imagination blended easily with his minor historical knowledge: "The ideal of the Young Arabs is the resurrection of a Moslem Arab State and eventually a Moslem Arab Empire somewhat along the lines of the empires of the Ommayads and the Abbasids."[196] In Yale's view, the strength of the Muslims' imperialist drive was matched only by their desire to oppress Christians. Muslims opposed the idea of a French mandate because France had "for centuries been the bulwark of Christianity in Syria."[197] Yale's arrogance, combined with an Islamophobic craze, provided the fuel for explaining away any possibility of Arab nationalism. Although he admitted that there were strong expressions of nationalism, Yale believed these expressions were not the same as genuine nationalism. The appearance of nationalism on the part of Christians was a result of their fear of Zionist takeover. It was the same fear shared by the Muslims of Palestine, who also wanted independence, but according to Yale, this was in order to dominate Palestine and be free of European control. Syrian Muslims wanted independence and unity with Palestine only because they wanted to reclaim what Saladin had taken from the Christians. The Druze and Greek Orthodox in Mount Lebanon only favored unity out of fear of Maronite domination and French culture. Yale admitted there were some Protestants in Lebanon who "sincerely" believed in Syrian nationalism, but this was only out of naiveté, for they did not rightly gauge "the forces working in the interior." The Muslims of Syria living abroad, in Egypt and America, might support Syrian national unity and independence, but that was because they were out of touch and did not appreciate how much danger the Christians of the area would be in.[198] In the cow-eyed docility among peasants and Bedouin, Yale saw that they did "not even understand the word Nationalism [sic]." They supported the calls for Syrian unity and independence only because they were "ordered to." The "effendi class," the feudal lords who colonial officials loved to blame, were in favor because they thought it the best way to guarantee the maintenance of their superior position over the Christians. "The program has pleased the Moslem clergy and fanatic because they see in it Moslem supremacy and independence. Among a few of the younger men there exists a vague but acute sense of nationalism, while the greater number of the younger men are fanatically Islamic," Yale reported.[199]

In contrast to the Arabs, Yale understood what nationalism really was. It was "a psychological force," something he could judge according to the "intensity of emotional reaction."[200] Nationalism for Yale was "a political philosophy" that "stirs their emotions so profoundly that loyalty to this philosophy becomes the dominant loyalty over-riding . . . all others."[201] It was not unlike the definition by Yale's contemporary, Emile Durkheim, of "mana" as a "physical force and moral power."[202] The uniformity of the Arabs' demands and the orderly way they presented them were insufficient evidence of true nationalist spirit, betraying a certain lack of collective effervescence. (Although Yale was doubtless not a reader of Durkheim.)

Albert Lybyer, on the other hand, was not convinced by Yale's assertions. He (like T. E. Lawrence) did not have much respect for Yale (but for different reasons unrelated to unseemly visits to brothels).[203] Lybyer suspected him of French-style chicanery in his attempts to skew the commission's findings along the way.[204] Dotted across his copy of Yale's report are question marks written in the margins. In contrast to Yale, Lybyer had recorded that the commission encountered "unexpectedly strong expressions of national feeling."[205] He was moved to spell out his doubts about Yale's account in various places on the pages, indicating he had not gotten the same "impression" as Yale.[206] At the section in the report where Yale's powers of eidetic reduction reached their zenith—his prose soaring with his own self-professed abilities to see beneath the "cloak" of Arab nationalism (which was only ever a "thin" cover, "torn in spots" but hiding "their real aims and purposes" that were spurred by "the hope of Moslem domination")—Lybyer asked in polite handwriting: "Evidence?"[207] But there was none. Not in any of Yale's copious reports, notes, and articles, squirrelled away across at least four US libraries for his own posterity did Yale provide anything that today's social scientist might accept as "data," "evidence," or ethnographic basis for his assertions. He, unlike King and Lybyer, simply understood "the eastern world and mentality"; he knew not to take "things at their face value." He did not lack, as his fellow commission members did, "that intuitive knowledge of the Oriental which comes from living with, rather than among Orientals."[208] He just knew.

William Yale thought he knew so much that he wrote his own independent report during the commission's journey. There he countered the consensus among Lybyer and the commissioners (and those whose opinions they were tallying). He sent it to Westermann in Paris—the man who got Yale the job on the commission—when the others had sent an update to Wilson.[209] Yale's contrary recommendations followed from his belief that there was not enough Greater Syrian nationalism to sustain a liberal and tolerant state. He called, instead, for the separation of Palestine from Syria for a national home for the Jewish people under the mandate of Great Britain and the separation of Lebanon under a French mandate.[210]

## American, Mostly Liberal, and Christian Experts

Yale was not fully a part of this "Wilsonian moment," as historian Erez Manela has dubbed it.[211] But it inspired many others to believe that a just basis for international relations would finally crystallize. Throughout the West and the Arab world, people shared an idealized image of the United States and Woodrow Wilson as the vessels delivering these rewards. This included Albert Lybyer, who was a liberal fan of Woodrow Wilson, his former teacher.[212] He was not alone in holding Wilson in such high regard at a time when, in the words of H. G. Wells, "humanity leapt to accept and glorify Wilson . . . he became a Messiah . . . the bringer of untold blessings."[213] But Lybyer might have been the only one to refer to him with a schoolboy adoration as *en buyuk celebi*—Turkish for "the greatest gentleman." He recorded so much about the president in his diary using this moniker that he scribbled the acronym "E.B.C." when describing Wilson's actions.[214]

Although his faith in his president never seemed to wane, he did express a deep anxiety about the possibility that force, politics, and the selfish motives of the Great Powers would determine the outcome of the peace conference and the fate of Syria, rather than the principle of "consulting the people."[215] King, Lybyer's fellow academic on the commission, who told the president that he hoped their work "may help in securing righteous settlements in the Near East," also had apprehensions.[216] He didn't want their mission to be viewed as hypocritical if the Paris Peace Conference had already decided the fate of the mandates. This would be an "intolerable position" that he did not want to be in.[217] He had a hunch that neither the French nor the British seemed "to have any idea of paying any attention to what the people themselves want."[218] Eventually King and Lybyer both became sufficiently convinced that their investigation was meaningful enough for them to take on the assignment. Perhaps the instructions to the commission, which directed them to become acquainted "as fully as possible with the state of opinion there . . . which might serve to guide the judgment of the [Paris Peace] Conference" assured them that their mission presented new opportunities for steering the negotiations in a liberal direction.[219]

Like Wilson, Lybyer and King were scholars who saw themselves as important and having certain insights because of their training and status. They were, in their own estimation, experts with a clear sense of the deeper forces driving the world. For Lybyer especially, the commission presented a new opportunity to jockey within the politics of expertise at play. He was pleased with his appointment as advisor to the commissioners. Westermann noticed, and derided him as someone who was "hoping to be King of the World or something."[220] Propelled by his ambitions, Lybyer confessed to his diary great concern with his own status, registering every verbal gold star or snub that he received. Perhaps with the optimism encouraged by the first day of the year, Lybyer considered himself a member of "The Inquiry" "fairly well established among the experts" at the beginning of 1919. He was obviously pleased when interlocutors found his work and arguments impressive, and made special note when King consulted him on "all important points" in their report drafting.[221] His keen social eye assessed his position based on dinner-table seating assignments; where he was placed relative to the high-status guests was duly noted in his journal. Although he wore his special riding suit for meetings with important people (cutaway coat, white vest, striped trousers), he struggled to "hold his own" amid the commissioners.[222] He would not let a cold deter his work, but made fussy appraisals of its progress. He tallied any social slights. When Mrs. Wilson neglected to invite him to a reception she was hosting, he suffered. "Not a red letter day," he sighed to his journal on that rainy Wednesday.[223]

Despite the occasional disappointments, Lybyer looked back fondly decades later. "Those were great days!" he wrote in a letter to one chronicler.[224] And throughout his time with the King-Crane Commission, he was happy with his experiences on the journey across the Levant. In letters to his wife, Clara, he wrote with appreciative tones about the "very Oriental" scenes in Jerusalem's Old City, and the "picturesque" groups of people waiting to present their demands in Bethlehem.[225] He bought coins along the way and mother-of-pearl beads for her, his "Dearest Girl." He also mentioned to Clara the women who sometimes raised their veils during their delegations' meetings, and to his diary he remarked on the "good-looking ladies."[226] Lybyer was thoroughly engaged in the work and found the conversations with the delegations fascinating. "Most interesting times," he wrote to Clara on a postcard depicting the gaudy Church of the Holy Sepulchre.[227]

In the midst of their research and his trinket shopping, Lybyer also found time to collect some water from the Jordan River and go to church with Henry King.[228] Of the nine men in the King-Crane group, seven had ties to Christian missionary activity in the Near East, and at least three were preachers themselves. King was a history professor, an ordained minister, and a fan of Woodrow Wilson.[229] Crane was a businessman and a Wilson donor.[230] They believed that it was noble work they were engaged in, this "important government mission" a manifestation of the moral superiority of America and its Christianity.[231] Their Christianity also mediated their social and political networks. Wilson's religious inspirations and Presbyterian missionary social networks were fundamental in the formation and authorization of the commission.[232] Wilson and many of those he appointed believed themselves to be part of a "nation uniquely blessed by God, indeed chosen by God for a 'redemptive' role in the world, ordained to serve as a 'New Israel,' whose providential mission it was to serve in exemplary fashion as a 'beacon unto the nations.'"[233] Members of the commission saw the landscape they were touring through Bible-tinted glasses, referring to some of the stops on their journey with their religious names. Amman was "Rabbath Ammon," and the village al-Majdal in Palestine was "Magdala." Unimpressed by that town, Commissioner King quipped that he "didn't wonder that Mary Magdalene left home."[234]

## Secularism and Skepticism

While the Americans were fully engrossed in their Christian fantasies and concerns, obsessed with the lurking threats that Muslim ambitions posed, the Arabs were seeking to cordon off religion from their political affairs. Historian Elizabeth Thompson has declared that "the 1920 Syrian-Arab constitution was the most secular and democratic to date in the Middle East."[235] Whereas Western international law focused on minorities and cultural difference as a fundamental problem for the new international order, the Arabs who were presenting their political proposals to the commission took it as a given that minority rights would be protected.[236] What they were less certain of, however, were the Westerners' intentions. Even if, as historian Ussama Makdisi has observed, the problem of the Arabs' belief in "Wilsonian idealism ran deep," not everyone was so convinced by the American president.[237]

There were enough people who had doubts about the commission and about the sincerity of American promises that conflicting stories were swirling, echoes of which appeared in an argument carried out across the regional press. But hopes still soared. In a letter to the editors in *al-Muqattam*, one Issa al-Saqri from Yafa disputed "the rumors about the American government . . . that it agreed with the Zionists over their immigration to Palestine and that everything of relevance to Syria and Palestine is agreed on a priori." Al-Saqri was sure they were wrong. Others may think that "the American Commission's visit is nothing but an attempt to blind the people," but he did not believe that the United States would reject their request for an American mandate (if they had to have one), because it "comes from the hearts of the Syrians in the homeland and abroad."[238] One group asked if "Mr. Wilson still held to his Fourteen Points and the right of a people to self-determination," and if "the Peace Conference had decided definitely against an independent Syria."[239]

A contributor to *Lisan al-Hal* seemed torn between expecting the worst and hoping for the best:

> We stand confused between assurances by the countries that the guardian country would be a helpful teacher, rather than being an exploitive investor, and this strong rush and friction to win the guardianship. If they tell us that they are doing this for countries they wish to colonize and exhaust their goods and wealth, our confusion would recede. This is because profit motivates them to rush. What is confusing and surprising, however, are their claims about competing for the development of the country, even if this costs money and men. They are competing both to benefit and get benefits. And this is a sublime feeling and we have no doubt about their promises.

In contrast, 'Awni 'Abd al-Hadi, who Faysal had appointed director of the Arab delegation at the peace conference, was more certain. He had developed a decidedly cynical view of his Western interlocutors there. "As for the politics that go on these days in the [peace] Conference, they are the ugliest of politics. The words of freedom, justice, and rights are nothing to these political men but words of trickery, hypocrisy, nothing else," he lamented in a letter to his brother.[240] Faysal was inclined to agree and thought "that the Great Men of the World are best admired at a distance."[241] Those located farther away had their doubts too. Rashid Rida, a well-known writer and Muslim reformer who produced a publication loudly critical of European imperialism, feared that universal rights and international law might be applied unfairly, even while he praised Woodrow Wilson's democratic proclamations.[242]

There was plenty of cause to be wary in the long list of broken promises that had been doled out to the Arabs over recent years. Before Wilson and Balfour, there was the Hussein-McMahon correspondence, with its apparent support of Palestinian independence that had so far been unimplemented by the Western powers. In 1915, Sir Henry McMahon, the British high commissioner in Egypt, offered Sherif Hussein of Mecca an independent Arab state if he would help the British fight the Ottoman Turks. It was implied in the correspondence exchanged during 1915–1916 that Palestine was included in the promise. Around the same time, and unbeknownst to the Arabs, Great Britain and France agreed to divide Ottoman territory into British and French spheres of influence—with no provision for Palestinian independence. As that secret document, known as the Sykes-Picot agreement, was made public (thanks to the Bolsheviks who published it in *Pravda*), the British were making yet another pledge, this time to help the Zionists make Palestine their "national home."[243] In historian Avi Shlaim's words, "Even by the standards of Perfidious Albion, this was an extraordinary tale of double-dealing and betrayal."[244] Although the British did much to try to pretend otherwise, in private and sometimes in public, members of the government admitted that their support for the Zionists project in Palestine was contrary to McMahon's promise, and was thus a stain on Great Britain's "honor."[245]

These skeptics in the Arab world were not alone. When the League of Nations covenant was agreed in Paris, Thorstein Veblen, the unconventional economist and dissector of the "leisure class," condemned it as a ploy. He recognized it as being "a political document, an instrument of realpolitik, created in the image of nineteenth century imperialism. It has been set up by political statesmen, on political grounds, for political ends, and with political apparatus to be used with political effects."[246] Somewhat more pithily, a writer in Arabic suspected that financial gain was the real motive for Western states that wanted to be a mandate power.[247] In that, they were not far off the mark. The British thought there was oil at the eastern shore of the Dead Sea, which is why they wanted that territory included in the Palestine over which they would have a mandate.[248] William Yale, still in the employ of the Standard Oil Company during his commission work, "quite naturally" told a Standard Oil director "about matters that came to [his] attention . . . which concerned the oil interests of the Standard Oil Company in Palestine, Syria and Mesopotamia."[249] Yale is the man who believed Wilson's fourteen points to be nothing but "wartime propaganda," and the King-Crane Commission to be merely a camouflage, "a blind to deceive the natives."[250] At least one of his fellow commission advisers believed that Yale's employers' hopes for oil profit shaped Yale's interpretations of the facts and his analysis of the Arabs' political demands.[251]

People voiced other suspicions about colonial meddling too. Some wondered if state actors' visits to the region were really intended to lead Christians to think they had something to fear. Faysal expressed concerns about the discord-producing effects of the French in Syria in his presentation to the King-Crane Commission.[252] What Nasim Sbei'a found in his reading of French newspapers troubled him as well. He took up many column inches of *al-Muqattam* to insist on the separation of religion and state, and warn against those who were stirring up sectarian friction for purposes of divide-and-rule.

> We, the Syrians, have no choice but to maintain what we have repeatedly said before witnesses: that we do not want to have religion interfere in the affairs of our country and we do not accept in any way . . . and that our future government would be Syrian, civil, constitutional, and detached from any religious character. We also stated that it is not an Islamic government. Rather it is Syrian democratic government. Thus, we say now that this government won't be Christian; rather, it is Syrian and democratic. This is a right granted to us, just like other nations, after achieving freedom that was won in the battle. Thus, we are not giving up on this right. Both old and young among us are well aware of the fact that, once our religious

differences interfere in our common living affairs, the outcomes would be most detrimental for us, our nation, and our country. It would leave us like a ball to be kicked by different players. Thus, we now demand a new era in which our word is united, just like others before. Let everyone know that stirring up religious antagonisms among us will no longer be beneficial, and that laughing at us is a matter of the past and won't happen again. Let everyone of us pray to his god according to his religious rituals, this in the mosque, that in his church and that in his synagogue; in security.[253]

## Conclusion

The range of scholarship, commentary, and polemic on this period at the end of World War I is vast.[254] The era marked the beginning of the end of British imperial power, the rise of American influence in the Middle East, and the parallel rise of Zionism.[255] Likewise, scholars have thoroughly studied the question of how imperial hubris propelled the divvying up of the postwar spoils, and have examined the geographical and aerial imaginations by which its spores found fertile ground to grow across the Middle East.[256] Much of that work has focused on the secret dealings and political shenanigans of prominent political figures, mostly European and American men.

Rather less considered have been the Arabs upon whose lands the Westerners were trouncing with their pledges, plans, and boots on the ground. This chapter has offered an account of *their* hopes and expectations, their maneuverings and motives, to show how intent they were on securing their political independence and grounding their future polity in liberal values.[257] Historian James Gelvin has argued that what "accustomed much of the population to at least an attenuated form of political participation" was the mobilizing efforts of Faysal's Arab government, which was seeking to convince the King-Crane Commission of the sincerity and unity of its demands for independence.[258] But the political involvement was in fact widespread, bringing people from all walks of life into a lively civic conversation, drawing on already deeply entrenched participatory political habits.

The period around the end of the Ottoman Empire being one of fading, fluid, and inventing identifications, people anticipated different results from the future, and their political views were multiple and shifting.[259] For some, the Great War marked a sharp break and presented new social and political

horizons. Many Palestinians were focused on the specificities of their conditions that came with the challenges that Zionism posed, leading them to de-
vise a distinct set of Palestinian nationalist tactics for obtaining a unique national future.[260] Their democratic traditions encouraged an active debate over
correct bases for political identity, authority, and representation. Their collective discussions about the obligations of governments to minorities reflected
a consensus that religion should be entirely separate from government.

With its probing questions, the King-Crane Commission underscored
issues of minority rights according to liberal principles. The focus of Arab
representatives to the commission was on those same international legal
principles—self-determination, protection of minorities—which they presented in logical arguments, relying on the promises inherent within international law. The report of the King-Crane Commission, written mostly by
Lybyer and King, reflected much of the Arab majority's demands.[261] It recommended that Jewish immigration be limited, and that a single Syrian state
that included Palestine and Lebanon be established under King Faysal.[262]
As Lybyer wrote, implementation of the Balfour declaration would require
force, which would go against the principles that the Allies were supposed
to be fighting for.[263] The King-Crane Report also recommended that the
United States act as mandatory power for this new state. In his telegram to
Wilson summarizing their report, Crane encouraged the president to heed
the recommendations by assuring him that the report was "founded on vital
human facts." But he did not.[264]

The US State Department classified the report as a secret document, and
it may or may not have reached President Wilson after it was submitted in
mid-August—there was no copy in his strong box.[265] He may not have considered it much even if he did receive it, as he was very busy with losing the
argument for US participation in the League of Nations at home, which left
him exhausted and ill.[266] Wilson's stroke on September 25, 1919, sealed the
irrelevance of the commission report at the time. Two copies of the King-
Crane Report were left with the peace commission delegation, but it was not
publicly circulated, save for a few editorials in the US press about the recommendations that had been leaked.[267] The full document was finally published
in 1922 by *Editor and Publisher* magazine, with summaries and translations of
the report published in Arabic newspapers soon thereafter.[268] Some members

of the commission believed that the State Department and "the opposition of the Zionists" led to the report's suppression.[269]

Although the King-Crane Report had no political impact on the European and American powers deciding the fate of the Near East at the time, it has had a lasting legacy. It exists as a reference point for Palestinians and others to prove the existence of their movement and political peoplehood in the period of Zionism's infancy. Jamal al-Husayni, Palestinian political leader during the British mandate, told William Yale in a letter more than four decades later, "I know, it has helped a lot."[270] It did not help the Palestinians achieve independence, but in its peripatetic and thorough fact finding across the length and breadth of Palestine (and beyond), the King-Crane Commission helped convince Arabs in the region that they shared common ground with Western political values in holding representative government to be a supreme value. All sides professed a belief that homogenous nations that ruled democratically and protected minorities would and should be sovereign, and that "the will of the people" and international law would guide world politics. When it came to the Near East, though, none of this turned out to be the case in practice.

Henry King thought that the investigation played an important role, and the terms in which he expressed this are revealing: "I think our trip has been very worthwhile, and that we have gotten results that could not possibly have been gotten without such a commission." He said, "The people will certainly feel that they have been consulted and cannot help having a somewhat different attitude on that account."[271] Feeling like they had been consulted would encourage the Arabs to accommodate themselves to whatever outcome the Western powers imposed. But this, too, did not happen.

Arab hopes in international law and the liberals who proselytized it were disappointed after World War I. Despite the reasonably expressed uniform demands for absolute independence that the King-Crane Commission recorded, and despite the commission's proposal that the Arabs be assisted in developing their independent polity, the Great Powers granted the mandate of Palestine to the British, who ruled Palestine while supporting Zionism under the aegis of the League of Nations until Israel gained an independent state in most of the territory in 1948.[272] A full cycle of the hope and disappointment that would mark future international interventions in Palestine was complete: collective hopes inspired by imperial promises and lip service attention to public opinion, met with keen attempts by Arabs to prove their liberal worthiness of respect from other liberals, followed by assessments of their political readiness and Arab disappointment at the political promises left unfulfilled. The King-Crane Commission was a first rotation in the cycle of self-representation, investigation, and disregard that would repeat itself throughout subsequent Palestinian history.

# CHAPTER 2

# Universalizing Liberal Internationalism

## The Arab Revolt and the Boycott of the Peel Commission

IN 1936, the British appointed the fateful Royal Peel Commission as a means to calm the disturbances that had broken out across Palestine—what would become a three-year-long rebellion known as the Arab Revolt. By the end of the revolt, possibly more than five thousand Palestinians were killed, and almost fifteen thousand wounded. At its height, approximately twenty-five thousand British servicemen were deployed to police an Arab population of slightly more than one million.[1] Many Palestinians had decided enough was enough. They had experienced nearly two decades of British mandatory rule; had the League of Nations serially ignore their pleas for representative government and self-determination; watched tens of colonies with some 370,000 Jewish residents grow across their country as Arab peasant landlessness increased; and seen five major investigative commissions come and go.[2] Arabs were declaring publicly that they had "no hope in the fairness of the government and thus, they see no point in cooperating with its Commission," as Palestinian leader Hajj Amin al-Husayni explained in the pages of *Filastin*.[3] For months, Palestinians boycotted the Peel Commission, until political pressure from leaders of Arab states and violent suppression of the revolt by the British finally forced them to give in to yet another investigation.

The boycott of the Peel Commission is one of the few examples in Palestinian history of a collective refusal to take the bait of international law's official mechanisms. Although it was only a temporary hiatus in the longer history of continual liberal engagement that this book tells, the significance of this boycott is only heightened by its rarity. The refusal of an international commission highlights how much frustration had to build before this repudiation could happen. But it also shows both how intertwined Palestinian politics had become with the liberal order, and how necessary a contextual change was to boycotting the commission and refusing the Western order that it symbolized. What had changed to allow this refusal was Palestinians' view of their political horizons, how they imagined the audience to whom they could make their entreaties.

Arab rejection of the Peel Commission was both enabled by and contributed to the transnational development of an anticolonial consciousness. In the interwar period, international solidarity that formed around the fight against colonialism offered a model and means of struggle that the subsequent focus on international law largely displaced. (That is, until postcolonial shifts at the United Nations delivered a new context for solidarity politics from the 1960s onward, as Chapter 4 explains.) The boycott of the commission and the Arab revolt were part of an attempt to transform the liberal framework that international law and the League of Nations had policed, offering a different universalizing discourse not subsumed by the League of Nations and its articulations of international law.[4]

Although their main concern was to assert their status as a nation and claim the rights that were attendant on that status, Palestinians were also taking part in an international debate. With appeals to values deemed central to liberalism—with calls for justice, human rights, and their "natural" national rights—Palestinians launched their campaign of civil disobedience alongside more militant challenges to British forces. Within the liberal internationalism of this moment—too often misunderstood as an interwar dynamic of the West exclusively—Palestinians' anticolonial struggle against the British and Zionists came to be a motivating symbol for Arabs, Muslims, and others. Together they were battling Western imperial ambitions that thwarted their independence. Theirs was an attempt to establish a collective understanding of the correct criteria for sovereignty, which for Palestinians included adherence to liberal values that should guide an international system that was actually international and truly liberal. Palestinians called on and summoned into being a broader anticolonial liberal public opinion that was set to become a worldwide political force.

## The Conjuncture That Enabled a Boycott

As with all remarkable historical events, a confluence of factors enabled the boycott and the Arab revolt. National and international dynamics came together to produce this break with the hegemonic system.[5] In the lead-up to the Arab Revolt of 1936–1939, the economic situation had worsened for most Arabs in Palestine. Wages were down, and unemployment had increased.[6] British proposals for representative government had come to naught. There had been outbreaks of violence, partly in response to increasing Jewish immigration. The British had armed the Zionists, whose structures were coming to resemble a state that excluded the Arabs. And the traditional, mostly elite Palestinian leadership had fallen into disarray, while an increasingly mobilized nationalist youth contingent was pressing for stronger forms of resistance. New political parties also were being established.[7] Such were the factors contributing to this pressurized conditions. All was set up for an eventful outburst.[8]

On the international level, the Arab Revolt and Peel Commission came as the League of Nations experiment was crumbling and the storm clouds of world war were gathering again. Japan had already withdrawn from the league in 1931; Germany did the same in 1933; three years later, two Latin American countries (Honduras and Nicaragua) notified the league of their withdrawal; and league condemnation of Italy for its annexation of Ethiopia that same year (the Abyssinia Crisis) led that Mediterranean country to leave in 1937, along with Paraguay that same year.[9] One can read a sense of panic in the snippy tones with which league officials discussed the Palestinian crisis, a crisis that had ruptured the alliance of the British and the league.[10] The tectonics of regional and local political authority was shifting for the Arabs of Palestine too. Although it staged a "great international argument over imperialism's claims," the League of Nations became just one of many forums for demanding and asserting political ideas, having lost some of its appeal as a hub of political interaction.[11] The stranglehold on Palestinian politics that the elite leadership had maintained for so long was also weakened, as not only youth, but also workers, peasants, and the Arab Independence Party

[*Hizb al-ʾIstiqlal al-ʿArabi*] expanded Palestinian civic activism.[12] These were people motivated and able to coordinate a popular mobilization.[13]

The class and gender boundaries of political activity had been breached. Palestinian society in all its diversity—including peasants, women, students, workers, and the educated middle classes—were demanding fundamental change and fulfillment of their nationalist claims. They were doing so through liberal categories of rights and collective and individual freedom. They called for self-governance and democratic representation, and they made demands for economic and social progress and national equality.[14] Youth were studying "the Magna Charta, the English Bill of Rights and the rest of British history—to say nothing of the French, American and Russian Revolutions," Khalil Totah observed from his perch as a school director from Ramallah in 1936. They had gained a "potent political education" from "the law schools, newspapers, parliamentary procedures etc." and this was, in Totah's estimation, bearing "political fruit."[15]

The mannered elites of liberalism's domain—both Arab and Western—had to make way for more pointed refusals of colonialism, grounded in universal appeals to universal values. The time for a fight—its inevitability predicted by Khalil Sakakini during the King-Crane debates—had arrived.[16] In the words of a leader of the revolt, the Arabs had finally gotten "fed up with yesterday's friend."[17]

## A World Audience with Common Enemies

A goal of colonial histories, as David Scott has insisted, is to understand not simply whether or how the colonized accommodated or resisted their conditions. More central, Scott writes, is the question of how "(colonial) power altered the terrain on which accommodation/resistance was possible in the first place."[18] Perhaps even more important is the question of how the colonized experienced this alteration and perceived the possibilities it opened up for resistance. How did opportunities for solidarity appear to them? The meaning and impact of the transformations in legal and political institutions wrought by the colonizers could never be the product of colonial intentionality alone.[19] To understand what allowed—or compelled—Palestinians to resist engaging with an investigative commission and pursue other avenues for political change, it is necessary to consider how they were reading the world of political tumult that made other political avenues seem possible.

Through new channels of communication and transnational political interaction among the colonized, the idea of "the world" came into being as a new and significant political interlocutor for Palestinians—an audience that has remained a key interlocutor throughout the decades of their seeking independence.[20] Now more diverse and not as dominated by Western actors, "the world" emerged as a justifying source and platform for Palestinians' humanist calls for justice, for rights, and for humanitarianism as a guiding political ethos.

A growing regional press gave access to information about what was happening elsewhere, with greater publicity for colonial and anticolonial activities reaching more people. This included daily Arabic newspapers that now circulated widely in Palestine, throughout the Arab world, and beyond.[21] Demand for imported publications increased as events throughout the region heated up. Papers from Egypt and Lebanon were brought into Palestine, and Palestinian newspapers discussed what was being written in publications, including those from India, Brazil, the United States, England, and various parts of Europe.[22]

The broadsheets became an interactive and popular forum for public communication.[23] They discussed mass anticolonial demonstrations and strikes under way in Egypt and Syria in 1935 and 1936. Alongside the Moroccan movement for national independence, which was extolled in Palestinian newspapers, the strike in nearby Syria resonated particularly in Palestine, and calls to extend the revolutionary movement into Palestine circulated widely.[24] "Palestine occupied the conversation in Syria, the same way Syria occupied conversation in Palestine," a newspaper article recorded in 1936.[25] That Iraq had gained formal (albeit nominal) independence was widely referenced in Palestinians' arguments justifying their own demands for freedom. They also noted that France had signed independence treaties with Lebanon and Syria, while the local press reported on both the Libyans' struggle against the Italians as well as the Algerians' battle against the French.[26] They had seen these "Arab-speaking countries getting a semblance of political justice from the British and the French so why not Palestine—and by the same methods of

strikes, non-cooperation and civil disobedience?" Khalil Totah asked rhetorically of his interlocutors in London.[27]

Palestinians were paying attention to anti-British and anti-French politics elsewhere too. They looked to the Indian fight against the empire for
lessons. Palestinian teachers disseminated these lessons in their classrooms
and drew from Gandhi's tactics of noncooperation as a model for their own
protests, as Egyptians had done before.[28] In the view of one newspaper contributor, the Indians put on an ideal performance, but the "unarmed, poor but
patient" Palestinians surpassed it in "condemning oppression."[29] Not long
before the Palestinian revolt began, a general strike in Syria in 1936 prompted
sympathy strikes, demonstrations, and donation drives across Lebanon, Iraq,
and Palestine, where the press covered the Syrian events "exhaustively."[30] Palestinian editorialists chastised their leadership's lack of initiative, holding up
the Syrians as a model of proactive collective struggle.[31]

People sensed that the world was in crisis.[32] Farther afield from the Middle East, communists were fighting the fascists in Spain, communists were
rising up against the French in Vietnam, and strikes in Morocco were coordinated with labor unrest in France, all disruptions to imperial calm.[33] But
disruptions to this calm brought threat as well as hopeful openings, including
severe economic hardship across the globe that prompted worker strikes and
hunger marches. Palestinians were not spared. And they perceived this crisis
as more than a breakdown of some ideal prior order. It was understood as
evidence of the weakness of the imperial structure and the superficiality of
its liberal promises.

## The Abyssinia Lesson

The outrageously violent takeover of Abyssinia (today's Ethiopia) by Italy was
one manifestation of these cracks in the system, and Palestinians were paying
close attention. It had "affected Arab consciousness," Khalil Totah observed.
It was giving the Arabs a "now or never" feeling, he wrote.[34] Headlines excoriated the Western states and League of Nations for "doing nothing" for Abyssinia, while groups such as the Abyssinia Solidarity Committee in Egypt
ran donation drives.[35] Throughout May 1936, as Italy pounded the country
and emperor Haile Selassie fled, the Arabic press in Palestine recorded the
Abyssinians' attempts to defend their country. They also documented the

limp British response, including a lord's recommendation to form a commission of inquiry into the war.[36] At the League of Nations in 1936, Haile
Selassie sought support for his nation against the Italian aggression, reminding the delegates in Geneva that "fifty nations asserted that aggression had
been committed in violation of international treaties."[37] The raison d'être for
the League of Nations' existence was thrown into doubt, while the perfidious
nature of Great Britain was made ever clearer.[38]

The outlines of a shared enemy emerged in the Abyssinian story, as an
article in the Arabic daily *Filastin* exemplified: "The fall of the Abyssinian
Empire adds one more victim to the list of British deception. Britain that
claims to be friend of the weak nations breaks its promises and deceives these
nations. It let [the Abyssinian Empire] fall without offering any assistance.
Rather, it was busy bargaining about its share from the bounty."[39] The author saw that the British had deceived the Abyssinians as they had deceived
the Arabs, the Armenians, the Greeks.[40] (Arab observers might not have
known just how closely the Abyssinian case hewed to their own, because the
agreement between the French and British foreign ministers to concede the
majority of Abyssinia to Italian Prime Minister Benito Mussolini was secret, as had been the British and French agreement to parcel out the Levant
among themselves.)[41] In testimony to the Peel Commission some months
later, George Antonius, formerly assistant director of the Education Department in the British Government of Palestine, would present this imperial
convergence as an opportunity for England: "What Italy has done to Abyssinia is the same as the British in Palestine. And we've seen the world anger
at the Italians. Now is the chance for you to remove the oppression. It would
be the most noble action to take."[42] But they did not, which only reduced
British esteem in Palestinian eyes further.

The "sad, pale" Abyssinian emperor who arrived in the Palestinian seaport
town of Haifa "in a heart-breaking condition" was labeled in the Palestinian press a "living martyr," drawing him in to a shared collectivity united by
victimhood and respectful solidarity with it.[43] Palestinian notables and heads
of the Christian church welcomed him along with crowds in Haifa and Jerusalem. People flocked to see him, crying in sympathy for Selassie and his
people who fell prey to the same treasonous power that threatened the Palestinians themselves.[44] The Arabic press explained that the British and their

fake promises were behind the emperor's fate, "and then they let the emperor come to Palestine, which is another victim to their treason."[45] From these events another editorial concluded, simply: "The British empire is falling."[46]

The hypocrisies of the liberal order were becoming increasingly plain. That the League of Nations was cover for a "League of Empires" seemed clear.[47] It was evident in the Europeans' common venality and brutality. As a contributor to *Filastin* opined, the European countries that compete to spread their "civilizational message" in the East do not enact the ideals of a civilized world, for they are merely slaves to power. France, Italy, and England competed to "perform the message of the white man without faith in God, blindly and with harshness, led by a desire for material gain." The nature of their "message of civilization" was evident in Italy's violent behavior in Abyssinia. As the Abyssinian emperor observed conditions in his temporary refuge, the British attempts to put down the Palestinians' rebellion reminded him of the violence meted out to his own people.[48] The real message of human civilization was in Palestine, the unnamed writer in *Filastin* insisted, where nationalism and dignity were expressed in their revolution against oppression and in their civil disobedience in the face of the tyrant.[49] Ham-fisted British and French imperialism, and their willingness to stand aside as Italy invaded another country, ensured a shared understanding among the colonized and created the conditions for wide solidarity.

## Palestine Stirs the Arab World

The interwar period was a particularly fertile time for creative political reconfigurations to slide into place. Also significant is the way that people grasped and portrayed their own context, how they identified the chinks in the imperial system and the transnational solidarities that helped them believe they could achieve liberation. An increasing number of scholars have been considering the dynamics of internationalism in this era, which included transnational and regional circulation of political activists and radical ideas.[50] That research has drawn attention to the proliferation of international organizations and activist societies, such as the League to Combat Imperialism and the Women's International League for Peace and Freedom, that together constituted, in historian Daniel Gorman's view, a progressive "internationalist movement" moved by "liberal" internationalist ideals.[51] The energetic networking of anti-imperial activists in Paris underscores the importance of metropolitan cities where diaspora intellectuals convened and plotted, making that city a "headquarters of agitation of the French colonial peoples, where black, brown and yellow men [could] argue their case for freedom."[52] In addition, pan-Africanism, Black internationalism, pan-Islamism, the Khilafat movement, and pan-Arabism were movements and ideas bringing people into collective action across national borders.[53] Even if, as in Cemil Aydin's estimation, the threat and opportunity of a "unified Muslim world" was only a "racialized illusion," these ideological and social networks were key nodes of anticolonial activism.[54] In a region bubbling with anticolonial action challenging the struggling centers of imperial power, Arabs' horizons of possible action were prized open.

Abyssinia's fate provoked the support of Arabs across the region, but it was Palestine that really became a crucible of concern and solidarity in the Middle East. This is part of what encouraged the Arab Revolt and the boycott of the Peel Commission. People across the region understood themselves to be together in facing shared dangers and aspiring to common nationalist goals of independence and universal goals of peace. An article from the Egyptian magazine *Rose al-Yusuf* and reprinted in the Palestinian newspaper *Filastin* expressed it clearly:

> The Palestinian revolution has stirred the Arab world. The Palestinians have the right to live in liberty, away from this slavery practiced by British rule. Success of the Balfour Declaration is a failure of those who support peace. It raises concern in Palestine, a worry that extends to every Arab country that is aware of the dangers to which the Arab people are exposed, and which would lead to revolutions against colonialism. Every Arab nation cannot stop the feelings that motivate them to support Arab Palestine because the Palestinians supported every Arab nation. And because Palestine occupies a sacred place for the Arabs. When Palestine fights British colonialism, it is fighting the enemy fought by every Arab nation aspiring for independence. Cooperation amongst these nations is to serve one goal.[55]

The exchange of solidarity had been happening back and forth across many vectors for some years.[56] Hajj Amin al-Husayni, mufti of Jerusalem who was appointed by the British to be head of the Supreme Muslim

Council, convened an Islamic congress in Jerusalem in 1931.[57] The 145 delegates who attended hailed from twenty countries (including some Shi'a participants, a testament to the pan-Islamic, cross-sectarian nature of the gathering). Although the British limited what could be said, speakers framed the Palestinian cause at the center of the congregation's attention as a Muslim concern. The discussions and resolutions of the congress were pro-Palestinian, but also addressed the anti-Muslim policies and colonial activities faced by their coreligionists elsewhere, from Russia to Libya to Morocco.[58] The executive council of the congress protested these conditions to the League of Nations and Foreign Ministries, affirming their people's unity in opposing "every kind of colonization."[59] By November 1936, a "Palestine Conference" would draw thirty-five thousand Indian Muslims in New Delhi, who decided to boycott English products. It was just one of many examples of the "Muslim world" upset at British actions in Palestine, from Indonesia to Afghanistan.[60]

## International Public Opinion

Those horizons were dotted with a novel and nebulous setting called "public opinion." With the West's drive to democratize world politics after World War I—or to look like they were—the "moral force" of public opinion became another political tool to wield. In Woodrow Wilson's vision, rational discourse could mobilize it, and the League of Nations could channel it, all toward the goal of peace.[61] Although usage of the concept has a long history, the first Gallup and Roper polls in 1935 gave public opinion added reality and political weight.[62] Susan Pedersen, on the forefront of a recent surge of scholarship on the League of Nations, has argued that, despite the colonial continuities embodied by the league, "legitimacy" was necessarily a crucial concern for the rulers who used the League of Nations to enhance their own and the league's authority, and public opinion was the crucible in which that legitimacy manifested.[63] Western public opinion was a reference point for political justifications; it was deemed a basis for the production of international law, and Western activists and politicians of the time sought its support.[64]

The meaning of public opinion, however—what political actions it could justify, what modes of sovereignty it could legitimize, the range of views that constituted it—was not so limited. The dynamics of public opinion in this period have mostly been examined from the perspective of the West, but its significance did not stop at the boundaries of Europe or the United States. A diverse public mattered to the Palestinians resisting British and Zionist colonialism. They already believed that Palestine, as the home to three world religions, belonged "to all humanity." As Palestinian Quaker Khalil Totah told the British high commissioner, solving the problems in Palestine "could render a great service to humanity, civilization and Christendom at large."[65] For Palestinians and their Arab supporters, the legitimacy of their fight depended on how the strength and sincerity of their nationalist convictions were being assessed by Arabs, Muslims, and a world public. Activists writing in support of the Palestinian cause from throughout the Arab world also invoked this global audience. In a missive penned by the chairman of the Palestine Defence Society in the northern Iraqi city of Mosul, he

> hereby call[ed] the world to witness that we share with our kinsmen in Palestine their living feelings and their convictions, their faith in the righteousness of their national cause, and their sufferings, and that we admire their holy struggle in which we support them to the furthest limits, sparing no effort to that end, their cause being our own cause and their misfortunes being our own misfortunes.[66]

And these feelings of solidarity saw no geographic hurdles. "The distant deserts were not obstacles between our revolutionary souls and your proud lions," a prolific military leader of the revolt in Palestine proclaimed. "It made our struggle a duty and motived us to belittle ourselves for the path of Allah to have the world be witness to the unity of the homeland, the hope, and the blood everywhere in the Arab countries."[67]

This world was perceived to be a vigilant and judgmental one. The revolt was a "test of your steadfastness, your will, and strength," the Palestinian Arab Women's Committee wrote in a communiqué encouraging the revolutionaries. "Your unity, solidarity, and strikes will shake the world as it is making the breath of all Arabic speakers tremble with praise and astonishment."[68] The Palestinian leadership of the Arab Higher Committee (AHC) conjured a discerning world impressed by Arab bravery: "Your sacrifices that make the nation proud prove to the world that the Arab does not tremble in the face of attacks."[69] Showing a strong, united, nationalist refusal was seen to be a criterion of sovereignty itself. In a rousing statement from the leadership of the revolt, armed resistance was portrayed as the ultimate form of communication to convince the world of Arab rights:

> To arms! And show the entire world that the Arabs would not sleep on their grievances and that the Arab homeland is one, and Palestine is part and parcel of that sacred homeland. Make it clear that neither the British government, nor any other group or government has rights to Palestine that contradict the rights of the Arab people, holders of the legal rights to the country, or diminish their absolute sovereignty.[70]

Although the League of Nations had been the locus for making arguments about political worthiness, participants in the Arab Revolt knew that this rebellion was the significant battle for credibility and for national legitimacy. Through it they offered a critique of the "implicit organization of the world and its inhabitants" that had reigned until then and presented an ontological argument about their relation to the idea of freedom.[71] This was a struggle to define what kind of people each side thought they were dealing with.

Contemporary Arab analysts recognized clearly the colonial efforts to discredit Arab resistance. They saw these caricatures of themselves as laughable, but also dangerous, because political support or enmity is built out of narratives of deeds as much as the deeds themselves. An article published in the anti-British Egyptian newspaper *Al-Ahram*, and discussed in the Palestinian daily *Filastin*, examined this process carefully. With keen deconstructionist attention, the author of the original essay, titled "Newspapers of Colonialism and Their Ridiculous Campaigns," picked apart the various bogeys trotted out in the Western press—from communism and fascism to basic greed—which were espoused by the Westerners as the "real" motivations behind Arab anticolonial activities. The colonial press, the *al-Ahram* author observed, writes off those Egyptians, Syrians, and Palestinians who are willing to sacrifice themselves in resisting oppression. It portrays them as being no more than greedy Arabs who can be bought. The rebels are dismissed as being ignorant and easily manipulated, misled by communist, German, and Italian "conspiracies." According to these colonial campaigners, "the noble feelings of the people of Egypt, Syria, Palestine, Iraq and other eastern countries are non-existent. To them these people do not have feelings, personality, or substance. . . . These newspapers want to present these people as giving no significance to liberty, rights, independence, and national dignity." It was the correspondent's duty to warn readers about these spurious claims.[72]

It was a diverse audience to whom Palestinian nationalists thought they had to prove their political credibility and humanity. The Muslim world and Arab world were a continual address for them, as were world and English public opinion. The Arab Christians of Palestine called especially to "the Christian world" to save the holy places from Zionist danger.[73] At a conference convened early in the strike, Hajj Amin al-Husayni directed part of his speech to "the Arab world," including Muslims and Christians, and to "the Muslim world," telling them that the dangers facing the Holy Land threatened them all.[74] Echoing this feeling of shared threat, poets in other countries penned verses praising the revolt in Palestine, glorifying its military leaders, invoking a unified Arab struggle. Kuwaiti poet Saqr al-Shebeib encouraged the Arabs to stand by the "youth and old men" fighting: "And their assistance has become an obligation, with what you maintain of previous things or gold nuggets. If you, sons of the Arabs, help them, you help your own selves, and not someone else, out of the hands of evil."[75]

## The Revolt Symbolizes Pan-Arabism

And the Arabs responded. The revolt became a symbol of pan-Arabism itself. This encouraged the rebels and the spirit of the commission boycott. Volunteers from various Arab countries, including veterans of the Syrian Revolt against the French, came to Palestine to fight against the British for the idea of Greater Syria.[76] Among them was Fawzi al-Qawuqji, who became a rebel leader in Palestine and was declared (or declared himself) "Commander in Chief of the Arab Revolt in Southern Syria."[77] His statements were poetic, inspiring:

> To arms. It then pleases and honors me, my fighter brothers from the general Arab revolution in Southern Syria "Palestine," to invite the capable Arab cubs to carry arms . . . in order to fulfil the national aspirations and save dear Palestine from the hazards of slavery, Zionist invasions and British greed. Arms to defend the first of the two Qiblahs and the second of

the Two Venerable Sanctuaries, the birthplace of Jesus Christ, the prophet of peace and the one who calls for goodness among human kind.[78]

In many of his communiqués, al-Qawuqji showed the diversity of the revolutionaries. He publicized the participation in battle by Druze, Iraqis, Jordanians, and people from Homs and Hama (in present-day Syria), all sacrificing for this united Arab goal of saving Palestine.[79]

Assuring Palestinians that a united Arab conscience was being stirred by the injustices and the threat to Palestine as a "sacred homeland," al-Qawuqji wrote in a communiqué that "the Arabs feel agitated and the conscience is leaping." The Arabs were there together to fight the "barbaric 'Balfouric' promise, and illegitimate promises that contradict natural rights and human and divine justice."[80] In proclaiming Palestine to be an Arab issue, "an issue of the dignity and nobility of the Arab kings, and princes, and the whole Arab nation," nationalists made it so.[81]

While the armed struggle was a main focus of support coming in from the Arab world, solidarity with Palestine and the Palestinians took many forms and came from many quarters. Palestinian students sent greetings to Syrian students who demonstrated in solidarity with Palestinians.[82] The Iraqi Jewish intellectual elite professed solidarity with Arab brethren in Palestine; Palestine support committees and protests formed in Morocco and Tunisia; and collections for Palestinians were taken up in Bahrain and Kuwait.[83] The Muslim Brothers in Egypt were particularly active. They collected money for Palestinian fighters and victims of British violence, sent letters of protest to the League of Nations and the British high commissioner in Palestine, and encouraged Egyptian workers to refuse to work for the British in Palestine.[84] They organized a "High Committee for Helping the Distressed of Palestine" and distributed fliers that proclaimed: "Palestine Bleeds." These were posted as far away as Dubai and Najaf in Iraq and described the tortures of people in Palestine, calling on Muslims to fight.[85] Friday sermons in Egypt's mosques called for solidarity with Palestine, while students at several Egyptian universities organized "Palestine Day" events, where musicians, actors, and poets contributed their talents to help collect donations for the distressed and "to spread pro-Palestine propaganda."[86] Attempts to do the same in Lebanon were banned by the French government, while similar donation drives were conducted by the Egyptian Women's Union, a women's group in Amman, and by groups in Syria, Saudi Arabia, Yemen, and Iraq.[87]

The British were vexed by these demonstrations of support for Palestine; they portended a serious mobilization against the British and against the empire. Their most immediate concern was that money being collected under humanitarian pretexts was being diverted to purchase arms for the rebels in Palestine.[88] Palestinians and other Arabs continued to insist, however, that the material conditions of their struggle were not paramount, but universal principles were. Palestinians' primary goal was for "people around the world to witness the oppression experienced by those Arabs, both Christians and Muslims" in Palestine.[89]

## Defining Human Rights and Demanding Sovereignty

The polite confines of a commission engaging political elites in civil conversation could not contain the aspirations or express the ideals motivating the Arab revolt. There was another layer of values at stake in this revolt. Participants were collectively asserting their national and individual pride, their dignity, their beliefs in equality and their political and social worth. These values underpinned Palestinian Arabs' sense of entitlement to a nation-state of their own. They undergirded their conviction that British domination of their country must end and propelled their continued ability and willingness to restate that conviction.

These refusals show how international law—the values associated with sovereignty, the debated criteria of political worthiness, the ideas guiding international relations and who counted as a national entity—was a space of action, a realm of performance. How liberal, national(ist), and anticolonial subjectivities were felt—embodied—in an interwoven way can be seen in every rhetorical barb or assertion of Arab pride, whether recorded in ink or asserted in action. There was no giving in to the idea that the English or the Zionists were superior in any way. The Palestinian nationalists knew that they had to prove their own consciousness of being a free people equal to any other. The revolt reaffirmed and enacted their people's worthiness of political independence. Each such assertion was a refusal of any colonization of consciousness.

Liberal humanist and universalizing notions of justice and dignity, humanitarianism and human rights were their reference points.[90] The strike itself was a "clear expression of the noble Arab nation's opinion," the AHC explained in a communiqué.[91] In public addresses encouraging and justifying the continued strike, the AHC described their audience as "a people calling for their right to a free, dignified life, equal to the advanced peoples of the world."[92] The usurpation of Arab rights was "a humanitarian catastrophe and a historic crime," the revolt leadership averred.[93] "So," the general leader of the Arab revolution called out his challenge, "let the history and the humanitarian world be witness to the European civility and colonization that annihilates the weak ally."[94] The strike communicated the people's will to achieve their demands, which Palestinians had been making for a long time: end Jewish immigration, end the transfer of land to Jewish colonialists, and establish a national government.[95]

Certain liberal ideals remained their touch points. During a large meeting, the women of Jerusalem put more details on the demand for an elected, constitutional, representative government; they insisted that this demand be met before any negotiations with the British proceed.[96] Human rights were also at stake. In a telegram sent by ʿAwni ʿAbd al-Hadi, a prominent Palestinian political figure and first secretary of the AHC who the British exiled during the revolt, he complained to the Permanent Mandates Commission in Geneva:

> The British authority in Palestine sends war soldiers to beat up unarmed residents of the Arab villages. They destroy all the contents of their homes, furniture, and supplies, including ripping and stepping on the Holy Book of the Qur'an and looting jewellery and money. The [British] authority ratified new laws to enable sending citizens into exile and to force those on strike to open their shops, in contravention of the most sacred rights of individuals and the promise of human rights [ʿahd huquq al-insan].[97]

Wasn't "maintenance of right and justice," after all, the stated purpose of the League of Nations?[98]

As shown in the terms that were used to justify their revolt, in what motivated the boycott of the Peel Commission, Palestinians continuously demanded that the question of Palestine be addressed with regard to international law. Palestinians' eventual engagement with the Peel Commission and future investigative forays reveal that, whatever the commissioners and the powers that appointed the commissioners understood themselves to be up to in each commission, the Palestinians they encountered repeatedly argued that international law should be the frame of reference for their work.

## The Limits of British Liberalism

To understand their rejection of the Peel Commission, we have to understand how Palestinians experienced and interpreted the nature of British power and their broader, transnational context. They understood British state violence—the arbitrary arrests, torture, destruction of houses—to go against right, justice, and the law. How the British dealt with the revolt revealed with alacrity the limits of their liberalism—or perhaps it revealed the violence that is always at the core of liberalism in practice. Palestinians declaimed their oppressors, announcing that British authority was illegitimate even by their own liberal terms. They presented examples showing that British power and authority resided in their force of arms, rather than their statesmanship or diplomatic honor. The Arab Women's Committee of Jerusalem pointed to the British liberal hypocrisy in a petition they sent to the Permanent Mandates Commission:

> Your Excellency must have heard of the Arab woman, who was compelled, under the pressure of Government's policy and the acts of oppression, to join the bands [of rebels] in the mountains, in order to avoid the barbarous acts which are committed by the British troops and was shot dead, as many other women were, by the troops, as victims of the unbearable oppression which is meted out to the people, in this twentieth century, by Great Britain who claim to be the leading power in the civilized world and protector of the oppressed people. . . . The Arab women were greatly surprised when Your Excellency said in the message, which you broadcast to the people of Palestine on 7 July, 1936, that Government did not use force wantonly and ruthlessly. We take leave to observe that the atrocious acts which were recently committed in Quleh village, where four houses were blown up with all the furniture and effects they contain, where seven other houses were cracked and where some children and women were killed, are not acts which would confirm Your Excellency's statement. It will not be an exaggeration to state that you do not act according to your statements . . . the

Arab Women in Jerusalem and Sub-District wish to . . . appeal to the British Government, in the name of justice and humanity, to put an end to this human butchery . . . and to cease to show discrimination in favour of the Jews.[99]

Perceptions of dignity and the dishonorable behavior of the British were the lava bubbling at the core of this contest. Challenges over national honor were posed through reports of military victories of the Arab rebels over their much better equipped occupiers. Contemporary Palestinian eyewitnesses recorded them in gleeful detail. The rebels, as described by contemporary observer Wasif Jawhariyyeh (who we'll meet again soon), "would not be defeated, and they upped their struggle across the country, inflicting humiliation on the colonialist forces in many sites."[100] It was typical for chroniclers of the day to list every village and town that sent delegations to participate in nationalist demonstrations, proving that the country was thoroughly saturated by nationalist enthusiasm. In an even more explicit report, Bahjat Abu Gharbiyya, an armed rebel even before the revolt began, listed what he considered to be every significant "battle" that occurred during each stage of the rebellion, naming the Arabs who took part.[101] Abu Gharbiyya noted that it "made the British crazy" [jann jununhum] when a rebel escaped capture.[102] Every rebel victory was a knock to British prestige.

There were still those who held out hope in diplomacy and in British willingness to live up to their liberal ideals. Educator and Quaker Khalil Totah was distressed by the violence. He urged his Quaker coreligionists in London to speak to their politicians: "As Friends and peace-lovers and again as Britishers jealous for the good name and repute of your country I hope you will be able to do something at this crisis."[103] The Arab Women's Union of Jaffa sent a telegram to the Women's League in London calling "all women of England to help them save Palestine from the Jewish invasion and save the British honor from the greatest disgrace."[104] A similar complaint from the Arab Women's Union in Beirut to the International Women's Union in London invoked "high humanitarian principles" to urge them to forward their views "to the English government and people."[105]

Among those Palestinians who had until then believed Britain was just and civilized, many now knew the British pretensions to liberal purity were only superficial, as they became victim to the vengeful criminalization of their nationalist resistance to British/Zionist colonialism.[106] The military courts were busy night and day convicting people of participating in the revolt.[107] Hanna Naqqara, a lawyer from Haifa, recalled the moment when he realized that the courts in which he was trying to defend Palestinians accused of taking part in the revolt were staging "show trials." The British tried four youth for traveling in a car in which one gun was found hidden under a seat. According to the laws in place, at most one person could have been charged with weapons *possession* (not *carrying* a weapon), which was not a capital offense.[108] The British sentenced the four to death.

Abu Gharbiyya, the fighter, also worked as a journalist and assiduously covered the tragic farces going on in the British military courts. He watched as an Arab lawyer, who had traveled from Gaza to Jerusalem to volunteer his services, tried to defend Palestinians in the dock. In a case involving an entire family of defendants, the British military judge forbade the lawyer from asking most of his questions, and in less than two hours, a sentence was handed down that condemned one of the defendants to death, several others to life in prison, and seven years in prison for the accused children. Jewish lawyers explained the situation forthrightly: "The military court was not put in place to be applied to Jews; it was put in place to apply to Arabs."[109] The British government produced a rule of law that provided, in the analysis of one historian, "the veneer of legal respectability" for the brutal reprisals against Palestinian civilians, carried out "with all the energy of good bureaucrats obeying orders."[110] When an innocent man from Halhul (near Hebron) was captured, tried, sentenced, and executed in forty-eight hours, the hypocrisy of British justice was clear for Abu Gharbiyya to see. "And we used to sing the praises of British justice!" he declared, outraged, in his memoirs.[111]

Evidence with which to challenge British claims to justice was everywhere. In an early instantiation of the "human shield" tactic, Arab prisoners were bound in wagons attached to the front of trains to "take the blow" from any possible sabotage by landmine. One soldier recognized it as being "rather a dirty trick, but we enjoyed it."[112] Not all British were quite so gleefully sadistic. The ease with which they carried out what they called "judicial homicide" (fifty-four executed in 1938 and fifty-five recorded in 1939) left at least one official feeling guilty, mean, and "green."[113] His troubled conscience did not diminish these extremely harsh prison punishments, nor any of the other British attempts to repress the rebellion. In towns and villages where insurgents were most active, government forces demolished houses, arrested citizens randomly, and looted.[114] The British thought this was most effective because it "had a certain amount of moral effect on the villagers concerned . . . a quick and conclusive form of punishment and one that is understood by the Arab mind."[115]

British suppression of the revolt was not the Arabs' first taste of imperial injustice. Life under the British mandate was not just lived and suffered in nationalist abstractions. Lack of collective freedom, of political independence, and economic restrictions created by biased government policy were experienced in personal ways too. Some of this can be captured in numbers: Arab laborers were paid 30 percent to 50 percent less than their Jewish counterparts by the port authorities in Haifa, for example. Arab laborers in the quarries earned less than the minimum wage set by the administration and even less than a standard set six years before by the British 1928 Wages Commission.[116] But such systemic unfairness produced the texture of everyday life too, setting the parameters of individual experience patrolled by the mundane indignities of daily life under the mandate. This was a context in which an Arab could be imprisoned for laughing at a British policeman. And was. (It didn't matter that the man was actually laughing at his success in burning down a business as part of the revolt.)[117] It was an era in which an Indian officer of the British army could deny a Palestinian Muslim entrance into the courtyard of the Dome of the Rock with no explanation.[118] And did. It was a time when an Arab clerk in the civil service could be ordered by his British boss to buy the British boss's wife a birthday present. And what happened next . . .

## What the Canary Sang . . . and Drank

Wasif Jawhariyyeh, a musician, frequenter of cafes, enthusiastic drinker, snooker player, and party maker, was an Orthodox Christian from Jerusalem. He worked in the Finance Department of the British mandate administration, much of the time in a state of mild inebriation.[119] He knew the ways of British Empire: "their habit has always been to lie, deceive, and spread propaganda for the benefit of the empire." But he had to make a living and managed to work his way up to the position of Jerusalem financial manager. According to his own account, he did so with a great deal of merriment, doing what he could to take the piss out of these arrogant English lords of the manor as he went. He described in his diary an encounter with Lewis Andrews (1896–1937), British district commissioner for Galilee during the mandate.

> Once, on the occasion of his dear wife's birthday, he [Andrews] wanted to offer her a canary. And who could have seen to this but Wasif Jawhariyyeh? When my friend Matia Marrum entrusted the mission to me, it was accomplished immediately. The man who dealt in the purchase and sale of canaries . . . came and brought with him an exquisite yellow canary in a beautiful ornate cage. . . . The governor, who did not know me at the time, came and liked the canary when he saw it, and then said to Hassunah [the bird seller], "Can this bird sing?" Hassunah answered, "Yes, sir, he does." But the governor wanted to be mocking and went on. "What does he sing? 'Muhammad's Army Came with the Sword'?" He said this while looking at Hassunah with contempt, then turned to Matia and me and smiled. I said to myself that he was in need of a Jawhariyyeh-style reply, particularly since Hassunah was too scared to answer. So I said, "Your Excellency, he is singing 'O darling, I want to go back to my country.'" At this he remained silent and seemed bitter. Then he said to me, "Could you keep it and feed it until the morning of my wife's birthday?" I answered, "With pleasure. I will even give him a glass of arak to drink." Then, he went back to his room while staring at me, drinking my face in. I learned later from Matia Marrum that the governor asked him a lot about me.[120]

Andrews, considered one of the most important of the British authorities in Palestine, was known for his extreme hatred of Arabs and active support of Zionism.[121] He was shot dead by Arab rebels in September 1937.[122]

In Abu Gharbiyya's estimation, Andrews's assassination gave the British an excuse to destroy the Palestinian leadership. They exiled most of the AHC to the distant isles of the Seychelles, felt by some as an embarrassing blow to their dignity.[123] And the British more concertedly joined forces with armed Zionist groups. British repression of the rebellion increased in ferocity, as home demolitions, collective punishments, killings, and executions became more and more frequent. But in the midst of all that, more-diplomatic efforts were employed to quell the rebellion.

## The Elites' Good Manners—Not Good Enough

For many Arabs in Palestine, especially those fed up with the political inefficacy and apparently self-serving nature of their own traditional leadership, the courteous discourse and polite exchange of elites' views would no longer set the terms of the debate. In a remarkable letter that nationalist Akram Zuʿaytir penned to the British high commissioner, he challenged the colonial conception of the Arabs. "You may think that the nation has lost its dignity, vitality, and self respect."[124] But they had not succumbed to their colonizers, he assured the commissioner. "I am an Arab man who sees his duty towards the Arabness, Muslimness, and humanity of the country that is fighting for the sake of independence and freedom. My country has been cursed and its dignity besmirched." As much as this letter was a rebellious threat seething with contempt for the British, it was also a diatribe against the elite of his own society, the Arab sellouts he saw among the traditional leadership collaborating with the mandate. Zuʿaytir warned that, unlike these people, he was not fooled by the liberal chimeras that the government offered. "I am not a candidate running for the fake and imaginary legislative council. Instead, I am one of those who has despaired of Britain's justice, who has been made resentful and spiteful of it."[125]

The letter is a promise of things to come as it poked at British colonial arrogance and revealed consciousness of the class markers that united the liberal elite, native and foreign. "I think that when you compare my approach to theirs [the elite leadership,] you would almost confirm that I lack manners while they demonstrate good manners . . . or you almost believe that I lived in poverty and I have no idea what courtesy or its principles are."[126] It was not an issue of proper comportment, Zuʿaytir insisted, but one of individual and collective self-respect. Zuʿaytir spelled out the communion of the nation and the individual that made the revolt seem like an inevitability. "So how can I, as an individual, not feel my dignity injured and cursed, living in a country that is not respected." In a portentous statement on the eve of the general strike, he told the high commissioner, "I feel that this insult will not be cleansed by articles, speeches, protests, meetings. . . . You cannot do anything against those who are ready to die."[127]

And many were. In his memoirs recounting this period, Hanna Naqqara described the revolt as being the first time that Palestine witnessed full public participation in the national movement. A contemporary observer noted the same, sensing that "the whole population is resentful and ready to burst out."[128] The coming together of village and city was an express principle of what some of the activists were calling a "new national movement."[129] The exponential increase in Jewish immigration threatened the future of Palestine as an Arab country.[130] They knew the Zionists were there to establish a Jewish state that would deprive the Arabs of their rights.[131] This, Naqqara wrote, is what compelled the Arabs to express their grievances—and their fear—through a strike and with weapons.[132] The commission boycott was another part of that expression.

## Boycotting the Royal Commission

From as early as March 1936, only a month into the general strike, the British government announced that they would form a Royal Commission of Inquiry. A precondition that the government set for the commission's arrival was that the Arabs stop the revolt. An indication of what was at stake for Britain's honor, dignity, and authority, they insisted that this was a "decision of His Majesty's Government" and should not be understood as a sign of weakness or a form of conciliation.[133]

After the British issued a schedule for further Jewish immigration in 1936, the AHC called on the people—the "nation that has proved to the world its political maturity, and the strength of its national faith"—to boycott the Royal Commission.[134] This also might have been because the AHC president was receiving two hundred letters a day warning the Palestinian leadership that they should not stop the revolt to let the commission come.[135] Among them was a letter that Ahmad al-Shuqayri (a Palestinian nationalist whom we will meet in Chapter 3) spent a night writing to the head of the AHC, warning him not to "let the country fall into the British trap and stop the revolution without serious guarantees" and reminding him of the disappointing experiences they had had with previous commissions.[136] Beyond this friendly advice, nationalists of the Istiqlal [Independence] Party had been challenging the traditional Arab leadership, exacerbating the AHC's "credibility problem."[137] The leadership knew that accepting the investigative committee would turn the masses against them. One of the AHC members, 'Awni 'Abd al-Hadi, voiced a more politically principled stand against accepting the commission because he saw in this refusal, with the public's mood and solidarity at its current fever pitch, "the last opportunity to force the British to change their policy."[138]

## Fed Up of British Commissions

This was a unique moment of malleability in the international legal hegemony over Palestinian political imagination. Polite diplomacy and international legal structures had gotten the Palestinians nowhere, and more and more people were proclaiming that in public. They were "sick of promises" from the British.[139] In a petition on behalf of the Arab Women's Committee of Jerusalem, sent to the League of Nations Permanent Mandates Commission in 1936, these activists explained how the roller coaster of being superficially listened to and then substantively ignored over the previous nineteen years led to the revolt. They gave voice to the hopes and disappointments that British investigative commissions had instilled throughout the years of the British mandate: "In consequence, the Arabs were led into a state of despondency which impelled them to brave danger and to prefer death en masse to gradual annihilation under a policy which has no precedent in history."[140]

With every period of Palestinian revolt against the Zionist takeover of their homeland throughout the preceding two decades, the British had responded in boilerplate investigative form. Commissions had become His Majesty's reflex reaction to trouble of this kind, in Palestine and across the empire. For eighteen years, all they did was disperse, deflect, and reabsorb the volatility back into liberal dynamics of reasoned discourse and reasonable talk.[141]

The international legal project of developing international institutions that would coordinate international society, civilize conflict, organize trade, and ensure progress, order, and justice in international politics had only brought the Arabs more oppression, instability, and uncertainty.[142]

Palestinians' boycott of this commission threw a spanner in the imperial works. 'Izzat Darwaza, Palestinian nationalist and diarist, recorded the Zionists' shock at the Arab move, while the British were greatly confused. Their newspapers covered the issue intensely, and tried to belittle the boycott by claiming it was a result of pressure from "extremists."[143]

Although the Arabic press reported hopefully that the commission might decide to end Jewish immigration, the majority was not buying any of it. They knew this investigative commission was just an attempt by the British to extricate themselves from the current crisis.[144] A lawyer from Haifa commenting in the newspaper *Filastin* encouraged the boycott of the commission, explaining this refusal to engage as being a means of communication, such that "the High Commissioner and the Colonial Secretary would understand that challenging the Arab Nation is futile."[145] The fact that the commission would not directly address the terms of the mandate, which were the root of the problems, and that the British issued more certificates for Jewish immigration—which the Palestinian leadership had thought would at least be paused for the duration of the commission—made clear to the Arabs that the government was not acting in good faith.[146]

Leaders of the rebellion vowed not to be lulled by false promises [*al-wu'ud al-kadhiba*] and even declared as a fundamental principle of the revolt their refusal to be sucked into yet another investigative commission.[147] They knew commissions to be a means to "lull and split the ranks" of their people [*takhdir wa tafriq al-kalima*].[148] They "refused to fall for the propaganda."[149] Lack of faith in such investigations was widespread because people had come to understand that "the government sends these commissions to gain time, to dope the nerves." They believed "that the idea of sending a new commission is merely a political one and has nothing to do with the boiling sentiment in the country."[150] Others saw it as a form of "vengeance" and an indication of "the government's carelessness about the feelings of the Arab nation."[151]

Hussein Fakhri Khalidi, mayor of Jerusalem at the time, reported that the Arabs were made "speechless" by the British announcement of a commission, "as they have not forgotten the several commissions that were dispatched to the country" to no good effect. He recorded the sense of futility that such British initiatives inspired. "These commissions spend weeks

and months, researching and digging up published reports, issued recommendations, government announcements and its white papers. None of the
[commission] recommendations that favored the interests of the Arabs were
implemented."[152]

The AHC replied that they, too, no longer had any trust in commissions
of inquiry. And anyway, the Arabs' demands were quite clear, requiring no
further investigation. "Great Britain should by now have a fairly clear understanding of Arabs' demands, from the commission of inquiry reports that
have been released over the last 20 years."[153] As Darwaza explained, "Britain
had sent more than enough commissions over the years, and they have grown
tired of it."[154] If eighteen years of fact-finding was not enough, then another
commission was not going to change things, a delegation from the National
Committee told the British acting governor in Gaza.[155] Their decision not to
cooperate with the investigation was thoroughly covered in the Palestinian
press.[156]

Although the majority of Palestinians adhered to the commission boycott
"across all classes and political leanings," some did so with ambivalence.[157]
Raghib Bey al-Nashashibi, member of the umbrella AHC and head of a
party that opposed the al-Husayni family's political domination, urged the
leadership to present their views to the commission at least informally, but
he was outvoted by those who pointed out that this would make the boycott
pointless.[158] Another who was unsure about the commission was George Antonius. He fretted about the dilemma, and resolved to give evidence to the
commission only if invited directly. What convinced him to abstain from
providing evidence was what had convinced the majority of Arabs to boycott
voting for a legislative council: it prevented any change to the mandate charter that promised to facilitate the production of a national homeland for the
Jews in Palestine. Antonius likewise objected to the narrow terms of reference of the royal investigation, which made it "practically impossible for any
independent witness to give evidence with due regard to the broader aspects
of the problem. . . . They are so narrow as to preclude the possibility of the
Royal Commission working out a real solution." If he was invited, he would
begin "by explaining to the Commission the grounds of my criticism of their
terms of reference; and, having made my criticism and its implications as

clear as I can, to give evidence on questions on which the Commission might desire to hear me."[159]

## Pressures against the Boycott

That the boycott was an effective political move is reflected in how much outside pressure was being put on the Palestinian leadership to meet with the commission. One of their British supporters, Frances Newton-Welcomb, advised them to see the commission, because "otherwise the Arabs would lose the British affection ('atef) and it will make the work of their friends harder."[160] Other sympathetic Englishmen made similar efforts, which were echoed in the English press and translated in Arabic newspapers.[161] The British governors of Nablus and Jenin even convened meetings among villagers in those areas to try to convince them that the commission would be a good opportunity for the Arabs.[162] A great deal of effort went in to scupper the commission boycott. The British put pressure on their Arab underlings in many locations across the Arab world, which cascaded down to the Palestinian leadership.[163] After meeting with the British ambassador, the Iraqi foreign minister conveyed to his king, Ghazi, that he wished the AHC would reconsider its decision to boycott the Royal Commission because such a continued boycott "would result in disagreeable outcomes" and might end up benefiting their opponents.[164]

It was when the Arab kings and princes got involved that the Palestinian leadership started to buckle. But it took some effort by, among others, Emir Abdullah of Transjordan, Great Britain's "trusted tool."[165] Their first effort to convince the Palestinians to play along was unsuccessful. They tried to convince them that this commission would not be like all the others because it was a "royal" one that would include important personalities who would not be influenced by anyone.[166] The argument that they should "rely on the good intentions of our friend the British Government and their declared desire to see that justice is done" while the Arab leaders continued to try to promote their cause did not initially persuade, and it cost the AHC an expensive long telegram (twenty guineas!) to explain why.[167] They clearly did not like running the risk of irritating their more sovereign Arab brethren by saying no, and they traveled to Baghdad, Riyad, and the Hijaz to convince the kings of the politically principled and pragmatic reasons behind their boycott position. In Riyad they found the king motivated by his wish to avoid angering his British sponsors.[168]

Finally, after six months of an economically draining and physically grueling strike and revolt, and with more pressure from the leaders of Saudi Arabia, Iraq, Transjordan, and Yemen, who continued to reassure the Palestinians of British friendship, they gave in to being forced to present to the commission.[169]

## Conclusion

After years of working toward autonomy under the Ottomans and then years of upheaval in the Great War, by 1919 Palestinian representatives had come to believe they were on the cusp of a bright horizon, leading themselves to an independent political future through representative government and self-determination. They had a constitution at the ready. They were making headway toward women's rights to vote and gaining greater access to education, and ever greater autonomy generally.[170] Their presentations to the King-Crane Commission demonstrated how great were their expectations. They had until recently been self-respecting members of the Ottoman Empire, in which Palestinians became members of Parliament on an equal basis with Turks.[171] They knew the mechanics of parliamentary democracy from the inside.[172] That was still a mostly elite affair, but national politics was grabbing the imagination of an increasingly literate, media-consuming society whose collective opinion increasingly mattered and so helped constitute a political public.[173] So when the rugs were pulled out from under their plans for a liberal, democratic future, by no less than Great Britain that claimed to run on liberal principles, in an era that espoused liberal internationalism as its guiding light, of course they objected. That the British and Zionists were actively conspiring against their progress was proof that these supposedly advanced societies were not living up to their own professed ideals. It was all so offensive. And disappointing. "We have despaired of anything called British honor," nationalists proclaimed again and again.[174]

The League of Nations was mostly an imperial affair run by and for Western states. The provincial nature of its proclaimed universal values of liberalism was clear to those who were suffering from them. The limitations that the Permanent Mandates Commission put on Palestinians' (and others') free political expression were obvious, inscribed in the rules that forbade any challenge to the terms of the mandate itself.[175] The league had no credibility—at least for Arabs—as a true representation of "the international" that could mediate objectively and ensure the rule of international law. Western hegemony over the institutional order and its symbolic significance had become unhinged. At the same time, other internationalist energies and inclinations were percolating, giving Palestinians the context in which to expand the audience for their political claims, providing a broader range of solidarities.

Contrary to how the story of the Peel Commission is usually told, what is more interesting for this book's telling of the life of international law and liberalism in Palestine is that the events around this commission seemed temporarily to loosen the ideological straightjacket of Western-dominated liberal international law that had so far tied this conflict's portrayal, enactment, and management. It was especially the Arab and Muslim solidarity for Palestinians that enabled the boycott. Historians recognize the Peel Commission as one of the most significant for Palestine because it put partition formally on the table of political options, and because its report made public the British government's recognition that the mandate's contradictory promises were unworkable.[176] What is more significant is the boycott of the commission. It shows that international law as arbitrated by commissions, by the League of Nations, and by a version of liberalism defined by well-mannered gentlemen—those engaged in what they defined as rational discourse—no longer exhausted Palestinians' tools and terms of nationalist claim making.

The Arab Revolt and Palestinians' boycott of the Peel Commission were not a refusal of international law, not a rejection of liberalism, but an insistence on them. Liberal values of national and human rights based in human dignity had long been part of Palestinian political vocabulary, and nationalist aspirations for political sovereignty defined their political objective since cracks in the Ottoman Empire made it possible. But after two decades of speaking this language and articulating this goal to the nonrepresentative government that ruled them, a new communicative mode became necessary. Popular resistance that disrupted the colonial status quo, it turns out, was a language the British could hear.

The Palestinian leadership did finally give in to pressures on them to engage with their investigators. And the liberal mechanisms delivered again what they had been dishing up for years. The commission's recommendation to partition Palestine into two states—giving the Zionists the most fertile parts of the country and suggesting massive population transfers (primarily of Arabs) as a means to purify the ethnic makeup of these suggested polities more thoroughly—set off a wave of protests throughout the Middle East.[177] The revolt was reinvigorated after the commission report was released. The British responded with the most illiberal of tactics: "vicarious punishment," or collective punishment, meted out with a rapid hand, regardless of guilt or due process.[178] Those who claimed to be the adjudicators of liberalism's bounds always declaimed Palestinian resistance, violent or otherwise, as unacceptable. But their resistance did something specific to poke through the liberal balloon; it revealed more starkly the inhumane cruelty of the British Empire, the fragility of its hold over Palestine, and the superficiality of British commitment to its claimed liberal values. The Peel Commission was a flailing attempt to reassemble the liberal-colonial order that would reduce Palestinian resistance to forms of liberal-legal pleading.

The Palestinians' ultimate participation in the Peel Commission after so much disappointment and refusal highlights a core puzzle of this book: what is the attraction of the liberal-legal mode? Ahmad al-Shuqayri declaimed the AHC's decision to give in to the kings and princes demanding their engagement with the commission. He lamented it as a win for the older generation of politicians who still believed in British promises. He saw it as a loss for his generation of young men who recognized themselves to be victims of British trickery.[179] But more than a reassertion of a generational and political hierarchy, Palestinians' attempts to sway the members of the commission reveal how powerful was the need to have their say and how amenable was the commission forum for doing so. They wanted to exercise their right to represent themselves as political agents who were "fighting for constitutional and fundamental rights."[180]

The language of liberalism and the legalistic aura of the commission provided them with a ready arsenal of rhetorical weapons to be wielded on a clear stage set by people promising an unbiased hearing. In presenting to the commission, 'Abd al-Hadi elaborated on the source of these rights: their collective and individual humanity that made them equal to all others. "We are a nation like all other nations." No nation would willingly allow another people to enter their country and turn them into a minority without rights, he told the commissioners. "We are humans, we feel, we sense, and we have rights, a culture, a civilization. . . . The Arabs believe that they have their ancient civilization and they bear the strongest nationalist feelings, just like the most advanced nations of the world. . . . We are today living like animals. But we are humans, and have the rights of humans [*huquq al-bashar*], and natural rights to govern ourselves."[181]

Palestinians had made a genuine break with the imperial-liberal order as policed by the League of Nations and Western powers. In becoming a core object of concern within a movement of global anticolonial solidarity, they had activated a world audience that went beyond colonial countries and their liberal legal modalities. It was a direct challenge to the British to change their "parochial mentality," as one writer in *Filastin* explained.[182] The boycott and global mobilization was a significant counter-hegemonic challenge.[183] One that heralded a possible alternative order of politics based in shared anticolonial sentiment and transnational mobilization. The Palestinian leadership's eventual submission to the pressures on them to engage with the commission marked a defeat of that challenge.

# CHAPTER 3

# The Humanitarian Politics of Jewish Suffering

## The Anglo-American Committee of Inquiry

THE PALESTINIAN LEADERSHIP was finally persuaded to give testimony to the Peel Commission. In his presentation before the Peel Commission, Akram Zuʿaytir emphasized the difference between universal human rights and context-specific legal declarations, elaborating on the meaning, extent, and basis of these human rights: "The Palestinian Arab natural right to independence exists regardless of the mandate charter, or British promises, or President Wilson. Our right to freedom is the same as our right to life, based on our humanity, dignity, self-respect."[1] Much of the rest of his testimony was an attempt to convince the British of the sincerity of the Arabs' nationalism, of the depths of their feelings, and of the level of their conviction that diplomacy was no longer the way to convince them of anything. "We've spent 18 years protesting, screaming, being in pain, writing reports, sending delegations, and meeting with Commissions of Inquiry. But it has all been without results. The government in this country ignores our rights, so the Arab has despaired of justice, and has expressed that despair wonderfully. That despair has led them to revolution . . . the Arabs have been waiting for the British to realize the depth of that despair."[2] The realness of their feelings, their frustrations, the depth and sincerity of their nationalist commitments were persistent themes in Palestinians' communications with the British.

Palestinians remained consistent in their arguments and political logic. The Westerners trying to solve the problem of Palestine, however, made

shifting demands, brandishing different criteria throughout their investigations. From William Yale's disappointed expectations of Arab nationalist
enthusiasm, the "psychological force" he found insufficiently proven by the
Arab's lackluster "emotional reactions" during the King-Crane Commission,
to the royal commissioners' fluctuating requests to acknowledge the British
mandate's beneficence, Palestinians were being told to prove their worthiness of nation-state sovereignty in vacillating ways.[3] By the time of the Peel
Commission, there was a concern that too much nationalism was making the
Palestinians uncooperative. In the British Parliamentary debate of the Royal
Commission report, Lord Snell drew attention to the commission report's
commentary on Arab nationalism: "The Report says: 'Arab nationalism in
Palestine has been artificially puffed up by methods which the Government
should never have allowed. Only a little firmness is needed to deflate it.'"
Snell regretted that so little had been done in the way of tamping down
the nationalist inflammation of the population. In the lord's estimation, it
was only the manipulations of self-interested actors that caused the "decent-
minded . . . chivalrous, hospitable, and kindly" Arab peasant to develop "hos-
tility against his neighbour."[4]

In the Anglo-American Committee of Inquiry, international law was
mediated by affective assessments of a different sort. For nearly two decades,
the people investigating Palestine had been demanding more and then less
nationalism from the Arabs. Here Palestinians were required to provide evidence of "reasonable" political stances adjudged through emotional performances of different kinds once more.

## Suffering and Sympathy: The New Political Epistemology

The demands being made of Palestinians altered yet again after World
War II. Clear in the Anglo-American Committee of Inquiry (AACI) are
shifts in the overlying and underlying principles guiding assessments of Palestinian readiness for—indeed, deservedness of—sovereignty. Most distinctive is the newly crystallized political epistemology of suffering, sympathy,
and humanitarianism that comes into the frame.

The Anglo-American Committee came at another important moment
in the development of international law.[5] World War II created the conditions in which sympathy for Jewish suffering would become a core virtue of

liberalism. For many, the brutality of the Second World War, and especially the destruction of European Jewry, was a blow to any faith in humanity. It prompted international legal innovations that were espoused in the name of restoring that belief.[6] Legal professionals declared themselves to have a "special responsibility" for "revitalizing and strengthening international law" as the "spirit of man cries out for a better way of life."[7] The Preamble of the United Nations Charter signed in 1945 declared itself to be a reaffirmation of "faith in fundamental human rights, in the dignity and worth of the human person, in the equal rights of men and women and of nations large and small." It promised "to establish conditions under which justice and respect for . . . international law [could] be maintained," putting justice and law on equal footing. The United Nations Charter reasserted the liberal principle of self-determination that was at the heart of the League of Nations; it prioritized the promotion of "human rights and fundamental freedoms."[8] The abstract individual central to this new regime—made manifest in legally relevant ways in the UN Charter and in the 1948 Universal Declaration of Human Rights—was one whose rights and dignity required protections from indiscriminate suffering and political repression. Institutionalized in this liberal-legal nexus of declarations and organizations was a humanitarian sensibility that required sympathy—and its expression—of a particular sort.

For this committee of six Brits and six Americans dispatched in 1946 to "examine the question of European Jewry and to . . . review the Palestine Problem in light of that examination," self-determination and tolerance of minorities remained important concerns as they had been during the King-Crane Commission, but the worry about the strength of nationalism began to take a different cast. Now, nationalism that was too hardy had come to be seen as a serious problem.

It is in the Anglo-American Committee of Inquiry that international law is revealed most starkly to comprise a habitus of a particular sort, and here that the policing of affect most blatantly becomes part of how international law is implemented. We see Palestinian representatives struggling to reassure their interrogators of their humanity and the sincerity of their sympathy for the Jews, while trying to maintain a collective focus on legal and democratic values. Despite these fickle Western concerns with perceived degrees of Palestinian nationalism and sympathy, the focus of Arab representatives was resolutely on international legal principles: the promises that the end of empire would yield self-determination to the Arabs in Palestine; that protection of minorities should and would be a commitment of the representative, constitutional Arab authority that would govern them; that citizens would share equal rights and duties; and that their inherent human dignity entailed universal, natural human rights, including the right to economic and national sovereignty. But their efforts did not align with the new political epistemology governing this moment, in which proof of a properly humanitarian subjectivity required a prioritization of sympathy above all else.

Sympathy for Jewish suffering became in this moment the barometer of liberalism—and expressing that sympathy alongside acquiescence to Zionist demands for Palestine became the required stance of the good liberal. The AACI was not just a tribunal for deciding whether the Palestinian Arabs or the Zionists had the right to claim Palestine as their national home, or for distinguishing whose rights were natural or more just. It was an authorized and authorizing venue for the assertion of humanity as a prime value for world governance. The Jews and their Zionist dream had become the symbol of that humanity in need of rescue and confirmation. The Jews, not the Arabs, were endowed with world-historical significance. The Jews, not the Arabs, represented universal values. For the Palestinians, no amount of liberal-legal argumentation or appropriately expressed sympathy for Jewish suffering could make their own suffering or their political requirements equal to that of the Jews.

Like all commissions to Palestine, the AACI was part diplomatic mission engaged in a kind of political negotiation, and part investigative body intent on reporting what its members took to be the relevant political facts. Swirling around this inquiry, alongside its ostensible goal of achieving political progress, were debates about the criteria for political sovereignty. To be deemed worthy of sovereignty was attendant on attaining political credibility, which in turn entailed a sympathetic demeanor. The AACI, like all commissions, was a forum for the assertion of credibility and for the performance of particular kinds of identity and morality.

The debates through which the principles of political identity, legitimacy, sovereignty, and democracy were defined and demonstrated at this moment flowed through many cross currents eddying with anxieties over how to steady the global order after the Holocaust. Maintaining the co-constitutive nature of international law and civilization was a significant concern for many, and it shaped Palestinians' engagement with the Anglo-American Committee as much as it did that of the Western powers and Zionists.[9] Together, Palestinians, Arab leaders, Zionists, the British, and the Americans debated how to fulfill humanitarian ideals that prioritized helping the displaced Jews of Europe.[10]

The Palestinians had identified the crux of the dispute as it was being framed in this moment quite clearly. At root were two points of view, they said: either the majority (Arabs) in Palestine should be accorded their democratic rights; or that right could be sacrificed and the result of Europe's barbarity could be shunted off, and its victims given a state in Palestine in the name of "humanitarianism."[11] The Palestinians' main goal was upholding democratic principles that recognized the Arabs of Palestine, the majority in the country, as having political rights. The Anglo-American Committee was a setting in which the different contestants sought to limit or expand the place of humanitarian claims within those negotiations at a time when principles of the modern "humanitarian regime" were being established.

The Anglo-American Committee of Inquiry was an early international performance through which the authorizing discourse of suffering was legitimated anew as a political tool in global politics. A humanitarian structure of feeling formed the way Westerners discussed the issue of Palestine and the Jews, as it became an overriding criterion in Zionist claims for Jewish independence.[12] As anthropologists Peter Redfield and Erica Bornstein have described it, humanitarianism is "a structure of feeling, a cluster of moral principles, a basis for ethical claims and political strategies, and a call for action."[13] It is a magical mix of emotion declared beyond reproach that provides and justifies the impulse and cover for political action. This deployment of humanitarianism in the AACI trumped the Palestinians' legal liberal arguments. These new expectations index a shift in the political epistemology, one that left Westerners unable (or unwilling) to believe that Palestinians could be both politically reasonable and humanly sympathetic, because to do so would have upset the hierarchy of suffering that made realization of the Zionist dream a fulfillment of universal values.

## To Commission or Not to Commission . . .

There had been public debate about the committee's legitimacy and the problems of cooperating with it.[14] Expressing bewilderment at yet another commission to Palestine, an article in *Filastin* argued that the "Arabs have every reason to oppose the commission, for it is their right to reject mass Jewish immigration into their country, and they will not stand to have this right scrutinised and subjected to investigation by anyone, and neither to have it approved or cancelled as the British government sees fit."[15] There were also deliberations among Palestinian political representatives about whether to cooperate with the committee.[16] On one side were those in support of engagement from the outset. Musa ʿAlami, a Palestinian political independent and head of the Arab Office that was advocating for Palestinian political rights, still believed that the British had a sense of justice. He did not want to repeat the mistake he thought the Palestinians had made in boycotting the Peel Commission, which left their presentations underprepared.[17] ʿAlami played a significant role in directing the work of the Arab Office that would produce "a vast documentation of every aspect of the problem of Palestine" (over one thousand pages in English) that was submitted to the AACI.[18]

In contrast to Musa ʿAlami's enthusiasm and confidence in the British was the pessimism of Hussein Fakhri Khalidi, former Jerusalem mayor and secretary to the AHC. He thought that the Arabs would suffer from cooperating with America, given its strong ties with Zionism.[19] ʿAwni ʿAbd al-Hadi was just as dubious, having learned something about the Great Powers as assistant to Prince Faysal during the Paris Peace Conference, where he spent time "in the company of the greatest of men, men who strive every day to change and manipulate the map of the world." About these politicians he wrote in his memoirs: "The most successful among them is he who finds the best means by which to rob a nation of its political life."[20] More than a quarter of a century later, as a member of the AHC, he suggested to that group of Palestinian political party representatives that they write to the United Nations to object to the Anglo-American Committee's existence and shape. What was its authority? What right did it have to examine questions of Jewish immigration to Palestine? Or to involve Arab states in the investigation? Why were the United States and Britain the only nations sending investigators?

Palestinians were not alone in their initial hesitation toward the inquiry. In Egypt, some advocated a rejection of the commission on tactical grounds. The Arabs should rebuff the AACI, the editorialist for the Egyptian newspaper *al-Wafd al-Masri* contended, because recognizing the committee would imply a recognition of the legitimacy of its final decision, which would weaken the Arabs' position.[21] Some members of the recently formed Arab League shared this opinion.[22] They asserted that participation did not give the Anglo-American Committee the right to decide the Palestine issue, "nor the right of Great Britain and the US to handle this problem exclusively."[23] As the debate over how to deal with the committee continued, the Arabic newspaper *Filastin* reported the news of the committee's formation in great suspense-building detail, with several articles promising that the names of the members would be announced soon.[24]

With the Anglo-American Committee, the push-me-pull-you dynamic exhibited in earlier years became set as the pattern of Palestinian representatives' approach toward investigative commissions. Although in this case it tilted quickly toward engagement, their wary uncertainty would remain throughout this committee's existence. But engage they did, advocating for the Palestinian case for independence through what they thought were the political givens of liberal internationalism. As was true throughout the King-Crane and Peel commissions, during the AACI, Palestinians returned to the principle of natural national rights to assert their political claims to Palestine. They based those claims on their centuries-long presence as a distinctive people in Palestine, but also on what they took to be universally valid international legal principles. Their rights to Palestine were, in their view, established by international law's preservation of the principle of self-determination and liberal notions of representative self-government. They carefully presented their case for an independent, constitutional government and representative democracy as the solution to the problem of Palestine.

Again.

The deliberations over how to interact with yet another tribunal on the Palestinians' fate, and the extensive news coverage of the investigative group's

establishment and progress reflected intense public anticipation and interest in the Anglo-American Committee across the political spectrum. Just as
the Aguda Israel World Organization, a proponent of a binational solution
in Palestine, followed the inquiry "with breathless attention," Arabic newspapers, too, assiduously followed the committee's work as it traveled from
the United States onward, hearing testimony in Washington, DC, London,
Jerusalem, and the displaced persons camps of Europe.[25] After the committee was announced in 1945, a single newspaper, *Filastin,* published sixty-six
articles about it in its November and December issues (including an article falsifying rumors about it). Many people believed this committee was
important.[26]

What attracted attention were the obvious concerns about the committee's eventual report and recommendations. Also at stake for Palestinians, for
others in the Arab world, and for their leaders were questions of fundamental
political principle. As 'Awni 'Abd al-Hadi highlighted with his doubts about
the right of the Americans and British to determine anything about Jewish
immigration to Palestine, these were issues of political legitimacy, authority,
and representation. Articulating Palestinians' contention that the Westerners'
involvement was illegitimate, Jamal al-Husayni insisted "that the Palestine
Arabs cannot bind themselves finally by the Committee's decisions, even if
they are prepared to put their case before it."[27] Challenging the tendency of
Western powers to arrogate to themselves the authority to make vital decisions about the futures of others was at the core of Palestinians' anti-imperial,
anticolonial struggle from the beginning of their battle with Zionism.

## The Arab Liberals Presenting the Palestinian Case

They undertook this battle driven by a shared commitment to achieving a liberal, democratic, and independent Palestine. After the Palestinian and Arab
state representatives decided to cooperate with the committee, and despite
his 1919 prediction that there would be "no hope for the weak, unknowing
countries, neither today nor tomorrow," 'Abd al-Hadi threw himself into the
preparations.[28] Putting his Sorbonne-trained legal mind to the task, he urged
the Arab Higher Committee to meet until they could produce a unified Arab
approach and develop compelling presentations to this commission.[29] Most
of those involved in presenting the Palestinian case were self-evident—and

in many cases self-proclaimed—liberals. In addition, many were already or would go on to become influential figures in Palestinian politics. The perhaps most significant contributor to constructing and presenting the Palestinian case was Albert Hourani, an Oxford historian of Lebanese heritage. Although he developed a liberal Arab nationalist sensibility as his education about the Middle East deepened, Hourani described himself as originally an unquestioning English liberal.[30] Much has been made of Hourani's liberalism in recent scholarship, but he wasn't the only participant easily described as liberal.[31] A range of Palestinian representatives helped make their case to the Anglo-American Committee, some of whom—like Albert's brother Cecil Hourani—were self-declared liberals. Among others with a similar outlook developing the Palestinian presentations were Charles 'Issawi, Yusif Sayegh, and his brother Fayez Sayegh, all of whom, along with Ahmad al-Shuqayri, would go on to work in different capacities at the United Nations.[32] These were all educated people (mostly men), who both professed and enacted liberal principles and sensibilities throughout their lives.[33]

Others—such as Ahmad al-Shuqayri and Jamal al-Husayni—both demanded liberal resolutions and framed their claims in liberal values, while also challenging the liberal-legal institutions that could be used to justify an illiberal solution to Palestine. Al-Shuqayri, an overtly rebellious anticolonial activist who appeared before the committee, was one whose liberal values were seen to be in tension with his demeanor. Albert Hourani was not happy with al-Shuqayri for his "unnecessarily loud, explosive, and threatening performance"—probably because it was not in accord with liberal etiquette requiring calm discourse to prove its rationality. Nevertheless, the substance of his speech emphasized values of freedom and representative government that were familiar and acceptable to other liberals.[34]

Jamal al-Husayni apparently had been eager for the Anglo-American Committee of Inquiry to hear what he had to say. Maybe it was because this member of the Arab Higher Committee and cousin of the Mufti wanted to be counted as a "competent witness," as called for by the terms of reference of this commission.[35] More likely, it was because of the urgings of Egyptian politician Azzam Pasha. In his own testimony as the first secretary-general of the Arab League, Azzam Pasha assured the committee that he believed them to be friends, "enlightened people who are after the truth."[36] Eventually al-Husayni became so convinced that the Arabs should present to the commission, "to take the opportunity to demonstrate the justice of their cause before the world," that he announced to the Arab press his eagerness to share his views with the committee to "demonstrate the justice of their cause."[37]

It is not clear if Azzam Pasha's advice benefited the Palestinians in this case.[38] One of the US secretaries for the committee thought Jamal al-Husayni's presentation was "rigid" and "unimaginative."[39] Richard Crossman, one of the British investigators, recorded that al-Husayni "added nothing new" to what they knew of the Arab case. Perhaps even more damning, American diplomat and committee member William Phillips guessed him to be "on the verge of the DT [delirium tremens] from drink."[40]

There were obvious tensions between Jamal al-Husayni's personal style and the liberal substance of his presentations. And, more so than many other Palestinians with prominent roles presenting to the investigators, the extent of his commitment to liberalism was unclear. Al-Husayni was a recognized political leader of the notable urban elite. On the debit side of his liberalism ledger was the fact that he would not condemn his cousin, the Mufti, for his infamous dalliances with the Nazis, as family loyalty and political priorities caused him to make what Commissioner James McDonald recognized was a courageous but strategic mistake. It left a black mark, overshadowing the Palestinians' credibility as a whole.[41] Jamal al-Husayni did, in some respects and contexts, profess and exhibit liberal values, however.[42] He took part in parliamentary bodies and contested candidates in political parties of elected representatives.[43] In his earlier pro-British years, he lobbied the government and in 1923 won its recognition of the legitimacy of a representative Palestinian body, the Executive of the Palestinian Congress.[44] The British considered him a "reasonable and pragmatic representative" then.[45] He was also keen to present the Palestinian case before the latest institutions of liberal internationalism, the United Nations Organization and the Security Council.[46]

Across this range of both faithful and wary liberal positions, however, was a steadfast adherence to the core tenets of liberal tolerance, democracy, and equality. But the committee interpreted this persistent commitment as an obstructive intransigence. Despite their liberal commitments and the detailed democratic proposals that the Arabs offered as a solution to the problem of Palestine, as the commissioners' reactions to the Arabs' presentations show, it was the tone of their interventions more than their substance that mattered.

## Committee Formation and Membership

Around the same time that Palestinians and others in the region were considering whether to engage with the Anglo-American Committee and how to do so, others with stakes in the game were haggling over who the committee's members would be. Although the British foreign secretary Ernest Bevin had announced the committee's formation in the House of Commons in November 1945, which was reported in the Arabic press, it wasn't until the following month that its full membership and remit became clear.[47] On December 10, in a carefully coordinated and precisely timed public announcement, US President Harry Truman explained the Anglo-American investigative committee's terms of reference.[48] First among these was to "examine political, economic and social conditions in Palestine as they bear upon the problem of Jewish immigration and settlement therein and the well-being of the peoples now living therein." The committee was also to examine the position of Jews in Europe, and to "consult representative Arabs and Jews" and other "competent witnesses" on the problems of Palestine. The twelve commissioners were given one hundred twenty days to make recommendations to the US and UK governments for "interim and permanent solution[s]" to these problems.[49]

The statement listed the committee's team of investigators, which included an American and a British judge as its rotating chairs. Joseph Hutcheson, a US fifth circuit court judge from Texas, knew his Bible and wasn't afraid to quote from it. Sir John Singleton, the UK chair, was high court of justice, having obtained a third-class degree in law (the lowest possible without failing) at Pembroke College, Cambridge University. The British members included Richard Crossman, a socialist Labour MP who often wrote letters home to his wife during Arab presentations to the committee; Sir Frederick Leggett, chief industrial commissioner, who Bevin believed to be a stellar negotiator;[50] Wilfred Crick, an economist and lecturer at the London School of Economics; and Lord Robert Morrison, Labour peer. Rounding out the British membership was Major Reginald Manningham-Buller, who was a Conservative MP with a blue-blood education from Eton and Magdalen

College, Oxford, where as a student he imitated his future teacher, John Singleton, and took a third in law. (His daughter, Eliza Manningham-Buller, would go on to become director of the UK intelligence agency, MI5). Harold Beeley, "tall, lean, [and] donnish,"[51] a secretary to the committee, was an adviser to Bevin and a professional historian.[52] The others included, among the Americans: William Phillips, an American diplomat with a snazzy dressing style; Frank Aydelotte, former president of Swarthmore College and head of the Institute for Advanced Study in Princeton; Frank Buxton, editor of the *Boston Herald*; Bartley Crum, a San Francisco attorney who proved to be a controversial character; and James McDonald, former League of Nations high commissioner for refugees who was already on record as a Zionist advocate. Evan Wilson was a secretary.[53]

To this distinguished collection of gentlemen, al-Shuqayri said in his testimony, "Our case rests on our natural right, our inherent right to live in our country in freedom and security, to revive our potentialities and capacities and to contribute our full share in world civilization and progress," assuring the committee that his views were "generally representative of public opinion."[54] "It is the true import of democracy that no one man is entitled to decide the fate of another man; not even twelve men are entitled to decide the fate of a nation," al-Shuqayri said.[55] In an exchange with the British chair of the committee, Justice Singleton, al-Shuqayri defended his own liberal democratic background, pointing out that Palestinians had constituted 10 percent of the Ottoman parliament and noting that his own father-in-law had been a parliamentarian.[56] Perhaps in order to suggest his liberalism was more authentic than that which was claimed by European countries, al-Shuqayri disturbed Singleton's equanimity when he declared that he had spent most of his youth in British prisons and concentration camps.[57]

There was a mix of dispositions, personal and political, in the group of twelve committee members. The democratic liberalism, defensive imperialism, socialism, and Zionism were evident in how they approached each other, the witnesses, and the issues. The Christianity of Hutcheson and McDonald was also central to their outlook, but resulted in very distinct approaches to their committee work. The down-home, jokey Hutcheson was a self-proclaimed liberal who recognized that the Arabs made reasonable arguments. McDonald, whose contacts with Zionists throughout the committee's work have

been described as "discreet" but were not,[58] exhibited strong support for Jewish nationalism, which was noted by his fellow commissioners and was obvious during the hearings and deliberations.[59] His support of the Jews may
have been messianic, but he was also influenced by his frustrations at being
unable to mobilize more powerful forces against the Nazis before the Holocaust.[60] Bartley Crum was also pro-Zionist from the start. Like McDonald,
Crum had been recommended for the committee by Truman's secretary,
David Niles, who was himself a Zionist activist. And also like McDonald,
Crum leaked information about the committee's work to benefit the Zionists.[61] Richard Crossman claimed repeatedly in his diary and memoirs that he
and other British people had a tendency to be "pro-Arab," a claim that surely
most Palestinians would have challenged.[62] If there was any pro-Arab or anti-
Zionist inclination in Singleton and Manningham-Buller, it came more from
a concern to protect the holdings and prestige of the British in Palestine than
from any desire to see Palestine an independent Arab country.[63]

The Palestinian representatives had started preparing well before the official announcement of the committee's composition. Already on November
24, Albert Hourani, the historian who was enrolled by Musa ʿAlami to lead
the preparations for the committee, had drafted a memo on how to organize
their presentations for the investigation. He took an information-heavy approach. He proposed including a "historical and factual section" refuting Zionist arguments, explaining how Arabs see Palestine, and a summary of previous commissions and "how they lead logically to the White Paper."[64] (The
British White Paper of 1939 articulated the government's policy in Palestine
that included some restrictions on Zionist expansion.[65]) But the Palestinian
presentation was to be far more than a rehashing of the past and its grievances. It would also proffer a democratic solution. Hourani and the team at
the Arab Office that organized the bulk of the Palestinian submissions to
the committee also developed detailed proposals for a constitution for a self-
governing Palestine, which included the provision of full citizenship for the
Jews in such a state.[66]

Most scholarly treatments of this committee focus on the political log-
ics of the major players, especially British Prime Minister Attlee, Bevin, and
Truman.[67] Figuring heavily in historians' reckonings are Truman's personal
connections to Zionists (including Eddie Jacobson, his former business

partner from Kansas City, and David Niles, his personal secretary).[68] The very organized and active Zionist constituency in the United States, Truman's concerns for the Jewish vote, and the US commitment to retaining control over Middle East oil are also oft-noted dynamics.[69] The difficult economic situation of Great Britain in need of American support after the war, the waning British Empire—or, as Crossman put it diplomatically, "a revolution from suzerainty to friendship"—and the British desire to keep the Arabs on their side inflected the behavior and attitudes of UK officials.[70] But the motivations, hopes, and expectations that brought hundreds of Palestinians and other Arabs, Zionists, non-Zionist Jews, British colonial officials, and others together to debate and make their political claims known were much more complex than such a meager real-politick accounting could capture.

Their motivations were political, but also human; they were self-serving and materialist, as well as moral and idealistic; they were reacting to recent history, but also steeped in hopes for the future. The destruction of human life wrought by World War II threatened the liberal international order and assumptions about humanity upon which it hinged. The report on the Jews in DP camps that Earl Harrison produced for the US president in the autumn of 1945 is what "by all accounts . . . stirred Truman's sympathy of the Jews."[71] Harrison's report asserted a hierarchy of suffering that helped nationalize the Jews.[72] The report stated: "Jews as Jews (not as members of their nationality groups) have been more severely victimized than the non-Jewish members of the same or other nationalities." Harrison "alerted [Truman] to an issue that would arouse the political as well as the humanitarian emotions of the American public."[73] Truman later wrote to the Saudi monarch of "humanitarian instincts" that made "the tragic situation of the surviving victims of Nazi persecution" a "worldwide problem." "It seems to me," he wrote to King Ibn Saud, founding monarch of Saudi Arabia, "that all of us have a common responsibility for working out a solution."[74]

The "magnitude" and "poignancy" of the Jewish plight, in Truman's words, demanded a global response.[75] Truman, described by those who knew him as a "humanitarian and a bible reader," continually expressed compassion for the refugees to his Jewish constituency.[76] He reassured them that he would push for the opening of Palestine to mass Jewish immigration to relieve their suffering.[77] He urged the American chair of the Anglo-American Committee to produce a report that would recommend "an affirmative program to relieve untold suffering and misery."[78] Whether Truman encouraged or reflected a particular sensibility that was becoming dominant, Protestant humanitarianism in the Middle East during this period was marked by an "identification with Jews as symbols of historical injustice. . . . The Jew was now the lovable symbol of injustice and violence in the world," requiring the "fulfillment of history's atonement" to them.[79]

## Refusing Suffering as Political Currency

The moral valence attached to the suffering of the Jews was considered to be something historic and universal. Christian Zionist activism directed this sympathy to Jews in politically significant ways. James McDonald, one of the American members of the committee, was one such tireless advocate for Jews, for Zionism, and after the state's establishment, for Israel. Similar to the views of fellow American Frank Aydelotte as well as several who presented to the committee, McDonald believed that the "threat to Jews was not only a hideous wrong but also created a world problem of overwhelming significance. It was that, not only for the sake of the Jews, but for the larger cause of freedom, justice and equal treatment of all human beings, everywhere."[80]

The question of why and how suffering conferred political rights was still being debated, however. It was an explicit matter of contention in this period and throughout the committee's hearings. Humanitarian emotions were a form of argumentation, and what such emotions could do and justify were part of the political contest. The calibration of suffering as political currency occurred through moral and economic discourses, as well as through discussion of political threats and challenges to national prestige and personal reputation. Many recognized the transactional logic that had become intertwined with the humanitarian impulse and rejected it. Egyptian politician and scholar Mohammad Zaki 'Ali Pasha said that Palestine should have received independence after the war, and if the "Jews were terrified or persecuted in Europe, the Arabs cannot be asked to pay indemnity for that."[81] For some, the principle of compensation for Jewish suffering was not in question, but the important issue was the nature of the payment and who was responsible for it. Saudi monarch 'Abd al-'Aziz ibn Sa'ud, speaking with President

Roosevelt on February 14, 1945, told him that the Jews deserved to be compensated by having "the choicest land and homes of the Germans who had oppressed them. . . . What injury have Arabs done to the Jews of Europe? . . . Let the Germans pay."[82]

When Ernest Bevin seemed to be pushing back against the inflation of this currency, he was scorned as being insensitive to the Jews. He had said he was "very anxious that the Jews in Europe shall not over-emphasize their racial position . . . if the Jews, with all their sufferings, want to get too much at the head of the queue, you have the danger of another anti-Semitic reaction through it all."[83] (He was referring to queues caused by shortages in England.[84]) Despite this public relations slipup, Bevin was fully aware of the political uses that were being made of Jewish suffering at the time. He sought to convince the Arabs that, in light of this, it would be in their own interest to make a humanitarian gesture of letting Jewish refugees into Palestine: "Complete closure of Palestine to further immigrants at Arab instigation would be regarded throughout the world as an ungenerous action on the part of the Arabs and would doubtless be found to have created an unfavorable impression when the Palestine problem is eventually discussed by the United Nations."[85] The British were not seeking Arab acquiescence to Jewish immigration just to protect the Arabs, however, but primarily to shield themselves. The British government desired "that the emotional appeal of the Jewish problem should not become a propaganda weapon against Britain in the US."[86]

Others who presented at the AACI hearings in London disputed the criteria by which political privilege was being given to the Jews.[87] Similar arguments were occurring in public discourse too.[88] It was Arab representatives who made this argument against the political calculus of suffering most forcefully though. Because of their location in the United States, the Institute for Arab American Affairs (IAAA) knew firsthand how the scales were tipping. They condemned as "hypocritical" the expressions of sympathy for the Jews by those who "refuse to admit them into [their] own country." This argument was also circulating in the Arabic press.[89] Putting an even finer point on it, the IAAA described its mission as one of promoting friendship and goodwill between the United States and the Arab world "based on the founding principles of the United States and the UN Charter of self-

government and self-determination." They drew attention to the politicization of Jewish suffering in one of their pamphlets: "The support of Zionism
has become an all too easy way of appearing a friend of the persecuted Jew,
and a cheap means of enjoying the comfortable glow of big-hearted humanitarianism at the expense of the Arabs."[90] The institute in 1945 had already
beseeched the US president to be wary of Zionists who were exploiting Jewish suffering for political ends.[91]

In his testimony to the committee, the Saudi leader deployed some demographics to make a similar point, calling US President Truman a hypo-
crite in all but name:

> The President of the United States . . . demands the admission in the name
> of humanity of another 100,000 Jews into this small and overcrowded
> country of Palestine, at the expense of the weak Arabs. He demands their
> admission into this country where every square mile would have to take 44
> of them, while at the same time Mr. Truman would not accept in his vast
> and rich country more than 39,000 or at the rate of one immigrant to every
> 75 square miles.
>
> For the champions of right and justice who fought against tyranny to
> act in this manner and to proclaim such policies is most regrettable. For
> this is a clear contradiction of right and justice and we will not comment
> on it any further, but leave it to the conscience of humanity and history to
> give their verdict on it.[92]

Whereas Zionist supporters sought to universalize the plight of the Jews,
and universalize the Jews themselves as a world-historical race for which
humanity was responsible, Arab argumentation universalized, and sought
to internationalize, the Jewish refugee problem specifically. "The problem of
Jewish refugees is a universal problem," and its solution must be based on
"universal principles of equity and equality among nations," the IAAA argued.[93] Using diplomatic terms, Musa ʿAlami "contended that the refugee
problem was a universal one. The Arabs were willing to contribute their share
to solving it," he said, "but they could not do so before they [had achieved]
their political rights."[94] An editorial in *al-Difaʿ* reminded readers to "not lose
sight of the universal humane nature [of the problem; not to] turn it into a
racist program that meant aggression against another people, the Arabs. The

overall refugee problem, not just the Jewish one, was a humanitarian problem that the entire world should resolve."[95] In his testimony to the committee, Fadel Jamali, director general of the Ministry of Foreign Affairs of Iraq, re-iterated the point: "As for the question of refugees, I think that all humanity should contribute, and it should be dealt with on an international level."[96] The insistent message was that Jewish refugees should not be cared for in Palestine alone.

## Let Arab States Share in the Humanitarian Scheme

What a "world solution" meant for some Arab representatives was rehabili-tating Europe so Jews could go home.[97] In the view of Palestinian represen-tatives and other Arab leaders, this international response also included the Arab states. Arab leaders repeatedly told Western heads and the committee that they were willing to contribute their share to solving the refugee prob-lem. A Syrian minister of foreign affairs wrote an aide memoire expressing sympathy with the homeless Jewish refugees and saying the Arabs were will-ing to share in "any humanitarian scheme which helps persecuted Jews to secure a peaceful life."[98] Egyptian foreign minister 'Abdel Hamid Badawi Pasha, a jurist and co-signer of the UN Charter, said Egypt and other Arab countries were prepared to help with the Jewish problem, adding that the rest of the world should be too.[99] The Arabic press reported on these offers and recorded Palestinian representatives' support for the idea. Arabs would be willing to work with other nations to solve the issue of European refugees if they had assurance that the Zionists would not take over Palestine and turn it into a Jewish state.[100] There were so many offers from Arab countries to accept Jewish refugees that US President Truman thanked Ibn Saud and told him how "heartening" it was.[101]

There was no discussion of these proposals among the Anglo-American Committee members, however. Neither has scholarship on the period recog-nized the offers from Arab states to house Jewish refugees.[102] That the Zion-ists were fully opposed to proposals involving anywhere other than Palestine no doubt influenced the marginalization of these proposals.[103]

What is irrefutable is that the Palestinian Arabs and their supporters understood that the humanitarian crisis of the Jews was real. They repeatedly acknowledged it publicly and expressed sympathy for it. They agreed that the crisis did need to be solved with international initiatives. Not at the Palestin-ian Arabs' expense, but, according to Palestinian-American Fuad Shatara, by "humane people of all countries."[104] That the problem of refuge for the Jews was a global responsibility was an argument Palestinians had been making for a while, and it became all the more intense after WWII. Their stance was clear: humanitarian need was significant but did not entail Jewish political rights in Palestine.

Arab interlocutors of the AACI sought to distinguish the humanitarian issue from the politics of Palestine. It was an uphill battle, given that so many Americans had "mixed up in their minds their natural and profound sympa-thy for the homeless Jews of today with the proposal for the establishment of a Jewish political state in Palestine," as Virginia Gildersleeve, a dean at Bar-nard College in New York, observed.[105] While recognizing the condition of Jews "in Europe and Hitler's massacres and persecutions which make every human heart repel those deeds," Jamali implored the committee to "separate entirely and completely the question of refugees, the humanitarian problem, from political ambitions and political desires," a stance echoed in both the Transjordan's and the Saudi Legation's missives to the committee.[106]

Expressions of sympathy for the Jews preceded almost every Arab argu-ment presented to the committee made in oral testimony and their written submissions.[107] It was as if the Arabs knew that no argument could be heard unless presented on a pillow of compassion. Proving their humanitarianism and their very humanity required embedding their arguments in empathy. As one Palestinian told the committee during the Jerusalem hearings: "To both the Americans and British as Allies we wish to tell you this: We as much as you, pity and sympathise with the Jews." He went on to point out, as had many others, that they had "taken into Palestine more than Pales-tine can take and we have contributed more than our share towards their relief."[108]

Despite these repeated expressions of compassion, which had been ar-ticulated and were documented throughout the Arab world for a long time, the Palestinians' humanitarianism remained in doubt.[109] Throughout the committee's interrogations of Palestinian witnesses, they prodded and chal-lenged the sincerity of the Arabs' sympathy. An exchange between members of the committee and renowned Princeton University historian Phillip Hitti demonstrated the Westerners' dubiousness and their apparent inability or unwillingness to see the political significance of increased Jewish immigration to Palestine. Despite Hitti's attempts to pick apart the inextricable link that had developed in public discourse and politicians' minds between the question of a Jewish state and Jewish refugees, despite his lessons on the power of historical legacy in Palestine, the committee members repeatedly tried to constrain political imagination, to ring-fence debates over resolutions to the current moment of humanitarian emergency, corralling all plans into resting on a solution in Palestine.

In the questions of Singleton and Hutcheson to Hitti, the judges explored points made in the Middle East expert's memorandum in which he stressed the importance of keeping the problem of Jewish refugees separate from the claims for a Jewish state. Singleton quoted the memorandum: "We appreciate the importance of the human problem of displaced and destitute Jews, and we wish to share in its solution." He then asked Hitti to clarify that he was speaking on behalf of the Institute for Arab American Affairs, and not for all Arabs, which Hitti confirmed.[110] Singleton added a somewhat ambiguous statement expressing his "hope that you will have all the help we can get to solve the human problem.... I draw attention to it now as something I think we ought to have."[111] With this, the question of humanitarian responsibility was broached, after which Hutcheson took over the questioning by quoting Hitti's memorandum at length:

> Reading from the first page of your memorandum, you say "It is likewise clear that the immediate object of concentrating on Palestine as a place of refuge, is for the political purpose of achieving a majority after which the de facto majority will automatically establish a Jewish state in Palestine. The question, therefore, so far as it affects the political future of Palestine, is whether a humanitarian purpose in which all right-thinking people will concur, shall be allowed to create a political revolution in which a present Arab majority of two to one shall be politically subordinated to an immigrant group, contrary to all international precedent...." It is your view that the present conditions are being seized on by the Zionists and used for the purpose of carrying out their prime desire to make a Jewish state?
>
> DR. HITTI: Yes, sir.

The rest of the discussion with Hutcheson involved an epistemological tussle in which the liberal judge struggled to reduce the current problem to one of the immediate crisis for the Jews. Hitti patiently sought to maintain a historically extended purview, to help the Westerners understand the problematic nature of their expectations. He underscored the importance of understanding the context, one that was more complicated and of longer duration than the committee members seemed willing to grasp.

> HUTCHESON: If that assumption were removed . . . if the conception of
> a Jewish state or a Jewish Commonwealth disappeared by some change
> in the opinion of the Zionists or by a public law which prevented such
> consummation, would you say that the great humanitarian purpose to go
> to a place where the people are ready to receive them and are in sympa-
> thy with them would be opposed and prevented by the Arabs, Moslems,
> and Christians? In other words, let us look on Palestine as a place fitted
> by long preparation for the reception of Jews. . . . Would you say that
> the sentiment of those now opposed to political Zionism would subside
> enough to permit that great humanitarian purpose to be achieved? ·
> HITTI: Frankly, no, sir. I am answering from the standpoint of the
> Arabs. . . . If you permit me, I may remark that your question, Your
> Honor, is hypothetical. . . . And because it is hypothetical, it can't be
> answered in practical terms. I mean to say so much emotion has been
> stirred up, blood has been shed for many years, and there are psychologi-
> cal elements and tensions over the years that no matter how much you
> tell the people in the name of mercy, admit more Jews, you cannot over-
> ride that background. There was a time, Mr. Chairman, in which that
> could have been done very well. I was teaching in the early twenties in
> Lebanon, and there were hundreds and thousands of Armenian refugees
> coming from Turkey. I happened to be on the committee of the Near
> Eastern Relief, and I visited those places where those Armenians lived,
> and I know how everybody welcomed them and did everything they
> could for them. At the same time, every time a Zionist landed in Haifa,
> everybody looked upon him with suspicion, not because he was Jewish,
> not at all, but because he came with the idea "this is my country. It has

been my country and I am coming to reclaim it." It was an immigration different from all other immigrations.

HUTCHESON: You mean they treated it as immigration for conquest?

. . .

HITTI: Absolutely. . . . If your question was raised twenty years ago, I have absolutely no doubt that the people of Palestine, the Arab people in general, would have said "Welcome" to the Jews. . . . [But today] the people would say "No."

HUTCHESON: In order to carry out the objective of the state, no, but in order to relieve the suffering in recognition of what they have undergone, would not the Arab say yes out of a spirit of generosity, if they could be assured that the Jewish state was out?

HITTI: If you can convince them, you will go a long way towards the solution of the problem, because in the mind of the Arab, every Zionist coming in is a potential warrior.

At this point, Lord Morrison stepped in to pursue Hutcheson's line of questioning, asking Hitti what was meant in the memorandum by the assurances of support for a solution: "We appreciate the importance of the human problem of displaced and destitute Jews, and wish to share in its solution." Hitti explained that two years ago, he had appeared before a committee of the US House of Representatives where he "said definitely and clearly that as an American citizen, I would not be adverse to having Jews and any suffering people admitted to the United States. I still maintain that we here as Americans should do our share towards the solution of this problem as Americans." Returning to expose American hypocrisy, Hitti remarked, naming himself as a US citizen: "Our legislators and our governors have been making many gestures and declarations about forcing Palestine to take more Jews, but I didn't hear anyone of them raise a finger in [sic] behalf of the Jews to the extent of lifting the barriers so some Jews can be admitted to the United States. . . . I think we should be ashamed of ourselves for not having done it before." None of his interrogators addressed this challenge directly, but in Buxton's question, he emphasized Hitti's insistence that "the gates of Palestine should be closed to the Jews." To this Hitti responded by clarifying

that, given the history of bloodshed, "it will be very difficult for us, if not
impossible, to convince the Arabs that those forthcoming Jews are coming
under a different banner."

Hutcheson, in trying to get Hitti to concede a point, revealed his own
deeply Christian and liberal views, as he would throughout the committee's
work and in his reflections on it afterward. He said to Hitti:

> Two or three days ago I read how the Jewish fellows state the basis of their
> neighborly views, and it is said in the Bible that you must love your neigh-
> bor as yourself, so if all that comes together, wouldn't there be a reasonable
> place for accord in something like this: Permit the population of the Jewish
> section to be increased by this pitiful remnant—this remnant remaining in
> Germany and Austria—and then let the thing stop with such reasonable
> immigration allowances as proportioned to any country. Why should you
> think when the spirit of compromise is being involved, that bar should fall
> absolutely on the present status? Why not let some of these hard-depressed
> ones come in and use that as a basis?

In response to this idealistic portrayal of what "balance" could achieve, Hitti
reiterated his opinion, that "if you can convince [the Arabs]," it could be. But
when Hitti posed the direct question about how many Jews Hutcheson himself would let into the United States, the judge's playfully vague response that
he "would be awfully liberal with them!" garnered only laughter.[112]

When the conversation (which this period of the hearings with Dr. Hitti
seemed to have become) addressed more seriously the issue of Western
countries' immigration policies, Hutcheson affirmed that the United States
"should do something." According to an opinion poll from the period, most
Americans agreed that more Jews should be let into the United States.[113]
Hitti affirmed Crossman's suggestion that Arab opinion on Jewish immigration to Palestine might soften if the "Western Powers were willing to make a
very big gesture and do a big job in taking in refugees." The secretary general
of the Arab League had already said as much during his visit to London in
October 1945. Arab interlocutors regularly confronted the committee with
the suggestion that Western countries should take in Jewish refugees and
apparently received no answer to the question of why they would not.[114] But

rather than pursue this alternative home for the Jewish refugees, McDonald steered the discussion to ancient history.

Despite McDonald engaging Hitti in a long and abstruse debate about Amorites and Canaanites and the Old Testament, Phillips averted this hijacking of the conversation and returned to the question of humanitarian relief for the Jews. He asked how to change Arab opinion toward it.[115] Hitti replied forcefully: "Action." History had taught the Arabs to look on the promises from the West with suspicion, Hitti explained, so only immediate action from America or England could make a difference. (He would make the same kind of argument more than ten years later, explaining to American legislators that only sincere action on behalf of the "legitimate national aspirations of the Arabs" could win Arab respect back for the United States.)[116] "How can we convince the Arabs that they should offer a sacrifice if none of us is offering any sacrifice?" Hitti asked, reasserting himself again as one of the Western "us." Instead of a reply, Hutcheson (one imagines him grinning wryly because the committee "found that question difficult"[117]) thanked the professor "especially for that historical debate between you and McDonald."[118]

## International Law and Liberal Comportment in the Jerusalem Hearings

By the time the committee reached Palestine, this somewhat jovial atmosphere in the hearings had diminished. Richard Crossman reported in letters to his wife (written while Arab representatives were presenting testimony) that the committee members had descended into a "fairly bad, bickering mood."[119] The majority of the Arab representatives that the committee would hear—who Crossman described as "poor inefficient, idle, corrupt political leaders who are wasting our time"—appeared before them in Jerusalem, where the committee heard seven hours of hearings every day. It was "a bit trying" and left the committee "very testy and bored." 'Awni 'Abd al-Hadi's contribution was, in McDonald's view, "a very dull, labored and nervous presentation of historical data" that tried the committee's patience, as did the claim that the Jews took the most fertile parts of Palestine.[120] Aydelotte also considered the Arabs' testimony in Jerusalem to be "old stuff."[121] Their only interest was "to get the hell out of Palestine and to start finishing the job."[122]

Crossman found himself mostly on his own, evidently fed up with his fellow investigators who he found "silly and petty," and in the case of the two chairmen, "crochety [*sic*]" too.[123] This testimony fatigue may explain something of how irritably the committee received the Palestinians' representations. But the themes in their questioning and attitudes toward their Jewish and Arab interlocutors remained consistent throughout the course of their mission—perhaps being revealed only more starkly among some tired commissioners in these final days of their investigations. During their mission, they were, on the whole, impressed with the creativity of the Zionists and by their economic development in Palestine; they were deeply moved by the suffering of Jewish displaced persons in the camps they visited throughout Europe.[124] Several of them dismissed the Arabs as "intransigent" and their leadership as corrupt, and pitied them their dusty poverty. Some commissioners thought the Palestinian and Arab leaders did not represent their people, dismissing them as a "set of charming degenerates."[125] The orientalist racism of some committee members sustained their political opinions throughout. And yet, many of them considered themselves to be liberals or, as in the case of Richard Crossman, a liberal socialist.[126] Basic racism may help explain the fact that the liberal motivations and goals of the people involved in this committee ran counter to what they recommended in the end. But it is a conundrum bigger than this.

The Anglo-American Committee reveals how the correct expression of sympathy for Jewish suffering became a performative requirement for the good liberal in the politics of this period. Although the Anglo-American Committee, like other commissions to Palestine, made claims to function according to rules of objectivity, with legalistic processes and according to international legal principles, the actual means of adjudicating and their categories of assessment functioned otherwise. Crossman explained to the British prime minister that the committee "tried to be a straight and honest jury."[127] What the jury read was more than the facts, however. In the midst of their explicit debates about how to develop a balanced accommodation between the Zionist and the Arabs of Palestine, committee members actualized *implicit* norms and made unspoken demands for standards of comportment that showed the correct balance of reasonableness and sympathy. The Arabs were accused of falling short.

Palestinian representatives, although expressing both their reasoned arguments and their sympathy for Jewish suffering, hewed forcefully to a liberal legal approach, manifesting a firm belief in the idea that the objective rules of law would produce fair results, that law is universally accessible to all, and equally, that law can be a break on power.[128] In their interactions with the committee, they returned, again, to history, logical reasoning, and international law to ground their demands for independence, and to challenge the legitimacy of British and Zionist claims. Although there was novelty in their references to the new instruments of international law such as the UN Charter that had developed in the legal ferment after World War II, the message remained consistent: Arabs should rightfully be politically independent in—and have sovereignty over—Palestine because of their long history in the land and centuries of Arab sovereignty there. The British had no right to give Palestine to the Jews, who were interlopers trying to take over a country based on spurious historical claims with the aid of Western intervention. The "national home" that the Balfour Declaration referred to was just a "vague expression that bears no definite meaning in International Law," the Arab League argued.[129]

In addition, the logic of the Zionists' argument was faulty, they explained. To contend that because the Jews ruled over Palestine two thousand years ago and should therefore be sovereign there again today would logically lead to the assertion that the Arabs, likewise, "should have the right to acquire Spain, parts of France, Italy, and Sicily" where they used to rule. And both the British and Americans should be expelled from their own countries.[130] In contrast to this deficient reasoning, the Arab League reminded the committee that the Arab legal claim was based on a treaty from 636 CE between the Caliph Omar ibn al-Khattab and the Byzantines, when Arab control over Jerusalem was established. The Balfour Declaration had no *legal* validity because it was only addressed to an individual who represented neither a state nor a government. It was merely an "expression of sympathy towards the Jewish aspirations," as Balfour himself wrote in a letter to Rothschild.[131] Not only was the Balfour Declaration inconsistent with prior promises that the Great Powers made to the Arabs, but it was also invalid because it went against the League of Nations Covenant Article 22. It was contrary to the principle of self-governance outlined there, as the committee read in multiple written submissions.[132] Fayez Sayegh argued that it contradicted "elemental rights of nationalism and national self-determination." Touching on the most important principles of the emerging global order in one sweeping sentence delegitimizing the basis of British and Zionist control in Palestine, Sayegh dismissed the Balfour Declaration as "a sin against humanitarian conscience as well as against the principles of national existence and international behaviour and cooperation."[133]

The recounting of broken treaties and the mandate's unfulfilled obligations had become standard in Palestinian debates with their Western interlocutors, and much of their written submissions to the Anglo-American Committee covered this ground again, underscoring the illegitimacy of the Balfour Declaration that was at the heart of the League of Nations mandate that gave Britain control of the country. Citing "the UN Charter of self-government and self-determination,"[134] throwing the committee's liberal principles back at them, the Palestinian presentation pointed out that the Balfour Declaration had "no basis in the consent of the population."[135] The legal irrelevance of the Balfour Declaration was an argument that the committee would hear again.[136]

In making their case to the committee, Palestinians invoked, but did not always rely on, legal arguments and these international documents and norms. Sometimes they called them directly into question:

> I must make it clear that our right is not based on treaty or pledge. . . . As we know, pledges are often framed with backdoors and loopholes. . . . I shall not refer to Article 22 of the Covenant of the League of Nations . . . [nor] to President Wilson's twelfth point. . . . Nor do I intend to refer to the . . . King-Crane Commission of 1919, or . . . to the Atlantic Charter. These instruments recognize but do not create our right to independence. If the recognition is withheld, our right still remains and shall remain.

In this rhetorically clever testimony, Ahmad al-Shuqayri, "a very ambitious rising lawyer" and the future head of the PLO, offered a critique of the malleable and political nature of human-made law.[137] He brought out into the open the forces of political expediency at play, framing the Palestinian case as one of "our natural right, our inherent right to live in our country in freedom and security, to revive our potentialities and capacities and to contribute our full share in world civilization and progress."[138] The deconstructionist critique of international law was a common element in many of the Palestinians' presentations.[139] Although they admitted their doubts about the Westerners' legal instruments, they also professed their faith in the commission's "sense of justice" and their hope in the international legal system that was supposed to guide the commission's work. They were not duped or naïve, but nevertheless expressed faith in the system and actors judging them.[140] In the words of Cecil Hourani, a member of the Arab Office, they "felt that [they] were part of a new phase in Arab history in which all the Arab countries would emerge into independence."[141] Such hope, both skeptical and optimistic, motivated Palestinians' involvement with international institutions.

The Arab Office, the small public relations team for the Palestinians that took the lead in presenting the Arab case, consistently drew on legal arguments. The methodical research that their team undertook to convince the Anglo-American Committee of their rights to independence also included historical arguments and economic proof that Zionist claims to be developing Palestine for the benefit of the Arabs were false claims.[142] The Arab presentation was not merely critique and refutation, however, nor merely an assertion of rights. It also included a specific proposition for a democratic solution. In testimony before the AACI, Albert Hourani reminded the committee that the

> Arab people . . . has again and again emphasized that the only just and practicable solution for the problem of Palestine lies in the constitution of Palestine, . . . into a self-governing state, with its Arab majority, but with full rights for the Jewish citizens. . . . A state which should enter the United Nations . . . on a level of equality with other Arab states; a state in which questions of general concern, like immigration, should be decided by the ordinary democratic procedure, in accordance with the will of the majority.[143]

The government Hourani proposed would be "representative of all Palestinian citizens on a level of absolute individual equality." As the Arab Office laid out its vision, it emphasized the rights of Jews who were already in the country as legal citizens. They would remain in Palestine as citizens with full civil and political rights, not just a tolerated minority existing "by sufferance of the majority." This vision for the future was one in which "Palestinian citizens, Arabs and Jews alike, [would] have responsibility of the welfare of the whole people of the country."[144] Other documents outlined the formation of the government through constitutional and legislative assemblies, provisions for an electoral law, and other guarantees that should be, they said, "embodied" in a UN General Assembly resolution.[145]

Self-government. Religious tolerance. Equal citizenship. Democracy. All were touchstones of the new liberal international legal order heralded by the formation of the United Nations. Palestinians' deployment of international legal norms shows their location in a liberal framework shared with the commissioners. But the terms in which the commissioners rejected the Palestinians' arguments reveal the limits of those shared principles. Beyond the bounds of liberal reason, there was another political epistemology in operation—that of moralized suffering. The Janus-faced comportment demanded of the Palestinians required one aspect showing a balanced stance, demonstrating reasonableness and a compromising attitude, and the other manifesting humanitarian sympathy for the suffering of the Jews.

## Judging Intransigence and the Humanitarian Structure of Feeling

Despite Palestinians' assertions that the humanitarian crisis did indeed need to be solved (but not at their expense), members on the committee were mostly unimpressed by the Arabs who appeared before them.[146]

Regardless of the other Palestinian presenters' demonstrations of reason and sympathy, the Westerners dismissed their case as being "mostly a repetition of the standard Arab argument that Palestine was Arab and the Jews were interlopers." The Americans and British did not interpret the Arab arguments about self-determination as a principled and consistent political stance. Rather, they found them "rigid and unimaginative."[147] They considered the Arab "intransigence" and "overstatement" to be unhelpful and distasteful.[148] And it stood in contrast with what they perceived to be the Zionists' balanced, moderate approach. Richard Crossman expressed his appreciation for these qualities when he praised Chaim Weizmann's testimony.

In Crossman's view, Weizmann was "the first witness who has frankly and openly admitted that the issue is not between right and wrong but between the greater and the lesser injustice."[149] Aydelotte extolled Judah Magnes's testimony as "the high water mark of our hearings" for it "was a rare embodiment of quiet reasonableness in a land where reasonableness was too often interpreted as weakness or even treason."[150]

Belief in the Arabs' intransigence was circulating in public discourse in the United States in this period too. It echoed most forcefully in McDonald's commentary.[151] Although he knew no Arabic, he claimed to decipher the Arabs' intransigent ways through mere observation. In his diaries he recorded his impressions of the Arab spokespeople:

> As the testimony went on, I kept my eyes on Prince Faisal. He showed intense interest and at crucial moments seemed to me to indicate that he was one of the most uncompromising of the group. I could imagine him being completely unyielding. . . . On the whole, the Arabs made an impression of such unyieldingness that it would be impossible to win them by any sort of compromise.[152]

Leaning his lanky frame back into his chair, peering down his aquiline nose, he knew just by looking at them.

Other commissioners did have cool words of praise for some of the younger spokespeople, especially Albert Hourani. They were impressed by his intelligence and eloquence.[153] But the force of his testimony was weakened, his credibility tarnished, because he fell short on expressing enough of one crucial emotion: sympathy. He neglected to express it in the right way. When one of the commissioners questioned him on the Arabs' demand that Jewish immigration to Palestine stop, the commission's secretary reported that Hourani "would not agree to the admission of a single additional Jew to Palestine—not even the aged and infirm among the displaced persons."[154] Indeed, the Arab stance was clear: the doors of Europe and America should be opened to the victims of the European war, not the politically fragile Holy Land.[155] The Arabs recommended that the refugee problem should be "adjudged by the United Nations . . . at the equal expense of all its members."[156] Again, reassuring the committee that they understood the plight of the Jews, Hourani explained that "Jewish refugees and their misfortunes in the world is a question which is sympathized with by everybody who has any humanitarian feeling . . . [and we] participate in this feeling and this sympathy towards the Jewish situation, and the oppression which they have suffered in Europe . . . as much as, if not more than, any other nation in the world, but we do not wish to . . . join this position to the Palestine question."[157]

Sympathy for the displaced Jews of Europe, their suffering which Hourani said he felt "deeply," could not be addressed as if their distress existed in a political vacuum. "It is unhappily impossible," Hourani explained, "to consider the question of immigration simply on humanitarian grounds. . . . The question of [Jewish] immigration into Palestine must be seen in its general political framework." This was a time when some Palestinians believed coexistence with the Jews already in Palestine was still possible. They thought mass immigration to Palestine would spell the destruction of that shared existence, tip the demographics, and create the conditions for the declaration of a Zionist state and political oppression of the Palestinians.[158]

But what struck the committee was "this completely intransigent stand," rather than Hourani's argument.[159] What Hourani actually said in response to Manningham-Buller's question about whether the Arabs would admit old, sick Jewish people into Palestine was that the question was not "adequately posed" because it "implies there is no other possible asylum for those people." When Manningham-Buller asked the same question again—"I was only asking whether the Arabs would be prepared to open their doors to elderly Jews who had relatives now in Palestine as a humanitarian measure"—Hourani again objected to the way the question was posed, pointing out that refugees in Europe had other choices besides going to Palestine and dying. "There are other possible asylums," Hourani observed. "I insist that the Arabs are not responsible."[160] With that, the committee became convinced that sympathy and malleability were the missing "anthropological capacities"—what Uday Mehta called the characteristics demanded of non-Western peoples by liberal thinkers—that proved the Arabs' "political incompetence" and human inadequacy, disqualifying their claims.[161]

Despite being described as a "hot-head" himself,[162] Judge Joe Hutcheson reviled the passions of the nationalists he had to listen to, so irritatingly repeating their "extremist" assertions that their side had the one and only correct solution to the Palestine "problem child," as Hutcheson called it.[163] In

his pondering of written submissions to the commission, mentions of violence, threatened in more and less veiled terms, propelled his pencil onto
their pages with double underlinings and question marks in the margins.
These contestants' passions that led them to "speak only in terms of bombs
and carnage," their "hardness of hearts" that could brook no compromise, got
under the judge's skin.[164] In these conditions, he believed, only the principle
of justice could fly above the fray, "until the question has been stripped of its
political and opportunistic aspects." When the facts could be examined from
the perspective of "abstract and universal justice," free of political consider-
ations, then a real solution could be determined.[165] It was only this judge's
liberal view that could bring justice into being. For what was justice but "the
end of governments and of civil society . . . the constant and perpetual dis-
position to render to everyone his due," as Hutcheson wrote in an essay on
"racialism."[166] Intransigence was a vice that liberals could not tolerate. And
unwillingness to bend political principles for the sake of Jewish vulnerability
was a cruelty that could not be forgiven. Cruelty, after all, is a cardinal vice of
the liberal, perhaps the most important one.[167] Although the specific qualities under scrutiny have changed over time, they are, as Mehta has identified, always available as a mechanism for denying self-determination to the
colonized.[168]

The humanitarian structure of feeling was an ideological-emotional system gaining prominence in political discourse well before the end of the
Cold War (when many scholars belatedly date the rise of humanitarianism's
diplomatic centrality).[169] This deployment of humanitarianism—specifically
the activist humanitarianism that has since come to stand as "a core value of
liberalism"[170] functioning as "the continuation of politics by other means"[171]—
obscured the Palestinians' arguments grounded in legal terms. Because of
their continuing commitment to the ideology of international law and assumptions about liberal legalism—repeating arguments based in a notion of
rights and tolerance of diversity—Palestinians did not fulfill the performative
demands of the humanitarian liberal that were now prominent.[172]

So long as Palestinians deployed their liberal-legal arguments to deny
the Jews sovereignty over Palestine and claim an Arab state—even one that
would constitute, in the words of Ahmad al-Shuqayri, "a marvelous evidence
of tolerance," in which the Jews already in Palestine "who are ready to display

their loyalty to this State will automatically acquire full rights of citizens in a democratic state, in spite of the fact that they were admitted to the country against our protests"[173]—no profession of democratic ideals and no amount of sympathy expressed for Jewish suffering would be enough for their Western judges.

The Arabs *had* fully appreciated the power of the humanitarian claim, and they sought to challenge it, trying to separate its emotional pull from political reason by calling out what they saw as the Zionists' and commissioners' inappropriate politicization of suffering. But in their reasonableness—part of the liberal's moral sensibility[174]—they had violated the "conventions of sympathy," a feature of political discourse about Jews in World War II that would soon become widely entrenched.[175] They could not perform the correct combination of reason and sympathy, compromise and compassion, because their political reason and rationale ran contrary to the scale of the compromise being demanded of them. These interchanges with the committee reveal the implicit standards of judgment that could be called on to help justify political decisions that denied Arab demands for independence.

Among the final recommendations of the committee was to issue certificates for the immigration of 100,000 Jews to Palestine. Citing America's moral leadership, Judge Hutcheson justified it as a humanitarian necessity.[176] Although this fulfilled the Zionist demand and would put them forward on the path to obtaining a majority in the country, the committee report also asserted that neither Jew nor Arab should have dominance in Palestine. They thought their report demonstrated a fair "live and let live" attitude, as the American chair of the committee described it.[177] The Western adjudicators did not publicly admit that it would be politically decisive to grant certificates of immigration to the Jews as an expression of sympathy and compensation for Jewish loss. But they knew it. The American secretary to the committee knew that the fundamental issue was not the form of the future state, but rather who would be the majority, because that would ultimately determine the issue, and he told the committee as much in a memo.[178] Obscuring this significant point, the committee echoed the ill-considered claims of Earl Harrison. In his 1945 report to Truman, Harrison cited the Jewish Agency's call for 100,000 immigration certificates as "reasonable." Harrison wrote with apparently minimal understanding of the political ramifications of his recommendation for the Arabs. He wrote: "if there is any genuine sympathy for what these survivors have endured, some reasonable extension or modification of the British [limitation of Jewish immigration to Palestine] ought to be possible without too serious repercussions."[179] Reasonableness and "compromise" were what the commissioners thought was needed, chastising even Western interlocutors who did not "recognize that there are two sides to th[e] question."[180]

## Liberal Entanglements

Judge Hutcheson thought it fair and correct that Jews and Arabs should have "equal rights and voice" in the Palestinian government, a status he believed could only develop under a trustee that would bring about "a balance between the two elements in the population."[181] This required setting an immigration level aimed at reaching equal numbers of Arabs and Jews despite the demographic disparity at the time. By 1946, enabled by the British mandatory government, Jewish residents owned 7 percent of Palestine's total land and constituted 31 percent of the population. (The Jewish population had constituted only 10 percent of the population in 1914, before the British mandate implemented its policies encouraging Jewish immigration to Palestine.[182]) And now the AACI wanted to facilitate further Jewish expansion. Hutcheson thought they could bring a political balance to Palestine through population equity. At the same time, and without apparent consciousness of the irony, he expressed outrage at the Zionist demand for just a little more than equity. Zionists wanted help in accelerating Jewish immigration to Palestine until Jews reached an outright majority and then could capture control of the state. Hutcheson fumed that this "is so contrary to the fundamental principles of self-determination and does so much violence so that there is something vicious in stacked elections and controlled plebiscites, that it is quite plain that . . . those who accept it are either not just men or they are uninformed."[183] He did not see that what he was advocating in his equity plan—policies that would enable increased influence of Zionists in the country—was about the same thing.

Hutcheson's perspective reflected a common tendency to view the Palestine problem as one that existed between two claims that were equally just, equally right, and therefore required an equalizing balance.[184] Hutcheson's inability to appreciate structural reasons for present conditions, structures that had historical roots and political motivations, stemmed from his version of liberalism. A reasonable balance in the here and now fulfilled his liberal criterion of fairness, but required bracketing out the longer history and broader context of Palestine as an overwhelmingly Arab country.[185] That this had been even more so until British imperialism and Zionist colonialism transformed it did not seem to figure in his thinking. When a commissioner did acknowledge the mandate, it was usually to reassert the mandate's own terms of reference, including the Zionist provisions of the Balfour Declaration.[186] By instituting "balance" in the moment, Hutcheson could overlook his own role in trying to stack the elections and control the plebiscite by instituting a trusteeship.

The sentiment was crystalized in the committee report's third recommendation: "That Jew shall not dominate Arab and Arab shall not dominate Jew in Palestine. That Palestine shall be neither a Jewish state nor an Arab state."[187] Indeed, who could argue against a prohibition on ethnic domination? But what their recommendations and reasoning obscured was a history of British mandatory policies and practices expediting Jewish colonization of the land, thwarting Palestinian resistance to it, blocking democratic developments, denying self-government.[188] This blindness was enabled by a fetishization of the idea of balance as the goal of the reasonable subject and by a historically foreshortened view. But Palestinians knew that a trusteeship was a form of government that would never be "any more neutral than the mandatory government, unless an uncertain wavering from side to side be called neutrality," as Albert Hourani quipped.[189]

The Anglo-American Committee and its "solutions" facilitated the repression and dispossession of Palestinians from their lands and rights in multiple ways. And it did so in a way that allowed the commissioners to bask in their balanced approach to instituting "equality."[190] The Anglo-American Committee permitted—indeed encouraged—well-intentioned liberals like Frank Aydelotte to believe they were doing good and spreading good. The committee members' self-satisfaction resulting from their liberal performances grew because their personal integrity and national identity were tied up in their commission work. Their liberalism was a shared subjectivity among many of them. Like others he would work with on the Anglo-American Committee, Aydelotte believed deeply in many liberal ideals. He was a great fan of Woodrow Wilson. He hosted a League of Nations technical group at the Institute of Advanced Study.[191] He thought democracy was not just a "material order; [but] a spiritual point of view."[192] There was ideological and temperamental variety among the other eleven commissioners, but several of them shared Aydelotte's liberal outlook. Texas judge Joe Hutcheson called himself a "Liberal of the Jefferson, Madison, Lincoln, Wilson school;" a "lover of liberty."[193] This, he said, "is the way of freedom, the way, too, of personal and national integrity, character and honor."[194] He seems to have taken on board Truman's admonition that the world was expecting a report "that is in accord with the highest American tradition of generosity and justice."[195] Exhibiting his tendency toward self-assured pontification, Hutcheson made "an eloquent defense of America's 'moral' record in foreign affairs" in his deliberations with the committee.[196] His strong faith in the "American way of liberalism and justice," superior to any "European, bastardized ideas of Liberalism," was only bolstered by his equally strong faith in the law "as liberator" and "the bulwark of all freedom and prosperity."[197]

Commissions demanded the performance of an idealized liberal national identity on a public stage (so much so that it angered Crossman when British misrule was in the cross-hairs).[198] In private, too, the commissioners' liberalism shaped how they saw themselves as ethical individuals. Especially among Hutcheson, Aydelotte, Crum, and Crossman, their liberalism was part of how they formed and shared a common self-image.[199] In exchanges with each other after their work ended, Aydelotte reiterated his continued conviction in the rightness of the commission's recommendations.[200] He praised those who agreed with their recommendations, labeling them approvingly as moderates.[201]

Hutcheson agreed: he thought their report could "satisfy the just claims of both Arab and Jew" and a solution would have been "well under way" had their report been implemented.[202] (Aydelotte and Hutcheson kept up their mutual praise for their balanced approach in letters they exchanged after the report's release.)[203] Hutcheson believed that his role as a judge, and his role as a member of the committee, was to "recommend what is moral and just."[204]

Crossman defended their report as being "based upon a full consideration of both points of view and a deliberate if reluctant choice of the lesser injustice."[205] They looked back fondly on their time on this committee and thought highly of themselves for embodying liberal values in their report.

This is how the ideology of liberalism has worked in many contexts. It lets those engaged in performing its principles believe—and as important, feel—that they are virtuous by living up to what were, to them, objectively positive values, even when "tough choices" were involved. The committee members were gratified by enacting liberal standards, as their personal correspondence and memoirs exhibit, brimming with moments of self-congratulation and with expressions of faith in their own rightness, their own justice.[206]

What is peculiar to the power of liberalism as an ideology is its ability to produce and justify injustice in the name of justice, while inspiring an emotional dimension of feeling righteous and rational at the same time. "Self-government is a great thing," Aydelotte avowed, "but Palestine is not the place for it."[207] Liberals determine that democracy is appropriate only for some based on readings of others' apparent sensibilities, noticing their unsuccessful enactments of predefined liberal virtues, as they thought they had in locating the Arabs' intransigence. In Palestine, it was Jews who the commissioners and others determined were vulnerable and most in need of legal checks on cruelty, a requirement of a liberal order.[208] The AACI members thought their committee's recommendations would inscribe those values in a new political arrangement. Arabs' fears were not understood to be existential.

Anthropologist Elizabeth Povinelli has observed that many characterizations of liberalism "miss the [work] done by minor emotions and discourses such as doubt and irritation and failures of faith. . . . They authorize, authenticate, and guarantee Truth in liberal regimes of critical rational reflection. . . . These [are] feelings of moral right."[209] This self-congratulatory (self-)fulfillment within the investigative commission as an institution of liberalism—an open space for "the repetition of [liberalism's] key verities"[210]—is what allowed them to work so hard and feel so good about expediting colonial dispossession. Their faith in liberalism allowed them to misrecognize their part in bolstering and justifying repression and keep their "feelings of moral right."

## The Liberal Middle

It may be easier to understand the part liberalism played in the workings of the committee than to recognize its role among Palestinian representatives, because common assumptions about liberalism and about Palestinians usually put them in separate pens of thought. But Palestinians, too, were entrenched in this liberal discourse, which rolled consistently from their tongues and pens as they interacted with the committee. They demanded representative government and liberty, and spoke of their national rights. Palestinian educator Khalil Totah encouraged the committee to "settle the Palestine question in the same way you would settle it in England or in America. That is by the ballot. . . . The Jews are clamoring for democracy. England has suffered and has bled in two bloody wars for democracy. I say let the people of Palestine, including the Jews . . . more than half a million of whom are in Palestine . . . let them vote."[211] Calling the committee's own legitimacy deeply into question, Palestinians' invocations of liberal principles were voiced to challenge their adjudicators in their own terms. But for many of them, these were their terms too. Palestinians' democratic demands, their belief in the logic of their arguments, their reliance on reason, and their faith in the reasonableness of the Great Powers and international law came from their own liberal backgrounds. It was a faith that came from their own sensibilities and beliefs, and in the case of some who were involved, their Western legal training as well.

Among those most deeply involved with representing the Palestinian case were men firmly entrenched in the colonial liberal middle. They were middle class or elite with prestigious academic backgrounds. Some were professional intermediaries between the British and the colonized, working with the mandatory government. Along with others in the Arab Office, Musa ʿAlami, Albert Hourani, and his brother Cecil Hourani considered themselves to be "decent, liberal, approachable people," as Cecil Hourani, the former director of the Washington branch of the Arab Office, told me in an interview. ʿAlami, who initiated the development of the Arab Office that did the most to present the Palestinian case, was the son of a Jerusalem mayor and would become Palestinian representative to the Arab League. He had studied law at Cambridge University and took a position in the legal department of the British mandatory administration, and was briefly Arab

secretary to high commissioner Arthur Wauchope in 1933.[212] He was friendly
with British foreign minister Ernest Bevin who, according to Cecil Hourani,
"had considerable respect for ['Alami's] judgment and wisdom."[213] 'Alami
wrote passionately about the democratic principles that must be at the foundation of any program for Palestinians to secure their freedom, the rights and
duties of citizens—whose first duty is to know their rights—in a representative federal government.[214]

The same democratic values appeared in Albert Hourani's proposals for
a democratic Palestine with equal rights for Jews, which the Arab Office
presented to the committee.[215] Historian Wm. Roger Louis characterized
Hourani's approach to the Anglo-American Committee as being driven
by Hourani's belief "that men of common sense investigating the problem
would quickly conclude that a small territory such as Palestine could not
possibly provide a solution to the Jewish refugee problem."[216] Such respect
for common sense and rationality—a feature of the liberal sensibility that
"centers on the idea of humans as rational beings who are naturally free and
equal and whose consent is therefore necessary to any form of rule"—had
motivated Arab cooperation with the British for years.[217] The denial of Palestinians' self-representative government was simply unreasonable, and their
presentations to the Anglo-American Committee was yet another effort to
demonstrate that.

Despite the Palestinians' invocations of democratic principles or assurances of their willingness to institutionalize tolerance in the constitution
of their Arab state—modeled as it would be on the British and American
constitutions[218]—the commissioners, like many who would come after them,
did not accept these Arabs as their liberal equals. For every argument the
Palestinians put forward that accorded with their own liberal values, they
found evidence of Arab "stubborn unyieldingness,"[219] violence, and hard-
heartedness that excluded them from the community of nations, if not the
human community itself.

## Conclusion: The Overwhelming Appeal of Humanitarianism

It is by now well recognized that representations of suffering are a central feature of human rights politics, that a "global meritocracy of suffering" in which images of pain are a "species of rhetoric" can justify political

interventions that encroach on state sovereignty.[220] As earlier chapters show, the suffering of "others" has long been a prompt and an excuse for Western actions in the Palestinian-Zionist conflict. Already in the 1930s, Palestinians recognized how Zionists sought to make political use of Western sympathy for the blighted conditions of Jews in Europe. After World War II, the Arabs more forcefully argued that the Zionists were inappropriately politicizing their suffering and that their supporters were intentionally eliding the question of why Jewish suffering and homelessness should be resolved in Palestine, rather than Europe. Europe, after all, was the source of the problem. But Arab refusal to take responsibility for the results of Western anti-Semitism did not go over well with the committee.

The pivotal issue for Arabs and Zionists revolved around what political identities and interventions could be justified by suffering in the name of humanitarianism. It might have been only in an offhand way that Alan Cunningham, the British high commissioner in Palestine, recognized that the "tragedy of Europe gave added emphasis to the Jewish demands."[221] But the European tragedy ultimately was used to determine and defend the political decision to grant key Zionist demands in opposition to all democratic principles and procedures. Ernest Bevin counseled the committee to find "a balance between equity, humanitarianism, and world peace."[222] Those who made these decisions thought of balance in a specific way, making them deaf to some important moral assertions of the Arabs. They opposed, in word and deed, the formulation of Fayez Sayegh, who declared in his submission to the committee: "To seek to alleviate the sufferings of the Jews, by causing equal sufferings to another people, is not only an *unreasonable* attempt . . . nor only an imprudent attempt . . . but also and primarily an *unjust* attempt."[223] But attempt they did.

Many factors coalesced to make the Palestinians lose the argument. The power of the Jewish constituency in the United States and Truman's concern for winning "the Jewish vote" is one well-documented reason (although the US administration tried to deny it).[224] But a much less analyzed dynamic was the production of a humanitarian structure of feeling that swayed the discourse, pushing it into synch with Zionist claims. Similar to what Lauren Berlant has found to be "the core practice of democracy in the United States," the international political sphere that coalesced around the Anglo-American Committee was not an "ideal scene of abstraction-oriented deliberation, but

[a] scene for the orchestration of public feelings . . . of politics as a scene of emotional contestation."[225] And in this contest orchestrated within the Anglo-American Committee's proceedings, it was sympathy that brought the suffering of the Jewish refugees and the demand that Palestine be their new home to center stage for the United States. To Westerners, the "humanitarian case" of the Jews, according to Commissioner Crossman, had "an almost overwhelming appeal."[226]

Like the committee members, those who were involved in presenting the Palestinian case thought they had done a good job. In al-Shuqayri's opinion, it was the best presentation of the Arab view that had been made in decades.[227] The forceful and coordinated performance did not yield fulfillment of Palestinian demands, however. In the peaceful surrounds of Lausanne, "one of the loveliest spots on earth," which Aydelotte called "a kind of return from the frontier to civilization again," the committee drafted its report. After being energized by rounds of golf and walks around a nearby lake, relieved to be hearing Swiss French after so much irritating Arabic and Hebrew,[228] the committee members developed their ten recommendations and issued their report in April 1946.[229]

Although some recommendations were crafted to encourage more balance in the economic and educational status and relations between Arabs and Jews in Palestine, the most controversial recommendation is also the one that received the most attention: that 100,000 certificates be issued to increase Jewish immigration to Palestine. Some of the committee members were upset when US President Truman made a public statement about the urgency of admitting 100,000 Jews to Palestine because it drew most of the focus to that one recommendation and away from the report as a whole.[230] In the end, most of the committee members agreed with that recommendation, even if some of the English tried to attach conditions to Jewish admission to Palestine, such as disbanding the Hagana, the Zionist fighting force. Aydelotte and others disagreed with imposing any such stipulation because the "poor Jews in the concentration camps" were not responsible for organizing the Hagana. He believed that their recommendations, written in the same place that a treaty dictating the compulsory exchange of Greek and Turkish minorities was signed just twenty-three years earlier,[231] included elements "in favor of the Arabs" that carefully balanced that out.[232]

The Arabs did not agree. What stirred their ire, in addition to "the refugee bombshell," as the British ambassador in Saudi Arabia referred to it,
were recommendations that Jewish immigration to Palestine should not be
dependent on the Arabs' approval, and that all laws limiting sale of Arab
land to the Jews be abolished—together a revocation of the White Paper.[233]
Like ʿIzzat Darwaza, the Mufti, Haj Amin al-Husayni, believed the report
to be extremely biased, exhibiting neither truth nor integrity nor logic.[234]
(Even David Ben-Gurion recognized that the Arabs got a bad deal.[235]) The
Institute of Arab American Affairs chastised the committee for not ceding to
the Arab demand that Palestine be organized "within the frame of the same
democratic principles which operate in [the United States and Great Brit-
ain]." They tried to make their democratic point again: "The same fundamental and inalienable human rights conceded those nations must be conceded
the Arabs of Palestine."[236]

The Anglo-American Committee of Inquiry did not determine the political future of Palestine. No commission has. But like all commissions of
inquiry, it had many side effects. Unique to this commission was the forceful
way it circulated and cemented humanitarian sympathy toward the Jews as
a political-moral value and sidelined once again Palestinian demands for a
democratic resolution to the conflict.[237] In not resolving the Palestine problem, the AACI also created the space in which the United Nations could
take over as the primary forum in which the problem of Palestine would be
managed.

The AACI and other earlier commissions that surveyed Palestine before
the establishment of the State of Israel was established functioned more as
opinion takers and diplomatic mechanisms. The commissions discussed in
subsequent chapters that came after Israel's statehood was confirmed, and
since the UN was established, have focused in a more technical way on issues
of international human rights and humanitarian law. With this concern for
determining the "facts" of legal violations, international law opened itself to
the contributions of new kinds of people. Witnesses, victims, lawyers, human
rights NGO workers, and other kinds of civil society activists became more
vocal contributors to the debates that commissions staged. This opening of
international law to a wider range of participants was part of what re-excited
faith in it.

# CHAPTER 4

# Third World Solidarity at the General Assembly

## A UN Special Committee on Human Rights

IN 1947, the United Nations Special Committee on Palestine (UNSCOP) was formed to deal with what the British left behind. That year His Majesty's government had finally given up on what Gen. Sir Alan Gordon Cunningham, high commissioner for Palestine, referred to in a draft of his statement to UNSCOP as "this somewhat complex country."[1] In May 1947, the UN General Assembly (UNGA) called for the constitution of a special committee "to prepare for the consideration of the question of Palestine."[2] The committee met a few weeks later and by mid-June was in Palestine to conduct investigations.

After so many British commissions that led them nowhere good, and after temporarily rejecting the Peel Commission and seriously debating whether to engage with the Anglo-American Committee of Inquiry, it was this special committee that the Palestinian leadership fully boycotted. In contrast, the Zionists offered a thorough and well-organized presentation to the committee. UNSCOP awarded them with a recommendation that mandatory Palestine be divided and the Jews be given 57 percent of Palestine (the most economically developed parts, specifically), despite the fact that the Arabs outnumbered the Jews by almost two to one and Jews had registered ownership of only 5.6 percent of the land.[3] Given the very thorough presentations that Palestinians had made to previous investigators with little effect on political results, it seems unlikely that Palestinian engagement would have changed the outcome of this committee.[4] General Assembly Resolution 181(II) to partition Palestine was the continuation of what legal practitioner and scholar Ardi Imseis has described as "international rule by law," cementing the UN's "two-state framework as the legal cornerstone of the UN's position on Palestine against the wishes of the country's indigenous majority."[5]

The war that ensued between the Zionists and Arabs throughout 1948 and 1949 left some 750,000 Palestinians as refugees, dispersed among neighboring Arab countries.[6] Israel was recognized as the latest state to become a member of the United Nations, while Jordan and Egypt took control of the West Bank and Gaza Strip, respectively.[7] Those roughly 150,000 Palestinians who remained in what had become the state of Israel were transformed almost overnight into subjects of a military rule that denied them the most basic political and civil rights.[8]

The UN's role in Palestine then became the humanitarian one of trying to care for the enormous population of refugees, a task undertaken by the United Nations Relief and Works Agency for Palestine Refugees in the Near East (UNRWA), and mediating peace between Israel and the Arab states, which the United Nations Conciliation Commission for Palestine (UNCCP) never fully accomplished.[9] In 1948, the UN bestowed the Palestinians with the legal crystallization of what has become one of their most piquant demands and nationalist rallying points, General Assembly Resolution 194, which enshrined Palestinian refugees' right of return. The approximately 5.3 million Palestinians living as refugees today are evidence of that resolution's nonfulfillment.[10]

A second central pillar of Palestinians' international legal discourse came in response to the Israeli military occupation of the West Bank, Gaza Strip, East Jerusalem, Golan Heights, and Sinai Peninsula in the summer of 1967. By November of that year, the UN Security Council passed Resolution 242, emphasizing "the inadmissibility of the acquisition of territory by war."[11] US President Richard Nixon affirmed in a speech to the UNGA that the United States supported Security Council 242, which "charts the way to that [Middle East] settlement," and declared the "sovereign right of each nation in the area to exist within secure and recognized boundaries."[12] Swedish diplomat Gunnar Jarring was appointed special representative on the Middle East question to work on implementing Resolution 242. His role was, in Jarring's assessment, "a very very long affair with hundreds of meetings without result."[13]

For Palestinians, transformations at the United Nations prompted hope for better results. The UNGA was where a growing number of recently decolonized nations started to rally together to produce anticolonial and antiracist international legal innovation. It prompted renewed optimism that the liberal legal order might finally include them as a national people whose political and individual rights would be realized in an equal and independent state. By 1963, there were 34 African states in a membership of 113.[14] With the UN Declaration on Granting Independence to Colonial Countries and Peoples (1960), they had begun remolding the United Nations "to create institutional platforms for their Third World agenda."[15] Human rights as part of that agenda also prompted "genuine optimism." Third World diplomats' intention to pursue that agenda was institutionalized in two special committees on decolonization and apartheid, which were created in the early 1960s. They gave voice to the group of new states' aims, displaying an experiential understanding of the evils of colonialism and racism, and a determination to uproot them.[16] Many of the resolutions and declarations they produced spoke directly to the Palestinians' plight. The UN came to symbolize a new version of "the international community" and its solidarity with the Palestinian struggle.

The grounds of the UN's symbolic role were cemented in its founding documents from the beginning. It was not set up to enforce the moral values enshrined in its charter or the subsequently passed Universal Declaration of Human Rights. This lack of enforcement capacity was thanks to the United Sates in particular, which made sure that at the heart of the system there was a "basic inconsistency" between the UN's lofty goals and its practical capacity to realize them.[17] Although justice, equality, and human rights sparkle throughout the articles of the UN Charter, the praise of "eternal human values" and declarations of rights principles was ever only intended to be symbolic. It was mostly mere rhetoric intended for idealistic Western activists and public opinion—those needing to be convinced of the legitimacy of this novel international institution.[18] The world's dominant states were only willing to join the UN because it had no real power, no authority to encroach on their sovereignty.[19] Human rights were incorporated into the charter in an intentionally vague way, as "embellishment," as ornamental "preambular principles," enshrined in formulations that would ensure their unenforceability and maintain Western state sovereignty.[20] The Great Powers intended the United Nations General Assembly in particular to be nothing more than a talking shop, a place, in the words of US President Franklin Roosevelt, for "small nations to blow off steam."[21]

The significance of this symbolic function has been insufficiently explored, especially by anthropologists, for whom symbols were once their stock and trade. Much critical analysis of the United Nations highlights the gap between the "quantitative accounting" of UN reporting and the subjective experiences of violence, but misses out on some longer-term processes that must be taken into account to sharpen the critique. The growing body of social science work on the UN narrowly condemns the flattening effects of the UN's bureaucracy and its "technical approaches that focus on forms, procedures, and the organization of data into categories."[22] This work is commendable for drawing attention to the effects of bureaucratic methods and to the unequal power that characterizes the relationship of UN investigators and apparatchiks to the victims of torture, poverty, and others who seek UN protection or recognition. But other kinds of relationships symbolizing solidarity and support, such as those that developed over decades among Third World governments and peoples, have also had political and ideological effects. Investigating these historically rooted social, symbolic aspects of the United Nations is required to see beyond the micropolitics of the halls of Geneva and the cynical realpolitik of interstate relations.[23]

## "The Over-All International Struggle"

The point and thing that I would like to impress upon every Afro-American leader is that there is no kind of action in this country ever going to bear fruit unless that action is tied with the over-all international struggle. You waste your time when you talk to this man just you and him. So, when you talk to him, let him know your brother is behind you, and you've got some brothers behind that brother. That's the only way to talk to him, that's the only language he knows.

This is what Malcolm X said three months after visiting the Gaza Strip in 1964. Whereas colonial officials in whatever context have clung to the idea that "violence is the only language the native understands," Malcolm X understood that solidarity was the only way to be heard by the oppressors, the only way to force meaningful change in an unjust system. He would be murdered some months after this speech highlighting the ties of African-Americans with the Third World "over-all international struggle," but the work toward internationalist solidarity among African-American and Afro-Asian activists would only intensify throughout the decade. As historian Michael Fischbach's book, *Black Power and Palestine*, details, the Palestinian struggle for self-determination in the 1960s and 1970s became an energizing symbol of a "wider battle against imperialism and white settler colonialism."[24] It would become a focusing symbol of Third World solidarity more generally too.

The General Assembly was a distinctly vociferous body articulating the terms and goals of Third World solidarity. It was a space of debate in which national representatives and regular people contested the meaning, morality, and political significance of international law. Examination of the discursive contests within it provides a unique lens for exploring the changed nature of international law as it became a language of solidarity in a period of rapid decolonization that spurred an effort to move the liberal legal order away from its Eurocentric roots. International law has never been an impartial arbiter, as scholarship on its role in the imposition of imperial control has amply demonstrated.[25] Its principles and their enactment have never been based solely on objective rules functioning apolitically, although its pretense has always been that. The claim of the distinction of law from politics is to the liberal-legal order what the blood-brain barrier is to the human body, a barricade sealing off earthly contaminants from higher, nobler realms. Unlike the physiological system, however, the anthropological one of social life is more malleable, permeable, and fraught.

With the emergence of postcolonial solidarity as an important dynamic within the UN came people who insisted on pointing to the real messiness of politics and law. In the hallowed halls where "the international community" met, they named the beneficiaries of the prior structure's pretexts and challenged them publicly to put humanitarian concerns and international legal principles ahead of narrow national, or imperial, interests—to make international law truly universal. This, too, was political—a feature of how international law functions as a "hegemonic technique."[26] And the implementation of these ideals was irregular, at best. But new principles of anticolonialism and antiracism were now central reference points requiring response from all, sustaining faith in international law among those whose liberation depended on them.[27]

These new manifestations of international law at the UN heralded an expansive liberal legalism that seemed more genuinely universal. A closer examination of the words and deeds of those brought together in the General Assembly, however, reveals a cloudier picture. On the one hand, one might glean in the intensely sympathetic support for Palestinians among those from the Third World a basis for future solidarity politics. On the other hand, that the words did not develop into enough material support to make a dent in the Israeli occupation suggests that the UNGA, international law, and Third World solidarity were talking shops—sometimes resonant, sometimes cacophonous, but mostly words.

It is also in this phase of international law's development that we first see the enactment of some kind of faith—or at least a performance of faith—in the redemptive power of knowledge and witnessing. Just as more technically legalistic renderings of Palestinians' experience under Israeli military occupation were forefronted in UN investigations, so too did testimonies by Palestinian victims, and then testimonials about them in the UNGA, come center stage as a primary mode of international legal encounter and interaction. Although the formulations and enactments of international legal principles changed shape, the ultimate results remained consistent. They were consistently ineffective, at least from the perspective of Palestinian efforts to secure national independence and freedom from the military occupation, or even merely to gain protection against its systemic abuses.

## UN Special Committee to Investigate Israeli Practices Affecting the Human Rights of the Population of the Occupied Territories

Over the decades since it was established in 1969, the UN Special Committee to Investigate Israeli Practices Affecting the Human Rights of the

Population of the Occupied Territories (hereafter "Special Committee" or UNSCIIP) has been one little noticed but significant venue in which Palestinians' conditions of life under occupation have been addressed.[28] The Special Committee was officially established by a two-thirds majority of the UNGA to investigate violations and analyze the nature of the military occupation when Israel occupied the West Bank, Gaza Strip, East Jerusalem, Golan Heights, and Sinai Peninsula in the summer of 1967.[29] In summoning Palestinians to state their case and provide proof of their abuses, the Special Committee served three important functions. First, it promulgated the argument that Palestine was a political—not solely humanitarian—problem and therefore required a political solution. Second, the Special Committee also gave members of the UN the opportunity to confirm their Third World solidarities, their proud refusal of imperialism, and their support for human rights. And third, it provided a forum in which Palestinian hope in international law could be recited, thereby sustaining the UN as a world-utopian project.

It could be said that this Special Committee has been of minor significance because it eventually stopped garnering much attention at the UN, from the Israeli government, in Palestine, or in the rest of the world. In some phases, the committee members themselves ceased to see any point in repeating the catalogue of abuses that remained an unchanged and fundamental feature of the Israeli military occupation, and issued truncated reports.[30] After twenty-one years of the Special Committee's reports, at the height of Israel's repressive measures against the first *intifada*—or uprising against Israeli occupation—one UNGA member wondered aloud if the "information contained in the Committee's report was intended to awaken the conscience of the world or simply to serve as material for ritual interventions."[31] That the Special Committee has never seen its call for the end of the Israeli occupation answered, and the attendant human rights abuses continue unabated, provides one gloomy answer to his question.

Despite this—and in some ways, because of this—UNSCIIP deserves analysis. Uniquely, UNSCIIP offers a subaltern perspective of international law. As legal scholar Balakrishnan Rajagopal has noted, "ignoring the role of the local as an agent of institutional transformation is . . . inseparable from the hegemonic nature of international law as an elite discipline."[32] The insight into various "local" perspectives that UNSCIIP gives allows for a more thorough appreciation of the subaltern voice, a step in challenging the international legal hegemony that Rajagopal has named. Considering the subaltern perspective is also a way to better understand the power of international law's grip. The Special Committee illustrates one answer to the central conundrum of "how international law and justice are imaginatively linked in practice . . . how international law works in the world."[33] Palestinians' interactions with UNSCIIP show that international law works through the sympathetic words of solidarity spoken by UN delegates and enshrined in their resolutions, sustaining hope in the "international community" that repeatedly announces its care for the subjugated and abused.

The analytical usefulness of the Special Committee also lies in its dogged longue durée. Its continuous existence since 1969 provides a uniquely steady lens onto changes and continuities within the international legal apparatus and its machinations in Palestine over time. Given the changes in global political leanings since the 1960s, perhaps less surprising are the transformations, such as the bold condemnation of the Zionist project as one of racial domination that was typical in discussions of UNSCIIP's early reports, in striking contrast to the criminalized taboo around such equations today.[34] More notable are the continuities: one thread weaving unbroken throughout the committee's existence has been spun by the expressions of faith to it from the Palestinians who gave testimony, proclaiming their hope in the UN. In maintaining this conviction, Palestinians have helped sustain international law as a belief system.[35]

## The UN-Palestine Mobius Strip and the Generation of False Hope

Debates about this committee's work reveal how many at the UN believed that solving the Palestine issue through international law was synonymous with the mission of the UN itself.[36] The chair of the Special Committee in 1970 argued that the violation of "several thousands of innocent persons living under military occupation . . . should be the concern of the entire membership of the United Nations."[37] For many in the UNGA, Palestine represented an unfulfilled promise of universal rights and self-determination. The Special Committee was another setting in which belief in the inextricable link between Palestine and international law deepened.

The Special Committee is just one of many UN forums in which this dynamic is evident.[38] The UN General Assembly became a hothouse of hope in the 1960s and 1970s, fostering in Palestinians an expectation that there was an "international community" that cared about their predicament and could wield international law to do something about it. I argue that this is a false hope because international law has not achieved practical change for the better for Palestinians and, absent the political will to enforce it, cannot achieve it. It is not an insincere or cynically strategic hope, but a faith placed in a system not designed to enforce systemic, political change on the ground. What the UNGA has done is inscribe liberatory and humanitarian values as a show of solidarity.[39] To be sure, expressing support for Palestinians and ensuring self-determination in Palestine has not been the only motivation or target of this new international legal language—ending South Africa's apartheid regime was for many years the primary focus of the Afro-Asian block.[40] But the reassertion of norms that spotlight universal human rights and self-determination, and that restate humanitarian values and prioritize the protection of civilians, happened consistently and in a great deluge of resolutions, speeches, and committees dedicated to the Palestine question. This has given Palestinians reason to believe in the UN and international law.

Solidarity with Palestinians was manifest at the UN in many ways, from recognizing the "inalienable rights of the Palestinian people" in 1969 (with similarly worded resolutions passed by the General Assembly in 1971, 1972, and 1974[41]), establishing a committee on the exercise of those inalienable rights, to launching an International Day of Solidarity with the Palestinian People in 1977.[42] While international solidarity with the people of Palestine has accompanied their struggle for independence from the beginning, by the 1960s and 1970s Palestine had become "hard-wired . . . into the circuits of the struggle for global justice."[43]

This was a period of peculiarly robust enthusiasm, as Palestinians had come to symbolize both the victimhood of imperialism and Third World resistance to it, a time when outrage and revolutionary fervor were at a peak pitch globally. Palestinian activists intentionally sought to channel that spirit into solidarity with their cause.[44] They fired the imaginations and inspired the cultural production of artists across many genres and geographies, cultivating a "liberation aesthetic" that enacted and encouraged sympathy and solidarity with their people and "the revolutionary will."[45] Creators of cinema, performance, and plastic arts in the Arab region and well beyond saw world significance in the Palestinian cause. "The Palestinian Revolution is a productive source for the cinema or television artists' works aimed at changing modern man's course and deepening his self-confidence and psychological and intellectual faculties by mastering his destiny, present and future," the manifesto of a Baghdad film festival pronounced in 1973.[46] The global reach of this commitment to artistic and political interconnection was evident in the 1978 International Art Exhibition for Palestine that happened in Beirut. The festival's catalogue featured a cover page in seven languages; the Exhibition for Palestine traveled (in part) to Japan, Iran, and Norway; and featured pieces by artists from South America, Europe, the Middle East, Europe, and Asia.[47]

Although the UN was not the sole venue in which Palestinians cultivated world solidarity, Palestinian representatives considered the UN's political significance to be weighty indeed. Alongside the first International Day of Solidarity with the Palestinian People, 1977 also saw the PLO called into the General Assembly as an observer, three years after the dramatic "gun or olive branch" speech by PLO Chairman Yasser Arafat.[48] Because this controversial leader of a nonstate entity was recognized as a legitimate representative of his people and invited into the UN as such, the fact of that speech—rather than the speech itself—has been proclaimed the Palestinians' greatest diplomatic victory.[49] Highlighting the common sense of how interwoven are the UN and Palestine, PLO leader Shafiq al-Hout, who helped write that speech, believed that the invitation to the PLO was "as much a victory for the UN as it was for Palestine and its people," as it "upgrad[ed]" the UN in allowing it to "better exercise the role for which it had been created."[50]

In the heyday of Palestinians' armed resistance movement, the UNGA also reaffirmed "the legitimacy of the peoples' struggle for liberation from colonial and foreign domination and alien subjugation by all available means, including armed struggle."[51] It ultimately acknowledged the proclamation of the State of Palestine by the Palestine National Council on November 15,

1988.[52] These and the many other resolutions and investigations have made the United Nations into a mirror reflecting Palestinians' identity and demands, and a megaphone, communicating their plight and their claims, amplifying them with the proclaimed legitimacy of the UN that represents universal norms and fosters international legal order.[53] Just as the Anglo-American Committee represented the Jews as a human problem that was the world's responsibility to solve, the UN has represented "the Question of Palestine" and Palestinians' rights as a universal issue for all to care about. For many Palestinians, it has offered not just a venue for publicizing their predicament and making political demands; the UN has held out a horizon of a peaceful future in which Palestinians' freedom and independence is recognized, arousing again a false hope in a political solution organized by international law.

## The Many Valences and Voices of Solidarity

Much of what Third World delegates in UN meetings did was tell Palestinians, in a way the Israelis would hear, that their brothers were behind them—as Malcolm X insisted was important. The plenary meetings of the UN General Assembly have been a particularly fulsome setting in which delegates from tens of countries have asserted their anticolonial and pro-Palestinian stance; a place where they acknowledged "the tragedies and the untold sufferings undergone by the Palestinian people," as the delegate from Nepal said in 1975 in terms similar to many others.[54] On being invited by the UNGA president to address the assembly in 1971, soon after Bahrain became a member of the UN, that country's minister for foreign affairs took the opportunity to announce both Bahrain's own high moral-political standards and its support of Palestine:

> Pursuant to its respect for the principle of equal rights and the self-determination of peoples, Bahrain is greatly concerned and conscious about the destiny of peoples who are still struggling for self-determination and independence. It therefore lends its full support to the rightful demand for freedom and full independence of the peoples of such territories still suffering from colonial rule. In this context, and with the same breath, Bahrain entirely supports the legitimate and inalienable rights of the people of Palestine to recover its usurped land and to live in peace and

security in its own homeland. . . . Bahrain thus appeals to the conscience of all peace-loving nations of this world Organization to view this chronic problem of Palestine, as well as the Golan Heights and Sinai, in the light of humanity and justice and to seek a satisfactory solution for it on the basis of the highly revered principles of the United Nations Charter.[55]

The war in the summer of 1967 that ended with Israel's military occupation of the rest of historic Palestine provoked a particularly strong tide of expressions of solidarity. In reminding his colleagues that the UN Charter condemned "conquest as a means of acquiring territory," the Algerian delegate analyzed the Israeli occupation as being motivated by

> the expansionist policy: more and more immigrants, more and more territory, more and more centres of colonization, more and more arrogant obstinacy in completely denying the identity of Palestine. If we are to talk of recognizing the right to live, is it not high time, precisely when the people of Palestine are yearning for a new lease of life, to grant it this right, elementary perhaps, but nevertheless absolute? . . . The hard fact is that the Palestine problem raises all the questions involved both in colonialist settlement and in the antithesis of liberation and domination.[56]

As the UN delegate from the United Republic of Tanzania explained that same year in a speech at the General Assembly, his compatriots saw their own situation or possible future predicament reflected in that of the Palestinians'. In his excoriation of the UN for its lack of action in response to the occupation, he worried:

> We cannot help fearing that, if tomorrow or next week one or another of us were to experience a similar situation, then the Assembly would react in a similar manner. Where, then should lie the hopes of the smaller nations in the protection promised by the Charter, of this Organization? Where, then should the countries of the Third World look for a safeguard against rampant imperialism, colonialism, and international forces of neocolonialism?[57]

He thus called attention to a fundamental feature of international law, a discourse in which a violation against everyone in a structurally analogous position becomes "a matter of concern for the political community itself."[58]

The Palestinian intifada against Israeli military occupation that began in 1987 (and lasted for several years) also prompted a further chorus of solidarity. In a 1989 Special Political Committee meeting, the Bulgarian delegate directly echoed words of Palestinian nationalism:

> The continuing intifadah was proof that the Palestinian people's struggle for freedom and national independence could not be halted. Regardless of the casualties, the intifadah would continue until peace and justice were achieved in the Middle East. . . . Bulgaria was convinced that the just cause of the Palestinian people would ultimately triumph.

Endorsing the uprising, the Bangladeshi representative praised the "valiant intifadah of the Palestinian people [that] had served to mobilize world opinion against a brutal suppression of freedom."[59] Although the levels of material support that these and other states that had expressed solidarity was uneven, with their speeches they sustained a certain unity of concern and principle.

For many across the Third World and elsewhere, Palestine—among the last and most overt unfulfilled anticolonial movements—came to stand for ideals, identities, and aspirations beyond Palestine itself.[60] Like the Arab Revolt that motivated a broader anticolonial fight in 1936–1939, and alongside the anti-apartheid movement, Palestinians' liberation struggle in this period of Third Worldism was seen as a linchpin for a global revolution against imperialism and white racism. As Fischbach has shown, for black activists in the United States, where one's solidarity lay in the Arab-Israeli conflict became a barometer of political identities, "a crucial reference point by which they created and articulated their respective visions of identity, place, and struggle in America."[61] Solidarity with Palestinians also became a currency of revolutionary credibility; international legal innovations became one form of that currency, and the United Nations an important forum in which it was exchanged.[62]

Fischbach's is a remarkable contribution to a wave of recent scholarship that documents and celebrates the Third World solidarity that blossomed in the period after the Bandung Conference of 1955 and stretched to include those fighting racism in the United States.[63] The place of Palestine in that gossamer web of solidarity has been both central and unsteady. The "Spirit of Bandung"—articulated in Indonesian President Sukarno's declaration: "Let a new Africa and Asia be born"—has been hailed as a moment of "unknowable potential" that spoke "to a vision of a new international order" in which peoples of color would halt and reverse their economic, cultural, and legal conquest by Euro-American powers.[64] Although there was tension around the topic of Palestine, certain delegates at Bandung won the argument that they should acknowledge the rights of Palestine's Arabs. The conference itself would be seen as a failure if Palestine was not addressed, as the Chinese delegate had insisted.[65]

In addition to affirming the "Universal Declaration of Human Rights as a common standard of achievement for all peoples and all nations"—according to some thereby "planting the seeds for a new international law"[66]—the final communiqué declared their support of Palestinian rights. But it also "called for the implementation of the United Nations resolutions on Palestine and of the peaceful settlement of the Palestine question." It was left to the Syrian representative, Palestinian lawyer Ahmad al-Shuqayri, to point out the problem of referencing the United Nations, which had "succeeded in eliciting a resolution that partitioned the Holy Land against the express wishes of the people concerned."[67] But his protests went unheeded and the unspecified UN resolutions remained the balustrade for the conference's statement on Palestine. This ambiguous approach to Palestine and other issues has caused some to insist that the Third World solidarity symbolically birthed at Bandung was mythical, and the Asian-African Conference merely "a forum for lofty but vacuous invocations of 'solidarity' . . . a romantic, thoroughly depoliticized slogan."[68] But solidarity manifests in many ways, and even lofty slogans can be powerful—mainly in being seen to be so.

Perhaps more so than at Bandung, the solidarity that was institutionalized in the UN Special Committee was potent, especially in the first decades after the General Assembly's decolonized demographic shift. Because pro-Israeli viewpoints dominated the public and political discourse in the West and justified Israeli military occupation as somehow benevolent while denying Palestinians' political identity, that UNSCIIP challenged these narratives was for Palestinians a political boon. The Special Committee did this in a variety of ways, offering more sympathetic portrayals of the Palestinians as victims of an unjust and inhumane system, through both the "objective" language of international law and impassioned speeches at the UN rostrum.

In addition to direct refutation of Israel's claims that the occupation benefited the Arabs, it also framed the Palestine question as a political one of settler-colonialism in need of a political solution. Although committee members sought to maintain their focus on humanitarian concerns as separate from political issues—and announced their commitment to that distinction—the solution they proposed to the problem of systematic human rights abuses was the very political one of ending the military occupation that began in 1967. And delegates often refused to condone the distinction between politics and humanitarianism. In 1989 the Albanian delegate reminded his colleagues that his country "had always adamantly condemned the inhumane Israeli practices, which should be seen not as a humanitarian problem but as the application of a political programme."[69] The debates that UNSCIIP reports occasioned were, likewise, pointedly political.[70] As the Czechoslovakian delegate stated baldly, "The occupation of Arab territories was in any case nothing but an attempt to expand the territory of Israel with a view to establishing a solid imperialist base in the neighbourhood of the Arab countries."[71] At the same time, they defined it as a question "of and for humanity": a matter of justice and moral principle.[72] The Egyptian representative equated support for Palestinians' "inalienable right to self-determination" with morality itself: "The Arab peoples, and indeed all peoples who strive for a just peace, take pride in their determined support for the just cause and the noble struggle of the people of Palestine."[73]

While giving UN members a stage on which to assert their own moral integrity, the Special Committee both echoed Palestinians' insistence on their national identity and provided them a platform on which to perform their political reasonableness. The proof of their liberal credentials that the committee recorded was then translated into the form of the UN report, encased in the lattice-work of prior UN resolutions supporting their claim for human rights and self-determination.[74] All of which was then defended and reconfirmed in General Assembly debates.

## UNSCIIP Begins

Once the representatives of Ceylon, Yugoslavia, and Somalia were appointed to the Special Committee, they began their work in New York, one year after the General Assembly's decision to establish it. These countries had been supportive of the Palestinian cause within the framework of the UN and beyond.[75] Yugoslavia in particular, which had staked out a leading role for itself within the Non-Aligned Movement (NAM), was supportive.[76] Ceylon—which would become Sri Lanka—was too. Their stance was partly related to their tea trade with the Arab market and partly to the fact that Muslims in Sri Lanka were "closely identified with the Arab cause, and alienation of this minority was a political liability" that no Sri Lankan government could afford.[77] The position of solidarity deepened in 1970 when the opposition (United Front) leader Sirimavo Bandaranaike came to power as the new prime minister, moving Sri Lanka's foreign policy more emphatically in line with the nonalignment movement, as strong ties were established with Yugoslavia.[78]

An impediment to the Special Committee's work, which it described as a "major obstacle," was the refusal of the Government of Israel to cooperate with it, a refusal that remains unaltered until today.[79] Despite this obstruction, the Special Committee forged ahead, placing notices in local newspapers calling forth: "Any person who has knowledge of practices affecting the human rights of the population of the territories occupied by Israel."[80] Through forty-six meetings held in seven cities—including in Arab countries, Geneva, and New York—over a period of nearly three months, the three members of the Special Committee heard from 146 people during its first round of investigations.

In addition to hearing testimony, they collected press reports, written evidence from individuals, letters and reports from human rights organizations, and statements by the Israeli government. They listened to accounts from those who had suffered torture in prison and could tell of seeing the effects of torture on their fellow prisoners. They asked witnesses about their impressions and observations, for accounts of "feelings of the population," and about the "atmosphere" to judge how benevolent the occupation really was. Challenging any notion of a beneficent occupation were allegations of rape, testimony about summary execution, protracted curfews, mass deportation and expulsion especially of community leaders, collective punishment, prolonged administrative detention, and looting of shops and homes by Israeli soldiers. The members of the Special Committee sought to determine if the violations they learned about were a result of a deliberate policy by Israel, which they found most of these to be (with the exception of looting). As an indication of how much interest there was in this committee's work, at least some of its 1970 hearings were broadcast on Jordanian television.[81]

The Special Committee concluded in its first report "that the occupying Power is pursuing a conscious and deliberate policy calculated to depopulate the occupied territories of their Arab inhabitants." While recognizing that the "ideal manner in which violations of human rights could cease would clearly be by the termination of the occupation itself,"[82] the committee recommended that until that happened there be "supervision by an independent authority . . . an arrangement whereby the Third and Fourth Geneva Conventions will be enforced."[83] The Moroccan representative made an observation at the 1970 UNGA Plenary in which the UNSCIIP report was discussed. The committee's findings prompted "a serious anxiety" among those who debated it, he said, "caused by the situation in which the peoples in these territories must live." The Iraqi delegate declared the report to be "a clear indictment of the inhuman practices of the Israeli occupation forces in the occupied territories."[84]

For some, the Special Committee became a symbol of the UN's prestige as a whole, evident in the extensive debate about the Special Committee's early reports. During eight meetings of the Special Political Committee (the General Assembly's so-called Fourth Committee) in 1970, representatives from a variety of UN member nations elaborated their support of—or objections to—the first report and work of UNSCIIP.[85] Israel and other states expressed many concerns about the committee, stemming from purported irregularities of procedure and suspicions about its objectivity. The representative of Ceylon called attention to the emotions in the room, naming "the atmosphere of acrimony and controversy that had enveloped the Committee and its investigation." Speaking as chairman of the Special Committee, he defended it and suggested that those objecting were doing so for political reasons.[86] Among those in favor of the Special Committee's work, some delegates summarized highlights from the report and praised the committee members for pursuing their task despite the obstacles. Others rehearsed the history of Palestine's takeover by the Zionists and listed the impressive number of UN resolutions that had been issued on the topic already. Many sought to defend the committee and its report as objective and serious, pointing out the corroboration of their findings in the reports of other impartial bodies.[87] With an apparent tone of crossness, many rebutted Israel's claims that disparaged the committee as being a tool of Arab propaganda.[88] In defending the Special Committee, the UN, and the Palestinian cause, the significance of each was once again equated.

## Affect and Fact in Anticolonial International Law

Although much has been written about the way colonial powers have read and policed affect as a means of statecraft, less consideration has been given to the role of emotional assessments in anticolonial dynamics.[89] As Ann Stoler has written, colonial "'political rationalities' were grounded in management of affective states, assessing appropriate sentiment and those that might fly out of control. . . . The making of the moral and the ambiguities over which sensibilities it required were at the center of political debates on colonial ground."[90] The same could be said for the anticolonial grounds of the UNGA. At stake in their debates were not only national demands and visions for world political futures, but also personal and collective morality. The performance and patrolling of emotion was central to how they did this.

The exchanges in the Special Political Committee were carried out in frank, and often frankly outraged, language. The Albanian delegate said that the "innumerable crimes" to which the population of the occupied territories was being subjected "outraged all of progressive mankind."[91] A few delegates' reactions to the abuses suffered by Palestinians were emotional and, in some cases, physical. The representative from Senegal spoke of his time on a related Special Working Group of Experts that "had heard evidence of such repugnant atrocities that certain members of its secretariat had been nauseated."[92] In condemning Israel's occupation of the Holy City, the Jordanian delegate highlighted the passion he felt toward Jerusalem in calling attention to his own self-restraint: "I must pause here to say, in as quiet and unemotional a way as I can, that there will be no peace in the Middle East so long as the Holy City of Jerusalem remains under the domination of Israel. . . . I say it because it is an accepted truth in the mind and heart of every Arab-Moslem and Christian."[93]

The rhetorical tussle between affect and fact carried on throughout these debates. The chair of UNSCIIP dismissed Israel's vilification of the committee as being "the product of emotion rather than reason, and [had] no foundation in fact."[94] In a similar move, undercutting another's words as being the product of emotion, the Israeli representative dismissed the Kuwaiti delegate's rebuttals of Israeli arguments. The Israeli delegate "would not reply," he told the assembly, "to the other points raised by the representative of Kuwait, whose remarks had been prompted by anger because the truth was unpleasant to him."[95] The Kuwaiti representative did not deny his anger but explained it, retorting "that his anger had not been provoked by the truth but by the lies of the Israeli representative."[96] As the years of UN debates passed, the derogatory comments among the antagonists became increasingly blatant, and the rancorous atmosphere thickened.[97]

Fluidly weaving together insult and sarcasm, logic and sympathy in his speeches was Fayez Sayegh. A Palestinian spokesperson who grew up near Tiberias, an academic, and a diplomat who acted as the representative for Kuwait, Sayegh spoke often in defense of Palestinian rights. An active and sharp debater in the Political Committee, he regularly showered his Israeli counterpart with waterfalls of facts, challenging the Zionist narrative that painted Israel's military occupation as a boon to the Arabs.[98] "If one were to believe the representative of Israel, Israel was to be thanked for occupying the Arab territories and should be requested to annex still more territories," Sayegh goaded in a 1970 speech. He followed this with a list of the many ways the occupation was destructive of Palestinian prosperity and security.[99]

At the same time, Sayegh continually pushed back against any Palestine exceptionalism, reminding his audience of UN delegates in compassionate terms that the principles at stake were universal. He rebutted Israel's argument again:

> Finally, it was suggested [by Israel] that this resolution [confirming the Special Committee report] was an unbalanced resolution. My delegation has submitted and submits again today that the charge that this is an unbalanced resolution is born either of maliciousness or of foolishness, or perhaps of both. For there can be no meaning to the requirement that a resolution on the occupied territories should be two-sided. There are not two sets of occupied territories—Israeli territories occupied by Arab States, and Arab territories occupied by Israel—and therefore there cannot be

two-sided resolutions. There is only one set of occupied territories, and the requirement of two-sidedness does not obtain.

In conclusion, I wish to address myself to those delegations that voted against and those that abstained, and say: I earnestly pray that none of you will ever know the meaning of foreign occupation. I earnestly pray that you will be spared foreign occupation. But should you ever find yourselves under foreign occupation, whoever you may be, my delegation will always be among the first to sponsor the maintenance of international law, the protection of human rights and the conduct of international investigations in the territories under occupation.[100]

At one moment the declamation of emotion was a clear rhetorical barb; at the next, the mobilization of affect an expression of solidarity.

It is difficult to assess the mood of each session through transcripts, impossible to determine when delegates were expressing and evaluating emotion with intentional performativity or punctuating a stance through accidentally unchecked sentiment. Evident even in transcript form, however, is the fact that emotions were a dynamic aspect of UN politics and a part of the performances of personal and national character that delegates enacted.

## Objective Evidence and Sympathetic Sufferers

The majority of disputants, however, held firm to the language and performance of objectivity, evidence, and international law. The enactment of liberal-legalism was plain at every stage of this committee's work, from the investigative interviews to the text of the report to the discussions of it among delegates. Even in the midst of the highly personal but almost uniform expressions of indignation, the UN members who supported the Special Committee's work emphasized the priority accorded to the principle of objectivity. "The Special Committee had acted with complete objectivity and impartiality and had scrupulously applied the recognized legal norms and procedures," the Polish representative opined in words similar to those of many others.[101] In defending the Special Committee, the delegates were protecting the UN mission itself; securing Palestinians' rights was a defense of international law.

This was a period in which some in the UNGA believed they could reshape international law. Mexican diplomat Peon del Valle declared in a plenary of that assembly that a "kind of 'anti-colonial law' . . . based on the principle that the interests of the inhabitants of Non-Self-Governing Territories are paramount . . . seem[ed] to be emerging in the United Nations."[102] How the UN dealt with the occupation was seen as a crucial element in this progress. George Tomeh, the Syrian diplomat, celebrated the Special Committee's report that "would be a historic development in international law as applied to human rights."[103] As he and Sayegh observed, the occupation of Palestine was the first test of the Fourth Geneva Convention.[104] According to another Palestinian representative, the credibility of all that the UN stood for was at stake: "If the United Nations failed to uphold its Charter, the International Bill of Human Rights and the Genocide Convention in Palestine, it would show the world that its high-sounding principles were sheer hypocrisy."[105] The notion that Palestine has helped international law progress remains popular today.[106]

The UNGA and Special Political Committee meetings saw similar debates over UNSCIIP in subsequent sessions. Each debate at the Political Committee ended in the production of a draft resolution—decrying Israel's actions and confirming and upholding the Special Committee's recommendations—which was then passed in the UNGA.[107] The terms of excoriation and solidarity have been duplicated from year to year. Those who supported the Special Committee insisted that its investigations were objective and just. They held firm to the idea that revealing an objective truth could lead to the preservation of human rights. UN delegates and Palestinians both insisted on this undefined but inextricable connection between the act of recording the truth of abuses and their rectification. This notion—expressed just as forcefully in 2018 by the high commissioner for human rights quoted in the Introduction of this book—that proof of violations would lead to ending them was fundamental to the meaning of international law itself.

Orators at the UNGA worried over the fragile foundations of the UN's collective norms and recognized that cracks in the thin veneer of credibility that the organization required jeopardized their mission as a whole. As a delegate from Mali argued in 1969, if Security Council Resolution 242 was not imposed, the council would "lose its prestige, to the great detriment of the international community." He called on the permanent members of the Security Council, "to do everything in their power to strengthen the authority of the United Nations which, despite everything, is still the hope of mankind in these troubled times."[108] That their work had to be more than mere words was a clear theme in their conversations. How to get from words to action and meaningful change was, however, not so obvious.

## A Liberal-Legal Matrix

The Special Committee has investigated, interviewed, and issued reports on the human rights situation in the occupied Palestinian territories annually since it was established forty years ago.[109] In so doing, it has brought hundreds of Palestinians (and others) before it to testify and conveyed those details of the military occupation in the language of international human rights and humanitarian law to the UN. It became a matrix pulling a steady stream of Palestinians into the UN's instantiation of the liberal-legal order, continually reinstilling hope in the UN and international human rights and humanitarian law among an ever-wider array of Palestinians. In addition to hearing from officials and politicians, UNSCIIP members talked to, among many others: a housewife who observed looting; a school headmistress who was deported to Jordan and separated from her husband in the West Bank; a deported student; a teacher who had been imprisoned and deported; a dentist who had been mayor; a lawyer; a farmer; tortured prisoners; one surgeon who had been imprisoned; and another who had treated cases of torture. There were many others from "humble" backgrounds, as the committee described them.[110]

The diplomats and jurists of the General Assembly invited Palestinians onto the international stage to testify to the crimes against them and make their political arguments, but they summoned them to do so within the confines of specific liberal subjectivities. Reflecting the shifting political epistemologies of global governance, these included categories recognizable today, such as the human rights victim and humanitarian sufferer.[111] They hailed other kinds of subjects too: the revolutionary but reasonable freedom fighter, the peace-loving youth, the legal expert, and the NGO worker among them.[112]

Special Committee reports have adhered to the terms of international law, each report referring to the trail of resolutions and declarations that name the international legal principles that were its terms of reference. They were the outcome of hours of testimony and reams of documents that the committee members analyzed.[113] In keeping with the semijudicial nature of UNSCIIP's remit, throughout the hearings the committee members sought to gather credible evidence from eyewitnesses, and regularly disciplined those giving testimony when they ventured into the realm of hearsay. A testy exchange between a witness and a committee member in 1974 illustrates their sense of the epistemological stakes. After the witness's multiple attempts to relate what his family told him about incidents of abuse, the committee member repeatedly explained that they could not accept hearsay evidence.

> We daren't go before a tribunal and say that we heard this unless we can produce a person who has seen it. If you are not in a position to indicate who said it and if I am not in a position to interrogate that person, then the evidence is of no value to me. . . we cannot put evidence into our records unless it is evidence that will stand the usual test of credibility.[114]

Although witnesses and petitioners sometimes referred to the text of the international laws that Israel was breaking,[115] committee members sought to maintain a hierarchy of authority for themselves as the official interpreters of the law. One member disciplined a witness for interjecting legal interpretations into his testimony. When the witness—a surgeon who had been expelled from the West Bank—declared that his expulsion was "contrary to international law," the chair replied: "Please give us the facts and allow us to determine the law on the subject. Thank you." When the witness asserted that his expulsion into a dangerous area "was done intentionally," the chair replied more forcefully: "May I please ask you not to give your own opinions and draw your own inferences. That is for us to do. You merely state the facts, [name], because we want to get many other things out of you and I don't want to spend time on matters which really are only our concern."[116] Although the invocations and expressions of fact and emotion, evidence and trauma testimonial were fluid in the work and discussions of UNSCIIP, the professional boundaries of international law remained a guidepost throughout.

In an unusually frank disclosure of process, the committee's 1970 report revealed the performative evaluations that were part of how they scrutinized evidence: "Throughout the investigation the Special Committee endeavoured to pay special attention to the demeanour of witnesses as a measure of their credibility and to sift actual experience from invention."[117] The emotional control of one witness impressed them so much they drew attention to it explicitly in the report:

> Mr. Ahmed Khalifa's evidence (A/AC.145/RT.9) was particularly impressive because, when he testified before the Special Committee, he did not give the impression that he was moved by rancour towards his former captors. Despite his experiences he seemed to have retained his objectivity and sense of proportion. This was manifest in his description of his own ill-treatment and that of his fellow prisoners.

According to Khalifa's testimony, throughout his more than two years of detention in three Israeli jails, he had been suspended by the wrists for prolonged periods, attacked by dogs, and severely beaten.[118] According to Israel, this prisoner had been a member of a political faction, considered by that government to be "one of the most extreme terrorist organizations."[119] Regardless of whether the committee knew that Israel categorized Khalifa this way, they presented a Palestinian victim of torture as righteous, in an almost Christian mode.

As with earlier investigative commissions, in which commissioners interpreted witness comportment in whatever way supported his preferred political assessment of Palestinian (lack of) readiness for sovereignty, members of the Special Committee often summoned Palestinian victims to present themselves in a sympathetic light that would support their bid for freedom. Through the committee's investigations, they were massaged into the liberal subjectivity that might allow them to be heard and understood by a skeptical audience: reasonable, peace-loving Palestinians who were willing to reconcile with the Israelis despite their years of suffering under occupation.

During the first intifada, the Special Committee received testimony from injured Palestinians. In one meeting, most of the committee's interlocutors were paralyzed or partially disabled from being shot or beaten by Israeli forces. While one of the Special Committee members began the interviews with standard questions about the circumstances in which the injuries were received, another member pursued a line of questioning that evoked the personal dimensions of the Palestinians' experiences. He also repeatedly asked witnesses if they were optimistic about the prospects for peace. He ended most of his exchanges by asking each witness if he had hope in the future and whether he would be able to "forgive and forget," if peace were achieved. Most responded that they would.[120]

These questions gave Palestinians an opportunity to express their sense of grievance, to assert their nationalist aims and convictions, and to confirm their politically reasonable stance.

> I believe that the Palestinians are a peace-loving people: they do not love violence, but they have had to resort to violence because they found that this was the only way to regain their liberty, to achieve independence and to hoist their own flag, like other people . . . because they are peace-loving, they have made concessions. They are ready for peace with Israel.[121]

Reflecting the narrowed political demands of the official PLO line, a witness assured the committee: "All we want is to establish a Palestinian State in the West Bank and Gaza," reminding them that Arafat was ready to recognize Israel.[122] One respondent admitted that he was not optimistic in the short term, but assured the Special Committee that Palestinians would not stop struggling until their rights were achieved.

## Sincere Hope in the World

The world is imagined as an entity out there with the power to change the status quo. With every invocation of "the world," these Palestinian witnesses pronounced the Special Committee, and the UN, to be the rightful conduit of global humanity's principles of equality and justice. Others were hopeful that they would "regain the right to self-determination, the right to live like all other peoples in the world." Another stated: "I have great hopes. I know it is not easy to achieve all this, but with pressure on Israel exerted by the whole world, it may be possible to reach some solution."[123]

With each interaction of the Special Committee, the threads braiding Palestine, the UN, international law, and universal justice together became ever more tightly interwoven. Without being prompted by leading questions, Palestinian witnesses often sought to expand the significance of their conditions, rendering it into a universal, human problem of justice, as so many in the Special Political Committee debates did. A West Bank mayor expressed his hope that his appearance before the committee "might contribute not only to the defence of my friends and my relatives, . . . but to the defence of mankind in its entirety, because the Palestinian people is an example of mankind; a people which has been subjected to suffering for almost thirty years now, without having committed any crimes."[124] Creating an equation of international law and justice, some begged the committee members "in the name of justice and in the name of humanity and in the name of human rights" to do what they could to prevent the torture of their family members.[125] Another highlighted the global significance of the Special Committee's work, praising its "nobility and grandeur." He continued: "And thus I cannot refuse to appear before you . . . because your task is a noble and humanitarian one, that of defending those who have no other means of defence at their disposal other than their faith and public opinion, the best part of it which is represented by organizations such as your own."[126] The committee members themselves saw their work in this universal perspective: "We can only assure [the witnesses] that we shall assess their evidence and evaluate it, and, in arriving at our final conclusion, we hope we shall be of some service to the cause of humanity," one of the investigators pledged.[127]

The Special Committee and the Palestinians they spoke with had firm hopes that their efforts would make a difference for Palestinians and, therefore, for the UN and the world. In testimonial after testimonial, Palestinians declared their faith in the committee and what it stood for. One witness declared the committee to be a conduit to the world. And like many UN delegates, he confirmed his faith in the significance of establishing the proof of violations to be communicated. He hoped that through the committee, his voice would "[reach] the United Nations and world conscience . . . we are equally sure that the candid voice of truth which you have heard here and elsewhere will reach, through you, the General Assembly and the world forum to reveal and expose practices in violation of human rights in the occupied territories involving acts of systematic, cold-blooded torture, collective punishment, merciless reprisals and other atrocities."[128]

Throughout its first three decades, UNSCIIP was the inspiration and recipient of hope and gratitude. A reader might object that such expressions of hope and faith in the UN could be discursive ploys, "just rhetoric," buttering up the one who might be able to grant a request. And, indeed, the problem of interpreting sincerity and cynicism in the archives is a tricky one.

It is difficult to know what every interlocutor believed was at stake or what they intended with their words. But it is hard to read anything but hope and genuine gratitude in the speeches presented before the Special Committee. Consider what a witness for the committee in 1988 avowed:

> I should like to say that I am proud and happy to be here before you and to have testified. . . . Therefore I should like to thank you for having listened to my testimony, and with all my heart and with all sincerity I hope that this testimony will, through you, reach every honourable and free person in the entire world. I hope there will be more pressure in the end to put an end to the practices from which we suffer day to day. I hope that this meeting will yield a real ray of hope, to enable us together, we and you, the representatives of an official circle, to move towards a peaceful solution to our Palestinian cause, if you can bring pressure to bear on international public opinion, so that the Palestinian people will achieve its legitimate and just rights, so that the refugees may return and we may establish our independent state.[129]

More than just their words of hope and Palestinians' own insistence on their sincerity, it is the repetitive persistence of their expressions of faith that indicates how much the Special Committee represented. Throughout the 1970s and 1980s, people who presented to the Special Committee told them that they were grateful just to have the chance to explain their conditions. A teacher who had been imprisoned and then expelled from the West Bank thanked the committee for allowing her to "speak on behalf of the Palestinian women, to describe the sufferings which we have undergone because of the Israeli occupation . . . so that [this committee] might make law known, to safeguard human values."[130] Many understood themselves to be speaking as representatives of the Palestinian people and were thankful to have an opportunity to express themselves on their behalf.[131]

In these, as in many other speeches to the Special Committee, the witnesses nominate "the world" as their intended audience. Through their invocation, "the world" comes into being, with the UN recognized as its legitimate representative. A mayor from the West Bank implored the Special Committee: "I hope you will convey this truth to the whole world, so that the whole world will know that there is still a Palestinian people which is undergoing tremendous suffering."[132]

The lack of improvement in Palestinian conditions of life under occupation, the untrammeled advancement of Israel's settler-colonial project, made the audience that the Special Committee gave them all the more important, a relief from the desperation caused by feeling unheard. A witness thanked the committee

> on behalf of my people, the Palestinian people, for the trouble you have taken . . . [it is] difficult for you to understand how much the trouble you have taken means to my people. In the seven years of Israeli occupation they have come almost to despair of world opinion and world action. . . . Israeli authorities . . . have been transgressing human rights . . . resolutions of the UN . . . and not a single international body has been able to stop them. . . . So we consider the activity of your distinguished Committee as at least a ray of hope for us in the future of humanity.[133]

## Conclusion: Ordinary False Hope

As conversations sparked by Special Committee reports show, while in the confines of General Assembly Plenaries, UN delegates divulged their concerns about the fragile edifice of shared norms that only precariously props up the world organization. Although legal scholar Sundhya Pahuja has observed that fatigue had set in by the late 1980s, UN delegates were sharing their sense that the world doubted the UN's efficacy—and therefore, credibility—much earlier.[134] That the principles proclaimed by the UN might be "mere idle words" was a worry of the Republic of Gabon's representative in 1967. His apprehensions were reflected in his assurance to the UNGA that his country would "do all in its power . . . to see that self-determination and peaceful coexistence" would be made into "living realities, the outcome of the application of the rules of a system of morality which the United Nations must establish in all its details."[135]

In 1969, Angie Brooks, the Liberian president of the UNGA, observed "the gradual decline of the United Nations in the eyes of public opinion." In a remarkable speech, she prodded colleagues who had been lulled into a false sense of accomplishment, at those who were reassured by the insularity of the UN's formalistic machinery:[136]

> We have sometimes failed to realize that neither oratory nor agreements between delegations, nor even resolutions or recommendations have had much impact on the course of affairs in the world at large. The sense of satisfaction, upon adoption of a resolution pleasing the purposes of one delegation or of a homogeneous group of delegations, has helped to perpetuate the mythology of achievement, so that many of us tend to go happily from one agenda item to the next without seriously considering the possibility or even probability that the resolution adopted will not be implemented. We have lacked and we do lack in this respect a sense of reality.

She nevertheless retained the hope embodied in the UN, rallying her colleagues to their collective mission: "The United Nations could and should and does have all the potential to become the only saving device that the world can invent."[137]

Like the two metal balls swinging in a Newton's Cradle, General Assembly delegates and Palestinians confirmed their mutual reliance and shared faith in the perpetual motion machine of the United Nations. Palestinians unwaveringly reinforced the mechanism with their expressions of hope. As both defender of Palestinian rights and UN diplomat, Fayez Sayegh embodied and articulated this codependence. Recalling the universal prohibition of the acquisition of territory by force as part of the UN system, which was "a system of law and order," Sayegh asserted that the Arabs' demand for Israel's withdrawal was "the only rational demand, and the only demand consistent with a system of law and order." It was only such a system of law and order that provided "any hope of peace."[138] The "United Nations system represents a progressive concept of world order, . . . which is the only hope of mankind today," he said, nearly two decades after that body condoned the partition of his country that led to the expulsion from Palestine of his family and that of thousands of others.

Like that of many of his compatriots, Sayegh's hope was probably a blend of many kinds. It was a hope that would allow compromise and coming to terms with devastation, filled with something akin to the "residual hope" that anthropologist Peter Redfield has identified among disillusioned humanitarian workers. It was also a more "ordinary" hope, categorized by Ayşe Parla as one "that verges on expectation, one that is emboldened by a sense of entitlement."[139] In all its variations, as Parla's ethnography of Bulgaristanlı migrants in Turkey so convincingly shows, hope is as much "a way of resisting immobility and marginalization as it is a tool of governmentality."[140] The hope that Palestinians have invested in the UN—in its proclaimed universal principles, in the international laws that are supposed to enforce them—is a refusal of their banishment to the margins of the international community. The UN has been an aspirational space, not just a forum in which to make an appeal to "the world," but the source of confirmation of their equal participation in it. Palestinians' presentations to it are an instantiation of that worldly—in the senses of real, global, and universal—significance. The UN Special Committee has offered a permanent world stage from which they and those in solidarity with them have affirmed Palestinians' inclusion in "the universal," and their worthiness of rights and sovereignty that is supposed to flow from it.

The solidarity spoken at the UNGA has been powerful in suturing international law more deeply into the Palestinian political imagination, reinforcing its authority as a tool of governmentality, but has been impotent in changing the political realities. By maintaining an argument that the problem of Palestine is a political one, but with an exclusive focus on the occupation, the Special Committee has replayed a limited political vision that ignores the longer history and context of the conflict. Unlike many other human rights portrayals of the Palestinian situation—whether by NGOs or the UN[141]—Special Committee members have remained resolute in their argument that human rights violations must be understood in their structural context, a stalwart voice insisting that Israel's military occupation is the root cause of rights violations in the occupied Palestinian territory. "In dealing with violations of human rights, you can never overlook the deeper causes of these violations, the sources of injustice," the director of the UN Division of Human Rights said at a Special Committee meeting in a speech on behalf of the secretary general.[142] And in its resolutions, the UNGA has repeatedly "reaffirmed" "the fact that occupation itself constitutes a grave violation of the human rights of the Palestinian people in the occupied Palestinian territory."[143] However, it has never addressed the initial UN partition of Palestine that created Israel and legitimized the expulsion of hundreds of thousands of Palestinians, and it has cordoned off Israel's actions against its Palestinian citizens, leaving them unaddressed in their investigations.[144]

So far, although it has generated some material forms of assistance and morale boosting, the solidarity spoken at the UNGA has not coalesced in a way that would create the structural changes necessary for the protection of Palestinians' individual and collective rights. The delegate from Ecuador identified plainly the political hierarchy that explained this when he confessed that his country "was not in a position to act as it would have wished." He continued:

> Like many other third world countries, [Ecuador] had to confine itself to its role of spectator. In view of the absence of the necessary political will on the part of those who did have the means to bring about a true solution to the problem, third world countries could only demonstrate their deep solidarity with the Palestinian cause and continue to offer what support they could within the Committee, and confine themselves to denouncing the existence of a double standard in the work of the United Nations when it came to taking effective and concrete decisions on questions which had not held its political interest, while in other circumstances it had acted with a swiftness and an effectiveness that had surprised the international community.[145]

As the years dragged on and the Israeli military occupation became only more entrenched, the work of the Special Committee became a ritualized routine, a point that UN members themselves sometimes observed. It was again the Ecuadoran delegate who remarked in the Special Political Committee's discussion of UNSCIIP's report in 1991:

> The issue under consideration was one that, despite its importance, had produced so much repetition that it was becoming routine. For years it had been constantly repeated that the rights of the Palestinian people and of the other Arabs of the occupied territories were being violated by acts of violence, the demolition of houses, the forced displacement of the population, the closing of schools and other educational institutions, discrimination in the administration of justice, the installation of new European Jewish settlers in the territories occupied by Israel, and many acts of the

occupying Power which violated the Geneva Conventions, the Universal Declaration of Human Rights and the International Covenants on Human Rights, as well as a number of resolutions and declarations of the Security Council.

Although the emphasis of the discussions in the Special Political Committee shifted from year to year, reflecting contemporary political developments and Israeli actions, the format remained similar, with delegates of sympathetic countries noting the continuing deterioration of the human rights situation and criticizing Israel's violations. Sometimes they echoed the sentiment of the Saudi delegate, who "hoped that all the parties concerned had the will for peace and that the principles of justice, freedom and the right to self-determination would prevail."[146]

By the 1990s, NGO staff were among UNSCIIP's standard witnesses, some appearing year after year to provide their briefings on the worsening human right situation in the occupied territory. UNSCIIP's significance diminished as a tool for drawing attention to Palestine: it dissipated as the UN established ever more mechanisms for documenting and declaiming the occupation and, as the human rights industry boomed, flooding many discursive spaces with the narratives and images of Palestinians' rights violations.[147] "Ritually and unfailingly," as the Ecuadoran delegate put it, UNSCIIP's interlocutors at the UNGA called for an end to Israeli settlement building and its withdrawal from the occupied territory. "Just as unfailingly," he added, "the resolutions adopted on the question remained a dead letter."[148]

The United Nations and the hopes that Palestinians have invested in international law have been a tool of governmentality that both promises advancement and keeps people in their place.[149] The Special Committee and other UN mechanisms have encouraged many Palestinians into the echo chamber where their right to have rights is proclaimed with no power to enforce it. The implementation of any of these principles and judgments on the ground requires other pressures, political mechanisms, and foremost the political will by those with power to pursue them. The magnetic proclamations keep a stream of Palestinians engaged with a perpetual motion machine that remains in one place.

# CHAPTER 5

# The Silences of Democratic Listening

## The Mitchell Committee

THE OFFICES OF the Negotiation Support Unit (NSU) were professional and looked pretty slick when I visited them in 2001, befitting the processes of political professionalization that the team offered. The NSU was created in 1998 when "permanent status" negotiations were getting under way between the Palestinians and then Israeli Prime Minister Ehud Barak's government. Britain, Norway, and other European donors funded the NSU to provide legal, technical, and public relations assistance to the Palestinian leadership. Modern, with clean lines and white walls, their offices in Ramallah resembled those of boutique law firms I've seen in New York and DC. It was in these offices that the NSU team prepared the memos, analysis, and talking points that the Palestinian leadership needed in their negotiations with Israel. And many of the people working with the NSU resembled people one might meet in an East Coast law firm. They were young professionals (many in their thirties) and graduates of prestigious law schools such as Yale, Stanford, Oxford, and Georgetown University. The NSU team comprised a mix of mostly Arab-Canadians and Arab-Americans as well as Palestinians and others who grew up in Palestine and other Arab countries. These sharp and hard-working legal advisors constituted what one member positively considered a foreign ministry. Another called it "the one centerpiece of Palestinian diplomacy." It was precisely their sophisticated demeanor and mostly Western backgrounds that made them effective diplomats for the Palestinians in this period that marked the last gasps of the Israeli-Palestinian negotiations.

One of the very last of those gasps was the Mitchell Committee, an international fact-finding group that took up much of the NSU's time as it sought to develop recommendations for furthering the peace negotiations.[1] This investigative commission is remarkable, not for what it achieved politically—as history shows, such commissions rarely precipitate noticeable political change in and of themselves—but for what it exposed of international law's captivating allure and cold impotence. In the space where Palestinian representatives tried to impose international legal principles as the correct framework for determining a resolution to the conflict, the Mitchell Committee patiently recognized that "fear, hate, anger, and frustration have risen on both sides."[2] While Palestinians described their position as "respond[ing] to Israeli allegations with facts," and insisted on "the legal obligations that flow from" Israel's role as an occupying power,[3] the committee encouraged Palestinians and Israelis to "appreciate each other's problems and concerns."[4]

As reflected in the committee's final report, the interchange ended up being a dialogue of the deaf, as the language of international law was deflected by a committee of "democratic listeners" who prioritized the enactment of liberal communicative ideals over the assertion of legal principles. They instantiated what anthropologist James Slotta has described as a "liberal communicative framework," a paradigm that functions according to several principles, including "(1) communicative openness; . . . (2) equality of communicative opportunity; and (3) the ability to communicate freely, that is, without coercion."[5] A crucial final ideal of this framework, unremarked by Slotta, is that of balance. At least in the case of Israel and Palestine, the essential counterpart to the equality of communicative opportunity is according equal attention, concern, and weight to "both sides" and their feelings.[6] The Mitchell Committee was the embodiment of the international community intent on fostering conditions for peace through facilitating understanding, if not sympathy, between the Israelis and Palestinians. Their methods of democratic listening were to be a vital feature of this process. For the core committee members, the Palestinians' and Israelis' inability or unwillingness to understand their opponents' narratives and perspectives was, in the diplomats' view, central to the conflict. And it was their job to understand and convey those narratives across the political divide.

A significant part of this balanced approach was an equal expression of compassion. The Mitchell report marked a moment in which sympathy for Palestinian suffering went mainstream. Remarkable in this report—all the more so for having been penned by an American—was its recognition of the Palestinians' lived daily realities under occupation. It drew attention to "the humiliation and frustration that Palestinians must endure every day as a result of living with the continuing effects of occupation, sustained by the presence of Israeli military forces and settlements in their midst, or the determination of the Palestinians to achieve independence and genuine self-determination."[7] Just as sympathy for the suffering Jews became the requirement of the good liberal after World War II, showing a balanced compassion for the feelings of all was the mark of the new millennium's properly sympathetic liberal subject.

Similar to previous commissions such as UNSCIIP—which evinced a shift toward according greater sympathy to the Palestinians' plight while demanding both facts and evidence of legal violations, as well as proof that Palestinians were the right kind of peace-building subjects—so too did the Mitchell Committee display a receptiveness to especially sympathetic stories of suffering. Palestinians' presentations to the committee likewise struck a balance of kinds of engagement, producing legal argumentation as well as testimonials of victimization. Palestinian representatives insisted that their situation be addressed within a legal framework—as they had been insisting throughout their history of dealing with commissions. But here, they highlighted specifically international humanitarian law more so than during earlier investigations. Although representatives of international powers (especially the United States) had a decidedly more ambivalent attitude toward international law, by this time there was a very thick dossier of UN resolutions and legal precepts on which Palestinians could draw to ground their arguments, making this approach seem all the more appropriate and reasonable.

## Pride in Liberal Communication

All sides walked away after the committee's report was concluded feeling like they had done a "good job," although their report did not quell the violence and no path to peace was forged. There was a strong consensus among the investigators and staff that their work "could make a difference," that their team had been "a good group," that they "had done a pretty good job" and inspired optimism.[8] Many who I interviewed about the committee's work praised the committee's chair, US senator George Mitchell, for his diplomatic abilities. He, in turn and unprompted, praised his colleagues on the committee as being "really impressive, engaged, interested, and a wonderful group of people to work with."[9] In his opinion, the committee and its work were very good, and he found validation in the fact that it was widely praised.[10]

As previous chapters have noted, a similar sense of achievement, maybe even righteousness, was expressed by investigators in earlier commissions. That people could be so gratified by accomplishing nothing highlights the potency of commissions, their ability to lure so many into a trompe l'oeil of political action. The stage that commissions provide for the enactment of liberal values—of objectivity and fairness, democracy and balance, equal political opportunity, sympathy—allows participants to perform these ideals and then inscribe and inflate them for consumption by the public in a report. That the political circumstances that called for the commission were left stuck and deteriorating mattered little when the principle of democratic listening has been enacted.

In performing this democratic listening, the Mitchell Committee gave Palestinians from all walks of life a chance to tell their story. It was an opportunity that seemed significant, given the high profile of its chair, Senator Mitchell, known for his successes in negotiating peace in Northern Ireland. The international community, as represented by the committee, received these stories with openness and sensitivity. Together, all the participants in the committee's work—including the investigative staff, the Palestinian lawyers and representatives, and witnesses providing testimony—constituted a "liberal communicative framework" in which tellers (or supplicants) and benevolent hearers could take pride in their practice of liberal democratic principles.[11] The final report was lauded as a "triumph of evenhandedness over passion."[12] It was a model iteration of "balance" that has become an ideal for Western depictions of the Palestinian-Israeli conflict, imposing false equivalences between occupier and occupied in a way that allowed apparent even-handedness to displace international legal principles and ignore prior agreements.[13]

As with all investigative commissions, although it did not produce the desired political results, the Mitchell Committee did have many effects. One was to create proof of the international community's democratic objectivity. By showing that they had engaged with a variety of groups within both Israeli and Palestinian societies, they made a convincing show of their sincerity and good-faith efforts at finding a political resolution. It drew more Palestinians into contact with "the international community," encouraging them to contribute to the international management of their lives. With their broad, almost ethnographic fact-finding method, the committee gave people a reassuring sense that they were being listened to. This desire for validation, always central for Palestinians who have been written out of so much history (its telling overtaken in the West by Zionist narratives), was particularly acute in this period when so many had laid the failure of the peace negotiations at the Palestinians' feet.[14] The committee also opened another channel in which Palestinians could reassert their contention that the precepts of international law should be the core of the solution. The NSU's team of lawyers responded to this opportunity with diligence, hopeful that the committee would affirm the relevance of international humanitarian law to the management of the occupation. But they were ultimately unable to infuse international legal principles into the Mitchell Committee's recommendations.

With this investigation, another shift in the role of international law becomes apparent. The Mitchell Committee pursued the form of legal processes and prompted legal argument, duly studded with values claimed as central to liberalism, highlighting democratic principles of fair and open political representation and rational argument. But it also included a new emphasis on empathetic listening as a means to reach meaningful understanding of all sides' frustrations and fears, which Palestinian representatives communicated accordingly. Whereas the Palestinians responded dutifully to these invitations, emphasizing yet again their commitment to international law while delivering a sympathetic presentation of Palestinian concerns, the substance of the committee's report and its results proved international legal arguments to be once again impotent in the face of liberal notions of balance and ideas of what was politically pragmatic and feasible. In its conservatism and feebleness, the process benefited the status quo, which supports the Israeli occupation. For the Palestinians, international law remained at the core of their political arguments. For the international diplomats attempting to create the conditions in which political negotiations might proceed, although international law was referenced, it was not regarded as a core lever for achieving political change. The ultimate irrelevance of international law was not new, but the initial show of democratic listening was.

The power of democratic listening is found in the mutual gratification it entails. It was the way the committee's liberal investigators demonstrated their virtuous good-faith efforts, enacting liberalism's principle that upholds the importance of listening to various views, while focusing on the violence of the moment and ignoring the historically embedded structures of an American-backed settler-colonial movement.[15] And it was a way Palestinian representatives could take satisfaction in making themselves heard.

## The Negotiations Support Unit and the Second Intifada

An intensification of violence is usually what has prompted the investigative impulse. If violence reaches a level or an audience not considered acceptable within the liberal order, the reassuring presence of an investigation is dispatched, ostensibly to support a just solution, but usually leading to the reestablishment of the status quo. There is a false but common assumption that violence is abhorrent to liberalism, that reasoned discourse and peaceful negotiation are the prioritized values of liberal ideology. "Just war theory," the Responsibility to Protect doctrine, the UN committee to define aggression, and international humanitarian law are a few examples of liberals' prioritization of orderly, rule-bound, and acceptable violence.[16] The Mitchell Committee, like all investigative bodies in Palestine, was part of a process of redefining acceptable and unacceptable violence. The violence that had become unacceptable was Palestinians' collective effort to dislodge a suffocating status quo through the second intifada.

### The Negotiations Support Unit

Even if the NSU's office and staff appeared like any global legal team, their conditions of work and their goals were not so New York. Their operations were located near the City Inn Hotel in Ramallah, the town that was the closest thing to a metropolis in the West Bank. When I was first getting to know some of the people involved with the NSU while conducting research for my PhD thesis in 2001, the term "City Inn" had become synonymous with "clashes" that were a central feature of the second intifada, the Palestinian uprising against Israeli occupation. These clashes, and the violence that escalated from there, were the Mitchell Committee's fact-finding target.

Although the City Inn Hotel was operational before the intifada began, it certainly lost business after. The clashes that clustered there began as confrontations between Palestinian youth, who were mostly boys and young men throwing rocks, and Israeli soldiers armed with guns, bullets, and tear gas. These confrontations became a regularized ritual during the second intifada that began in September 2000. They often occurred at friction points like checkpoints and areas at the border of "Area A," the label for locations in the West Bank that were ostensibly under Palestinian Authority (PA) control. Venturing past the City Inn, especially on a Friday afternoon after the midday prayers on Muslims' holy day ended, meant risking inhalation of tear gas or getting caught in the path of an Israeli rubber-coated steel or live bullet.[17] Some months into the intifada, some of these clashes also included exchange of fire between armed Palestinians and Israeli soldiers.

Although most on the NSU staff received a high salary, in comparison to local income standards especially, their material remuneration and nice apartments could not shield them from the violence that was becoming part of daily life in the occupied Palestinian territory. They were surrounded every day with the violence they were seeking to analyze and convey to the Mitchell Committee in international legal terms. The same violence I was seeking to understand in anthropological terms. My field notes from the period include observations about how heavy the gunfire sounded on each day, where it seemed to come from, what was going on that might have prompted the spike in confrontations. My feeble attempt to impose some mental control on a situation that felt out of control. An incident I recorded in my notes described what happened with one NSU member who lived in a particularly hot location, near an Israeli settlement that had become a target of Palestinian fighters. Agitated because of his proximity to the shooting, he called a friend of mine with whom I was having dinner. Another of his colleagues at the dinner party advised him not to leave his apartment. She told him to stay there and she would remain on the phone with him for reassurance. (This was the same steady, brave woman who would, months later, walk the deserted streets of Al-Bireh with me, searching for an open bakery during the Israeli army-imposed curfew in the next town over from Ramallah where we both lived. She could hear the low rumble of an approaching Israeli tank from miles away and walked upright like it didn't matter.) During this phone call, someone turned on the television, and we saw live scenes of the very firefight that was making their colleague anxious on the other end of the phone line. At the same time, we saw the red glow of bullet tracers whiz by the window, right outside the apartment in which we were gathered. My notes from this evening convey something of the normalcy of the absurdity that characterized many people's experience of the intifada: "Someone said, 'This is too virtual.' We saw some bullets, heard the guns from outside the window and from the TV, and it got boring, so we turned it off."[18]

The atmosphere of life was tense and intense, as was the atmosphere of the NSU's work. Most of the people I met from the NSU struck me as lively and energetic. They were also driven and committed people. Despite what seemed to be their envious levels of vim and vigor, they were also often pretty tired. The NSU team put in long hours doing the research, preparing the legal arguments for negotiating points that they offered the Palestinian leadership, and developing the talking points to represent the Palestinian position to the media. The important files they had responsibility for, on issues like water, refugees, settlements, and security, required them to become experts on topics that, in some cases, they had no previous knowledge of. In the eyes of the Palestinian leadership, according to one NSU lawyer, their job was to put their arguments "in nice words," but I think this lawyer and others would contend that they did more than that.

## Damage Control Post-Oslo

The NSU was part of the Negotiations Affairs Department that was originally headed by Mahmoud Abbas (Abu Mazen), who became president of the Palestinian Authority in 2005. (Sa'eb Erekat headed the NSU from 2003.) During the permanent status negotiations, most of their efforts were dedicated to developing legal arguments for the Palestinian negotiating team to finalize agreement on issues that the Oslo Accords had left open.[19] The

Declaration of Principles that saw Yasir Arafat and Yitzhak Rabin shake hands on the White House lawn in 1993, with US President Bill Clinton smiling on, was one part of a collection of agreements known as the Oslo Accords. They were named after the location in which Palestinian and Israeli negotiators confirmed an initial peace agreement on interim self-government arrangements under the auspices of their Norwegian hosts. The Oslo Accords established the framework that created the political and diplomatic background against which the NSU and Mitchell Committee had to consider their work.

According to one member of the NSU team, Naima, none of her colleagues thought the Oslo Accords were good, but they recognized that they were the framework they had to work with.[20] It seemed obvious to her and others at the NSU (and beyond) that political agreements would require a legal basis and that international law was an appropriate framework in which to embed them. Many believed that the fact that the Palestinian negotiators had signed the Oslo Accords without legal guidance was a cause of the agreement's many flaws. Naima thought that the NSU team all saw themselves as doing damage control. She told me that when she first read the agreement, she was struck by its legal weaknesses and thought that with all its loopholes, "anyone could drive a truck through this." Her main criticism was that the agreement lacked precision and was open to interpretation. Where issues were precisely defined, she told me, "they were things Israelis wanted, not what the Palestinians wanted."

The accords were dissatisfying to many others too. Not just for what they left unclear, but also for what they gave away or relegated to the sidelines. The accords ignored the rights of most Palestinians, including Palestinian citizens of Israel and Palestinian refugees, whose right to return home has yet to be realized.[21] After Arafat signed the Declaration of Principles, representatives of the countries of the Arab League gave him "a polite but cool reception."[22] The leftist Popular Front for the Liberation of Palestine (PFLP) also opposed the accords. In an interview with members of the executive committee of the PFLP four years after the agreements were signed, they decried the "so-called Peace Process" as "a lie, a big theater, [which had] the aim of pushing through security arrangements which benefit the major powers in the region and which guarantee the interests of Israel." They, like others, pointed to the lack of improvement in Palestinians' daily lives and the increasingly authoritarian PA as evidence of the agreements' problematic nature.[23] Among the most vocal critics of the Oslo Accords was Edward Said:

> [The Oslo "peace process"] has simply re-packaged the occupation, offering a token 18 per cent of the lands seized in 1967 to the corrupt Vichy-like Authority of Arafat, whose mandate has essentially been to police and tax his people on Israel's behalf. After eight fruitless, immiserating years of further "negotiations," orchestrated by a team of US functionaries which has included such former lobby staffers for Israel as Martin Indyk and Dennis Ross, more abuses, more settlements, more imprisonments, more suffering have been inflicted on the Palestinians—including, since August 2001, a "Judaized" East Jerusalem, with Orient House grabbed and its contents carted off: invaluable records, land deeds, maps, which Israel has simply stolen, as it did PLO archives from Beirut in 1982.[24] Such has been the upshot to date of Ariel Sharon's gratuitously arrogant visit to Jerusalem's Haram Al-Sharif [the Al-Aqsa Mosque compound] on 28 September 2000, surrounded by 1,000 soldiers and guards supplied by Ehud Barak—an action unanimously condemned even by the [United Nations] Security Council. Within a few hours, as the merest child could have predicted, anti-colonial rebellion broke out—with eight Palestinians shot dead as its first victims.[25]

This dissatisfaction contributed to the outbreak of the second intifada, and was also a defining feature of the context in which the Mitchell Committee was plunged.

## The Second Intifada

Sharon's visit and the anticolonial rebellion that it prompted—which was sometimes called the Al-Aqsa intifada after the holy place in Jerusalem where it began, but more typically came to be known as the second intifada—eventually claimed thousands of lives. Israeli military and settlers killed more than six thousand Palestinians. Among the dead were civilians, militants, army personnel, Israeli settlers, children, foreigners. They died from stray bullets, rubber-coated steel bullets aimed right at them, suicide bombings, tear gas inhalation, bombs.

But the second intifada was more than deadly violence. For Palestinians, it was a conflagration of mourning and resistance, creativity and stifled imagination, unemployment, demolished economic interchange, art and funerals, restricted movement and frustrated aspirations. It was curfews imposed by young Israeli men on bullhorns in military jeeps or unseen soldiers creeping through neighborhoods in tanks, rolling over cars and thundering through refugee camp walls. It was traumatized children wetting their beds at night and trying to "ventilate" their trauma through coloring workshops during "crisis intervention projects" that became a common activity for NGOs to host during the day. The intifada just kept going. But nobody could see where it was headed, and politically it turned out to be leading nowhere but worse.

The permanent status negotiations ended in early 2001, when Israeli Prime Minister Ehud Barak terminated the talks in the run-up to Israeli elections. At the time, Miguel Moratinos, the special envoy of the European Union to the Middle East at the time, compiled a paper at the request of the Israeli and Palestinian negotiators. In it they declared that the later stages of the talks being held in Taba, Egypt, "were unprecedented in their positive atmosphere and expression of mutual willingness to meet the national, security and existential needs of each side." The parties to the talks agreed "that they have never been closer to reaching an agreement and it is thus our shared belief that the remaining gaps could be bridged with the resumption of negotiations following the Israeli elections."[26]

The incoming prime minister, Ariel Sharon, did not restart the talks—but he started much else. His armed visit in Jerusalem, accompanied by Israeli armed forces and widely described as "provocative," popped a cork from a bottle that had been filling with pressure for years. It was not only the continuation of the Israeli settler-colonial occupation of the West Bank, Jerusalem, and Gaza Strip that fueled Palestinians' frustrations. (The number of Jewish settlers doubled during the first decade of the Oslo process and tripled in the second decade.[27]) The Palestinian leadership's inability to induce a real peace with Israel was also a source of frustration. Their failure to achieve true sovereignty had severely reduced their credibility in the eyes of many. Many aspects of the leadership's privileged lives increased the popular resentment toward them. Politically, their apparent willingness to act as a security force that prioritized Israeli interests over those of their own people was seen as particularly egregious. Socially, the stratification of society that saw PA officials designated as "VIPs" with "special privileges"—such as being able to move through checkpoints and borders without being accosted by Israeli soldiers—was another offense. And economically, their financial successes resulting from business deals with Israel stood out as unfair and immoral. The second intifada was an anticolonial rebellion that included among its targets the comprador that many saw the Palestinian Authority to have become.

The NSU team understood these dynamics very well. They knew the variety of attitudes that regular people had toward the Palestinian Authority forces and the leadership. Living in the West Bank, they had also experienced many of the same frustrations as other Palestinians deprived of their freedom of movement, subject to arbitrary violence, at the mercy of armed soldiers shooting and imposing curfews. They knew their job was to translate hard-to-believe facts of daily life (to many outsiders at least,) into terms Westerners could understand. International law was the language of commensuration they knew best.

## The Mitchell Fact-Finding Committee

Just a couple of months after the second intifada began, while the negotiations were still under way, yet another fact-finding commission was dispatched to Palestine. Officially called the Sharm el-Sheikh Fact-Finding Committee, US president Clinton called for this investigation at the conclusion of the Middle East Peace Summit at Sharm el-Sheikh. Better known as the Mitchell Committee after US Senator George Mitchell who chaired it, the investigation team released its report on April 30, 2001, about six months after it was established with a remit to develop recommendations for ending the violence and finding a path back to peace.

International law was a shared language for all the participants, but its significance, the weight it carried, was very different for each. This was the seesaw of liberalism—prioritizing international law in one moment, nation-state sovereignty the next; freedom of expression in one instance, prevention of incitement in another—in which the various values never quite teeter on a horizontal plane.[28] International humanitarian law grounded the Palestinian representations to the Mitchell Committee that were articulated by lawyers who tried to keep the Fourth Geneva Convention and UN declarations the tractor beam that would focus political efforts toward Palestinians' rights. But for the Western investigators, international law was, variously, a threat, a distraction, a political hindrance, or a droning language that they had heard before and could mostly ignore. These differences did not become clear until the report was issued, however. In the fact-finding process, the liberal communicative framework kept the Palestinian representatives and their investigators acting in a spirit of cooperation and occasional bonhomie.

## Professionals Speaking to "the Western Mind"

More than a common legal language, what brought the examiners and investigated together was their belief in the importance of democratic listening. The performance by both the committee members and the Palestinian representatives of their sympathetic, open-hearted, and open-minded approach created relations of trust. On both sides of the investigation line, there was a clear recognition that developing sympathy was a vital aspect of the interaction. This meant being sensitive toward their counterparts and toward the people who gave testimony. There was a common belief that the work of the committee happened on the interpersonal level, where the "facts" found their meaning. Many of the investigators thought that to achieve real understanding, the narratives, experiences, and feelings of all the people involved had to be attended to.

Those presenting the Palestinian perspective to the committee wanted their narrative, their perspective, to be heard and understood. This common understanding was developed through similar professional status, as well as a Western background shared by the committee members and the NSU team that guided them around Palestine. The Palestinian representatives produced clear and well-organized presentations for the committee, and the investigators recognized and appreciated this. Expressing themselves in the appropriate way in order to be heard by "a Western mind," as one committee staff member described it, entailed a performance of a class-specific habitus that the Palestinians especially had to enact. They intentionally cultivated personal relations with the committee members by spending time with them in social settings. They put effort into trying to "stoke empathy" among the diplomats. Their friendliness and educated, articulate manners facilitated this.

That the investigators and Palestinians shared a legal-professional deportment and enacted values associated with liberal democracy encouraged them all to believe they were doing their jobs effectively. Although professionalism eased the cultivation of sympathy, however, it could not equalize the imbalanced structures of politics.

## The Performance of Democratic Listening

Of those involved with the Mitchell Committee who I interviewed, none could quite recall how the idea for the fact-finding investigation came about. It seemed to result from a request from the Palestinian side for a UN investigation of the issues around Sharon's visit to the Temple Mount/Al-Aqsa complex. One committee staff member understood that the Israelis "were very suspicious of non-US actors overseeing the commission," and another reported that the Israeli Ministry of Defense feared that the committee would "recommend that certain Israeli uniform personnel be referred to some sort of international criminal judicial sort of thing." The compromise allowing the Israelis to dodge what they feared might be a more potent international intervention was US President Bill Clinton's appointment of a commission, which had a broad, less-defined mandate. This was intended to divert attention away from any UN commission that would stress Israel's obligations under international humanitarian law.[29] Although the Palestinian leadership wanted the commission, it was not until the Israeli-Palestinian negotiations ended without resolution that the fact-finding mission moved from being, as one NSU lawyer saw it, "a side-show" to being "the only show in town" after Sharon's election.

Alongside George Mitchell (a Democrat), the commissioners included Suleyman Demirel, former president of Turkey; Thorbjoern Jagland, Norwegian minister of foreign affairs (and former prime minister of Norway); former US senator Warren B. Rudman (a Republican and "a strong supporter of Israel's earlier right-wing governments"[30]); and Javier Solana, secretary-general of the Council of the European Union. The "principals," as they were referred to, served in their individual capacities but were also national and international representatives. In bringing together this international group, with the backing of the United States and under the chairmanship of George Mitchell, the committee imparted gravitas to its work and findings. It also reconfirmed the authority of "the international" in overseeing the Palestinian-Israeli conflict.

The principals each had staff that helped them conduct research in the field and, in some cases, assisted in drafting the final report. They mostly appointed people they knew and included some people who had previous knowledge of and experience in the Middle East and some who did not. American staff members included a former US Army officer of a Republican bent, US Senate staff, and a member of the Foreign Service. On the Norwegian team were people who had varying levels of experience with and knowledge of Palestine and other conflict zones. The principals and most of their staff were men and mostly middle-aged; all people who had made politics and the law their career. One was an MI6 agent, and at least two had, at the time of the committee or after, active commercial dealings in the Middle East as leading members of international business consultancies and project finance firms.[31]

Perception of the Mitchell Committee's integrity and "moral authority" was partially guaranteed by the stature of the five principals, especially the international reputation of Senator Mitchell, who *TIME* magazine named as one of the one hundred most influential people in the world in 2008. He was renowned for his "extraordinary diplomatic skills" and deft shepherding of the Good Friday Agreement, the pact that was to end the conflict in Northern Ireland. One Palestinian politician proclaimed Mitchell to be a good man.[32] "You could feel that he was a balanced man," he said, someone who was not influenced by outside pressures. Palestinian representatives who I spoke with uniformly praised the committee's balanced and open-minded approach. Some of these evaluations about the Mitchell Committee were familiar, common to talk about commissions the world over. That they should be "fair and objective" is a core claim, demand, and even prerequisite for investigative commissions generally. But what was unique in the Mitchell Committee's performance was its emphasis on a kind of democratic listening practice that included not just hearing a representative sampling of Palestinian society, but specifically a sensitive listening.

This entailed a democratic and researcherly thoroughness that was proved by listening to the views of a wide cross-section of people on the ground. The American team thought they had to be able to say that they actually did "visit the place where the incident took place that inspired the whole rebel-lion," even though visiting the Al-Aqsa Mosque complex stirred the ire of the Israelis and was seen by some committee members as an unwise provoca-tion. The validity of the report required that they "be seen being out there" among all the various groups so it would not be regarded as "just a high fly-ing report, made by some academics in Washington." For a Norwegian staff member, it was essential that the public knew the committee had observed things firsthand.

Unlike earlier fact-finding groups—like the King-Crane Commission, which tried to claim in the statistical language of positivist science that its investigations covered a "representative sample" of public opinion—the Mitchell Committee spoke about being good listeners. It was the quality of the hearing as much as the quantity that they thought mattered. The com-mittee members knew that they must publicly perform their openness as much as they had to be open to hearing multiple perspectives. It was an expectation of the Palestinians too. A senior Palestinian politician was con-fident that the committee could "send an important message to the people" that "the international community is prepared to hear their views," which itself could contribute to ending the violence.

Some members of the fact-finding team emphasized the importance of bringing a kind of ethnographic sensibility to their work. What these liberal listening subjects believed they had, and were required to have, was a certain empathy that would allow them to understand and respect the different sides' "narratives." One staff member who had extensive experience in the occupied Palestinian territory had lived there long enough to understand the sensitiv-ity that Israelis and Palestinians have to the language that is used to describe things. He knew about the heavy "symbolism" (in his terms) that different labels can carry. (The question of borders should be addressed as the neutral "internationally recognized" borders, for example, and not as Israel's "defen-sible" borders.) Walking in the shoes of people living through the conflict was an essential part of fact-finding because "unless you can really grasp the nature of the narratives, at least try to understand how people are processing these events," the facts become merely an almanac of happenings.

All participants in this fact-finding exercise knew themselves to be per-forming for different audiences. They understood that they had many messages to deliver, and that they must communicate in a variety of idioms. But each side across the investigatory divide had to prove their credibility according to different criteria, as has been the case in every investigative commission to Palestine. The Westerners and Palestinians had judged the demands of these performances in similar terms. They referred to similar liberal ideals that anchored these requirements within the democratic communicative framework. Having a voice and being heard "is a crucial part of being a free and equal political being."[33] Just as the Mitchell Committee knew they must try to hear democratically, the Palestinians wished to be heard, to have their narrative validated. It was part of what motivated their participation in the investigation.

## Hopes of Being Heard

The prospect of being heard is one of the carrots of hope that commissions dangle. The promise of being able to assert a narrative and receive a "fair hearing" is a particularly valuable and powerful one for Palestinians. As in many colonial contexts, the expurgation of "the native" happens across many registers, through a variety of genres. The freshest instance of such narrative suppression was the deletion of the Palestinians' positive contributions to the peace negotiations with Israel, which had been ignored or denied. The negotiations' collapse had been advertised as being the Palestinians' fault, yet another erasure of the Palestinian experience.[34] After that, the Mitchell Committee appeared as a crucial opportunity for the Palestinians to be heard on an international level.

Naima, an NSU lawyer, saw their presentations to the committee as a chance to head off what she expected the Israelis to say about the intifada.[35] She had predicted that they would try to take it out of political context and turn it into a story of racism, of Arabs hating the Jews. They would portray it as having been caused by there being "something wrong with the Arabs' DNA," she said a bit sarcastically. Another NSU lawyer explained his hopes that the committee would offer "a vindication of [their] factual narrative." He expected the committee to conclude that the Israelis' contention about the Palestinian Authority's responsibility for starting the second intifada was "not a correct story." He wanted them to validate the Palestinians' assertions "that the violence was both a reaction to Israeli intransigence at the negotiating table and to Israeli provocations after September 28, 2000 [when Sharon made his provocative visit to the Al-Haram Al-Sharif complex]. That it was not planned by the Palestinian leadership." The final report did in fact do this. To achieve this narrative confirmation, they knew they had to express the facts in the most professional way. As Naima said, they had to break down the false and typical narrative that framed everything as being a result of "Arabs hating Jews, all about a centuries-long conflict." Claiming the language of objectivity, they would present well-researched facts about deaths, injuries, and destruction caused by Israeli force, within a historical and legal narrative that would explain the Palestinian side of the story and its context.

And this they did. NSU lawyers who I spoke with expressed a palpable pride in the professionalism of their work, and they were widely recognized as being an impressive and effective group, especially in the period of the negotiations and during the Mitchell Committee's tenure. Members of the committee praised the NSU for its intelligent presentations. George Mitchell described the NSU staff members as bright and able. One American committee staff member said, "The Palestinian side was indeed quite systematic, prepared to interact with us, prepared to facilitate any kind of contacts we might want to have, very open, very above board." Their competence was especially apparent in comparison to some others who the committee met.

A few members of the committee described the off-putting behavior of their Israeli counterparts and some Palestinian political leaders. To illustrate this distinction between the NSU members and others of their interlocutors, one of the staff described for me a first meeting with members of the Israeli Ministry of Foreign Affairs. An Israeli spokesperson encouraged the committee to see themselves as being among those like themselves. The Israelis told them: "We are like you. We're the outpost of the democratic world. We share your values. We can talk openly." He claimed the liberal communicative framework to be an Israeli and Western one, explicitly excluding Palestinians from it. When this spokesman shifted to talking about the Palestinians, he showed the committee how different the Israelis really were—at least in the eyes of some on the committee's team. The Israeli Ministry representative warned them about the Palestinians: "When you come to the other side, you must understand what kind of people you are speaking to. They lie. That's how they are. You can't trust them. You can't trust a single word." The committee member commented to me that this racist commentary was "so gross" and went on to contrast this experience with those they had with the NSU team in Ramallah. These were "very pleasant people. They really *were* like us. From Canada, other Western countries. It was a highly sophisticated, relaxed team. More like us than what we had experienced in Tel Aviv."

The NSU team possessed the social capital and class habitus that allowed the committee members to sympathize with and like them. They spoke eloquently, with confidence and humor. They wore nice suits. But it was more than the NSU lawyers' good looks and charm that won over the committee members. What captivated many was their ability to translate the Palestinian experience in a way that could be understood and believed by outsiders. One of the staff told me he had been impressed by the Palestinians' self-representation to the committee because they did not "overdo" it. As someone who had lived in the occupied Palestinian territory and had studied the situation from close up, he had noted a tendency among Palestinians to pile on their stories of victimization and stress the Israelis' wrongdoings. While he acknowledged that what they expressed was "true," he also recognized that it could have a stultifying effect on listeners. "It becomes so massive. [What Palestinians tell you] becomes so much that you don't necessarily . . . You ask if it can be true. Or is it theater? It *is* true, but. . . ." In contrast to what one might hear on a typical visit to somebody affected by the occupation, instead of overwhelming the investigators, the Palestinians made a "factual impression" because, he said, they knew how to talk effectively to outsiders.

The NSU team worked hard to present to the Mitchell Committee reliable data within water-tight legal arguments guided by the precepts of humanitarian law, by reason and an ethos of fairness. They sought to ensure that even the testimony they facilitated be democratic, channeling it from a range of Palestinian individuals and political representatives. Presentations by political leaders and representatives seemed to have left the worst impression on the committee, however, with then president Yasir Arafat coming in top as the least effective interlocutor for the Palestinians. "You would try to ask him something, he starts with a couple sentences that make sense, and veers off onto something that gives the impression of him not being a rational, clear-thinking person. I felt sorry for the Palestinians having such leadership," one committee member told me. Several of the committee members I spoke with recounted a specific meeting that featured Arafat's tirade about the "Romanian" or "Roman" trees. Arafat had been referring to a recent incident when Israelis destroyed an olive grove. Burning and chopping down Palestinian olive trees is a practice common to both the army and Israeli settlers, a practice that has devastating consequences for the livelihoods of Palestinian farmers who rely on this crop.[36] Olive trees, with their firm and ancient rootedness in the land (dating back to Roman times), are also an important symbol for Palestinians, representing their steadfastness in inhospitable soil.[37] But Arafat had expressed the issue in garbled terms that required explication from the NSU staff in the room.

Some American staff members also commented on the meeting they had with Marwan Barghouti. Barghouti was a political leader in the mainstream Fatah party who had become prominent during the first intifada and was elected to the Palestinian legislature in 1996. Also active in the second intifada, Barghouti was convicted in 2004 by the Israelis on five counts of murder in a trial that the Inter-Parliamentary Union judged was not fair.[38] In their 2001 meeting with him, the Americans encountered Barghouti as someone "with blood on his hands," adopting the terminology Israel uses to demonize Palestinian violent resistance. Although one American apparently left the encounter feeling like "he wanted a shower after that meeting" because Barghouti "was a person that you knew was responsible for a lot of the violence," another acknowledged that Barghouti "told an interesting story" and had "an interesting perspective."

> If you set aside all of his alleged sins or acknowledged sins or crimes, he was a compelling person. There was a dynamic to his style. He defended what Palestinians had done violence-wise. He defended it with arguments that were attempting to justify the violence in response to Israeli transgressions or actions or something. And he did it in a way that I remember thinking, "If I didn't know. If I wasn't in this capacity. If I didn't know the Israeli side of the story, I would believe him, as a Palestinian citizen." He had the ability to make it seem like it was all justified. He was able to present the Palestinian case for violence in a straightforward way. I think he had the ability to convince others.

But this American's knowledge of "the Israeli side" compelled him to hear the evidence in a particular way. He recognized Barghouti as a political leader who might have to be engaged with, but was apparently not convinced by the Palestinian argument, reiterated by many, that armed resistance is a right guaranteed by international law.[39]

Beyond the meetings with what one NSU lawyer described as "the talking heads," the Palestinian team took the committee to see things in the West Bank and the Gaza Strip too. They included meetings with Palestinian business owners, officials, mayors, and "a good cross section of intellectuals," as an NSU member described them. They heard presentations by other experts employed by the NSU on core issues such as settlements, which was a major problem that the Palestinians wanted to stress to the committee. Hearing from Palestinian victims of Israeli shelling left a strong impression, especially on some members of the American team who had no prior experience of Israel and Palestine. As an indication of how underinformed at least one member of the American team was, he expressed shock that the US media did not convey the kinds of stories he was hearing in the occupied Palestinian territory.

What swayed each one of the investigators, at least in the moment of hearing testimony, was variable and to some extent overshadowed by their preconceptions and political leanings. The visceral and emotional way that some of the committee staff processed the information they received had various effects. From being physically repelled by an elected Palestinian leader to being filled with disdain or pity for another, these fact-finders were hardly neutral in their evaluations. One American staff member betrayed his bias most explicitly when he expressed surprise after I asked him if he had done any special research on Israel, realizing in the moment of my questioning that he had not considered there to be much need. What little information he received on Israel from CIA analyst briefings "fit the perception that you had an established government fighting against terrorist attacks," so it was not necessary to "second guess the [Israeli] government's decisions in particular instances." He spoke explicitly about the fact that because Israel was "an established ally" and because "it's a partner fighting against terrorism . . . there's less that we do analyzing what their government does."

On one field visit, the Palestinians took the committee to hear from a Palestinian businessman. He began by assuring them that he would not repeat an account of the complex problems his colleagues had described to the committee. Instead, he wanted to talk to them about taking his children to school. It was an example of how the NSU and other Palestinians sought to humanize their life under occupation, to relay this experience in a way their Western interlocutors could understand. It had an impact, as became evident when a committee participant recounted to me this businessman's testimony as if he had heard it only yesterday. The businessman told them:

> I take my kids to school. I go through two checkpoints. Then again in the afternoon when I fetch them. Everyday. And the Israeli [soldiers] there are usually the same. What happens to me most of the time: I get there, they verify my papers. They might frisk me. . . . It's no major problem. . . . But then there are the days when somebody decides, "Now we're going to show these guys." They put me on the ground. Made me lie down, face in the road. And then they started prodding me. Kicking me with their boots to check if I have got anything [hidden]. My kids are sitting in the car looking at this. They're looking at their father. Who is their father for them? Their hero. And they see how their hero is being treated by these people. Can you imagine what is left in them of anger and frustration and humiliation at that age? For no obvious reason.

"What we remembered was this story of this man," the committee member said to me. In a tone still tinged by remembered astonishment at the businessman's harrowing story calmly told, the diplomat assured me: "And he was right. He wasn't exaggerating anything. This very simple thing: How do my kids see this? That made an impression." It was one among many moments of sympathetic connection—a moment of listening and being heard—that influenced how investigators interpreted the broader situation.

The Palestinian representatives' methods of making their arguments heard worked in many ways. Points of international law presented professionally and stories of suffering appealed to different committee members, opening them up to an understanding of Palestinians' experiences of occupation. All the pieces of the "liberal communicative framework" were in place: the open, equal, free, and balanced listening. But being heard is not the central quandary of political change; it is liberalism's ideological obfuscation that makes it appear as such.

## Legalizing Politics?

International law is an effort to systematize the definitions of acceptable and unacceptable human suffering, to designate the humans who have the right not to suffer and those whose suffering must be tolerated. It is a field of contestation in which antagonists seek to impose their definitions of what is acceptable by aligning them with what is perceived to be right, just, and universal. As a language that pretends to be universal, international law offers Palestinians—as it does any subaltern group—a political Rosetta Stone that should translate their particular conditions of injustice into a language even Americans could hear.

But participants in the Mitchell Committee process held different perspectives on the significance of international law in—and in contrast to—politics. These discrepant views, which might be glossed as "realist" and "idealist," reveal something important about the faith that international law inspires in some and the ideological function it plays to obscure from consideration values and forces outside its own structure.[40] Many in the NSU were dedicated to international legal language and mechanisms because they believed that they accorded with Palestinian aspirations, which were in line with notions of universal rights and international norms. In every era of conflict with Zionism and Israel, Palestinians have looked to international law as a language to express and give credence to their political aspirations, which fit like a hand in a comfortable glove. As Chapter 4 showed, the decades of high Third Worldism fortified this symbiotic relationship even further, just as the saturation of international political discourse with human rights language did in the 1980s and '90s.[41]

In contrast, some involved in the Mitchell process believed that international law was a "drug" that left Palestinians flailing ineffectively within a self-referential system. And in the end, although the Mitchell Committee was exposed relentlessly to legal arguments, the report recommendations did not rely on international law. Instead, the report couched its analysis in a feather bed of sympathy for the frustrations and pains of the Palestinians and Israelis. It was aligned, finally, with the American perspective and the most recent political framework, the Oslo Accords, a set of agreements that also did not abide with international legal principles.[42]

## Injecting Palestine with International Law

From the accounts I heard from those who were involved in the Mitchell Committee, Norway played an important role in the committee's work, balancing the Zionist sympathies of the Americans with a greater firsthand knowledge of the Palestinian situation. The Norwegian government also helped establish the NSU. Alongside the governments of the UK, Denmark, the Netherlands, and Sweden, Norway continues to support the NSU financially.[43] The NSU was a novel experiment to boost Palestinian legal expertise that might allow them to compete on a more even playing field at the negotiating table with Israel. External evaluators praised the NSU for demonstrating to the Palestinian leadership "the benefits of utilizing professional legal/policy work as part of preparation for and conduct of negotiations."[44] Its establishment was instigated by a sense that the Palestinian negotiators did not have capacities equal to those of the Israelis. They had, it was believed by Westerners involved, neither the experts in international law nor the necessary machinery for collecting information required to back up their arguments. It was an explicit part of the NSU's job description to sensitize the Palestinian leadership to the need for a more professional approach to the negotiations.[45] The Norwegian government believed that if the negotiations were to have any chance at all, this imbalance in professional capabilities had to be addressed. The Palestinian negotiators needed the technical knowledge of key issues that were central negotiating points, such as water resources and water rights. In addition to the NSU's team of legal advisors, a bevvy of technical experts was also employed by Adam Smith International, the British contractor that managed the NSU.[46]

From the perspective of the NSU lawyers, a central component of their professionalism was the solidity with which they grounded their written submissions in international law. That they made their arguments with strong legal standing was a point of pride, a professional requirement, and, in their view, a testament to the rightness of their political and moral position. And yet, many of the American staff on the Mitchell Committee were unimpressed by the legal arguments and instead were most affected by the human dimension of the presentations and tours. They took the NSU's written submissions with a grain of salt, as one staff member told me, because he thought they knew what they could expect from both the Palestinians and Israelis. It was, the American said, just "cold, dry paper."

The unequal significance that different participants accorded to the cold letter of international law is contradictory in several ways. It was initially a European initiative to infuse Palestinian negotiating politics with legal expertise, expertise that was then dismissed as irrelevant by key Western players. Although this proficiency was appreciated, during the negotiations with Israel and the Mitchell Committee, the actual substance of the legal arguments was often disregarded.[47] But the legal form remained paramount. Although the committee's report insisted that the committee was "not a tribunal" and did not have the mandate to "determine the guilt or innocence of individuals or of the parties," there were many law-like features of the fact-finding process.[48] Some of that had to do with the people involved. Senator George Mitchell had been a justice before becoming a senator. One of his staff observed that Mitchell's approach to the committee's work was like that of a judge. As the committee discussed how to go about its work, an early idea was that the members would review "briefs" from both sides, which they did end up doing. They also heard testimony from regular people who had been hurt by the other side and talked with political figures and other spokespeople. Similar to the practice of bringing victim impact statements to sentencing hearings in the United States, the Palestinian representatives also introduced the committee to individuals who had been harmed in Israeli attacks to help the members understand the human dimension of the written materials and legal arguments they received.[49]

The people involved in organizing the Palestinian written submissions and testimony were also mostly lawyers. They too saw the process in a legal framework. In response to my question about why the Palestinian written submissions to this committee relied heavily on the Fourth Geneva Convention and international humanitarian law, one of the NSU lawyers said: "It's the law, and we are lawyers, and that's what one does. The law is very much seen as a genuine part of the Palestinian narrative. By using the law, we were using tools, terms that were at least familiar to the Palestinian leadership. It's in keeping with the traditional way Palestinians have done things." This work was in their "comfort zone," another Palestinian lawyer told me.

The legalism of the Mitchell Committee framework and Palestinian arguments to it was central to the fact-finding process, but not to the final report. And in that discrepancy lie important clues for understanding the ways legal norms function, how diplomacy and politics overpower law. Lawyers for the Palestinians insisted that international law should be the starting point, the framework, the moral basis for the committee's report, its recommendations, and any future negotiations. But, to the political people involved, the legal arguments were, at best, not something they could use and, at worst, a distraction.

International law was the mantra of the Palestinian written submissions. Their not-so-brief briefs insisted that international law was the correct "context in which facts must be examined." More than just the context or frame of reference, international law—specifically, Israeli transgressions of those laws—was at the very root of the conflict. "The current crisis is not a result of 'misunderstandings' as much as of a failure to recognize the universal applicability of international law," the Palestinian brief explained.[50] A Palestinian lawyer explained that their "whole focus was to make sure that we go back to the root causes, which is occupation, and that the UN has a basis for resolving the issue. [To show that] this is not just another conflict over disputed land. This has a history."

The second of the Palestinians' written submissions cited large spheres of Israeli activity that exemplified Israeli lawlessness, foremost among which was the acquisition of territory by force. Also highlighted was Israel's "use of illegal military orders and the sanctioning of unlawful policies," and "the routine flouting by Israeli military personnel of even these unacceptable standards," resulting in human rights violations.[51] Another of the documents explained that the Palestinians had no faith in peace negotiations because Israel has not upheld UN Security Council Resolutions 242 and 338, which called for the peaceful resolution of the Arab-Israeli conflict through territorial compromise.

An explicit goal for the NSU team was to obtain from the committee "normative statements" about international law. They wanted the committee to declare what many lawyers and previous UN resolutions and investigations had recognized: that settlements are illegal, and that the Fourth Geneva Convention applies to the Israeli occupation and dictates how they should manage it. The NSU knew that Israel's practices, during the intifada and before, were in breach of international law, and therefore, they asserted, "Palestinians have no fear of an unflinching and hard look at the root causes of this conflict or of a fair analysis of what has transpired within the context of international law."[52]

Omar Dajani was one of those involved in preparing these written submissions. He was part of the NSU during the negotiations and throughout the time of the Mitchell Committee, eventually going on to become a law professor at a university in the United States. His insider status afforded him details about how the Israelis and Palestinians framed their claims during the negotiations, which informed his analysis as a legal scholar. His evaluations and arguments offer important information about how international law functioned in this political setting. Even more, they yield insights into the way that faith in international law persists, including in Dajani's own convictions.

In his fascinating examination of international law in the Israeli-Palestinian negotiations, Dajani makes the case that "international law's influence . . . derives from the normative force of the ideas it embodies and its capacity to legitimize negotiated outcomes in the eyes of other international actors and domestic constituencies."[53] In other words, international law outlines standards of behavior based in certain principles and values, and those who are seen to uphold those standards in political negotiations can make people side with their negotiating position or derive legitimacy because those norms are seen as good and right.[54] In his widely cited article, "Shadow or Shade—The Roles of International Law in Palestinian-Israeli Peace Talks," Dajani recounts that the Palestinians consistently resorted to international law as fundamental principles for their demands or starting positions. The Israelis, in contrast, tended to reject international law as inapplicable or too vague. The Palestinians' position reflected the fact that international human rights and humanitarian law forbid many Israeli practices carried out against Palestinians in the occupied Palestinian territory.

At the heart of international humanitarian law, the Fourth Geneva Convention is a significant reference point for Palestinian claims. Among other prohibitions, it bans an occupying power from transferring parts of its population into the territory it occupies, as Israel has been doing by establishing settlements in the West Bank and, until not long ago, in the Gaza Strip. The existence of some 800,000 Jewish Israelis in the West Bank and East Jerusalem living in 240 settlements, or so-called "outposts," might be evidence enough that this international legal norm is more of a suggestion than a reality.[55] But the Fourth Geneva Convention relevant to the protection of civilians in times of war, alongside a long list of other international legal instruments, remain key pillars of Palestinian political discourse, fundamental principles used as reference points for their arguments.

Dajani's elaborate analysis makes clear that during negotiations both the Israelis and their American backers did not consider themselves bound by the international legal principles, which the Palestinians were trying to mobilize. Despite this and the fact that he recognized the force of international norms as deriving from the faith that is invested in those norms, Dajani still concluded his article with a plea to the international community to "clarify the content and implications of international legal rules . . . and to impose costs on the parties for noncompliance" as a means of extending the law's influence.[56] Like many other professionals in the field, Dajani maintains that there is a positive role for international law to play in achieving peace.[57]

If his academic writings are an accurate indication, Dajani's commitment to international law persists. But other lawyers at the NSU had lost faith in it. Among the latter was Rabih. He was, during the time that I knew him, considered by some colleagues to be among the more cynical of the NSU group. He had not personally expected much to come from the Mitchell Committee, he told me. What he anticipated was "what you expect from every other commission—to present something. It was interesting insofar as it obviously had high-level American backing, represented by the composition of the group. So we thought of it as a high visibility PR effort at that point." He had been working with the NSU for a year, and some among the Palestinian leadership were, in his words, "jaded." It was in this period that he was becoming, he said, "very political in my approach to things, less legal."

I have become very allergic to the law in dealing with the Palestinian-Israeli conflict. I think it's useless. That's the bottom line. It's a drug. It's where you go for your comfort zone. "The law is with me." Brilliant. But it's not about the law. It's about power. With the little power you have, how do you position yourself where you can actually shape [things].

Rabih's views aligned with those of a Mitchell Committee staff member. Although he was clearly and explicitly sensitive to the Palestinian situation, and he understood why they emphasized the moral and human dimensions of their plight, in his assessment of the Palestinian approach to this committee, the staff member gently criticized what he thought was the Palestinian overemphasis on law to the detriment of a focus on politics.

> As always the Palestinians were dumping international legal arguments on this. . . . There are some people who thought international law should be the end all and be all of an argument or political position. And others that recognize that politics is something else and happens somewhere else. International law can be part of the narrative, but it couldn't be the starting point for the Palestinians because it's not where the Israelis were.

This committee staffer reverted to a language of politics and pragmatism that construed political possibility as being defined by the stronger party, the Israelis. He recognized the Palestinians' desire to shape the report around Israeli breaches of international humanitarian law, but to reengage the political process, the conversation could not take international law's principles as preconditions.

In making the distinction between "political" and "legal," or between power and law, Rabih and some others were insisting on a theory of how political change comes about that was distinct from that of Dajani and other colleagues. Those with a self-declared "political" viewpoint believed that international law was either irrelevant or had to be set aside for political progress to occur. Those who insisted on international law as the necessary bedrock for solutions knew themselves to be part of a political process. But they had far less willingness to relinquish prior agreements and rights. They held on to their position because it was inscribed in international law.

## Conclusion: International Law as Belief System

It is here that international law becomes apparent as a self-referential belief system. The moral and political rightness of international law is clear for those, such as some Palestinians (and their advocates), whose existing political arguments and demands are supported by international law. Their political demands, which are specific and narrowly relevant to their own context, converge with law that is underwritten by a claim to universality, justified as being the result of international consensus. These Palestinians mobilize international law in a manner that upholds the "illusion of rational consensus around law that is meant to isolate law from power, morality, antagonism and the plurality of interests."[58] The double and apparently contradictory gesture, which partakes in the "fight for an international Rule of Law [that] is a fight against politics [that furthers] subjective desires,"[59] but on behalf of a specific political position, is not the primary object of critique among those like Rabih and the staff member who held the pragmatist position. What they derided or refuted is the "liberal impulse to escape politics" that happens through an assumption that international legal rules exist with authority beyond themselves, beyond politics, and beyond particular contests.[60] None of these participants would deny the essentially agonistic—political—nature of the problems to be solved in this context. What they differ on is the authority of international law and what role it should or could play in the processes of political resolution.

As previous chapters have shown, for many decades Palestinians have been insisting on international humanitarian and human rights law as necessary bases for a just peace. As each new crisis invites efforts by the international community to manage the situation, new generations of Palestinians and their representatives arrive to reassert the centrality of international law. With demands for Israel to abide by its "legal obligations and its responsibilities under the Fourth Geneva Convention relative to the Protection of Civilian Persons in Time of War of 12 August 1949," they repeated a version of these efforts to anchor the articulation of their political vision in international law during the Mitchell Committee.[61] And the results were much the same as what previous exertions yielded: more of the same destructive status quo.

Continual appeals to international law—despite its minimal returns—by people who were neither naive nor ignorant highlight two significant and intertwined dimensions of international law's allure. One is its status as a belief system, and the other is its power to convey a validated narrative. In explaining his argument that international law is a belief system, Jean d'Aspremont, a professor of public international law, highlights the self-referentiality of the "modes of legal reasoning that are constantly deployed by international lawyers when they formulate international legal claims about the existence and extent of the rights and duties of actors subjected to international law and the consequences of breaches thereof."[62] What this self-constructed, self-verifying system requires is a notion of truth that comes not by

> reason (rationalism) nor by experience (empiricism) but by the deployment of certain transcendental validators that are unjudged and unproved rationally or empirically. This set of validators . . . constitutes what the believers constantly turn to for 'revelation.' The self-explanatory nature of these validators is what allows these validators to acquire a transcendental character and be displaced outside the social praxis where they have been shaped.[63]

But in the case of Palestinians, the sources of belief and conviction are deeper than this. They return to the specificity of the Palestinians' history and claims. There is a self-professed tendency among lawyers in general to see the world through the lens of law and view its problems as able to be remedied by the application of legal rules. The addiction to law in the Palestinian context can be explained by something more specific, however. In particular, it is international law's lavish attention to Palestine and a Palestinian perspective that convinces many that it is on their side. As Chapter 4 discussed, international law has provisions against racism and colonialism; it has regulations that should protect civilians living under military occupation; and the UN has passed numerous resolutions bolstering Palestinian demands and condemning Israel's actions that adversely affect the Palestinians.

More than giving Palestinian demands a legal validation, international law offers a venue for the expression and confirmation of the Palestinian perspective. It provides a rebuttal to the forms of denial that run throughout Palestinian history—the denial of their political subjectivity, their national peoplehood, their national rights to independence and all individual rights, their innocence, their on-the-ground experiences of discrimination, dispossession, and violence. In hoping that the committee would issue "normative statements" about international law, representatives were hoping for confirmation of Palestinian positions, claims, and experience. They were hoping for the amplification of their perspective. And they were relying on an endorsement of international law's authority as an objective system.

The Palestinians of the NSU saw the Mitchell Committee as a chance for the activation of international law and a correction of the narrative of events, and even the narration of Palestine, in many ways. One lawyer told me: "We exerted a lot of effort trying to convey to them the frustration on the street that had brought this to pass. I think we wanted to win that point." In some ways they did win that point, insofar as the committee's report identified the lack of comprehension on the part of "some Israelis" of the "humiliation and frustration that Palestinians must endure every day as a result of living with the continuing effects of occupation, sustained by the presence of Israeli military forces and settlements in their midst."[64] But the misapprehension ran both ways, and the compassionate listening and understanding was always balanced.

As the report observed, the Israelis have feelings too, and "fear, hate, anger, and frustration have risen on both sides." For every "point" that the Palestinians may have won, the report doled one out to the Israelis as well. While acknowledging some crucial issues such as the need for the Government of Israel to "freeze all settlement activity, including the 'natural growth' of existing settlements,"[65] it chided "some Palestinians [who] appear not to comprehend the extent to which terrorism creates fear among the Israeli people and undermines their belief in the possibility of co-existence, or the determination of the [Government of Israel] to do whatever is necessary to protect its people." It scolded "each side" for their "perspective that fails to recognize any truth in the perspective of the other." The committee's balanced compassion was manifest in the form and content of the Mitchell Report, which presented for each summary of the PLO's "perspective" a corresponding description of the Government of Israel's. For every Israeli allegation recorded, the Palestinian denial was listed, too.

This may have been the committee's attempt to fulfill the mandate of the investigation as they understood it. According to George Mitchell, the directive was "to some degree contradictory: that we want you to find out what happened and report on it, but don't blame anybody for what went on."[66] The centrality of "a profound sense of victimization in both societies" and their "skepticism and even denial about some parts of the other's narrative" was the first thing Mitchell listed among his "conclusions about the current state of

Israeli-Palestinian relations."[67] Unlike the Peel Commission report, which argued that the British governed Zionists and Arabs with a balance ensured by its technocratic "government by arithmetic,"[68] or the British and Americans' derision of Palestinians' "intransigence" and their demand for compromise made in the Anglo-American inquiry, the Mitchell report displayed a balance of concern and understanding extended to all parties in the conflict. The result of democratic listening in this liberal communicative framework was an effective erasure of Palestinians' history being subject to a settler-colonial takeover of Palestine.

Political analyst Mouin Rabbani published one of the few critiques of the Mitchell report, in which he underlined its problematic ideological effects. The report, he observed, gave the impression that "the Committee was investigating a confrontation between equal forces, each equally responsible for the 'violence.'"[69] The report, and the investigatory process, was a story of incorrectly assumed equivalences on every possible level: an assumed parity among the Palestinian representatives and the Western investigators, lawyers talking to lawyers, professionals talking to professionals, all people in good faith seeking change for the better. Once again, this fact-finding commission brought together people who were sincerely committed to "trying to make a difference," people who were "sympathetic and nice," who "took things seriously," as one member of the Palestinian legislature described the Western investigators. They were "fair minded people without proclivities towards one side or the other," another Palestinian representative said. The committee engaged people in an exercise of "balanced" assessment and recommendation, and it was commended for so doing.[70]

There was an obscuring focus on the notion of balance—the idea that a "fair" and "objective" view of the situation and solution must give equal weight to the perspectives, emotions, and demands of "both sides." Such a focus always performs an insidious ideological function. Liberal commissioners' fetishization of the principle of "balance" enabled them to, as Israeli journalist Meron Benvenisti had predicted, "become one more instrument for stifling any initiative for examining the actions of Israeli security forces and for uncovering the truth lurking behind the propaganda smokescreen."[71] And they justified it within a liberal ethical framework such that they could feel good about doing so.

The Mitchell Committee displayed a mélange of commission approaches. It was a diplomatic endeavor that issued a technocratic report seeking to propose political solutions for the return to negotiations. But it was also infused with the sympathetic emotion that has become integral to the human rights approach of UN commissions. In the end, as with many commissions before, the contingencies of political life and its constantly shifting tectonics saw the Mitchell Committee's report swept away. During its investigation, both the Israeli and American elections replaced the government leaders who had signed on to the committee's formation with their more conservative opponents. There was no mechanism for implementation of the report's recommendations and no meaningful follow-through by the Bush administration. In the view of one diplomat involved in follow-up to the committee, this was because of a "fundamental disconnect between the two leaderships," which points to the basic weakness of investigative commissions generally.[72] The Mitchell Committee's report became a dead letter.

This was not a failure of liberalism, but an instantiation of it. It was not a bad-faith effort on the part of any participant in the process, each of whom undertook their mission with an earnest conviction that the revelation of objective fact might nudge the political dynamics in a positive direction toward a just solution—the faithful assumption underlying all investigative commissions. That the committee report's "triumph of evenhandedness over passion" could be so widely recognized and lauded illustrates how liberalism functions, obscuring the deep history of imbalance that underlay that moment's violence and rancor.[73]

# CHAPTER 6

# The Shift to Crime and Punishment

## UN Missions Renewing Hope in International Law

THE MITCHELL COMMITTEE LED to a "road map," released in 2003, which envisioned a process for achieving a permanent status agreement. It did not achieve that goal, and the second intifada continued with redoubled ferocity. The international community responded by sending commissions in April 2002 and November 2006, investigating Israeli attacks on the West Bank town of Jenin and Israeli shelling of Beit Hanoun in the Gaza Strip, respectively. The Arab League took part too, establishing the Independent Fact Finding Committee on Gaza to the League of Arab States in February 2009, which investigated violations of international law during the Israeli military offensive (Operation Cast Lead) against Gaza from December 27, 2008, to January 18, 2009. Its mission also included collecting information on the responsibility for the commission of international crimes during the operation. Two months later, on April 3, 2009, the president of the UN Human Rights Council established another fact-finding mission to report on the same incidents. The United Nations Fact Finding Mission on the Gaza Conflict, commonly known as the Goldstone Mission, investigated the 2008–2009 fighting in Gaza that left some 1,400 Palestinians dead.[1] In each case, the nature of the violence and the extent of death and destruction prompted the investigation. And in each case, international humanitarian and human rights law was the investigators' reference point.

International humanitarian law dictates rules of behavior in wartime that are supposed to protect civilians. Some critiques of these regulations maintain that international law promotes the violation of state sovereignty. Another standard critique, but from a different political perspective, is that international humanitarian law is used to legitimize state policy more than it limits state behavior or curbs state violence. The US Department of Defense Laws of War Manual, published in 2015, is a good example of this deployment of international law. It provides interpretations of international law that contradict the international humanitarian legal principle of "distinction" that requires fighting forces to distinguish between combatants and civilians. The guidance in this US manual permits "the incidental killing or wounding of such [medical and religious] personnel" if they are "in proximity to combatant elements." It also prioritizes mission success and protection of friendly forces over the protection of civilians.[2] It is an example of what critical political scientist Ian Hurd has argued regarding the ways that the hegemony of international law is manifest. Legal hegemony has not resulted in overwhelming compliance with international law, but in the "universality of law as source of justification and contestation." In setting the standards of evaluation and terms of debate, this hegemony reduces consideration of political and moral questions in international behavior, condensing the "language, institutions, and resources of contestation" to those of the law.[3]

Legalism's stifling reign over the Israeli-Palestinian conflict is evident in the standardization of international humanitarian and human rights law in the UN's frequent commissions. The black hole magnetism of law that pulls all categories of people and conflict through its "event horizon" does not reduce contestation to the one-dimensional pinpoints of its rules and institutions, however. Disobeying the laws of physics, law yields instead a supernova of diverse energies, particles, shockwaves, and turbulence that combine for a time and then fade.

The social complexity of international law comes into view as it is put into play in these investigations, shaping the epistemological and moral frameworks of evaluation and debate. The range of voices and forms of ethical deliberation in which participants assert the (im)morality of specific modes of violence, the innocence or criminality of certain categories of people, the significance of particular experiences, or the protected status of particular places animate international law as a language for naming human worth and social values.

The meanings of law and justice are questioned and asserted throughout commission proceedings, in the testimonials that the investigators hear, and in the arguments about the commissions' activities and results. Although commissions summon a wide spectrum of voices and narratives—from victims' tragic eyewitness accounts and human rights workers' evidence-based legal arguments to forensic experts' and international legal analyses—a shared idea of the relationship between innocence, crime, and what is legitimate punishment appears across them. Repeated throughout the various genres of testimonial and reporting are core premises of international law: that women and children are innocent civilians who should not be harmed, that violence must be regulated and directed, and that violence can be legitimate but only when aimed at particular targets.

Others have pointed to tensions between legal and moral aspirations as they are debated in similarly legalistic proceedings such as people's tribunals, where "'grammars of justice and legitimacy' that emerged between the 'legalist' and 'political'/'politico-ethicist' perspectives" competed.[4] What the interactions within investigative commissions reveal, in contrast, is the harmony of these "grammars." There is, in fact, a convergence of concerns, expectations, and beliefs underlying the assumptions expressed by commission investigators and the Palestinians who appear before them. There is a suffusion of moral discourse into international law as it is practiced through commissions, and this is what helps sustain Palestinians' and others' adherence to its terms and institutions. This discourse is built around common humanitarian values: Palestinians and their liberal investigators share a belief that morality, protection of humanity, and human suffering matter. In the back-and-forth of this discourse, the common moral substrate of international law becomes clear.

As the history of commissions laid out in these pages reveals, the laws and language of humanitarianism and human rights became increasingly prevalent in discussions of the Palestine issue after the UN's establishment. In the end, none of these commissions led to increased protection of civilians or human rights. But each offered a platform from which Palestinians could voice their suffering, their political demands, and assertions of rights, and from which representatives of international legal liberalism could hear them and express sympathy. Each commission was a forum in which representatives of liberal legalism could reassert the significance of humanitarian and human rights principles and express their belief in the rule of law that should protect and uphold them. They functioned to reinforce each other's convictions and keep hope in an international liberal order alive.

Beyond the rules of this sphere of international law (regarding the protection of human rights, the principles of distinction and proportionality), ethical principles were voiced in the testimony and reports that these commissions received. They were also woven throughout the reports that they wrote, and were asserted in the debates and controversies about them. That human suffering matters and should be stopped; that Palestinians are humans who should be treated according to universal human values; and that Palestinians deserve sympathy for their suffering were common themes, echoing a refrain long dominant in Palestinian discourse to the outside world.[5] The violent trouncing of those principles, in the Gaza Strip especially, prompted the outrage and desperation being communicated in Palestinians' testimonials, and the expressions of shock and horror being voiced by the commissioners who witnessed it. These ethical feelings and principled beliefs were deeply held and personally meaningful to those involved.

## Crime and Punishment

In the conversations staged in and around these commissions, there was also a growing discourse of crime and punishment. Its volume increased with mounting assertions that certain acts and forms of violence carried out by Israel should be categorized as war crimes. The idea that violence against innocents (especially children) was a way to prove that a crime had been committed was an assumption that appeared in Palestinian testimony around the events in Jenin and Gaza. The belief that such crimes should be punished became most pronounced in the widespread calls by Palestinians and international human rights organizations for intervention by the International Criminal Court (ICC). As legal scholars have observed, "it has become almost unquestionable common sense that criminal punishment is a legal, political, and pragmatic imperative for addressing human rights violations," an observation borne out in the Goldstone report's references to international criminal law.[6] In Palestine, these calls for criminal punishment of violations became more prevalent after the Goldstone report concluded that Israel (and Hamas) had possibly committed war crimes.

This commission was unique in many ways. The violence that prompted this commission seemed to have crossed a red line. Also distinctive were its public hearings, a first among UN fact-finding missions. This was done, in commission chairman Richard Goldstone's words, "to allow the face of human suffering to be seen and to let the voices of victims be heard."[7]

What was most significant about this commission, however, was the new and growing emphasis on the ICC as a possible international legal tool for ensuring accountability and ending Israeli impunity. With the centrality of the notion of "war crimes" in the Goldstone Mission findings and the focus on ending impunity in its report, this commission marked a turning point in the Israeli-Palestinian conflict and in Palestinians' international legal approaches to it. Although Palestine's membership in the ICC did not go into effect until April 2015, the press towards anti-impunity through international mechanisms had been developing for some years before that. This was a position that Palestinians, their advocates, and international human rights organizations began to take with increasing frequency.

The prioritization of international humanitarian and human rights law as a grounding framework for interpreting the experience of life under occupation remained constant. Commissions also continued to provide venues for mobilizing testimonials of suffering, venues where the power of witnessing was proclaimed to be redemptive. But it was the possibility of seeing individual Israeli perpetrators punished as war criminals that sparked hope. With the public discussion of the ICC generated by the Goldstone report, Palestinian hope in international law was renewed yet again. The ICC has become the latest answer to the common Palestinian appeal, "Where is the world?" Many believe it to be the one international institution that might enable the punishment of crimes and fulfill the moral demand for justice in Palestine.[8]

## The UN Commission That Wasn't:
## "Massacre" and War Crimes in Jenin

The Israeli attacks on Gaza in 2008–2009 were not the first time that the destruction of civilian infrastructure and killing of noncombatants prompted such pleas. As recalled in a report by the Palestinian refugee rights center, Badil: "The UN Commission on Human Rights, for example, has considered Israel's continued grave breaches of the 1949 Fourth Geneva Convention as rising to the level of war crimes since 1972 and affirmed this view during a Special Session of the Commission in October 2000."[9] The language of crime and punishment, of justice and humanity, resound every time there is a newly intensified bout of violence in Palestine. As the second intifada continued, the categories of massacre, war crimes, and even genocide emerged as a means for Palestinians to express their outrage and to request help from the outside world.[10]

The concept of "war crime" evokes the framework of international law, but in its usage by nonexperts and legal personages alike, it is infused with moral opprobrium and local history. The hegemonic language of international law, with its standardized rules and definitions, its references to resolutions and agreements, can never fully silence the nationalist, religious, and ethical-humanist values by which people evaluate and debate their conditions of life and death. This was especially noticeable in what happened in spring 2002 around Israel's incursion into the West Bank town of Jenin.

"The Battle of Jenin" took place less than a year after the Mitchell report was issued. This is how Palestinians came to refer to Israel's pummeling of that northern West Bank town. It left from 10 percent to a quarter of the Jenin refugee camp largely destroyed. Human rights organizations called for an investigation of the events, demanding that "sufficient numbers of criminal justice" be part of it.[11] The UN secretary-general sought to establish a fact-finding mission and appointed former Finnish President Martti Ahtisaari; former UN High Commissioner for Refugees Sadako Ogata; and former head of the International Committee of the Red Cross Cornelio Sommaruga to undertake the task. The UN Security Council adopted Resolution 1405 on April 19, 2002, that welcomed the "initiative of the Secretary-General to develop accurate information regarding recent events in the Jenin refugee camp through a fact-finding team."[12] Because of Israeli noncooperation, however, the investigators never carried out their mission. After Israeli stalling and objections, the secretary-general disbanded the fact-finding mission on May 1, 2002.[13]

By this time, Amnesty International delegates in Jenin had "found credible evidence of serious breaches of human rights and humanitarian law."[14]

Amnesty's director excoriated the "gratuitous, wanton, unnecessary destruction" wrought by the Israeli forces.[15] A Human Rights Watch team of three researchers also spent seven days in Jenin and found that "Israeli forces committed serious violations of international humanitarian law, some amounting prima facie to war crimes."[16] That organization had pressed the UN "for an impartial investigation, one that is empowered with prosecutorial powers," a possibility that Israeli government lawyers feared.[17] The lawyers advised the Israeli government not to cooperate with the UN investigation "until it was given assurances that those who testify will not be prosecutable."[18] It is possible that they received no such assurances, and in any case, Israeli cooperation was withheld.

Among the prosecutable crimes discovered by these human rights groups were the Israeli army's denial of humanitarian actors' access to the refugee camp, the use of Palestinians as human shields, extrajudicial executions, and disproportionate property destruction. Israeli bulldozers, tanks, and Apache helicopters were some of the army's tools that left at least fifty-two Palestinians (and as many as sixty-six) dead. Twenty-two Israeli soldiers were also killed during the ten-day Israeli incursion into Jenin in early April.[19] The devastation of lives and infrastructure was extensive. The Israeli army's "Operation Defensive Shield"—what Palestinians referred to as "al-ijteah al-kbir" (the big invasion)—sparked fears among Palestinians that the Israelis were going to fully and permanently reoccupy the West Bank. The destructiveness of this "operation" and Israel's blockage of international journalists, humanitarian aid workers, and medics led many to believe that a massacre had taken place.[20] The fact that the Israeli army was acting without much international observation may have motivated the UN's attempt at an investigation.

There was much discussion, among people in the West Bank and in the Western and Palestinian media, as to whether the term "massacre" was appropriate or helpful in describing the Jenin events. Although the term has no definition in international humanitarian law, it does have a meaning for Palestinians and in their history, most forcefully crystallized after the 1982 slaughter of hundreds, or thousands, of Palestinian refugees and others residing in the Sabra neighborhood and adjacent Shatila refugee camp in Lebanon.[21] The Christian Phalange militia murdered hundreds and possibly thousands of people under the flare lights of the Israeli army and with their knowledge. An Israeli governmental inquiry, the Kahan Commission, deemed Israeli leaders to be "indirectly responsible" for the killings. It determined that then–defense minister Ariel Sharon bore "personal responsibility" for failing to prevent the killings.[22] He was known throughout the Arab world as "the butcher of Beirut" for his overseeing of the 1982 Israeli invasion of Lebanon.[23] By the time Sharon became prime minister in 2001 during the second intifada, his history, including his role in the 1982 massacre, was well known in Palestine. He was already regarded as a war criminal.[24] In March 2002 Sharon gave the green light for "Operation Defensive Shield" that brought the army incursion into Jenin. He told his inner Cabinet: "The Palestinians must be hit, and it must be very painful. . . . We must cause them losses, victims, so that they feel a heavy price."[25] Sharon's reputation and the unprecedented scale of the Israeli attacks in Jenin (at least since the second intifada began) are part of what sparked fears that a particularly deadly attack had taken place. The uncertainty about what really happened in Jenin led to rumors that Israeli bulldozers deposited the bodies of Palestinian dead in unidentified locations or dumped them into sewers.[26] When human rights organizations reported on the killing of women, children, disabled people, and the elderly, one commentator in the Arabic press labeled Sharon the Herod of today, "one of the devils of his time."[27]

Despite Israel's serial refusal to engage with the international fact-finding regime of the UN, a range of organizations and individuals did collect facts through an array of methods and with a variety of purposes.[28] The moral tone is clear in their explorations of the intentions of those who were involved in military activities. The Israeli human rights organization, B'Tselem, collected testimony from Israeli soldiers and Palestinians who recounted the process of home demolition. They told of Israeli soldiers operating bulldozers to tear down Palestinian houses, sometimes knowingly atop people left inside.[29] Among the soldiers they interviewed, some delighted in the destruction and thought the Palestinians deserved all that and more, while others believed their actions were excessive. B'Tselem's report is replete with accounts of people killed without warning, shot while trying to obtain the basic necessities of everyday life—food, water, cigarettes. The report makes repeated reference to the innocent civilians who were killed in "Operation Defensive Shield."

As part of my doctoral research, I visited the devastated camp, too, and talked with residents there and in the town of Jenin. Among other sights, I was shown the location where Jamal Fayid, a paralyzed and mentally disabled Palestinian man, was killed when Israeli bulldozers demolished his house with him in it.[30] The moral outrageousness of such a death was the obvious point of the visit. For those showing it to me, the manner of Fayid's death encapsulated the immorality of Israel's violence.

It was a postapocalyptic scene that I toured, the people full of stories and the landscape full of stories-high piles of rubble from destroyed houses. Hundreds of buildings, including multifamily dwellings, were completely demolished or partially destroyed.[31] Exposed wiring and inner supports jutted out of the huge mounds of white rubble. Some four thousand to five thousand people had been made homeless.[32] As I passed through the town, I noticed groups of men sitting among the wreckage talking, seated around little fires, giving the dusk a surreal glow. A woman from the town of Jenin who accompanied me on this tour repeated multiple times, "Look! Look!" pointing out yet another hill of debris, apparently astonished by the scale of destruction in her neighborhood.

A couple of months later, during another visit to Jenin, I was instructed to look some more, to bear witness and convey these stories of pain, violence, chaos, and the incomprehensible immorality of the Israelis who caused it. A woman from the refugee camp who survived the April 2002 invasion bid me witness the results of that attack, showing me the scars on her legs from wounds sustained when a missile hit her house three months previous. She was offering visual proof of her attackers' low moral standing. She was also giving proof of her own humanity. We sat alone in an undamaged room of her house. As she rolled up the leg of her trousers, she exclaimed:

> I swear that while I was sleeping a rocket hit the house, and all the glass of the window was broken and fell over the bed! I will show you my leg that was injured by a piece of glass during that event, and I will show it to all Arabs. I didn't see it [the glass] at that time, and I didn't care at that moment because we were very afraid of the rockets that were falling over our heads. I felt pain in my leg, and when I looked at it later on, I found the cut and found that it was bleeding. But because of the heavy shelling, we

were very afraid, and I didn't give much attention to it. Could you imagine the feeling while the building was falling over our heads? It is not human behavior. We are human beings, and we aren't animals or cows to be dealt with in this way. The people around me saw the blood, and when they asked me about it, I discovered that I was injured, and it still hurts me until today, though it happened three months and twelve days ago. I still cannot remember what injured me exactly, and I still wonder what Sharon wants from us.[33]

As much as it was a condemnation of Israel's excessive violence, it was also a remonstration of the Arab nations: "I will show it to all Arabs." She, a woman, sustained these injuries. Her scars were a shocking physical sign and proof of what should be their shame for doing so little to protect their Palestinian brethren.

Palestinians collected their own stories of Jenin's destruction and resistance too. Across these discussions and representations, the meaning and significance of what is a war crime, what is a crime against morality, and ideas about what actions transgress human decency blend together. Everyone had ideas of what counted as relevant evidence and what its witnessing and recording could achieve. For Ramzy Baroud, the editor of a volume of essays titled *Searching Jenin*, the goal in collecting eyewitness testimonies of those who lived through the Israeli invasion of the camp was to "reveal the victims as they were and are—innocent, angry, grieving, proud, spontaneous . . . to uncover the lives and emotion behind the casualty figures." Through such grief-stricken testimonial, the accounts of Palestinian losses are verified, and the world is reminded "that the Palestinian voice has not been silenced and continues to long for freedom."[34] The stoicism of the refugee camp's residents, and especially the fierce resistance put up by the Palestinian fighters, gave Jenin camp and this episode in its history almost immediate mythic status. Throughout the occupied territories, Palestinians and others produced music cassettes and poetry honoring "Jeningrad" and "The Battle of Jenin." Annual commemorations took place in the camp to ensure that future generations would know what happened, and to reinforce the value of social and national unity that some believed was the most important lesson of the events.[35] Unlike today's humanitarian reports, in which resistance and persistence are neither recordable nor laudable qualities, Palestinians' recording of both the victimhood and suffering as well as the bravery and steadfastness were means of attesting to Palestinian humanity, their political subjectivity, their resistance, and their moral ascendancy.

Palestinian artists and directors produced films and collected testimonials, and some residents of the camp wrote their own accounts.[36] The documentary *Jenin, Jenin*, by Mohammed Bakri, preeminent Palestinian actor and citizen of Israel, was his response to being in a situation in which "reality impels you, and your human dignity obliges you, to respond."[37] For Bakri, like many others who have felt compelled to record and represent Palestinian suffering, seeing, hearing, and bearing witness are in and of themselves an enactment of a universal humanity. The film shows Bakri's interview with a resident who interprets the delay of the UN investigative commission: "In order to apply a simple resolution, which consists in bringing international observers, the whole world must beg Israel for its consent. . . . This is terrorism. Israel is not the terrorist, the whole world is the terrorist." In the view of this man, the "whole world" that is subservient to the occupying power, that seeks permission merely to look on as observers, bears collective guilt. It was a position that Palestinian human rights organization Al-Mezan echoed: "This situation is similar to giving a criminal the right to choose the judge."[38]

Academics also took part. They came to record testimonies, to document Palestinians' agency and resistance, and to analyze and critique the UN reconstruction of the camp.[39] Violence against women and children was held out as indubitable proof of Israel's crimes. Palestinian anthropologist Linda Tabar recorded one young mother's reaction to the cancellation of the UN fact-finding mission: "Tell them that I pulled my children out from under the rubble. Tell them that! This is not a crime?"[40] In her command, "tell them," the mother invoked the communicative function of humanitarian witnessing. The poignancy of her experience, a woman and her children subject to this horror, was assumed to be evidence enough of criminality.

From my months spent volunteering at a human rights NGO during this period, I knew these were felt to be urgent times. The sense of danger was pervasive. Even if people learned to adapt to the relentless violence, it was continually shocking. A member of the NGO also talked with me about the special evidentiary weight of another child who survived the attack on the camp. Affect, experience, and visual proof combined in her understanding of what made evidence effective. Along with statistics and facts about death and the extent of the destruction, what was needed to "reveal the Israeli crimes," she said, were "eyewitness accounts of what has happened—the Israeli crimes that have occurred on the ground." She described the NGO's rationale in bringing a girl to give testimony to the UN in Geneva: "First of all, she saw the facts. . . . The crime by itself, and the pictures that came out of what happened in Jenin, nobody could possibly see them without getting goosebumps. Nobody could see them without becoming sad. . . . You send numbers and fact about these crimes, and then a child comes along, eleven years old. She has seen crimes, lived through crimes. Her father was killed. She saw her father killed before her eyes. And she says, 'I saw these crimes with my eyes.' This gives a kind of credibility." The language of criminality was simultaneously an index of that sense of outrage, a demand for action, and an assertion of moral evaluation in legal language.

## Morality, Solidarity, and Hopeful Truth: The 2006 Investigation in Beit Hanoun

The Israeli leaders who oversaw the violence in Jenin and the rest of the occupied Palestinian territory suffered no legal repercussions for those deeds. The second intifada continued until 2005, after which the level of violence ebbed somewhat. Israel withdrew its military and settlers from the Gaza Strip in 2006, but it maintained effective control across the occupied territory, and its military occupation and the settlement project continued unabated.[41]

The next commission to investigate Palestine was the high-level fact-finding mission to Beit Hanoun, established after Israeli shelling of that Gaza town in November 2006. This shelling, in which nineteen civilians were killed and fifty-five wounded, occurred in the context of Israel's blockade of Gaza, imposed after the success of Hamas in the January 2006 Palestinian elections.[42] After Israel thwarted the Beit Hanoun mission's first three attempts to access Gaza via Israel, the two investigators, legal scholar Christine Chinkin and South African Archbishop Desmond Tutu, decided to travel to Gaza through Egypt.[43]

Throughout this commission's report, the authors underlined Palestinians' suffering and victimhood as an issue of moral and not just legal concern.[44]

With religious references, the report compares the mission to acts of Old Testament characters, thereby moralizing their work by placing it in the category of solidarity "witnessing:"

> The mission wishes to underline the importance of its travelling to Beit Hanoun to witness first-hand the situation of victims and survivors of the shelling, in particular to comprehend the deep distress of the victims of the shelling and of the population generated by the ongoing blockade. This depth of human suffering is only partially conveyed through the third-party reports on the situation. The mission felt it had to go to Gaza, even if reluctantly through Egypt, to express through its presence the solidarity of the international community with the suffering people, very much like the prophet Ezekiel sitting dumbfounded with his compatriots in their exile in Babylon, or the friends of Job in his suffering.[45]

Practicing an assemblage of fact finding and witnessing, these commissioners produced what anthropologist Peter Redfield has called "motivated truth" that emerges from an "overt combination of reason and sentiment . . . [and] a modified relationship with traditions of objectivity and neutrality whereby truth might be proclaimed in open association with a point of view."[46] An additional dimension of this motivated truth is the hope entwined within it, a hope—endemic to the humanitarian scene—that such sympathetic truths are an effective good in and of themselves. The Beit Hanoun report interspersed international legal analysis with personalized statements directed to and about the Palestinian victims of this shelling. It raised the possibility that the siege of Gaza and other Israeli actions there may constitute a war crime and crimes against humanity. And it placed this legal analysis in a context of quotes from witnesses and victim testimony that conveyed something of the emotional experience of those who lived through the attacks. The mission's expressions of sympathy and solidarity, and their characterizations of Israel's investigations into its army's behavior as being inadequate "from both legal and moral points of view" gave this report a distinctive tone.[47] It set aside the principles of neutrality and impartiality that are typical of the legal register in favor of a language of moral suasion. Its authors expressed a belief that bearing witness is both an end in itself and an act that can prompt some response. Despite the investigators being told "that survivors 'want justice, not sympathy,'" the mission report could provide only the latter. With admiration for their courage, the commission report offered Palestinians a placeholder for justice in the horizon of hope held out in the "eventually" time.[48]

Both of this mission's members expressed a faith in the future benefits of what they were doing. Confirming the importance that this mission placed on testifying, Christine Chinkin wrote in an essay reflecting on her fact-finding experiences in Beit Hanoun, "there is an importance in bearing witness." She affirmed its "heightened value where the person to whom [witnesses] are speaking has the moral authority and international standing associated with truth telling of Archbishop Tutu."[49] Together, Tutu and Chinkin professed their faith in this nebulous process during a press conference after their mission. "We are people of hope," Tutu explained. "You go on making your appeal, in the expectation that one day the one to whom you are appealing with [sic] hear, and show that we will not give up hope." Chinkin agreed: "If enough voices of integrity keep saying these messages, as Archbishop said, surely they will be heard eventually."[50] If the values and principles stop being voiced, "then it does vanish." In a discussion with me many years after her involvement with these commissions, Chinkin confirmed her continued belief in the importance of bearing witness: "Continued denouncing of human rights violations will be heard. You have to still believe it. You just do have to hope."[51]

There was little public discussion of the Beit Hanoun report. English and Arabic language press barely covered it. When Chinkin was asked to take part in the Goldstone fact-finding commission in 2009 that was established in the wake of another upsurge in violence in the Gaza Strip, she took it as a chance to pursue this "unfinished business." The hope that their recommendations "would be taken seriously" was part of her motivation to continue.[52]

## Goldstone's Ethical Listening

In the two years between Chinkin's first and second missions, Israel placed the Gaza Strip under a stifling blockade, which is still in place. As Israeli human rights NGO B'Tselem reported, the isolation of the Gaza Strip from the rest of the world had been "part of a longstanding Israeli policy" since the 1990s. Restrictions on the movement of people and goods in and out of the

Gaza Strip increased in the years after the outbreak of the second intifada. When Hamas won the elections and took control over the Gaza Strip in the summer of 2007, Israel installed a full blockade, with the cooperation of Egypt, "turning almost two million people into prisoners inside the Gaza Strip."[53]

The assault on the Gaza Strip (what Israel dubbed "Operation Cast Lead") began on December 27, 2008, and lasted through January 18, 2009. Israeli forces began with a week of airstrikes, followed by ground and air incursions by Apache helicopters and F-16 fighter jets. The shelling of family homes, use of white phosphorous, and bulldozing of houses and other buildings resulted in the loss of dozens of Palestinian lives every day. In three weeks, approximately 1,400 Palestinians were killed, including approximately 300 children; another 5,300 were injured, the vast majority civilians. Approximately 2,400 Palestinian houses were completely or largely destroyed, including public civilian facilities, ministries, municipal buildings, the Palestinian Legislative Council building, and tens of schools, factories, mosques, and civilian police stations.[54]

In the face of this destruction, there were calls for a commission, seen in this case as in many others as a first step toward accountability. BADIL, a refugee rights NGO based in Bethlehem, urged that the UN "dispatch an urgent high-level fact-finding mission to Gaza to investigate the countless gross violations of human rights and humanitarian law committed by Israel, which amount to war crimes and crimes against humanity, and to ensure that those responsible are held to account."[55] Eventually, after some haggling about its terms of reference, this UN mission, a team of four that included two jurists, a legal scholar, and a military expert, did go to the Gaza Strip to investigate the violence within the framework of "international law, the Charter of the United Nations, international humanitarian law, international human rights law and international criminal law."[56] Headed by Richard Goldstone, who is a former South African constitutional court judge and former chief prosecutor of the United Nations International Criminal Tribunals for Rwanda and the former Yugoslavia, the international legal and military experts on this team determined that Israel's attacks on Gaza were "directed, at least in part, at . . . the people of Gaza as a whole. It wasn't just self-defense: Israeli forces directly targeted civilians and civilian infrastructure during its 22-day offensive." In finding that the Israeli violence was disproportionate and targeted civilians, it raised the possibility of war crimes and crimes against humanity having taken place.[57] It also indicated that Hamas rocket attacks against Israeli civilians could be war crimes. It was not the first UN report to document Israeli war crimes and refer to them as such, but it was the first one to do so that was written by a team led by a self-declared Jewish supporter of the state of Israel. International legal scholar Richard Falk declared the confirmation of Israeli criminality by the Goldstone report "a major victory for the Palestinians in the legitimacy war."[58] In the view of one Palestinian commentator, that a renowned Jew wrote this report would be enough to put an end to any Israeli claims to "being a moral and utopian state."[59]

While voices of civil society and the human rights system seized on the language of accountability that was forefronted in the Goldstone report, focusing on the ICC as a possible way forward for the Palestinian cause, Palestinians who presented their case to the commissioners in Gaza had more varied and complex motivations, hopes, and expectations. Across the range of people who spoke, from human rights workers to victims who lost their family members, each took the chance to assert a moral interpretation of international law.

They also recognized the commission as an effort to alleviate what political philosopher Jill Stauffer has called "ethical loneliness." Ethical loneliness, she writes,

> is a condition undergone by persons who have been unjustly treated and dehumanized by human beings and political structures, who emerge from that injustice only to find that the surrounding world will not listen to or cannot properly hear their testimony—their claims about what they suffered and about what is now owed them—on their own terms.[60]

Richard Goldstone explained the public hearings of the commission as an effort at what I call "ethical listening." Whereas the Mitchell Committee engaged in a practice of "democratic listening," in which investigators emphasized an openness to listening to "all sides," which led to their balanced compassion, the intentions and affect of the Goldstone Mission were different. While similarly stressing their desire to hear from everyone, the UN commissioners—and Goldstone especially—accentuated the cathartic, humanizing, and communicative dimensions of hearing witness testimony. These commissioners constituted themselves as a channel opening the possibility of worldly sympathy with the Palestinians' suffering.

The hearings were an effort to "show the faces and broadcast the voices of the victims," a means to redress the international legal process that can dehumanize the victims who are "represented not by real people, by statistics, by numbers."[61] Many Palestinians appearing before the Gaza commissions expressed their gratitude at being given this chance to describe their experiences, at just being heard. Christine Chinkin also believed that there was an importance in bearing witness as a means to redress what she saw as law's tendency "to silence people's voices." International criminal law and trials focus so much on the perpetrators, she said, that "you don't hear the voices of the people against whom crimes have been committed."[62] This was the humanitarian ethos in action, in which legal professionals sought to humanize Palestinians as suffering victims, and in so doing recenter the lives that the legal bureaucracy was meant to protect.

For Chinkin, work on these commissions in the Gaza Strip was a chance to see and enact human rights in practice, beyond the limited confines of academia. An expert on public international law and international criminal law, she is renowned in the field of legal scholarship for her work on feminist international law, and she has been an important part of what she described as an "academic and activist movement that brought women onto the international agenda."[63] She has sought to marry international legal theory with practice and has brought her academic expertise on human rights into the public domain in many venues, including as a participant in the World Tribunal for Iraq.[64]

Bearing witness in this form was a way for Chinkin to raise awareness of what military operations "mean to people on the ground," to keep the situation in the Gaza Strip and human rights violations "on the agenda."[65] In the philosopher's formulation, this refusal to abandon the Palestinians, the refusal to let their situation recede from wider public consciousness, would be a tonic to ethical loneliness, which Stauffer describes further as "the experience of having been abandoned by humanity compounded by the experience of not being heard. . . . Being abandoned by those who have the power to help produces a loneliness more profound than simple isolation."[66] Although the commissioners may have helped alleviate Palestinians' sense of abandonment, they and their report did not end up alleviating the conditions on the ground that reproduce Israeli violations of their human rights.

The extent of the Gaza violence captured worldwide attention, prompting a variety of attempts to hear or stifle Palestinian voices. In a letter that sixteen preeminent international legal scholars and practitioners sent to UN Secretary-General Ban Ki-moon, they said they were "shocked to the core" by events in the Gaza Strip.[67] Describing themselves as "individuals with direct experience of international justice and reconciliation of conflict," they called for "an international investigation of gross violations of the laws of war."[68] The letter gained some attention in the Palestinian press, which attended to Western reactions to the Gaza events.[69] The scale of the destruction and the alarming way that Israel killed whole families and people praying in a mosque, among other civilians, provoked in many an "acute sense of frustration and outrage about the Israeli attacks . . . prevalent around the world."[70]

The Goldstone report's documentation of these and other acts and their categorization as possible war crimes is part of what raised the profile of this report for Palestinians especially. Palestinian human rights activists and others believed this report to be a "turning point," as commission member Colonel Desmond Travers also referred to it.[71] The Palestinian Committee for Human Rights, based in Gaza, stated that the report "represented an important landmark in the fight for human rights and the rule of international law in the occupied Palestinian territory, primarily as a result of its specific accountability-focused recommendations."[72] As a memorandum prepared by the Negotiations Support Unit for the Palestinian Authority noted, "the Mission followed investigative methodology similar to what an international criminal prosecutor would follow," which gave its findings additional credibility.[73] Travers confirmed that "the core message of the report is that there has to be an end to impunity to commit war crimes."[74]

Many held out hope that this investigation's findings might lead to a process that would hold Israel accountable for violations of international law at the ICC. Members of prominent human rights NGOs, commentators in Palestine and throughout the Arab region, political independents, Islamists, and secular people all expressed high expectations. An editorialist in the

Hamas journal *Filastin al-Muslima* was buoyed by the report, which was "a victory for the Palestinian people."[75] Another article in that same publication quoted a "UN expert" as saying that "the Goldstone report is the strongest in the history of the UN, confirming that the following six months would witness a change in reality."[76] As soon as the UN announced the Gaza fact-finding mission, Palestinian commentators began discussing the possibility of the ICC as an avenue of redress.[77] Egyptian journalist and longtime commentator on Arab affairs Mohammad Hasanein Haikal deemed the Goldstone Mission "effective" simply by virtue of the "wide discussion" it would open "at the Security council, at the General Assembly and the ICC."[78] And, indeed, wide discussion did ensue. This included a profusion of legal debate about the jurisdiction of the ICC and whether Palestine was a state that could bring a case under the Rome Statute (the treaty that established the ICC and entered into force in 2002).[79] In the midst of debates over the legal particulars, many continued to announce that this report heralded a shift in the paradigm of the conflict and how it was managed.

By the time of the Goldstone mission visit, the Gaza Strip had been under a state of siege for more than two years. The blockade that Israel imposed with the help of the United States, the European Union, and Egypt after Hamas was voted in to head the Palestinian Authority confined Gaza residents and cordoned them off from people and goods, isolating them within a small strip of land that had already been subject to decades of "de-development."[80] This left Gazans in a state of "alienation," the founder of the Gaza Community Mental Health Program observed. In his testimony before the commissioners, Iyyad Sarraj told them that the "very fact of public hearings gives Palestinians a feeling that in this world there are people concerned with justice and that we are not left alone."[81] Since the UN was established, its fact-finders have heard Palestinians communicate their satisfaction and gratitude for their mere presence, which offered a kind of validation of the Palestinians' experiences and narratives. But it was more universal than that too. Sarraj extolled the truth telling of the witnesses and the investigators as itself a valuable act. "This good or sane society needs certain basic values in order to be described as such. These values relate to saying the truth. Saying the truth is a very important role. . . . I believe this is also your role when you speak up before the world in order to show the Israeli crimes perpetrated against the Palestinian people, hoping to achieve the administration of justice."[82] Many who gave testimony drew a straight line between witnessing, truth telling, a hearing by "the world," and justice. Rashad Hamada, co-owner of the only functioning flour mill in the Gaza Strip that was destroyed by Israeli bombs, appeared before the commission to "appeal to the world and the Mission and the United Nations." He told them he was "hopeful that this will be the last fact-finding mission to come to our country to investigate crimes."[83]

Just as some lawyers believed the Mitchell Committee offered a means to convey the Palestinian experience of political injustice and explain how international law supported their demands, so too did many of those providing testimony in the Gaza Strip see the Goldstone mission as a way to tell their story to the world. One witness, Motee' al-Silawi, began his testimonial by thanking the fact-finding mission, "which allows us this opportunity to make the world hear our voice, to inform the world of our tragedy in the Gaza Strip." As earlier chapters have shown, "the world" has long been an addressee of Palestinian entreaties. Another witness exclaimed: "We call on the world, we call on the United Nations and we call on all those responsible in this area, in this region to find a solution to this conflict. Enough war, enough bloodshed."[84]

But many wanted more than a chance to make a statement. They wanted justice in the form of punishment. Hussein al-Deeb, from the Jabalya refugee camp, decried the effects of Israel's attacks in which he lost eleven family members (including eight women and girls):

> The most precious people you have in the world you lose within seconds and for no reason. This is why we come here today to speak before you. Why? Why did I lose my family? Why? What's the reason? I don't know what else I can add, but the shock is tremendous. . . . What we hope is that you will . . . portray the picture as you have seen it, and we hope that the criminal will be held accountable for his crimes.[85]

Palestinians who gave testimony came with clear purposes, even if the articulation of their hopes for redress was knotted with grief and outrage.

An elderly man, Mousa al-Silawi, recounted what had happened when the al-Maqadma Mosque was bombed, killing his son and fourteen others and injuring another forty people.[86] In his testimony he named the ethical principles and structures that should have been guiding events but were absent. "Where are the Arab countries? Where is Islam? Where is religion? Where is honour? And then I have to say: where is law? Where is the state? Where is justice?" To confirm the outrageousness of what happened, he announced that in all his ninety-one years "we have never seen anything of this sort." He called on God and the commissioners to "punish all the Arabs that have allowed this to happen, the governors, and the rulers who have let us down." Unable to move "the world" that should be responding to these pleas, that should be acting according to shared values, he invoked realms of greater power: "Where is rule? Where is justice? Where is Islam? Where is the government? Where is the whole world? What can I say?" Like many who appeared before them, he concluded his comments with words of appreciation to the commissioners.[87]

As if fearing that the scale of the calamity he saw would be too outrageous to be believed, in his testimony Motee' al-Silawi described the scene at the mosque with concrete and visceral detail:

> We saw uh, legs, uh, arms, blood. I swear to you, I swear to you that I saw this with my own eye. There was no more electricity and screaming was very loud. People were running away. . . . At that moment I cannot describe to you what I felt. It was frightful. . . . I was leading my father out. How can I describe to you? I—with my own foot I stepped on the head of a small child. Where is the world? Where is international law? Is this what the Palestinian people deserve, our children screaming?

Again the world is summoned as audience and arbiter:

> I tell the world, the world listening to me now: where is the law of international protection? Where are the Geneva Conventions on the protection of civilians in time of war? Where is democracy? Where is the right to worship that the European countries call for? Where is international law? A dog could die. A dog would die in one of the European countries or in Israel and there is upheaval because of the dog, but we see sheikhs dying, their body parts scattered around in a place of worship, and nobody looks at them. Where is justice? Where is justice? Where are human rights? . . .

And we hear about international law, about human rights, about the Geneva Conventions—where is all of that? . . . I tell the world, what crime did the children commit? . . . We call on behalf of all the victims we call from here, we call for our moral rights, our material and moral rights.[88]

In these narratives, the speakers' basic sense of justice and understanding of what is inhumane behavior presents international humanitarian legal principles of distinction and proportionality without naming them as such. Several of the Gazans who survived the attacks asked why the Israeli army shot at them, why they killed their children. Each recounted events in which soldiers targeted them deliberately, firing at children, women, people carrying white flags, people the Israeli soldiers had told to gather inside a house. They bespeak a common notion of crime and innocence based in a presumption that punishment must be legitimate and have legal and moral bases. Without naming them as such, they invoked the founding premises of international law: that civilians should be spared in fighting, and violence can and should be regulated.

Articulating clear ideas of who does and does not deserve punishment, these testimonials echo "a fundamental dictate" of the laws of war that prohibit "superfluous injury and unnecessary suffering."[89] Khaled 'Abed Rabbo, whose two daughters, ages two and seven years, were killed while his mother was carrying a white flag outside their house, explained:

This was execution. This was utter execution and I'm asking the world what crime did my children commit? What danger did they pose for the Israeli army? I myself was there. Why didn't they fire at me? Why didn't they kill me and not let me see my children die in front of my eyes? My children, until now, I cannot get myself to realize there I was looking at them while they were dying. . . . What crime did I commit? I have always been a peace loving person. . . . The Israeli army knows that I've never been a terrorist. I sent letters, more than 500, to different parts and I was asking why did it happen to me, why did they come to my house, kill my children without having committed any crime. What did I do? There was no war. It was cold-blooded murder of children. That was not just accidental. No, the soldier even chuckled, like I said. I know that Israel has a very sophisticated technology and that every operation it carries out is actually filmed and I'm asking Israel please broadcast the film of the killing of my children. Did you see my children carrying any rockets?[90]

Commissions arrive in Palestine at the very moment when the gap between justice and violent reality appears most dramatically wide and is experienced by many as deadly and existential. As anthropologists Sandra Brunnegger and Karen Ann Faulk have found in their study of Latin America, "definitions of 'justice' often emerge from the interplay between holistic visions of rightful redress and the practical limitations of available channels for implementing resolutions."[91] When *in*justice is (assumed to be) so obvious in the super-violent killing of children and old people who have committed no crime, commissions appear as a channel to rectify what is off-kilter. Commission members are representatives of the UN, an organization that in turn is seen as somehow embodying a virtuous, caring manifestation of "the world" that could end injustice and suffering. Even in the desperate questioning of their whereabouts—"where is all of that?" as Motee' al-Silawi asked—in the serial invocation of moral rights and international law, justice and human rights morality is merged with the law. Shared among testimonial givers and hearers is an assertion of the assumed existence of morality and law. Commissions promote this faith.

In continuing his appeal, the witness moved from the universality of international law to the universal principles of the world's religions and back again:

All religions respect people and respect places of worship, be it a church, a mosque or any place of worship. Any people respects that. Where are our rights? We need to exercise our rights, regardless of the means. . . . I reiterate: these are war crimes, perpetrated by the Israelis against unarmed people, civilians in the middle of a place of worship. These must be accountable, and before international tribunals, before the whole world we must declare these are war crimes, perpetrated against civilians, against innocent—what did our children do? What is their crime? What's the crime of our elderly, of our people, of our men, of our children? And now the children, they don't want to go to the mosque because they're afraid of being hit by a missile. We have to respect international law. And we say that in this world there is still an international law. If we do not exercise our right as the families of victims, then there is no international law. Where is the international law? Where are the Geneva Conventions?[92]

Al-Silawi identifies a norm that is at the heart of liberal notions of law: that the rule of law must be applied equally to and for all. If there is no protection for civilians or justice for victims, law is meaningless. In her reading of this witness statement, Roseanne Kennedy cites Laleh Khalili to argue that this "appeal to the international community in the language of dignity, suffering, and human rights indicates 'the profound influence of global politics on the production and reproduction of local memories. . . .'" Kennedy goes further to assert that international humanitarian law "provides [al-Silawi] with a political subjectivity, and human rights discourse provides the moral justification to make claims."[93] Rather than demonstrating a top-down flow of principles and subjectivities, however, al-Silawi's testimony reveals a convergence of values, a set of already shared standards and ideals.

A similar avowal of human, legal, and professional equality appeared in the testimony of Miriam Zakoot, the director general of the Culture and Free Thought Association. She reminded the commissioners of a string of international conventions, naming the Convention on the Elimination of All Forms of Discrimination against Women (CEDAW), the Nairobi and Beijing conventions, and the United Nations Security Council Resolution 1325 on Women, Peace and Security.[94]

> I'm aware of all those resolutions and conventions that were made to provide protection for civilians in time of war, mainly women. So are we as Palestinian women? Are we considered to be human? Where is that Resolution 1325 that has not been implemented? It was targeted at providing protection to civilians in times of war.[95]

Similar to the view of many discussants of the Special Committee's reports at the UNGA, Zakoot pointed out that Israel's repeated violation of UN Security Council resolutions, and the fact that it commits massacres and "considers itself above the law," calls the system into question. Arguing that "there is no point in adopting resolutions without implementing them," Zakoot approaches the commissioners as UN representatives, there to answer for the lack of implementation of these conventions. She goes on to explain the "crisis of confidence" between Palestinian women and the international community. Faith in the UN system cannot be restored, she told them, until the Security Council resolutions that are supposed to ensure protection for women and children are implemented.[96] This mutual conviction, which holds that international law is a realm that could and should protect humanity, civilization, and morality, is part of what maintains people's faith in international legal institutions and actors.

## Conclusion

While Palestinian human rights organizations galvanized their reporting and rhetorical resources in preparation for the mission's arrival in Gaza, there was evidence of less enthusiasm among the general population, and the hearings were broadcast on Palestinian television only briefly. Palestine's repeated witnessing of ineffective investigations had left Gaza residents cold. "Every time there is a war, they send a commission," a Gaza City moneychanger told one reporter. He said in tones of exasperation similar to those of Palestinians boycotting the Peel Commission in 1936, "We've seen so many inquiries come and go. No one cares anymore because nothing happens."[97] But once the hearings were over, the clear conclusions recorded in the Goldstone report led some to believe that Israel's impunity could be challenged. Although many recognized that Israel had dodged any demands for accountability in the past by conducting its own investigations that exonerated Israeli perpetrators, the Goldstone report, and Goldstone's personal credibility as a jurist and a person of the Jewish faith with Zionist attachments, made this time seem different. The conclusion that there was evidence that Israel and Hamas may have committed war crimes indicated that Israel might no longer be "a state above international law," and made the report, which one op-ed writer described as "an unprecedented condemnation document against Israel," seem like a watershed.[98] Although with different reasons and reactions, staunch Israeli supporters like Alan Dershowitz and Palestinian human rights workers shared this sentiment, expressing a belief that the Goldstone report was important in a way that previous human rights investigations had not been.[99]

Not all Palestinians lauded the report. Hamas leader Isma'el Radwan, for one, said the report was unbalanced and unjust. But the nature of his critiques reveals the shared ground of anti-impunity ideology beneath the report's authors and their appraisers. Radwan decried the report for lacking "courage" and "frankness" because it did not demand that those in charge of the Israeli military occupation be tried before "international war crimes tribunals for its atrocities and crimes against our Palestinian people."[100] The international legal and anti-impunity framework was not in question. Hamas representatives have repeatedly spoken in favor of engaging with the ICC. Even among those who recognize the politicized nature of the UN, the ICC stands out as a new opportunity. An analyst affiliated with Hamas who runs a Gaza think tank has called for efforts to ensure that the ICC remain neutral, uninfluenced by the balance of power. This was conceivable, he thought, because unlike the UN that has a bad reputation as an international institution due to the perceived US domination over it, the ICC was "staffed with accountable justices." As such, prosecution of Israeli war criminals through the ICC remained for him a possibility worth striving for.[101]

Despite Radwan's criticisms, the Hamas government in Gaza responded positively and proactively to the Goldstone report. Its deputy chief, Yousif Rizqa, said that his government accepted all international commissions, unlike the Israeli government that held itself above the law. The Hamas government in Gaza formed a Follow-up Committee under the Ministry of Justice and sought to engage with this commission "to make sure Israeli occupation will not go unpunished."[102] Four months after the Goldstone Mission presented its report to the Human Rights Council, the Hamas government's minister of justice, Mohammad Faraj al-Ghoul, issued their response to the report. It expressed hope that the UN investigation would lead to results and that its recommendations would be implemented. Much of the response document was an indictment of Israel's noncompliance with the Goldstone Mission's recommendations. It condemned the Israeli government for its use of internationally banned weapons, presented details about the destruction of homes in Israeli attacks, and informed readers about the detention of Palestinian legislators being held as political prisoners by Israel.[103] The Hamas government report also addressed the issue of rocket fire from the Gaza Strip, which was a main concern of the Goldstone Mission: "The Palestinian government has on more than one occasion called on armed Palestinian groups to avoid targeting civilians. . . . (The armed groups) struck military targets and avoided civilian targets, and any accusations related to this concern errant fire."[104] The ministry's report asserted that the Palestinian National Authority had implemented all of the commission's recommendations, but international and Palestinian human rights organizations judged Hamas's response inadequate, especially for failing "to address adequately the firing of indiscriminate rockets into southern Israel by Palestinian armed groups during the 22-day conflict."[105]

The criticisms of the Goldstone report went far beyond this. The damning findings were subsumed by the controversy that arose after the release of the commission's report. The fact that Goldstone, a Zionist judge, proclaimed the likelihood of Israeli war crimes provoked a blaring chorus of outrage and condemnation, not only of the report, but of Goldstone personally. Israeli president Shimon Peres said that "Goldstone is a small man, devoid of any sense of justice, a technocrat with no real understanding of jurisprudence." He condemned the South African jurist for being "on a one-sided mission to hurt Israel."[106] His was "a moral crime not only against Israel but also against human rights."[107] The Israeli minister of information, Yuli Edelstein, asserted that the Goldstone report would "revive anti-Semitism and backs those who deny the Holocaust."[108] In 2010, the US House of Representatives voted 344 to 36 to condemn the Goldstone report, which encouraged Israel and Hamas to conduct credible independent investigations of war crimes committed in Gaza.[109] Nicola Perugini and Neve Gordon argue that the report's publication "was no doubt a watershed in the anti-human rights campaign" in Israel, sparking a new wave of repression of human rights NGOs in that country.[110]

Although commissions often spark dispute, the bilious controversy that followed this one in response to its findings and their reconsideration by its chair reached an unprecedented level.[111] It produced such acrimony that it crowded out discussion of the report's actual findings, and of the desperate conditions in the Gaza Strip that had brought it into being in the first place.

Not much remarked upon in the reams of commentary about this UN mission were the public statements by commissioners Richard Goldstone and Hina Jilani about their own experiences as investigators in the Gaza Strip. Goldstone, who had been a sitting judge during Apartheid South Africa, said that meeting with victims of the violence in the Gaza Strip was "perhaps the most traumatic and emotional experience of my career."[112] He

said it would give him nightmares for the rest of his life.[113] Hina Jilani—
advocate of the Supreme Court of Pakistan, member of the International
Commission of Inquiry on Darfur in 2004, and member of The Elders—also
said she was "absolutely traumatised" when she was in the Gaza Strip, and
this despite having worked in the field of human rights for almost twenty-
five years in contexts where she had seen "terrible things and terrible suffering."[114] Despite these heartfelt expressions, the momentary spectacle of
Palestinian suffering made visible by the report was ultimately engulfed by
polemics about the commission itself, all of which was quickly outpaced by
political events on the ground.

Palestinian President Abu Mazen's freezing of the report at the UN created its own storms.[115] Goldstone's later profession that he believed Israel
had not intentionally targeted civilians as a matter of policy (a partial change
of position that has often been mischaracterized as a retraction) rekindled
the fires burning against the report as a whole.[116] Goldstone's reconsideration
surprised the other investigators and prompted them to publicly reassert the
validity of their original conclusions.[117] It is possible that the huge backlash
against Goldstone and his family led to his backtracking on the UN report.[118]
It is difficult to surmise any other reason for such a backpedalling from what
Goldstone had been so certain of after their investigations. Bill Moyers had
pressed Goldstone on the very point in an interview not long after the report's release.

> MOYERS: You wrote, quote, the military operation, this military operation
> in Gaza, was a result of the disrespect for the fundamental principle of
> "distinction" in international humanitarian law. So in layman's language,
> the distinction between what and what?
>
> GOLDSTONE: Between combatants and innocent civilians.
>
> MOYERS: And you're saying Israel did not do that, in many of these
> incidents.
>
> GOLDSTONE: That's correct.
>
> MOYERS: Did you find evidence that that is deliberate on their part?
>
> GOLDSTONE: Well, we did. We found evidence in statements made by
> present and former political and military leaders, who said, quite openly,
> that there's going to be a disproportionate attack. They said that if

rockets are going to continue, we're going to hit back disproportionately. We're going to punish you for doing it. And that's not countenanced by the law of war.

MOYERS: So they were doing, on the ground, what they had said earlier they intended to do.

GOLDSTONE: That's correct.

MOYERS: —so there was intention.

GOLDSTONE: Well, certainly. You know, one thing one can't say about the Israel Defense Forces is that they make too many mistakes. They're very, a sophisticated army. And if they attack a mosque or attack a factory, and over 200 factories were bombed, there's just no basis to ascribe that to error. That must be intentional.[119]

International public attention to the Goldstone mission controversy eventually waned. Palestinian and Israeli rights organizations issued multiple statements and letters urging implementation of the Goldstone report. In a letter to the UN High Commissioner for Human Rights on the occasion of her first visit to the region two years after the report's issuance, thirteen organizations wrote collectively to ask Navanetham Pillay "to give a voice to the victims of 'Operation Cast Lead' . . . to denounce the forfeiture of justice for Palestinian victims of international crimes in the name of politics and to publicly demand the implementation of the Goldstone report."[120] Palestinian and other NGOs had issued a statement with similar demands during the previous year too.[121] The Goldstone report had found that the blockade, "including Israeli acts that deprive Palestinians in the Gaza Strip from their means of subsistence, employment, housing and water," violated the Geneva Conventions and "might justify a competent court finding that crimes against humanity have been committed."[122] But the siege remained in place and conditions in the Gaza Strip continued to deteriorate. What happened to the report and what was done with its recommendations was not in the hands of the commissioners. But through its international legal performances, in the controversy that drowned out the details of the violations committed against Palestinians, the Goldstone Mission provided a screen of humanitarian concern for the ongoing siege on the Gaza Strip.

Despite the storms of controversy and recrimination that the report occasioned, commission member Hina Jilani maintained hope that it would contribute to "the further development in the honest and intelligent application of international law to situations that occur all over the world." She held up the Goldstone report as a positive contribution, as a record for history and for international law. "Whether the recommendations of the report are fully implemented or not," she said, Jilani believed that the report was important for showing "what has and has not been done by the United Nations on issues of peace and security that affect not just this region but almost all of the world."[123] Highlighting the international community's inaction might be the most significant contribution of a report that was looked to with such hopeful expectation for accountability and justice.

# Toward an Anthropology of International Law, and Next Time and Again for Palestine

Even if the words we use do not permit the acts they
describe to be played again, they can at least evoke
alternate outcomes, margins of freedom for possible
futures, if only by conveying a sense of human dignity
and working to measure the depth of sorrow and pain.

Arlette Farge,
*The Allure of the Archives*[1]

AS ETHNOGRAPHERS TEND TO DO, I have developed some kind of personal relationship with many of the characters who populate these pages, though I met only a few of them in person. The wry sarcasm of Fayez Sayegh impressed and amused me so much that I had to read out quotes to my partner, Fayez's nephew. The hubris of William Yale and the authoritarian grouchiness of Judge Singleton infuriated me as much as Texas Joe's civil rights sincerity and his blindness to its limitations. The tension of personal ambition and political goodwill in Albert Lybyer left me strained between appreciation for his anticolonial efforts and irritation at his petty self-regard. And the fire of the Palestinian women's righteous anger written into petitions to the Peel Commission bowled me over, and then flattened me with the knowledge that the deaths of their sisters-in-arms left nothing more than families without mothers, daughters, and sisters, not liberation.

Like some historians, I have tried to become familiar with these people, their "faces and pains, emotions and the authorities created to control them"[2] in order to articulate the past historically and, in Walter Benjamin's words, seize hold of memory "as it flashes up at a moment of danger."[3] And like any

anthropologist, out of respect and gratitude to those who have shared something of the dangers of their lives, even those who have done so without consent from the grave, I have been anxious to prevent any imposition of meaning upon them, and eager to allow their sense and sensibilities—including
those I found objectionable—to come through, not without interpretation,
but by some humble facilitation. In attempting this, the obverse of a magi-
cian's trick, I have included many long quotes of speeches and interchanges
between Palestinians and their interrogators, investigators, and sympathizers.
It is from a sense of humility, respect, conviction, and mission that I have attempted to smuggle them past the editor's scythe.

While the transcripts of words exchanged in the sometimes stilted frame
of a commission room may not bring the people who spoke them fully to life,
their words do, I think, reveal much of their humanity. Yet this is something
which, when it comes to Palestinians, astonishingly still has to be proven
today. Their considered arguments, their refusals to be baited, the heated and
calm assertions of what is right and what was at risk, the litanies of historical
facts that Palestinians brought to bear to try to convince those who might
see sense. They reveal how much (confident expectation, puzzle-piece logic,
sublimated anger, personal experience that made arguments known in the
bones) they deployed at every moment when it seemed like a system of terrible injustice might finally be righted, when a people might finally be freed,
a future opened up. I have sought to show how reasonable were their expectations when seen through the liberal lens; how emotionally satisfying and
maybe politically necessary were their hopes; how sincere were their desires
to be heard; and how enraging, how tragic, was the devastation of disappointment at each turn.

This effort at bringing the methods and intentions of subaltern studies to
a history of international law "from below" is meant to do something more
than recover the lives, aspirations, and agency of those largely written out
of history—although it has, I hope, done something of that too (and more
on which below).[4] It has also been aimed at revealing a record of hopeful
proposals that, had they been taken more seriously by those who had the
power to act on them, might have saved the lives of countless people. They
might have eliminated the chains of events that have left so many drenched
in the sorrow of dispossession and separation, abandoning them to exist for

generations with the simmering and sometimes explosive frustration of lives immobilized and deaths mourned under siege. How many today know, or could be induced to believe, that Arab leaders repeatedly and with avowed compassion invited refugee Jews to find harbor and home in their Middle Eastern countries after World War II? That Palestinians had detailed plans in place for a democratic Palestine with constitutional guarantees of equal citizenship for all, Jew and Arab, in 1919 and 1946? What the standard histories normally report (and condemn) are the Palestinians' refusals to agree to bad deals for partial autonomy and partition of their country. There is little record of the Zionists' and Westerners' refusals to agree to democratic solutions. With a nod to liberal values, let these pages help balance that historiographical scale a little.

Subaltern studies' research methods and attitudes produced a democratized historiography, a broadened view of the more diverse range of actors and movements playing starring roles in their own stories.[5] It opened up conceptions of where history happens and who makes it, away from the authorized versions that supported the already dominant. In proffering a critique of Whig history, it helped redefine the meaning of history itself. In this spirit, *A History of False Hope* has sought to expand understanding of international law, to recognize its functioning in the lives and imaginations of regular people. Finding it in the everyday of newspaper commentary and commission transcripts, in street banners and tapestries, in the words of Kuwaiti poets, housewives at the UN, and grandfathers in Gaza.

Anthropology's investigation of international law has only burgeoned in recent years, as bodies such as the International Criminal Tribunal for Yugoslavia, the ICC, asylum courts, and the human rights system have swept ever more people into international law's institutions and imaginative horizons.[6] This scholarship has brought ethnographic detail to a variable and not wholly joined-up critique of these systems: showing how culturally distinct notions of justice and forgiveness rub up against international legal procedure; how the sacralization of national narratives happens through legal scripts condoning the powerful; how court practices produce subjects like "the victim" as a social and political category; revealing the role of (sometimes racist) subjective valuations that determine what are supposed to be objective assessments—all of which belies any notion of legal neutrality or disinterest producing international law as an autonomous sphere.[7] International law, like all law, is an uneven field of maneuver in which people seek sanction for their views or make demands through more and less formal and articulated hierarchies of values and criteria of credibility. It favors the professionals and the well resourced. As anthropologists have shown, it is a lesson that those seeking recourse, compensation, or safety in these legal sites often already know, but must try to work within nevertheless.[8]

Bourdieu's rendering of law as a "social field" is one theoretical articulation that can partially help explain such ethnographic insights. His signal contribution has been to parse the systematized internal dynamics of "legal culture" that are in complex relation with the exercise of power outside the juridical field. He emphasized "the strange linguistic, symbolic, and hermeneutic world in which the struggle for authorized or legitimized interpretations of the texts of the legal corpus, and also the texts of legal practice, takes place."[9] Among anthropologists and critical legal scholars too, the relationship of law to politics, of international legal doctrine (the system's rules) as they are related to the extralegal contexts of application and dispute, has been a source of endless academic deliberation.[10] Some in these debates relegate law to the realm of the "epiphenomenal," considering it to be little more than a handmaiden of power. The renowned American legal historian Morton Horwitz offered a perplexed rejoinder to E. P. Thompson's legal-optimistic conclusion to *Whigs and Hunters*: "I do not see how a Man of the Left can describe the rule of law as 'an unqualified human good'!" Horwitz asserted that law is that which promotes formal equality but prevents substantive equality by cultivating "a consciousness that radically separates law from politics, means from ends, processes from outcomes," enabling "the shrewd, the calculating, and the wealthy to manipulate its forms to their own advantage."[11]

The puzzle of international law, however, cannot be reduced to its pretense to political objectivity, to international law as ideology producing false consciousness, or to a contest between "legal formalists" and "legal realists."[12] Nor is the dynamic merely one of the *intersections* of law and politics or law and society, in which the legal field is "vulnerable to" extralegal forces that "invade" the "semi-autonomous social field," as anthropologist Sally Falk Moore so famously put it.[13] The social dynamism *within* the semi-autonomous field that is law must be made central—and the emphasis should be more on the "semi" than the "autonomous." International investigative commissions reveal particularly clearly that it is the social (including the intellectual and moral, the embodied and emotional) that is at the very heart of the thing.

*A History of False Hope* intentionally treats the legal norms as the negative space of the picture. I focus instead foremost on the beliefs and actions of regular people as they try to shape the impact of international legal doctrine and interact in the institutions and social contexts in which it comes alive.[14] In concentrating on what they understood international law to be and what they thought it could offer, by tracing what attracted them to it, and by exploring how they tried to make do in the midst of international law's institutions and with its idiom, our purview is opened up to a distinctive understanding of international law's power and effects. That law leaves the door open to the disadvantaged and then convinces them of its fairness through formalized procedures and codified legal texts may be some of what ensures that the "tacit grant of faith in the juridical order [is] ceaselessly reproduced," as Bourdieu has described it. But that is only a very little part of the story.[15]

In seeking to explain how law functions in society and legal authority is exercised, Bourdieu has theorized the "juridical field" as a social field of struggle, where legal professionals and others compete "for monopoly of the right to determine the law."[16] This is conceptually similar to the move that Duncan Bell has made (as I discuss in the Introduction) in describing liberalism as an "actor's category," delimited by the totality of people competing to define what counts as liberalism.[17] Here the juridical field is confined to those already qualified as jurists. Like Bell, in expanding the conceptual apparatus to comprehend a narrowly self-defined field (liberalism, law) in a more complicated way, Bourdieu has maintained his focus on the mandarins who seek to police its boundaries. He limited the field of competitors to legal professionals, just as Bell attended to intellectuals and their texts. Likewise, those following Bourdieu who call for greater sensitivity to the "broader symbolic ecosystem" in which international law is constituted also tend to figure the competition to be one primarily among "interested elites."[18] The hierarchy of credibility that courts and law maintain—disqualifying the "non-specialists' sense of fairness," revoking "their naive understanding of the facts, of their 'view of the case'"—is thereby replayed in this theory.[19]

Palestinians' long engagement with investigative commissions reveals how much more we can understand about international law's power and functioning when we democratize our view of the field and track it over time. This move is especially crucial when considering international humanitarian and human rights law, in recent years in particular, because of the pretense in these fields to uphold the global democratization of law. The democratization I mean is evident not only in international law's universalizing reach or in the principles of egalitarianism that are at the core of these norms and guarantees—protection of civilians, the assurance of equal rights for all—as all law ensures a fair, ecumenical stance, or at least the appearance of one. Unique to this corner of international law these days is the catholic inclusion of the nonelite in the social-juridical field, where political spokespeople, victims of violence, NGO activists, and others are invited in to be heard by the legal cosmopolitans. They engage this variety of interlocutors through what I have dubbed democratic, sympathetic listening. If, as Ann Stoler has observed, "disdain ... and disaffection for thoughts and things native were basic to the colonial order of things," a big-hearted welcoming inclusiveness has become elemental to the formula of the liberal-legal order.[20] The hierarchy that places legal professionals and other experts at the pinnacle where narratives can be authorized still persists—recall how the chair of the UN Special Committee (in Chapter 4) disciplined witnesses, demanding they speak only of facts eyewitnessed, hushing them about hearsay and legal opinion. But the insistence within commissions that all should have the opportunity to tell their story, to be listened to, and to prove their political credibility helps people believe that they are viable contestants in this competition over the "monopoly of the right to determine the law."[21] However, of significance is not merely the fact of the invitation into this contest, but the nature of the interaction once everyone is in the ring.

Answers to the questions of what law offers, and how it attracts, are to be found in the social contexts, expressive opportunities, and human connections it lets blossom. Investigative commissions, as one spectacular format for the enactment of international law, bring people together in a framework that invites and praises reasonable discussion, solidarity, sympathy, and the elaboration of notions of justice and morality. A place where they can exchange promises that inspire hope. International humanitarian and human rights law especially opens forums in which the passions, aches, and anguish of political contestants can be expressed and amplified, as legal experts (those objective adjudicators or cosmopolitan sympathizers) hear and record those stories, relaying them (sometimes with compassion) to "the international community" out there. The power of liberal-legalism also resides in how it functions as a moral—and moralizing—mode that is gratifying to those enacting it. If, as anthropologist Didier Fassin has described it, "morality is duty plus desire," a good that we are not only obliged to do, but that we are also inclined to do, liberal morality allows the liberal to feel good about following their principles.[22] Investigative commissions provide a stage for performing them. Beyond the sympathy and satisfaction they can occasion, investigative commissions offer opportunities to tell one's story and elaborate a collective history. They give people the chance to "set the record straight" in a context that could both stamp it as authorized and also provide recognition and confirmation. Through these processes, international law channels and endorses people's meanings and morals, their feelings, and their performances of goodness and political competence. The gratification of these needs, too, is how international law rules.

The moments of history recounted here show the existential stakes that many Palestinians believed were hanging in the balance at each moment in which a commission was dispatched. They show the reasons for their refusals of the bad deals and for their offers of what they thought were fairer ones. Many of the Palestinians featured in these pages held tight to liberal values and employed international legal tools to make their case because they were liberals who believed these values and principles to be a means—if not *the* means—to justice. This history gestures at why such an embroilment with international law matters for what it has produced of repeatedly unfulfilled promises and hopeful expectations, not just because of the sadnesses and oppression that resulted, but also because of what it has occluded of other forms of action, argument, and resistance. As such, this book has offered a particular exploration of international law as ideology, a net of ideas and beliefs that cloaks the operations of power even while presenting instruments for ostensibly challenging and restraining power.[23] A producer of false hope.[24]

The evidence of history—international law's repeated failures to end the conflict or deliver justice—is enough of a damning critique. In my view, when it comes to Palestine, this dead horse requires no further flogging. Whether international law can be reformed into an effective counterhegemonic tool in support of Palestinian liberation is too broad a question because international law, political struggle and strategy, forms of solidarity, modes of encouragement and coercion are always in dynamic relation with each other and with history. There can be no such blanket prediction. There are those—especially legal practitioners and activists—who do not predict, but make a strong case for the need to improve international law, the need to implement it, the need to use it better, in general and for Palestinians. Despite liberal internationalism's weakness these days—its possibly immanent collapse provoked from the center that once claimed to uphold it[25]—many cling to their faith in international law. Some assert the inevitability of UN action against Israel, and many contend that international law can be a counterhegemonic force, a tool of resistance for all subaltern groups.[26] Those are different kinds of discussions, distinct from what are the critical provocations and nonprescriptive arguments I have made here.

To be sure, international law does not, and never has, defined the limit of Palestinians' political universe. International law has never been the only political tactic to which Palestinians—political parties, leaders, individuals, or movements—have made recourse. While Arafat's speech at the UN was hailed by so many as a mutual victory for the Palestinians and the UN's "causes of peace, justice, freedom and independence," his paean to the goal of world harmony came in a period of the PLO's active armed struggle. It also reminded the world that an alternative to the olive branch is the gun.[27] Just as some three decades earlier Ahmad al-Shuqayri and Jamal al-Husayni (rightly) predicted for the Anglo-American Committee that war would come if their demands for a democratic solution went unfulfilled. International law and its institutions often become unconvincing over time, as the events of the 1930s showed when Palestinians and other Arabs got fed up with England's civilizing commissions not delivering on their promises and opted for revolt—for a while. And more recently, resistance to military occupation during the two intifadas took many forms, from commemorative acts and art to stones and suicide bombings.[28]

If international law has not been the only network for funneling solidarity to the cause of Palestinian freedom, neither has violence been the only alternative to liberal engagement. Many configurations of transnational activism and globalist ideologies have brought people together in the hopes of resolving the conflict. The ideas of communism and binationalism have seen some Jews and Palestinians work collectively for a peaceful unification, almost from the moment that the idea of an exclusively Jewish state was proposed.[29] Internationalizing the Palestine issue was a goal of Amin al-Husayni's interactions with India's Khilafat Movement during the mandate, and other pan-Islamist activism has channeled material support and political solidarity to Palestine throughout its history of struggle.[30] The most recent innovation in Palestinian resistance to Israeli domination has been the Boycott, Divestment, and Sanctions (BDS) movement, a form of "radical democracy" which cofounder Palestinian Omar Barghouti describes as "a progressive, anti-racist, sophisticated, sustainable, moral and effective form of civil, non-violent resistance . . . affirming the rights of all humans to freedom, equality and dignified living."[31]

While recognizing the wide penumbra of Palestinian politics, *A History of False Hope* has demonstrated just how much energy—expended by people across all social strata—has been invested in the activities of international legal institutions. Despite the United Nations' fundamental role in creating the conditions that led to the Nakba—what Palestinians refer to as the disaster of their 1948 expulsion and Israel's statehood on their land—and despite the ongoing military occupation, the UN has endured as a premier forum in which Palestinians make their political claims on a world stage.[32] There have always been those who were more critical, who have considered the UN to be a Western club upholding only Western and powerful states' interests. The UN was, in the words of the Muslim Brothers, "nothing but a cloak of the greediness of the big imperialist states."[33] But because it is a site where "the world" is imagined, where humanitarian values are espoused, and where international law constitutes the terms of reference, many Palestinians continue to see the UN as a political and legal resource.

Perhaps more important, the UN persists as the embodiment of an international community that cares about the Palestinians' plight, where declarations affirming their national and individual rights are made and amplified. In his painstakingly detailed account of how "the Palestine question" was included and then dropped from UN agendas, George Tomeh, a Syrian representative to the UN, demonstrated how widely held was the view that the United Nations has the power to affirm Palestine as a political issue or erase it.[34] More than four decades after Tomeh penned that essay, it is clear that the UN maintains its magnetism. "We continue to talk to the United Nations," a Palestinian told me during my fieldwork in the West Bank in 2002, "in order to be recognized as part of the international community. In order to be recognized as human beings. Israelis refer to us as animals, snakes, bugs, but we are humans." The UN, its investigative commissions, resolutions, and declarations are seen to reflect and legitimize the Palestinian struggle for freedom and their very status as humans deserving human rights.[35]

Even many of the alternative modes of struggle are caught within, or at least imbued with, the international legal imagination. BDS is shaped by a rights-based approach and calls for a boycott against Israel until it meets its obligations under international law.[36] And there are many people who would not be deemed "liberal" by secular liberals—Palestinians who believe that Islam is the foundation for Palestinian liberation, for instance—who also believe international legal institutions like the ICC can render justice, and who have worked hard to show how human rights principles are incorporated into their faith.[37]

In the midst of this crosshatch of approaches to engaging with international law, there have always been, and continue to be, voices whispering for wariness toward it. Palestinians did, after all, greet every early investigative commission with trepidation (before they decided to engage). More recently, the whispers have grown into something more resounding, with a notable generation of intellectuals calling for a stance of "disenchantment" toward international law. As legal scholar Nimer Sultany has put it bluntly:

> Let us face it: it is not only that the reality of power often trumps humanist and universal moral codes like those expressed in the law of nations (e.g., international humanitarian law); it is also that these universal codes are often too abstract, contradictory and ineffective to be instrumental in advancing concrete outcomes.[38]

With perhaps more optimism, human rights attorney and legal scholar Noura Erakat likewise encourages advocates to "tempe[r] their faith in the law's capacity to do what only a critical mass of people are capable of achieving."[39]

And yet, as *A History of False Hope* has shown, many Palestinians and others have acted as if international law's methods could have an effect on their own, or that the support of Palestinian rights through international legal terms was a concrete positive outcome in and of itself. Palestinians have often turned to international law as if it is the end of the story, not as a singular instrument of what has to be a much larger and more complicated orchestra. This lack of strategy has been evident in every era, but the PLO/PA under Yasir Arafat's leadership is perhaps the most obvious instance. As someone active in the NSU during the time of the Mitchell Committee commented to me, "The leadership was flailing, as always. They engaged with the Mitchell Committee as if it were just another arrow in the quiver to be tossed about." When I asked another member of the team what plan had been in place to make use of the committee's report, he just laughed through his nose and shook his head. There was no strategy.[40]

Like Erakat, Sultany also argues that international law will remain ineffective unless it is part of a larger political vision: "Investing in the legal venue cannot be a substitute for direct political action and tools. Law is not free of politics and thus it cannot be an escape route from politics."[41] That this argument is so rarely articulated, that it even has to be made (when it is so obvious), provides some hint about where the ideological power of international law resides. Just as liberalism has been an ideology that can obscure structural reasons for some people's disadvantaged positions, international law—in its dogma and ideals—also blocks from view the political structures that obstruct or bring about change. International law functions in a way parallel to how liberalism "is *il*liberalism for all but a minority"[42]—that lexicon of blame dressed up as virtues that holds individuals accountable for their "failures," when every economic, political, and social deprivation has made their "success" an impossibility. International law ensures order especially for those who benefit from the existing one, while justifying the chaos of violent interventions and military occupation experienced by the many. That it does so under an umbrella of apolitical equal opportunity for justice only heightens the urge (for some) to wish to uphold it, to correct it, to induce real enactment of its ideals. Just as E. P. Thompson could avow that the "Rule of Law" is an "unqualified human good" at the end of a book that showed how powerfully English law served the ruling classes, so could Fayez Sayegh insist that the UN system embodied the universality of the rule of law and order. Through his decades in exile, Sayegh still insisted that only the UN could provide "any hope of peace" based on international law, even after countless unanswered appeals to it.[43]

In Palestine (laying down the gauntlet now), international law has been an antirevolutionary pacifying force. (Certainly, some will see that as a good thing, and others not.) For a hundred years, international law has been a black hole: the massive weight of its mechanisms, both ideological and institutional, have pulled energies and actors, ideas and motivations deep within it, suffocating their vitality. International law has channeled nationalist passions into "reasonable" discussion; expressed the ache for justice in the numb language of UN resolutions; condensed histories of agony, exile, repression, and dispossession into false assertions of balance in the here and now. The activation of international law through investigative commissions has been a dominant mechanism through which liberalism exercises its power: it spins a vortex that vacuums liberalism's bright ideals into itself where those who would be saved clutch onto it, eager to combine with it, to be lit—to be *seen*—by the brightness. And then it throws them back out, only to be caught up in the whirlwind again next time. "Next time" and "again" it has always been for the Palestinians.

# Notes

## Introduction: International Law as a Way of Being

1. As of November 2018, Israel killed 214 Palestinians and wounded more than 18,000 since the protests began on March 30, 2018. See "Gaza Protests: All the Latest Updates," *Al-Jazeera*, 2018, https://www.aljazeera.com/news/2018/04/gaza-protest-latest-updates-18040609250656i.html.

2. UN Human Rights Council May 18, 2018.

3. On Zionism as a colonial project, see Katz, Leff, and Mandel 2017.

4. The British used commissions in domestic and international politics with gusto. Studies of them are also numerous, offering varying levels of critique. See Block and Somers 2003; Clokie and Robinson 1937; Loades 1997; Shamir and Hacker 2001; Mongia 2004. Canada also has been prolific in its commissions. See Chua 1979.

5. Habermas 1984.

6. Asad 2015. To speak of legalism, legal liberalism, or liberalism as a "tradition" is to recognize their embodied aspects. It troubles the presumption that freedom and choice are fundamental to liberalism, to show the actual constraints inherent within law and liberalism that run counter to their proclaimed ideals and ideologies.

7. Marks 2009, 6. For a critical take on the laws of war that puts gender at the center of the analysis, see Kinsella 2011.

8. McBride 2016, 161, quoted in I. Hurd 2017, 2.

9. On doxa and orthodoxy, see Bourdieu 2013.

10. Sylvest 2009, 61–62.

11. On liberal legalism, see Hoffmann 2016; Hunt 1986; Levinson 1983.

12. On Palestinian conditions in Israel, see the information on Adalah's website, at https://www.adalah.org/en. On Palestinian refugees in Lebanon, see United Nations Relief and Works Agency, n.d.

13. On "the international community" as ideological formation, see Weeramantry and Berman 1999, 1528.

14. Mazower 2012, xv. In Duncan Bell's estimation, this doctrine had stabilized by 1860. See Bell 2016, 20.

15. Sylvest 2009, 3.

16. On global governance in the 1990s, see Mazower 2012, 370. For an anthropological approach to "global governance," see Cowan 2015 and Cowan and Billaud 2015.

17. Pedersen 2015, 61, 65; Niezen and Sapignoli 2017.

18. For a critical summary of the different ways historians have told the story of 1948 and its political implications, see Shlaim 1995.

19. For an anthropological account of the UN Relief and Works Agency that was set up to deal with the refugees, see I. Feldman 2018.

20. Normand and Zaidi 2008, 110.

21. Ibid.

22. Mearsheimer and Walt, 2006; R. Khalidi 2013.

23. United Nations Human Rights Council, "The United Nations Commission of Inquiry," n.d.

24. For a list of ongoing and recent UN fact-finding commissions elsewhere, see United Nations Human Rights Council, "International Commissions of Inquiry," n.d.

25. Accounts of the deep and mutual impact of the international legal system, the UN, and Palestine include: Allen 2013; Erakat 2019; I. Feldman 2010; I. Feldman 2018; Makdisi and Prashad 2017, 1–4.

26. Koskenniemi 1989; Anghie 2005; Hunt 1986.

27. Hoffmann 2016. For an elaboration of international law as ideology, see Marks 2000.

28. Pitts 2018, 6.

29. On the notion of habitus, see Bourdieu 2013; on the embodiment of ideology, see Mahmood 1996; on the "abstract embodiment" of Victorian liberalism, see Hadley 2010.

30. For a unique analysis of the universalism of international law, see Li 2020.

31. On international law and development, see Eslava 2015 and Pahuja 2011.

32. R. Khalidi 2006.

33. For a more complete chronicling, see Ghandour 2010, 123–65.

34. Gray 1995, 78.

35. Mehta 1999, 47–48.

36. Mehta 1997, 59–76.

37. Pitts 2000, 296.

38. Fitzmaurice 2012, 139.

39. Gray 1995, 86–87. Gray insists that liberalism is a single tradition because of the consistency of four elements within it: individualism, egalitarianism, universalism, and meliorism. Ibid., xii–xiii.

40. Mills 2017, 5.

41. Coleman and Golub 2008, 256.

42. Coleman and Golub 2008; Schiller 2015, 11.

43. On ideology, see Hall 1996, 41; Mills, 2017, 73; Asad 1979. It is precisely the malleability and the taken-for-grantedness of the concept of liberalism that reveals it to be an ideology, to be a political tool. This is evidenced in every usage of the word "liberal" without definition. Among those otherwise meticulous scholars who forego the work of defining liberalism are Joyce 2016 and Gorman 2012.

44. For a useful discussion of C.A. Bayly's approach to this problem, see Sartori 2017.

45. Bell 2016, 5, 70; Bell 2014.

46. Bell does trace the undulations in liberalism's contours as an effect of—and part of— political change over time. But his starting point—liberal ascription by self or other—erases the much wider field of political contest through which liberalism has moved, and the much more varied cast of characters who have constituted its proponents and adherents.

47. Mills 2017, xiv.

48. Pitts 2005; Bell 2011.

49. This work has been overwhelmingly concerned with European and American legal scholars.

50. Bell 2016, 9.

51. Hanssen and Weiss 2016a, xviii. Also see Hanssen and Weiss 2018.

52. Schumann 2008, 1–14; Abu-Rabi' 2004. Problematically missing the ideological imbrication of "the West and the rest," however, Abu-Rabi' views liberalism as "the product of historical conditions in Europe" that was, with difficulty, "transferred" into the Arab world, where it existed as "a cheap imitation copy" of the original and true European version (74). This idea that liberalism was transposed to the Middle East is echoed by Egyptian political scientist 'Ali-Addin Hilal. Hilal 1998. On the complicated and not necessarily liberal modalities of mission schools in the Middle East, see Makdisi 2008b, 15–28. The work on liberalism in the Middle East overlaps with scholarship on Islam. See, for example, Binder 1988 and Dalacoura 1998. These discussions, however, are not always billed as the study of liberalism per se. Much has been written on the claimed synergies or supposed incompatibilities of Islam with "human rights," what many consider a prototypically liberal notion. See, for example: A. E. Mayer 2013; Grote, Röder, and El-Haj 2016; Sachedina 2009; Oh 2007. For a critique of the framing of the question as one of "compatibility," see Allen forthcoming. Even for those who

have recognized that liberalism has been an intrinsic feature of politics in the modern Middle East at different times, there is a tendency to conclude that it has disappeared from the region. Either of the World Wars marks its demise. See E. F. Thompson 2015. But as *A History of False Hope* demonstrates, if we squint a different way, liberalism comes into view as a steady theme animating the political imagination and practices of a broad swath of transnational Palestinian society until today.

53. As Weiss and Hanssen point out, despite the title of his book, Hourani did not intend it to be understood as a study of Arab liberalism. Hanssen and Weiss 2016b, 12–13.

54. Gershoni 2016, 304; Hanssen and Weiss 2016c, 169.

55. Within anthropology, Elizabeth Povinelli's work on "late liberalism" has been among the most influential contributions to the theorization of liberalism. She understands late liberalism as a "social project" that emerged in the 1950s in response to legitimacy crises of liberal governmentality prompted by anticolonial, Islamist, and other new social movements. Without a fuller analysis of earlier crises in liberal governmentality (of the sort that Karuna Mantena and Jennifer Pitts have undertaken), however, Povinelli ends up overstating the novelty of late liberalism as a peculiar era of liberalism. Povinelli 2011.

56. Mantena 2009, 3.

57. Chatterjee 2011, 691.

58. Mantena 2009, 6–7.

59. Mantena 2007, 120.

60. Ibid., 131.

61. Sartori 2006, 625; Sartori 2014.

62. Sartori 2014, 5–6.

63. Sartori 2006, 624. In asking how the explicit articulations of liberal values by key thinkers circulate in the world and how they have been taken up to guide political action, Mantena and Sartori continue the work that Edward Said began with *Orientalism* in exposing liberalism's collusion with empire. See Said 1979. Also see Mehta 1997, 1999. Another analysis of liberal ideology in its material context is Bayly 2012. For a review of the literature on empire and liberalism, see Pitts 2010.

64. Hall 1996, 26–27; Asad 1979, 619.

65. Coleman and Golub 2008, 255.

66. Mahmud 2016.

67. Anthropology, as Naomi Schiller notes, seeks to "document and analyse the everyday effects, lived contradictions, impasses, and potentialities of liberal approaches to the individual, law, the state, reason, difference, property, and freedom (among other concepts)," to grasp "how liberal norms are lived and inhabited." Schiller 2015, 11–12. Also see Ansell 2015; Boyer and Yurchak 2010; Coleman and Golub 2008; T. Kelly 2018; Schiller 2013; and Mahmood 2012.

68. On anthropology's contribution to American racial liberalism, see M. Anderson 2019.

69. These scholars have left an important legacy, especially for the anthropology of Islam, by prompting a new subfield of "the anthropology of secularism" and also for our understanding of Western hegemony generally. Agrama 2010; Asad 1993; Asad 2003; Mahmood 2012. For a critique of Mahmood, see Schielke 2010. Scholars of postcolonialism have put forward an allied array of critiques of liberalism. See Chakrabarty 2000; Ivison 2002.

70. For related critiques, see Mufti 2015; Schielke 2014, 402–4.

71. Examples of this kind of international legal historiography about international law that focuses most intently on Europe include Duve 2017; Pitts 2017; Sylvest 2008. For a discussion of recent attempts to "globalize" the history of international law, see Pitts 2015. An exception to this Eurocentrism that attends to non-Europeans as important actors in this story is Lorca 2014. For a related example of international legal history that seeks to decenter the Euro-American frame, see work of the editors of the *Oxford Handbook of the History of International Law,* who made "overcoming Eurocentrism" a goal of this collection. Fassbender and Peters 2012. For some recent examples of this important focus on "legal politics" in the history of empire, see Benton 2002; Benton 2012.

72. For a recent study of the entanglement of international law with national and local administration, see Eslava 2015.

73. On the ICC, see Krever 2014, 67; C. Bassiouni 1997. For some recent discussions of the spate of UN investigative commissions, see Tonkin and Akande 2011; Heaven 2017.

74. On commissions of inquiry as mechanisms for the development of international law, see Darcy 2017; Rodenhäuser 2013.

75. See, for example, Buchan 2017; Herik 2015. For an assessment that recognizes the multiplicity of effects, including nonaction, that commissions of inquiry can have, see Nouwen and Becker, n.d. Draft on file with author.

76. Green, MacManus, and de la Cour Venning 2018.

77. Schlag 1998. In this view, legal reasoning obfuscates the simple truth that power lies outside, not within, legal form. The Report of the Independent International Fact-Finding Mission on Myanmar (A/HRC/39/64) was released in August 2018 showing the breadth of the genocide; it prompted no action by any world power to implement the report's recommendations. See United Nations Human Rights Office of the High Commissioner (OHCHR) 2018. See also Rahman 2018.

78. For a discussion of the Europeanism of international law and a review of scholarship on its role in imperialism, see Pitts 2012. Chimni provides a concise if general definition of TWAIL (Third World Approaches to International Law) as "a loose network of third world scholars who articulate a critique of the history, structure and

process of contemporary international law from the standpoint of third world peoples, in particular its marginal and oppressed groups." Chimni 2017. On TWAIL, see Anghie and Chimni 2004. For Marxist critiques of international law, see Knox 2013 and 2016. On IMAIL (Integrated Marxist Approach to International Law), see Chimni 2017. On the strained relationship between Critical Legal Studies and Marxist approaches, see Rasulov 2014.

79. Koskenniemi 2016, 105. Also see Burgis 2009, 53; Özsu 2009, 29; Koskenniemi 2002.

80. Anghie 2005. An earlier opener to this discussion was Koskenniemi 2002.

81. Anghie 2006a, 745; Anghie 1993, 447. Makau Mutua, another "TWAIL" scholar, began an article explaining the TWAIL approach with this sentence: "The regime of international law is illegitimate." He went on to write that the "Third World has generally viewed international law as a regime and discourse of domination and subordination, not resistance and liberation." Mutua 2000, 31. An oft-quoted observation from Mohammad Bedjaoui states that "classic international law 'consisted of a set of rules with a geographical bias (European law), a religious-ethical inspiration (it was a Christian law), an economic motivation (it was a mercantilist law) and political aims (it was an imperialist law).'" As quoted in Otto 1996, 339.

82. Andrew Sartori criticizes Mehta's core critique of liberalism's abstraction for what it contains of "an immanent propensity for colonial domination," because this critique reduces empire "to the single dimension of the pedagogical project of modernization or civilization" and is based on a reading of texts without placing them in context. Sartori 2006, 624, 634, 625.

83. Mehta 1999, 47–48.

84. Eslava and Pahuja 2012, 130.

85. Fitzmaurice 2012. Similar to many, Emmanuelle Jouannet asserts that international law is "simultaneously an instrument of domination and an instrument of emancipation." Jouannet 2015, 1. Sundhya Pahuja recognizes in international law "both an imperial and a counter-imperial dimension." Pahuja 2011, 1. While neither Jouannet nor Pahuja assess the efficacy of resistance through international law, they both explain how contemporary international law could be used as a tool of resistance. Jouannet describes international law as "the projection upon an international stage of the values and interests of international society's main players, at the same time being used by groups resisting that dominant order . . . it is as much the sword of the mighty as it is the shield of the meek" (1). He adds that by emphasizing the importance of human rights for all individuals, contemporary international law can be emancipatory in allowing for the adaptation of human rights to cultural particularities (112). He cites as the non-hegemonic use of human rights the 2011 revolutions of Egypt and Tunisia (109). In contrast, Pahuja argues that the new international legal order represents an anti-imperial

project that facilitated decolonization and was emancipatory (46, 58). For another call for more forthright investigation of law's normative valence, see I. Hurd 2017.

86. J. L. Comaroff 2006. There is a similar tendency to laud indigenous use of law against colonial regimes and capitalists, with proof of its efficacy as a tool of resistance being found in its ability to force changes in state policy, rather than in fulfilling indigenous goals. See Grossman 2001, 1–4; United Nations Human Rights Office of the High Commissioner (OHCHR) 2008. However, a slightly longer-term perspective shows how tenuous and temporary such victories tend to be. This is what legal scholars call "the implementation gap." Isa 2017. Another focus of anthropological studies of international law and global institutions has been on recovering "the messiness of global and transnational involvements and the local, on-the-ground realities with which they intersect," showing how international legal institutions can flatten out the multiplicity of notions of justice and rights across societies. Hinton 2010, 1. Also see Dembour and Kelly 2007.

87. Jamal Juma' 2006, "Globalizing the Occupation," *Electronic Intifada*, https://electronicintifada.net/content/globalizing-occupation/6079. As legal scholar Susan Akram observed, "Both the enthusiasm and opprobrium that followed the 2004 International Court of Justice's (ICJ) *Advisory Opinion on the Wall* seem, thirteen years later, to have been unwarranted and overblown." Akram 2017. For an overview of the opinion, see International Court of Justice, n.d.

88. Rabbani 2015.

89. I broached this issue in a discussion with civil society actors in Palestine about how they evaluated human rights successes and noted how narrow and limited they recognized these successes to be. Allen 2013, 20, 59–62. For a historical example, see Fitzmaurice 2012, 137. When serious attempts are made to empirically assess and even quantify how much good international law does, the studies are beset by simplistic methods that provide results that are easily countered. Katherine Sikkink is one of the most feted champions of liberal international law and provides one such example. See Sikkink 2011.

90. Dajani 2011; Erakat 2019; Falk 2006; Falk 2014; Hajjar 2017; Hajjar 2018, 356.

91. Özsu 2014, 278; Rajagopal 2003, 9.

92. See the contributions of Darryl Li and Nimer Sultany especially in Erakat 2011. Also see Sfard 2018.

93. Anthropology has begun to address this lacuna with ethnographic studies of international organizations and distinct streams of international law (primarily human rights and transitional justice mechanisms). See Anders 2014; Clarke 2009; Clarke and Goodale 2014; Dembour and Kelly 2007; Hinton 2018; T. Kelly 2009; T. Kelly 2011; R. Wilson 2005; R. Wilson 2011. An exception within socio-legal scholarship is Eslava 2015.

94. Eslava and Pahuja 2012, 203.

95. Important recent histories of international law include Benton and Clulow 2017; Benton and Ford 2016; Pitts 2018.

96. See, for example, Lorca 2014; Niezen and Sapignoli 2017.

97. Özsu 2014, 279.

98. On the spread of judicialization, see Comaroff and Comaroff, 2006; E. Hurd 2015; Moustafa 2018. For a critique of the hegemony of legalism in international relations that recognizes how normative notions of the "rule of law" bias outcomes such that they tend to favor the powerful and the status quo, see I. Hurd 2017. International relations scholars have also noticed the increased prominence of legalism in international politics. See Dunoff and Pollack 2013; Chinkin and Kaldor 2017. Some prominent scholars working within this discipline somewhat blandly summarize the legalization trend as a form of "institutionalization." Goldstein et al. 2000.

99. On December 20, 2019, the ICC prosecutor, Fatou Bensouda, announced that "there is a reasonable basis to proceed with an investigation into the situation in Palestine." See International Criminal Court, n.d.

100. Critiques depicting ideology in terms of false consciousness decry the arrogance inherent in the presumption that people do not know their own motivations and interests. See Marks 2000, 9.

101. Pirie 2013, 203.

102. For a self-proclaiming Marxist approach to commissions, see Chua 1979.

103. For arguments about the ways truth commissions produce a national narrative in service of the state and other powerful interests, see Grandin and Klubock 2007; Grandin 2005. Truth and reconciliation commissions are distinct in many ways from other kinds of investigative commissions. For a survey, see Hayner 2010. On Israeli investigative commissions that blot out certain unpalatable aspects of that government and the state's internal contradictions and tensions, see Maoz 2000; Shenhav and Gabay 2001. Important anthropological analysis of TRCs are found in R. Wilson 2001; R. Wilson 2005. For a less critical look at the role of investigative commissions in writing national history, see Molchadsky 2015. Matthew Keller analyzes British royal commissions as "a concrete form of governance that mediate between structures of state/elite power and the popular legitimacy necessary to maintain power in democratic forms of governance." Keller 2014, 208.

104. Ashforth 1990b, 4. Also, Ashforth 1990a. South Africa's use of commissions and its entrenchment of structures of black repression have been critically examined also by Krige 1997 and Sitze 2013. The South African Truth and Reconciliation Commission inspired a scholarly cottage industry, with Richard Wilson's being the most notable contribution in anthropology. R. Wilson 2001. The phenomenon of "transitional justice," of which TRCs are a part, helped construct a scholarly mansion. For notable

contributions, see Anders 2014; Niezen 2013; Hinton 2010. Also see Allegra Lab's collection of anthropologists reflecting on their work in this field: Allegra 2015.

105. Stoler 2009, 26. Also see Simon 2005; Sitze 2013, 133.

## Chapter 1: Petitioning Liberals

1. "Instructions for Commissioners, 25 March 1919, Future Administration of Certain Portions of the Turkish Empire under the Mandatory System (Secret)," in *Henry Churchill King Papers, 1873–1934, Reports and Correspondence*, Oberlin College Archives, RG 2/6, box 128/1, in King-Crane Commission Digital Collection (hereafter *King-Crane Collection*). http://www2.oberlin.edu/library/digital/king-crane/. For reviews of the extensive literature on this commission, see Reimer 2006, 129–50 and Patrick 2015. Patrick has tallied at least three hundred academic works that give substantive mention to the King-Crane Commission. Patrick 2015, 2.

2. Charles R. Crane and Henry Churchill King, "King-Crane Commission Report, 28 August 1919," in *King Papers*, in King-Crane Collection, RG 2/6, box 128/4, 1.

3. See the persuasive essay by bin Taʿama 1919, "La Quwwa illa bi-l-Itihad," *al-Manar* 21, no. 5 (August 26, 1919): 265–274. Echoing these sentiments was a brief opinion piece apparently from *al-Manar* editors: "Tadhkir al-Manar li-l-Fariqain," *al-Manar* 21, no. 5 (August 26, 1919): 249. This is a short letter urging Arabs to unite and take an active role in the Europeans' decision on their country.

4. Omar 2019, 1.

5. Wilson 1918b; Wilson 1918a.

6. Wilson 1918b, 8.

7. See, for example, Comaroff and Comaroff 1997, 4; Stoler 2010.

8. Cohn 1987; Cohn 1996; Fabian 2002; Stoler 2010, 4–5, 30.

9. Pels 1997, 164.

10. Mamdani 2001; G. Thomas 2007; Meiu 2015; Stoler 1995.

11. "Transcript of Albert Lybyer's Diary, March to September 1919," in King-Crane Collection, RS 15/13/22, box 17/8 (hereafter *Lybyer Diary*).

12. Tooze 2014, 8.

13. Zuʿaytir and al-Hout 1984, 7. For an account of earlier debates, see Makdisi 2002a.

14. Ayalon 2004, 105–7.

15. Ibid.

16. "The Sabotage of the East," in *Albert H. Lybyer Papers, 1876–1949*, University of Illinois Archives, Folder "April 1919" (hereafter *Lybyer Papers-Illinois*).

17. "Tadhkir al-Manar li-l-Fariqain."

18. For a few of many examples, see: "Mustaqbal Suriya, Clemenceau w-al-Amir Faysal wa-l-Lajna," *Lisan al-Hal*, no. 145–7792 (May 3, 1919), Col D; "Al-Lajna

al-Dawliyya al-Sharq al-Adna," *al-Muqattam*, no. 9202 (June 20, 1919): 4; "Qarar al-Mu'tamar al-Suri al-'Am," *al-Manar*, 21, no. 4 (June 28, 1919): 221–23.

19. Grossi, Milligan, and Waddelow, 2011. The "List of delegations received by the Commission" mistakenly spells the village of Deir Dibwan as Deir Diwan. See "List of Delegations Received by the Commission," in King-Crane Collection, RS 15/13/22, box 16/13, 4.

20. C. W. Anderson 2013, 82–83.

21. Hamada 1983, 16–22; Porath 1974, 88. Darwaza filled many roles: he became secretary of al-Nadi al-'Arabi; was elected representative for Nablus to the 4th and 7th Palestinian National Congresses; was a member of the Arab Executive Committee; secretary of the Nablus Muslim-Christian Association in the early 1930s; appointed general administrator of the Waqf in the 1930s by the Supreme Muslim Council; and was a member of the Istiqlal party. See Mattar 2005, 115.

22. "Petition from the Greengrocers and Spice Sellers of Tripoli," in *Lybyer Papers*, in King-Crane Collection, RS 15/13/22, box 16/4.

23. "List of Delegations at Nablus, 1919," in *Lybyer Papers*, in King-Crane Collection, RS 15/13/22, box 16/1.

24. "Conference, a Discussion at the American Delegation of the Peace Conference," *Crane Papers*, in King-Crane Collection, May 5–6, 1919. According to some legal thinkers in the interwar period, the challenge to the League of Nations was to creatively harness, but not suppress, the vitality of nationalism. See Berman 1993.

25. N. Smith 2003, 121. The negotiations in Paris were heavily influenced by Wilson's desire to make sure the deliberations and decisions were guided by "facts." Alongside the plebiscites and investigative bodies were technical commissions staffed by experts who were asked to determine the facts of "racial aspects, historic antecedents, and economic and commercial elements" of the peoples and regions under discussion. Franck 1990, 318–19; L. V. Smith 2018, 156.

26. Davison 1968. Motivation toward civic activism was enhanced with the 1839 Tanzimat decrees that established the equality of imperial subjects before the law and introduced the notion of the consent of the governed. Provence 2017, 13. Historian Andrew Arsan argues that the rise of civic activism after 1856 was in reaction to the Treaty of Paris, the Cretan rebellion, and the 1860 events in Mt. Lebanon and Damascus. Personal communication. In addition, by 1856 European recognition that the Ottoman Empire was part of European public law was marked in the Treaty of Paris. Palabiyik 2014; Kayaoğlu 2010, 109.

27. Davison 1968, 95–96.

28. For a parallel argument about the Ottoman modernization project that was "fully integrated into and inseparable from wider European trends and processes," see · Provence 2017, 13, 9–55.

29. Qasimiyya 2002, 75.

30. Seikaly 2016, 32, fn. 55; Campos 2011, 4.

31. Salim Tamari 2011, 3–4.

32. R. Khalidi 1984; Ayalon 2004, 62, 64. Three months after the announcement of the constitution in 1908, Palestine saw the publication of fifteen different newspapers between September and December. Salahat, "Sahafat Filastin fi-l-'Ahd al-'Othmani," *Aljazeera.Net*, August 24, 2017, https://institute.aljazeera.net/ar/ajr/article/550.

33. Qasimiyya 2002, 75.

34. Kayali 2008, 181.

35. Arsan 2012, 181; Mazower 2012, 22–23.

36. Arsan 2012, 173.

37. R. Khalidi 1997, 69–84; Abu-Manneh 1999, 40–41.

38. Özsu 2016a, 124. Jennifer Pitts discusses the many European contemporary interpretations of the capitulations, which "made them readable as generating a regular legal community with Europeans," producing "a fairly stable form of interstate law." It was only in the late nineteenth century that the Ottomans recognized the capitulations as "instruments of penetration by stronger Western powers." Pitts 2018, 31, 36.

39. "Al-Misio Picot," *Lisan al-Hal*, no. 151–7798 (May 12, 1919): 2, Col C.; "Notes on Conversation with M. George Picot, on April 17, 1919, by Captain William Yale," in *Personal Diary of William Linn Westermann*, Columbia University Archives, New York (hereafter *Westermann Diary*).

40. "Al-Mas'alah al-Suriyya wa-l-Ahzab," *al-Manar* 21, no. 4 (June 28, 1919): 197–207.

41. "Statement of Emir Faisal to the American Commission, 6 July 1919," in *Lybyer Papers*, in King-Crane Collection, RS 15/13/22, box 16/1; "Report on the Reception of the Islamo Christian Association," in Central Zionist Archives (hereafter CZA), L4/794. Faysal, who was son of Hussein bin 'Ali, the grand sharif of Mecca, was leader of Iraq from 1921 to 1933.

42. Darwaza 1949, 104.

43. Ibid., 112; *Lybyer Diary*, June 11, 1919; "Al-Lajna al-Dawliyya," *Lisan al-Hal*, no. 172-7819, (June 12, 1919): 2, Col B.

44. "Zulumat Ba'duha Fawqa Ba'd," *Lisan al-Hal*, no. 193–7840 (May 6, 1919), Col A–B; "No Title," *Lisan al-Hal*, no. 193–7840 (July 17, 1919): 1, Col A–B; *Lybyer Diary*, July 14, 1919.

45. Sakakini 2004, 179; *Lybyer Diary*, July 11, 1919.

46. Youhanna Khalil Dikrat, "An Address Delivered by the President of the Literary Society of Bethlehem, 20 June 1919, Digital Reproduction of Original Manuscript," in *Lybyer Papers*, King-Crane Collection, 15/13/22, box 16/4.

47. *Lybyer Diary*, July 14, 1919.

48. "Letter to Clara Lybyer, July 9, 1919," in *Lybyer Papers-Illinois*, RS 15/13/22, box 16/A.H.L to C.A.L. March–May 1919.

49. "Fi Yad al-Mu'tamar," *Lisan al-Hal*, no. 245–7895 (October 1, 1919): 1, Col A–B. See "Photograph of Delegation Waiting to See Commission, Hebron/El Khalil," in King-Crane Collection. On *Lisan al-Hal*, see Ayalon 2008.

50. "Al-Lajna al-Dawliyya," *Lisan al-Hal*, no. 151–7798 (May 12, 1919): 2, Col C; "Ma Hiya Niyatahum wa-Kayfa Yajib an Nakhtar," *Lisan al-Hal*, no. 179–7826 (June 24, 1919): 1, Col A–B; "Zulumat Ba'duha Fawqa Ba'd," 1. Watenpaugh recounts the commentary on the commission that ran in the Aleppan newspaper *Halab*. One headline read: "The joy of the nation is tremendous thanks to the blessed delegation." In contrast to my analysis, Watenpaugh interprets the consistent nationalist line expressed in this newspaper as a form of elite nationalist pedagogy. Watenpaugh 2006, 149–53.

51. *Westermann Diary*, 12 January, 1919, 21–23; "Emir Faisal's Talks" 1919.

52. Zu'aytir and al-Hout 1984, 28.

53. "Official Text of the Memorandum Handed by the Syrian General Congress to the American Section of the International Commission," July 20, 1919, CZA, L4/794-255 to 794-256. Also published in "Qarar al-Mu'tamar al-Suri al-'Am," 221–23.

54. Schumann 2008, 3.

55. "Interview King Crane Commission in the Corners of Palestine and East Jordan, June 1919," in Zu'aytir and al-Hout 1984, 23–24.

56. Ibid., 28.

57. Chatterjee 1993, 11.

58. Tams 2006.

59. "Qanoun Jam'yat al-Umam," *Lisan al-Hal*, no. 146–7793 (May 5, 1919): 1. On *Lisan al-Hal*, see Ayalon 2008, 561.

60. See the Covenant of the League of Nations, n.d.

61. William Yale, "An Analysis of the Syrian-Palestine Situation in 1919: The American Point of View" (MA thesis, Boston University, 1928), 7, in William Yale Papers, Boston University, box 7/1 (hereafter *Yale Papers-Boston*); "League of Nations Covenant, Article 22," n.d. For a critical reassessment of the category "nationalist" as it may or may not apply to Sakakini, see Bawalsa 2010.

62. Sakakini 1955, 175.

63. "Report by Captain William Yale, July 1919," in *Lybyer Papers*, King-Crane Collection, RS 15/13/22, box 16/1; "Notes on a Conversation with Emir Faysal on Feb 13, 1919," in Yale Papers-Boston, box 4/2; "Letter from Henry Churchill King to His Son, Lieutenant Donald S. King, M.D., 24 July, 1919," in *King Papers*, King-Crane Collection, RG 2/6, box 128/8.

64. Lesch 1979, 31.

65. Wilson 1918b.

66. Gelvin 2003, 16; Manela 2007, 63. Wilson's Fourteen Points became a foundational document in the settlement of the war, and its effect was immediately obvious from press reactions around the world. More than any previous statement, except the

declaration of US involvement in the war, it gave Wilson a pedestal on the world stage. N. Smith 2003, 125.

67. Manela 2007, 23.

68. "Mustaqbal Suriya wa-Sa'ir al-Bilad al-'Arabiyya," *al-Manar* 21, no. 1 (December 2, 1918): 33–38.

69. Antonius 2010, 287.

70. "'Telegram.' From the Inhabitants of the Districts of Antioch, Harim, Alexandretta, Jisr, and Eshouge," in *Lybyer Papers,* King-Crane Collection, RS 15/13/22, box 16/3.

71. See, e.g., "Protest to Wilson, 15 March 1919 from Palestinian Colony of San Salvador," in Zu'aytir and al-Hout 1984, 10.

72. Zu'aytir and al-Hout 1984, 2.

73. Ibid.

74. Gelvin 2003, 16.

75. *Westermann Diary*, 27 January, 1919, 28. Article 22 of the League of Nations was well-known and thoroughly publicized throughout the region. Yale, "An Analysis of the Syrian-Palestine Situation in 1919," 6. Wilson's famous Fourteen Points speech championing "self-determination" shaped the discursive framework of the commission's enquiry.

76. Berman 1993, 1794.

77. David Kennedy 1987.

78. Lorca 2011.

79. "Statement for the Press of Damascus, 26 June 1919," in *Lybyer Papers*, King-Crane Collection, RS15/13/22, box 16/1.

80. Other states in this category included China, Japan, Korea, Morocco, Muscat, Persia, Siam, and Zanzibar. Özsu 2016a; Özsu 2016b, 373; Rodogno 2016b. Japan demonstrated that some states could be recategorized. Ottoman interest in international law was already well established in the mid-nineteenth century. Even earlier the Ottomans were cooperating in coalition with the Russian and British empires to oppose the French empire that was viewed as an enemy because of its violation of international law. Kayali 2008; Aydin 2015, 164. For another way that civilizational discourse was shaping how Arabs and the Turkish were defining themselves and each other, see Makdisi 2002b.

81. Lorca 2014, 21.

82. Aydin 2015, 164.

83. See Sylvest 2013.

84. "The Mandate System," *UNISPAL* 1945, https://unispal.un.org/UNISPAL .NSF/0/C61B138F4DBB08A0052565D00058EE1B; Pedersen 2006, 561.

85. Among the Arab lands designated "peoples not *yet* able to stand by themselves" were Syria and Lebanon, Palestine and Transjordan, and Iraq, "provisionally recognised

as independent, but [who would] receiv[e] the advice and assistance of a Mandatory in its administration until such time as it is able to stand alone." "The Mandate System."

86. See "Raja᾽ Suriya," *Lisan al-Hal*, no. 137–7784 (April 22, 1919): 1, Col A–B.

87. Franck 1990; Wambaugh 1933, 13; citing Baker 1922, 109.

88. Pedersen 2010. Also see Maogoto 2014.

89. Berman 2013, 357.

90. Byrne 2016, 22.

91. Dikrat, "An Address Delivered by the President."

92. "Al-Lajna al-Amrikiyya," *Lisan al-Hal*, no. 179–7826 (June 24, 1919): 2, Col B; "Manshur al-Wafd al-Amriki fi Dimashq min al-Lajna al-Dawliyya," *Lisan al-Hal*, no. 183–7830 (July 2, 1919): 1, Col B.

93. "Historical Sketch by Albert H. Lybyer of the Commission's Visit to Syria, 1 August 1919," in *Lybyer Papers*, box 16/2, 21; also Darwaza 1993, 362; "Petition from Abraham Mitrie Rihbany on Behalf of the New Syria National League, 15 March 1919," in *King Papers*, King-Crane Collection, RG 2/6, box 128/9.

94. Ambrosius 2006, 141.

95. "Letter from Albert H. Lybyer to A. C. Coolidge, January 1923," in *Lybyer Papers*, King-Crane Collection, RS 15/13/22, box 17/12.

96. "Report by Albert Lybyer on the Peace Conference's Balkan Policy, 22 March 1919," in *King Papers*, King-Crane Collection, RG 2/6, box 128/2; "Report by Albert H. Lybyer on Tentative Conclusions from Jaffa, 13 June 1919," in *Lybyer Papers*, King-Crane Collection, RS 15/13/22, box 16/1, 19; "Letter to Clara Lybyer, 24 August 1919," in *Lybyer Papers-Illinois*, RS 15/13/22, box 16/A.H.L to C.A.L. March–May 1919.

97. "The King–Crane Commission, A Historical Footnote for the Record (handwritten, no date) (typed version, dated October 8, 1952, Durham, NH)," in *Yale Papers-Boston*, box 3/4, 7.

98. "Schedule of Commission Meetings with Delegations in Beirut, 7 July 1919, Digital Reproduction of Original Manuscript," and "Schedule of Commission Appointments and Events in Damascus, 26 June to 3 July 1919, Digital Reproduction of Original Manuscript," in *Lybyer Papers*, King-Crane Commission, RS 15/13/22, box 16/3.

99. "Schedule of Commission Meetings with Delegations in Beirut, 7 July 1919."

100. "Document Listing Significant Conclusions from the Petitions," in *Donald M. Brodie Miscellaneous Papers, 1919–1941*, in King-Crane Collection, box 1/3 (hereafter *Brodie Papers*).

101. "Letter from Albert H. Lybyer to A. C. Coolidge, January 1923," in *Lybyer Papers*, in King-Crane Collection, RS 15/13/22, box 17/12.

102. *Lybyer Diary*, July 3, 1919.

103. Howard 1963, 121.

104. B. N. al-Hout 1986, 103; Jeffries 2017, 270.

105. Porath 1974, 89–90.

106. "Al-Hizb al-Suri al-Mu'tadil," *Lisan al-Hal,* no. 182–7829 (June 28, 1919): 2.

107. "Masiruna, al-Lajna al-Dawliyya," *Lisan al-Hal,* no. 162–7809 (May 27, 1919): 1, Col A–B.

108. "Zulumat Ba'duha Fawqa Ba'd."

109. Gelvin 2003, 21. The King-Crane Commission heard it was happening. Lybyer thought the Muslim-Christian Association to be a well-organized party. *Lybyer Diary,* June 18, 1919.

110. Sakakini 2004, 176–77. Also see Darwaza 1949, 106.

111. B. N. al-Hout 1986, 114.

112. "Qarar al-Mu'tamar al-Suri al-'Am," 221–23.

113. H. S., "'Ala Abwab al-Imtihan," *Al-'Asima,* no. 37 (June 24, 1919): 1.

114. "Mata Tantahi?," *Lisan al-Hal,* no. 182–7829 (June 28, 1919): 1, Col A–B.

115. Gelvin 1999.

116. "Masiruna, al-Lajna al-Dawliyya," 1.

117. "Tablighat Rasmiyya," *al-'Asima,* June 24, 1919.

118. "Letter to Clara Lybyer, 17 July 1919," in *Lybyer Papers-Illinois,* RS 15/13/22, box 16/A.H.L to C.A.L. March–May 1919.

119. See, for example, "Photograph of Delegation at Hebron/El Khalil, 17 July 1919," in *King Papers,* RG 2/6, box 129/1.

120. Petitioners' appeals for complete autonomy were reiterated in these summaries. "Ihtijaj al-Suriyyun: Surat al-Talighraf Allathi Arsalathu al-Jam'iya al-Suriyya," *al-Muqattam* 21, no. 5 (August 26, 1919): 250–51; "Surat al-Bayan Allathi Qaddamathu 'A'ilat al-Shuhada' li-l-Lajna al-Amrikyyia fi Dimashq," *al-Manar* 21, no. 5 (August 26, 1919): 25; 'Issa al-Saqri, "Al-Lajna al-Dawliyya fi Yafa wa-Mustaqbal Suriya," *al-Muqattam,* (June 14, 1919); "Matha Qala Ahl Dimashq," *al-Muqattam* (July 10, 1919); "Al-Lajna al-Dawliyya fi Yafa, Qarar al-Yafiyyun," *al-Muqattam* (June 20, 1919); "A'mal al-Lajna al-Amrikiyya fi Haifa," *Lisan al-Hal,* no. 182–7829 (June 20, 1919): 2, Col D; "Al-Lajna al-Amrikiyya," *Lisan al-Hal,* no. 187–7834 (July 8, 1919): 2, Col B–D.

121. "Petition from the People of the Coast in Damascus, 25 June 1919," in *Lybyer Papers,* King-Crane Papers, RS 15/13/22, box 16/1.

122. Sakakini 2004, 175.

123. "Excerpt of an Article by Sheikh Mohammed Khoudry Bey, Undated, Digital Reproduction of Original Manuscript," in *Lybyer Papers,* King-Crane Papers, RS 15/13/22, box 16/3; "Notes Edited by William Yale about Sherif Ali Haidar, 1919, Digital Reproduction of Original Manuscript," in *Lybyer Papers,* King-Crane Papers, RS 15/13/22, box 16/3; *Lybyer Diary,* June 28 and July 8, 1919.

124. "Letter to Clara, 19 June 1919" and "Letter to Clara Lybyer, 9 July 1919," in *Lybyer Papers-Illinois,* RS 15/13/22, box 16/A.H.L to C.A.L. March–May 1919.

125. Gelvin 1998, 20, 264.

126. Sakakini 2004, 177.

127. Zuʿaytir and al-Hout 1984, 30.

128. "Petition from Muslim and Christian Delegates of Jerusalem," in *Lybyer Papers*, King-Crane Collection, RS 15/13/22, box 16/3.

129. "ʿAridat al-Jamʿiya al-Islamiyya al-Mesihiyya ila Muʿtamar al-Silm al-ʿAm Howl Tamasuk ʿArab Filastin bi-Biladihim wa-Rafadihim Fikrat al-Watan al-Qawmi al-Yuhudi wa-l-Hijra al-Sahyuniyya," in Zuʿaytir and al-Hout 1984, 8–9.

130. "Report from Commission to President Wilson with Key Findings," in *King Papers*, King-Crane Collection, RG 2/6, box 128/3.

131. "Historical and Political Report of the First Arab Palestinian Conference (Held between January 28–February 9, 1919)," in Zuʿaytir and al-Hout 1984, 15–16; C. R. Crane and H. C. King, "Paris Peace Conf. 181.9102/3: Telegram Mr. C. R. Crane and Mr. H. C. King to the Commission to Negotiate Peace," *Papers Relating to the Foreign Relations of the United States* (hereafter *FRUS*), *The Paris Peace Conference, 1919, Volume XII*, July 10, 1919.

132. Zuʿaytir and al-Hout 1984, 7.

133. Gelvin 1998, 183.

134. Zuʿaytir and al-Hout 1984, 23–24; B. N. Al-Hout 1986, 112.

135. Zuʿaytir and al-Hout 1984, 12. The note states that this protest letter represented "the credible popular opinion officially from the Nablus municipality."

136. "Historical Sketch by Albert H. Lybyer."

137. Zuʿaytir and al-Hout 1984, 7–8.

138. "Al-Muʿtamar al-Suri," *Lisan al-Hal*, no. 183–7830 (July 2, 1919): 2, Col C.

139. Darwaza 1949 1:110.

140. "Report by Albert H. Lybyer on Tentative Conclusions from Jaffa." "Paris Peace Conf. 181.9102/9, Report of the American Section of the International Commission on Mandates in Turkey," *FRUS, Volume XII*, August 28, 1919. The report of the first Arab Palestinian Conference averred that Judaism was a religion and did not entail political rights of "a people" (*shaʿb*). Zuʿaytir and al-Hout 1984, 15.

141. Where it did get sticky, Darwaza recounts, was when the discussion turned to the choice of a possible mandate. He was one among several others at the congress who wanted no mandate at all, while the majority agreed to seek technical and economic assistance from the United States. Some at the congress believed that Great Britain might be good for the job, but many opposed any assistance from France, knowing its imperialist interests in the region "contradict Arab national ambitions." Darwaza 1949, 116–17, 107.

142. "The Initial Law of the United States of Syria," in *King Papers*, King-Crane Collection, RG 2/6, box 128/5; Darwaza 1949, 113.

143. *Lybyer Diary*, July 3, 1919.

144. "Interviews of King Crane Commission in the Corners of Palestine and East Jordan June 1919," in Zuʿaytir and al-Hout 1984, 26.

145. Darwaza 1993, 386–87.

146. Makdisi 2008a; Campos 2011, 68–72.

147. On the 1860 massacre of Christians, see Fawaz 1994.

148. The fighting between Druze and Maronites in 1860 was a significant moment contributing to "an empirewide debate about the place of religion in a modern nation." Makdisi 2002a, 602.

149. "Masiruna, al-Lajna al-Dawliyya," 1.

150. See Tusan 2014, 54, fn7. On the "Minorities Protection Regime" and how the league dealt with Iraq, see Pedersen 2015, 277–82. And on the league's treatment of the minorities issue more generally, see Mazower 1997; Mazower 2000; Anghie 2006b; "Paris Peace Conf. 181.9102/9, Report of the American Section of the International Commission on Mandates in Turkey."

151. Mazower 1997.

152. Akka is now known as Acre. B. N. Al-Hout 1986, 113.

153. "La Quwwa illa bi-l-Itihad," al-Manar 21, no. 5 (1919); Lybyer Diary, July 1, 1919.

154. "Letter to Clara Lybyer, 3 August 1919," in Lybyer Papers-Illinois, RS 15/13/22, box 16/A.H.L to C.A.L. March–May 1919.

155. B. N. al-Hout 1986, 111; "Document Listing Significant Conclusions from the Petitions."

156. Sakakini 2004, 180.

157. Joyce 2016, 473; Clor 2010, 343.

158. Crane and King, "King-Crane Commission Report, 28 August 1919," https://wwi.lib.byu.edu/index.php/The_King-Crane_Report; "List of Delegations Received by the Commission."

159. The Muslim women specifically requested American governmental support in "above all, education," but they wanted it only once their independence had been recognized. See, for example, "Schedule of Commission Meetings with Delegations in Beirut, 7 July 1919" and the commission's agenda for the delegations from Homs, on 16 July 1919: "List of Delegations Received in Homs, 16 July 1919" and "Petition from Muslim Women of Beirut, 8 July 1919," in Lybyer Papers, King-Crane Collection, RS 15/13/22, box 16/3; "The King-Crane Commission Report: Syria;" "List of Delegations Received by the Commission."

160. Lybyer Diary, June 30, 1919.

161. "List of Supplies Needed by the Commission, by Albert H. Lybyer, 1 May 1919," in Lybyer Papers, King-Crane Collection, RS 15/13/22, box 16: King-Crane Commission (May–August 1919) Folder 1, 1919.

162. "Notes from an Interview with a Delegation in Jaffa, Met with Donald Brodie and Albert Lybyer, 11 June 1919," in Lybyer Papers, King-Crane Collection, RS 15/13/22, box 16/3.

163. Westermann Diary, 20 January 1919; "Zulumat Baʾduha Fawqa Baʾd."

164. H., "'Ala Abwab al-Imtihan."

165. This belief that the United States had no imperial interests in the region was widespread. See, e.g., 'Issa al-Saqri, "Al-Lajna al-Dawliyya fi Yafa wa-Mustaqbal Suriya," *al-Muqattam,* June 23, 1919.

166. John and Hadawi 1970, 137, 140.

167. N. Smith 2003, 113.

168. Satia 2006, 21.

169. "Report by Howard Crosby Butler on Proposals for an Independent Arab State," in *King Papers,* King-Crane Collection, RG 2/6, box 128/3.

170. *Westermann Diary,* 23 March 1919, 46–47. For another take on this episode, see Khalil 2016, 30–31.

171. *Westermann Diary,* 23 March 1919, 47.

172. "Memorandum from the American Mission to Negotiate Peace to Commissioners King and Crane," 18 April 1919, in *Lybyer Papers,* King-Crane Collection, RS 15/13/22, box 16/3.

173. "Abtal al-Tahqiq fi Suriya," *Lisan al-Hal,* no. 134–7784 (April 22, 1919): 1, Col E; "Mustaqbal Suriya, Clemenceau wa-l-Amir Faysal wa-l-Lajna," 2; "Al-Lajna al-Amrikiyya," *Lisan al-Hal,* no. 178–7825 (June 23, 1919): 2, Col C; Qasimiyya 2002, 75.

174. Britain, France, and Italy withdrew from the Commission, fearing that the inquiry "might infringe on their claims to the Middle East," leaving the Americans to complete the work on their own. Patrick 2011, 6.

175. Drayton 2011, 675.

176. Quoted in Bentwich 1965, 35.

177. The British who favored a commission did so because they thought it would quiet down the natives in Palestine. "Albert Lybyer to Harry Howard, 30 October 1940," *Lybyer Papers*, King-Crane Collection, RS 15/13/22, box 16/1.

178. "Transcript of Albert Lybyer's Diary, March to September 1919," April 12 and 21, 1919, *Lybyer Papers,* King-Crane Collection, RS 15/13/22, box 17/8.

179. N. Smith 2003, 120.

180. Ambrosius 2006.

181. "The Council of Four: Minutes of Meetings, March 20 to May 24, 1919," cited in Patrick 2011, 27.

182. *Lybyer Diary,* May 17, 1919.

183. "Notebook Concerning the King-Crane Commission, Written by Donald M. Brodie, Commission Secretary, Digital Reproduction of Original Manuscript," in *King Papers,* King-Crane Collection, RG 2/6, box 129/30, 57–64.

184. Gibbons 1919, 370.

185. Dominian 1917, 230. Dominian also argued that language exerts influence on nationality and geography, and a "scientific boundary" could ensure peace (vii), making geographical knowledge a useful tool for helping to solve the Eastern Question. There

were quotes from this book (which was written by a student of Robert College of Constantinople) in Brodie's notes.

186. "Notebook Concerning the King-Crane Commission," 57–64.

187. Stocking 1991.

188. Howard 1963; "Document by Albert H. Lybyer Listing Data Gathered, 1 May 1919," in *Lybyer Papers*, King-Crane Collection, RS 15/13/22, box 16/1.

189. C.f., Stoler 2009, 156.

190. "Report by William Yale, 1 August 1919," in *Lybyer Papers*, King-Crane Collection, RS 15/13/22, box 16/2.

191. Montgomery had the same approach. See: "Report by George Montgomery on Syria, 1 August 1919," in *Lybyer Papers*, King-Crane Collection, RS 15/13/22, box 16/2.

192. Howard 1963, 144, 163. This belief that Islam was incompatible with modern civilization was widespread in the West. It was a conviction bolstered by an orientalist imagination that had shaped American and Western interactions with the Middle East for a long time. See Makdisi 2010, 85; McAlister 2005; Said 1979.

193. "Report by William Yale, 1 August 1919, Digital Reproduction of Original Manuscript," 7, 18.

194. Sakakini 2004, 24.

195. "Report by William Yale, 1 August 1919, Digital Reproduction of Original Manuscript," 7.

196. Ibid., 21.

197. Ibid., 9.

198. "Yale's Letter to Westermann from Beirut, 8 July 1919," in *William Yale Papers*, Yale University Archives, box 1/6 (hereafter *Yale Papers-Yale*).

199. "Report by Captain William Yale, July 1919, Digital Reproduction of Original Manuscript," in *Lybyer Papers*, King-Crane Collection, RS 15/13/22, box 16/1.

200. Yale, "Reflections on Syrian Nationalism," in *The Near East: A Modern History*, in *Yale Papers-Boston*, box 5/3/319. Yale exemplified what Nathaniel Berman has identified as a key feature of internationalism in this period. See Berman 1993.

201. Yale, "Reflections on Syrian Nationalism."

202. Durkheim 1995, 192; Mazzarella 2017, 173.

203. T. E. Lawrence "does not like Wm. Yale because he said that Yale spent his time in Jerusalem visiting the brothels. 'Men of our set don't do that sort of thing.'" *Westermann Diary*, 12 January, 1919, 19.

204. "Letter to Clara Lybyer, 9 July 1919, Digital Reproduction of Original Manuscript," in *Lybyer Papers-Illinois*, RS 15/13/22, box 16/A.H.L to C.A.L. March–May 1919.

205. "Mr. C. R. Crane and Mr. H. C. King to the Commission to Negotiate Peace, Beirut, 10 July 1919, Received 12 July," in *FRUS*, 749.

206. "Report by William Yale, 1 August 1919," 10.

207. Ibid., 21–22.

208. "Harry Howard to Albert Lybyer, 24 July 1941," in *Lybyer Papers,* King-Crane Collection, RS 15/13/22, box 3.

209. *Lybyer Diary,* July 9, 1919.

210. Patrick 2011, 68.

211. Manela 2007, xi, 19. For a critique of Manela, see Omar 2019.

212. "Letter from Albert H. Lybyer to Woodrow Wilson, 22 April 1919," in *Lybyer Papers,* King-Crane Collection, RS 15/13/22, box 16/1.

213. Wells 1936, 82.

214. "Telegram from Albert H. Lybyer to an Unknown Recipient, 11 July 1919," in *Lybyer Papers,* King-Crane Collection, RS 15/13/22, box 16/2; *Lybyer Diary,* January to March 1919, January 1, 1919, March 2, 1919.

215. See, e.g. *Library Diary,* March 9, 1919, March 25, 1919, and April 24, 1919.

216. "Letter from Henry Churchill King to President Woodrow Wilson, 10 September 1919," in *Brodie Papers,* King-Crane Collection, box 1/ 7; "Copy or Draft of a Letter [Probably from Henry Churchill King] to Colonel Edward M. House, 21 May 1919," in *King Papers,* King-Crane Collection, RG 2/6, box 128/1.

217. "Copy or Draft of a Letter [Probably from Henry Churchill King] to Colonel Edward M. House, 22 May 1919," in *King Papers,* King-Crane Collection, RG 2/6, box 128/1.

218. "Letter from Henry Churchill King to Albert H. Lybyer, 1 October 1919," in *Lybyer Papers,* King-Crane Collection, RS 15/13/22, box 17/3, 2.

219. *Lybyer Diary,* 14 June 1919; "Instructions for Commissioners, 25 March 1919," 3.

220. *Westermann Diary,* 28 April 1919, 70.

221. *Lybyer Diary,* January 1, 9, 11, 1919; *Lybyer Diary,* May 27 and August 8, 1919; "Letter to Clara Lybyer, 10 August 1919," in *Lybyer Papers-Illinois,* RS 15/13/22, box 16/A.H.L to C.A.L. March–May 1919.

222. "Letter to Clara Lybyer, 26 June 1919" in *Lybyer Papers-Illinois,* RS 15/13/22, box 16/A.H.L to C.A.L. March–May 1919.

223. *Lybyer Diary,* February 2 and January 15, 1919.

224. "Albert Lybyer to Harry Howard, 30 October 1940, Digital Reproduction of Original Manuscript."

225. "Letter to Clara Lybyer, 18 June 1919" in *Lybyer Papers-Illinois,* RS 15/13/22, box 16/A.H.L to C.A.L. March–May 1919.

226. *Lybyer Diary,* June 28 and 30, July 3 and 18, 1919.

227. "Letter to Clara Lybyer, 20 June 1919," in *Lybyer Papers-Illinois,* RS 15/13/22, box 16/A.H.L to C.A.L. March–May 1919.

228. "Letter to Clara Lybyer, 26 June 1919"; "Letter to Clara Lybyer, 29 June 1919" in *Lybyer Papers, Lybyer Papers-Illinois,* RS 15/13/22, box 16/A.H.L to C.A.L. March–May 1919.

229. "Letter from Henry Churchill King to President Woodrow Wilson, 10 September 1919."

230. Howard 1963, 38.

231. Hoff 2008; Throntveit 2011.

232. Grabill 1971. The extent to which Wilson's religious faith informed his political vision and actions is a matter of great debate. See Throntveit 2011. According to Mazower's reading of the scholarship, Wilson "thought in biblical terms of covenants" and saw democratic politics as "a sphere of moral action." Wilson also had an "elitist commitment" to "democracy and public opinion as the bedrock of any living political order." Mazower 2012, 121, 126.

233. Brubaker 2015, 110.

234. *Lybyer Diary*, 1 July 1919; "Letter to Clara Lybyer, 26 June 1919." in *Lybyer Papers-Illinois,* RS 15/13/22, box 16/A.H.L to C.A.L. March–May 1919. In his diary entry dated June 25, 1919, Lybyer recorded the group's journey past Tiberias into Syria. As they passed the apparently unattractive town of "Magdala" (or al-Majdal), "King said he didn't wonder that Mary Magdalene left home." On the popularity of Holy Land biblical images circulating in the United States, see McAlister 2005, 17–18.

235. E. F. Thompson 2015, 244.

236. "Al-Mu'tamar al-Suri," 2; Anghie 2002. The protection of minorities in general was an important feature of liberal imperialism. Tusan 2014, 54, fn. 34. On the protection regime for minorities, see Pedersen 2015, 277–82. And on the league's treatment of the minorities issue more generally, see Mazower 1997, Mazower 2000, Pedersen 2007. The first "Minority Treaty" was signed between Poland and the League of Nations during the summer of 1919, coinciding with the King-Crane Commission. Anghie 2006b, 449–450.

237. Makdisi 2010, 127.

238. Al-Saqri, "Al-Lajna al-Dawliyya fi Yafa wa-Mustaqbal Suriya."

239. "Notes from an Interview with a Delegation in Jaffa."

240. Qasimiyya 2002, 75.

241. *Westermann Diary,* 28 February 1919.

242. Makdisi 2010, 126; E. F. Thompson 2009.

243. Loevy 2016, 321.

244. Shlaim 2010, 4.

245. A. Hourani 1990, 34–35; Spooner, 2015.

246. Hofstadter 1948, 270.

247. "Ma Hiya Niyatahum wa-Kayfa Yajib an Nakhtar," 1; Bulus, "Al-Mas'ala al-Suriyya wa-l-Ahzab," *al-Manar* 21, no. 4 (June 28, 1919): 197–207, 2; Suqary 1919; "No Title," *al-Muqattam*, no. 9203 (June 23, 1919); Makdisi 2010, 144, fn. 66.

248. *Westermann Diary,* 28 February 1919.

249. "Letter from Harry Howard to Albert Lybyer, 8 September 1941," in *Lybyer Papers,* King-Crane Collection, RS, 15/13/22, box 3. Lybyer expressed his doubts about Yale's loyalties in a letter to Harry Howard more than two decades after their mission. "Letter from Albert Lybyer to Harry Howard, 5 September 1941," in *Lybyer Papers,* King-Crane Collection, RS 15/13/22, box 3.

250. *Lybyer Diary,* June 14, 1919; "Albert Lybyer to Harry Howard, 26 October 1940," in *Lybyer Papers,* King-Crane Collection, RS, 15/13/22, box 3.

251. "Letter from Albert Lybyer to Harry Howard, 5 September 1941, Digital Reproduction of Original Manuscript."

252. "Statement of Emir Faisal to the American Commission, 6 July 1919, Digital Reproduction of Original Manuscript."

253. Nasim Sabe'a, "Hukumat Suriyya al-Dusturiyya," *al-Muqattam,* no. 9253 (August 22, 1919), Col. A.

254. Neil Smith gives an account of the development of the United States' "imperative for expansion" in the preceding period. He writes: "By the time of Woodrow Wilson's presidency, the frenzied pursuit of US economic interests across the world was generally clothed in the more medicinal rhetoric of moral global advancement." N. Smith 2003, 115.

255. The fact that Zionist political clout and the influence of their backers were always greater than that of the Arabs is not in doubt (even if some partisans continue to try to claim otherwise). Shlaim 2017; Segev 2000; R. Khalidi 2006

256. Loevy 2016; Satia 2014; N. Smith 2003.

257. Regarding the Hussein-McMahon correspondence, historian Tariq Tell notes that "George Antonius' (1891–1942) *Arab Awakening* remains to this day the only credible academic source in a European language in which the Hashemites' own version of the negotiations—drawn from its author's conversations with leading members of the dynasty—are given a sympathetic scholarly airing." Tell 2017. Also see Boyle 2001, 7–10.

258. Gelvin 1994, 648.

259. Salim Tamari 2011; Salim Tamari 2017; Halabi 2012. This was also the position of the chief of police and gendarmerie in Damascus, Gabriel Haddad Pasha, as he told it to the King-Crane Commission. "Notes from Commission Meeting with Gabriel Haddad Pasha in Damascus, 27 June 1919," in *Lybyer Papers,* King-Crane Collection, RS 15/13/22, box 16/3.

260. Salim Tamari 2011; Salim Tamari 2017, 10–15.

261. "Letter to Clara Lybyer, 31 July 1919," in *Lybyer Papers-Illinois,* RS 15/13/22, box 16/A.H.L to C.A.L. March–May 1919.

262. "Text of a Telegram from Commissioner Charles Crane to President Woodrow Wilson," in *King Papers,* King-Crane Collection, RG 2/6, box 128/1; King-Crane Commission Report, August 28, 1919.

263. "Historical Sketch by Albert H. Lybyer."

264. "Text of a Telegram from Commissioner Charles Crane to President Woodrow Wilson;" John and Hadawi 1970, 170.

265. "Memorandum from Donald Brodie, 1923," in *Lybyer Papers*, King-Crane Collection, RS 15/13/22, box 17/12.

266. Knock 1995, 251, 267.

267. Laurence Hilss, "Peril Is Seen in American Rule of Asia Minor," *The Sun*, August 31, 1919, 1.

268. "Taqrir al-Lajna al-Amrikiyya," *Filastin*, no. 85–544 (January 2, 1923): 3, Col E; "Taqrir al-Lajna al-Amrikiyya ʿan al-Sharq al-Adna," *al-Muqattam*, no. 10280 (December 29, 1922): 4, Col F. President Wilson allowed select newspapers to publish the King-Crane Report. "Taqrir al-Lajna al-Amrikiyya ʿan al-Sharq al-Adna," *al-Muqattam*, no. 10281 (December 30, 1922): 2, 1 Col E–F; "Taqrir al-Lajna al-Amrikiyya ʿan al-Sharq al-Adna 2," no. 10282 (December 31, 1922): 3, Col A–C; "Taqrir al-Lajna al-Amrikiyya ʿan al-Sharq al-Adna," no. 10283 (January 3, 1923): 3, Col A–D.

269. John and Hadawi 1970, 170; "Memorandum from Donald Brodie, 1923;" Howard 1963, 270, 311; "Letter from Henry Churchill King to Ray Stannard Baker, 6 May 1922," in *King Papers*, King-Crane Collection, RG 2/6/1, box 6.

270. "Concerning the Letter of Jamal Husseini of February 9th, 1962 from Palm Beach, Florida to William Yale," in *Howard W. Bliss Collection 1902–1920*, American University of Beirut, box 19/7.

271. Howard 1963, 154.

272. Crane and King, "King-Crane Commission Report, 28 August 1919, Digital Reproduction of Original Manuscript"; "Petition from the People of the Coast in Damascus, 25 June 1919, Digital Reproduction of Original Manuscript."

## Chapter 2: Universalizing Liberal Internationalism

1. Hughes 2009, 348–49, 314.

2. According to an official survey, in 1936, there were 172 Jewish agricultural colonies in Palestine: "A Survey of Palestine, Prepared in December 1945 and January 1946 for the Information of the Anglo-American Committee of Inquiry," 1946, 372. The total number of settlers increased from 175,000 in 1931 to 370,000 in 1936, see Krämer 2011, 240. Also on the Jewish population, see *Palestine Royal Commission Report* 1937, 294. For a list of British investigative commissions to Palestine, see the list of Major Commissions of Palestine at the front of this book.

3. Amin al-Husayni, "Lam Yabqa li-l-ʿArab Amal fi ʿAdl al-Hukuma," *Filastin*, 20, no. 109–3381 (November 13, 1936): 8.

4. The League of Nations Permanent Mandates Commission was the scene of much argumentation, where Palestinians tried to make their case for their right to

independence, exerting what historian Natasha Wheatley has described as legal "hermeneutic efforts" marked by an "(often obsessive) examination of what the mandate actually said." Wheatley 2015, 226.

5. For an eyewitness's estimation of the direct and indirect factors that led to the outbreak of this revolt, see Abu Gharbiyya 1993, 51. On the antecedents to the revolt, including the "rising tide of worker militancy" that fueled the revolt, see Lockman 1996, 208–9. On the making of events as events, see Sewell 1996.

6. M. K. Kelly 2017, 21. For an analysis of how the economic situation at the time influenced the revolt, see Kanafani 1972.

7. Naqqara 2011, 83–85.

8. Yazbak 2000; Abu Gharbiyya 1993, 51; Matthews 2006, 223.

9. Magliveras 1991.

10. Pedersen 2015, 356–57.

11. Pedersen 2015, 5.

12. C. W. Anderson 2013; C. W. Anderson 2018; Swedenburg 1995; Matthews 2006.

13. Matthews 2006, 223.

14. On Palestinian claims to citizenship, see Banko 2016.

15. "Letter from Khalil Totah to Sir Arthur Wauchope 1 June 1936," in *Khalil Totah Papers* (Haverford, Box 1, F3).

16. Sakakini 1955, 175.

17. al-Kayyali 1988, 435.

18. Scott 1999, 16.

19. On the role of law and political institutions in the production of colonized subjectivity, see, for example, Cohn 1996; J. Comaroff 2006.

20. The birth of Palestine as a global cause has been (I think incorrectly) dated much later, with Fayez Sayegh's 1965 publication of "Zionist Colonialism in Palestine" standing out for Yoav Di-Capua as one founding moment. With less historical specificity, John Collins asserts that "the Palestinian struggle has always been a global one," but mentions 1948 and the 1960s as important periods in this process. See Sayegh 2013 [1965]; Di-Capua 2018, 191; Collins 2011, 4.

21. Tens of Arabic newspapers were being published in Paris, New York, Rio de Janeiro, and Sao Paulo, Brazil. Arsan 2012, 175. The leading Arabic dailies in Palestine, *Filastin* and *al-Difaʿ*, sold 4,000–6,000 copies daily. Newspapers were read out loud in public at cafes, and other village gathering sites, such as marketplaces. The editor of *Filastin* delivered free copies of his paper to every village in Jaffa "to 'teach the peasants their rights.'" Three large dailies were published in the city of Jaffa alone, and the British were concerned about the Arab public that the press was helping to crystallize. See Ayalon 2004, 62–65, 106–7; Wildangel 2004, 81–94, 89, 90; Shubayb 2001. Radio was another news medium gaining force in this period. On the opening of the radio broadcast station during the mandate, see Stanton 2013.

22. See, for example, "Al-Hind al-Muslima Taghdab li-Filastin," *Filastin* 20, no. 81–3272 (June 18, 1936): 2; "Al-Sahafa al-Ajnabiyya Tudir Siyasat Biladiha," *Filastin* 20, no. 66–3257 (May 16, 1936): 3; "Filastin al-Tha'ira 'Ala Siyasat al-Ifna'," *Filastin* 20, no. 88–3279 (June 25, 1936): 7. An article published in Sao Paulo, Brazil; "Difa' al-Duwal al-Isti'mariyya 'an Haybatiha," *al-Rabita* 20, no. 91–3282 (June 28, 1936): 6. An article published in New York; "Al-Ghazw al-Yahudi wa-Wajib al-Lajna al-Malakiyya," *al-Huda* 20, no. 190–3381 (November 13, 1936): 2 and 7.

23. Ayalon 2004, 61.

24. Abu Gharbiyya 1993, 52; Wyrtzen 2016, 166; "Kayfa Bada'at al-Thawra fi-l-Maghreb," *Filastin* 20, no. 108–3299 (July 26, 1936): 3.

25. "Faransa fi Suriya wa-Ingiltra fi Filastin," *Filastin* 20, no. 86–3277 (June 23, 1936): 5.

26. Matthews 2006, 23–24; Wyrtzen 2016, 147.

27. "Letter from Khalil Totah to Palestine Watching Committee, London. 11 May 1936," in *Khalil Totah Papers*, Haverford College Quaker and Special Collections (hereafter *Totah Papers*), box 1/3.

28. Kahn 2011; Matthews 2003, 16. Palestinian courting of Indian support has a longer history. See O. Khalidi 2009.

29. "Filastin fi Yawm 'Isyaniha," 1; Elshakry 2013, 255.

30. Provence 2017, 229.

31. Ibid., 231.

32. Although here I am referring to people suffering from imperial domination, the imperialists were also aware that they faced a crisis, including Reginald Coupland, member of the Peel Commission. Coupland 1933.

33. M. Thomas 2005, 4; Wyrtzen 2016, 166.

34. "Letter from Khalil Totah to Palestine Watching Committee, London. 11 May 1936."

35. "Al-Duwal la Ta'mal Shai'an li-l-Habasha," *Filastin* 20, no. 61–3252 (May 10, 1936): 3; "Amwal Musa'adat al-Habasha li-Mankubi Filastin," *Filastin* 20, no. 76–3267 (June 13, 1936): 3.

36. "Al-Harb al-Habashiyya al-Italiyya," *Filastin* 20, no. 52–3243 (May 1, 1936): 4; "Al-Imbratur Yusir 'ala al-Difa'," *Filastin* 20, no. 53–3244 (May 2, 1936): 4; "Italia Satandam 'ala Khawd al-Harb," *Filastin* 20, no. 53–3244 (May 2, 1936): 7; "Akhbar al-Harb al-Italiyya al-Habashiyya," *Filastin* 20, no. 54–3245 (May 3, 1936): 3.

37. Matera and Kent 2017, 46.

38. "Al-Najashi wa-'A'ilatuhu Yughadirun Biladahum," *Filastin* 20, no. 55–3246 (May 4, 1936): 3.

39. "Al-Habasha wa-Akhawatuha Dahiyat al-Ghadr wa-l-Musawama al-Siyasiyya," *Filastin* 20, no. 56–3247 (May 5, 1936): 2.

40. "Al-Habasha wa Akhawatuha," 2.

41. Matera and Kent 2017, 46.

42. Zuʿaytir 1992, 275.

43. On the concept of martyrdom in Palestinian nationalism, see Allen 2009a; Allen 2009b.

44. "Kayfa Istuqbila Imbratur al-Habasha fi Haifa," *Filastin* 20, no. 60–3251 (May 9, 1936): 1; "Al-ʿAʾila al-Malakiyya Habashiyya fi-l-Quds," *Filastin* 20, no. 60–3251 (May 9, 1936): 4.

45. "Shaʿbun Shahid Yurahhib bi-Malik Shahid," *Filastin* 20, no. 59–3250 (May 8, 1936): 3.

46. "Britania Takhsar Kul Maʿraka," *Filastin* 20, no. 57–3248 (May 6, 1936): 2.

47. Pedersen 2015, 403.

48. "Filastin fi Yawm ʿIsyaniha," *Filastin* 20, no. 67–3258 (May 17, 1936): 1.

49. Ibid. For an account of Italy's brutality against Abyssinia, see Matera and Kent 2017, 63.

50. Jackson and O'Malley 2018; Sluga and Clavin 2017; Sluga 2013; Goswami 2012; Aydin 2017. On earlier manifestations of internationalism in the Middle East, see Khuri-Makdisi 2013; Arsan 2012.

51. On WILPF, see Cowan 2014; Gorman 2012.

52. Goebel 2017, 2.

53. Edwards 2003; Hodder 2016; Makalani 2011.

54. Wilder 2005; Matthews 2003; Aydin 2017, 136.

55. Fahmi 1936, 7; "Shukr Sumuw Waalidat al-Amir Talal," *Filastin* 20, no. 80–3271 (June 17, 1936): 4; "Mecca al-Mukrama wa-Musaʿadat Mankubu Filastin," *Filastin* 20, no. 81–3272 (June 18, 1936): 3. Arabs had been active in showing solidarity across the newly imposed political boundaries for a while. The bloody events in 1929 sparked by years of Zionist efforts to alter the structure of the Haram al-Sharif/Wailing Wall—a holy place of Jews and Muslims that had been peaceably shared among their worshipers until then—saw hundreds of Jews and Arabs killed in riots. The Arab world reacted, protesting the events and the Balfour Declaration that had set the stage for them. Boycotts of goods from Palestine were also being undertaken in Syria to express opposition to Zionism. And four years later, when the Palestinian leadership in the Arab Executive declared a strike and demonstrations turned deadly, solidarity protests happened in Damascus and other cities across the Arab world, while student and medical delegations from Syria, Iraq, and Egypt toured Palestine to witness the conditions and care for the wounded. Iraq announced a public holiday called "Palestine Day" and reactivated the Committee for the Defense of Palestine that had formed during the 1933 turmoil in Palestine. Wheatley 2017, 270. On Egypt's relationship to Palestine, see Jankowski 1980; T. Mayer 1983. On the Muslim Brother's activism for Palestine, see Gershoni 1986; "Wafd min Misr Yazur Filastin," *Filastin* 20, no. 75–3266 (June 12, 1936): 2; "Wafd wa-

Bi tha Tibbiyya min al- Iraq," *Filastin* 20, no. 79–3270 (June 16, 1936): 2; Provence 2017, 199–200, 214, 221, 231, 243; *Iraq Correspondence, Foreign Office* (British National Archives, 371/20016, 1936); Nafi 1998, 223–24.

56. Invocations of the "Arab world" and "Muslim world" were voiced partially as a leverage point against the British too. This warning was expressed across Indian and Palestinian newspapers and was heard loud and clear by British colonial officials. See discussion of two articles from the *Indian Eastern Times* in *Filastin*, "Al-Hind al-Muslima Taghdab li-Filastin," 2. The revolt leadership also made announcements to the "Arab and Muslim worlds" when warning Palestinian villages not to cooperate with the British. al-Kayyali 1988, 456.

57. Allen 2018; Freas 2012; Matthews 2003; Toynbee 1936, 101–2, 105.

58. Wyrtzen 2016, 149.

59. Toynbee 1936, 107.

60. Zu aytir 1992, 242. Another example of Indian Muslim solidarity for Palestine reported in *Filastin*: "Jam iyat al-Muslimin fi Bunjab," *Filastin* 20, no. 80–3271 (June 18, 1936): 3.

61. Ambrosius 2006, 144; Millen-Penn 1995.

62. Herberichs 1966; Noelle-Neumann 1979.

63. Pedersen 2006; Pedersen 2015.

64. Carr 1936, 855; Wertheim 2012, 214; Gorman 2012, 190.

65. "Letter from Khalil Totah to Sir Arthur Wauchope 1 June 1936."

66. Letter from Mustafa Al Sabunji, Chairman of the Palestine Defence Society in Mosul, to His Excellency the Ambassador, 19 April 1938, in India Office Records, British Library, IOR/L/PS/12/3348.

67. al-Kayyali 1988, 434.

68. Ibid., 384.

69. Ibid., 394.

70. Ibid., 435.

71. Trouillot 1995, 73.

72. "Al-Sahafa al-Ajnabiyya Tudir Siyasat Biladiha," 3; Nafi 1998, 201.

73. al-Kayyali 1988, 429–33.

74. Ibid., 391.

75. Waqayyan 2012, 181–82, 184–86.

76. Parsons 2015, 396.

77. Khoury 1985, 329; Parsons 2015, 400.

78. al-Kayyali 1988, 435.

79. Ibid., 438.

80. al-Kayyali 1988, 433–34.

81. Ibid., 458–59.

82. Ibid., 396.

83. Bashkin 2012, 104; Nafi 1998, 199. On activities in the Gulf and the British concern, see India Office Records, IOL/PS/12/3351.

84. el-Awaisi 1998, 30–33, 36, 43, 48–53; "Hawadith Filastin fi Masajid Misr," *Filastin* 20, no. 78–3269 (June 15, 1936): 2.

85. Memo from Aden to Ormsby Gore, Secretary of State for Colonies, 7 Oct 1936, India Office, IOR/R/20/A/3703, 1935. Also see Jankowski 1980. From these British records, it is not clear who was responsible for the fliers. 19 September 1936, India Office Records, IOR/R/15/2/165.

86. "'Atf al-Misryin 'ala Filastin," *Filastin* 20, no. 77–3268 (June 14, 1936): 2; "Tawassut al-Misryin li-Hal al-Qadiya al-Filastiniyya," *Filastin* 20, no. 78–3269 (June 15, 1936): 2; "Tanafus al-Misryin li-Musa'dat Mankubi Filastin," *Filastin* 20, no. 80–3271 (June 17, 1936): 2.

87. Memo from Police Office, Aden, to the Civil Secretary, Aden, 31 July 1936, in India Office Records, IOR/R/20/A/3703; "Awal Duf'a min Tabaru'at Suriya," *Filastin* 20, no. 77–3268 (June 14, 1936): 4; "Musa'ada Maliyya min al-'Iraq li-Mankubi Filastin," *Filastin* 20, no. 79–3270 (June 16, 1936): 7.

88. See, for example, "Telegrams from Mr. Mackereth and to Sir Maurice Peterson" June 2, 4, and 18, 1938, which reported the collection of money in Iraq "going to Terrorists in Palestine," in India Office Records, IOR/L/PS/12/3348.

89. "Unsuru Filastin wa-la Tahtamu bi-Ingiltra," *Filastin* 20, no. 80–3271 (June 17, 1936): 2.

90. On colonialism's un-Christian assaults against the concept of equal and universal human rights, see Marzuqa, "Hukm al-Nusraniyya 'ala al-Isti'mar," *Filastin* 20, no. 83–3274 (June 20, 1936. For mentions of British insults to Arab dignity, see Boyle 2001, 252; Hughes 2009, 324.

91. al-Kayyali 1988, 394.

92. Ibid., 404.

93. Ibid., 434.

94. Zu'aytir and al-Hout 1984, 449.

95. Ibid., 379.

96. Ibid., 386.

97. Zu'aytir and al-Hout 1984, 435.

98. "League of Nations Covenant, Article 15," n.d.

99. League of Nations 1937b.

100. Jawhariyyeh 2014, loc. 4894-4896.

101. Abu Gharbiyya 1993.

102. Ibid., 113.

103. "Letter from Khalil Totah to Palestine Watching Committee, London. 11 May 1936."

104. "Al-Nisaʾ al-ʿArabiyyat Yastanjidna bi-Muluk al-ʿArab," *Filastin* 20, no. 77–3268 (June 14, 1936): 2.

105. "Al-Itihad al-Nisaʾi al-ʿArabi Yursil Ihtijajan," *Filastin* 20, no. 77–3268 (June 14, 1936): 2.

106. M. K. Kelly 2017; Nafi 1998, 197.

107. For more on the military courts, see C. W. Anderson 2013, 904, 116.

108. Naqqara 2011, 87–88.

109. Abu Gharbiyya 1993, 117.

110. Hughes 2009, 318, 353.

111. Abu Gharbiyya 1993, 114.

112. Norris 2013, 179; Norris 2008, 34. For analysis of contemporary practice of human shield use, see Gordon and Perugini 2016.

113. Kirkbride 1987, 353–56.

114. For a contemporary account of the looting and home demolition, see Newton 1987, 357–66.

115. Provence 2017, 237.

116. Norris 2013, 173; Yazbak 2000, 106–7. On the dire economic situation of peasants and workers during the period leading up to the revolt, see Khalaf 1997, 107; Tress 1988.

117. Abu Gharbiyya 1993.

118. Jawhariyyeh 2014, loc. 2693–2706.

119. Ibid., loc. 3931.

120. Ibid., loc. 2597, 4807–4819.

121. Ibid., loc. 4805; Abu Gharbiyya 1993, 331–32.

122. It was never proved with certainty who killed Andrews. Nafi 1998, 252.

123. "Khalil Totah Diary, 1 June 1939," in *Totah Papers* box 1/3.

124. Zuʿaytir and al-Hout 1984, 408.

125. Ibid., 407; Zuʿaytir 1992.

126. Zuʿaytir and al-Hout 1984, 407; "Letter to the High Commissioner Arthur Wauchope, 18 April 1936."

127. Zuʿaytir and al-Hout 1984, 408.

128. "Letter from Khalil Totah to Sir Arthur Wauchope 1 June 1936."

129. Zuʿaytir and al-Hout 1984, 410; Atrash 2015, 287.

130. On Jewish immigration rates, which rose to 62,000 in 1935, see Simson 1937, 159.

131. al-Kayyali 1988, 382.

132. Naqqara 2011, 72.

133. "Royal Commission" 1936.

134. al-Kayyali 1988, 457; Darwaza 1949, 149–50. Palestinians had employed political boycotts as a means of civil disobedience before. In the early 1920s they boycotted consultative committee meetings and elections for an only partially representative

legislative body, refusing the unfair terms of the setup, rejecting them as sham structures that would serve only to legitimize the cards stacked against them. The more radical among them insisted on naming their actions during this rebellion "civil disobedience" to indicate it was an intentional rejection of the prevailing order and British state authority. Zuʿaytir 1992, 80, 100.

135. Public declarations of support for boycotting the commission were also published in local newspapers. See, for example, "Jenin Tuʾayid Muqataʿat al-Lajna wa-Tashku," *Filastin* 20, no. 190–3381 (November 13, 1936): 4; "Taʾyid Qarar al-Lajna al-ʿArabiyya al-ʿUlya," *Filastin* 20, no. 190–3381 (November 13, 1936): 5.

136. al-Shuqayri 1969, 158.

137. M. K. Kelly 2017, 22.

138. Mattar 1988, 75.

139. "Al-Siyasa al-Ingliziyya Talʿab ʿala Hablayn," *Filastin* 20, no. 108–3299 (July 26, 1936): 2.

140. League of Nations 1937b.

141. The Palin Commission of 1920 investigated the causes and course of the 1920 riots in Jerusalem during the Nabi Musa festival, but the report was not released. The Haycraft Commission investigated the causes of the riots in Jaffa the next year and drew attention to Arab resentment of Jewish immigration. The 1926 Bertram-Young Commission investigated relations between the Arab Orthodox community in Palestine and the Patriarchate. The British Parliamentary commission led by Sir Walter Shaw investigated the causes of the Haram al-Sharif/Western Wall riots in 1929 and recommended that land transfers and immigration be controlled to prevent future disturbances. In 1930, the Hope-Simpson Commission that investigated economic issues relating to land and immigration found that Zionist labor practices and inalienability of Jewish land purchase were contrary to the mandate. That commission's recommendations led to the Passfield White Paper, elaborating British policy limiting Jewish immigration, but it was withdrawn the following year. See Abboushi 1977; Verdery 1971; Shamir and Hacker 2001; Block and Somers 2003; Lauriat 2010; Ashforth 1990a; Mongia 2004; Stoler 2009; "East Africa: The Royal Commission" 1955; "Report of the Royal Commission on the South African War" 1903.

142. Joyce 2016, 476; Sylvest, 2013, 61–62.

143. Darwaza 1993, 150.

144. Qaddoura 1993, 23.

145. Kousa, "Istihtar Mustamir bi Karamat al-Umma al-ʿArabiyya," *Filastin* 20, no. 70–3261 (May 25, 1936): 11.

146. "Antonius Letter to Rogers, 15 December 1936; Written from Institute of Current World Affairs Letterhead, from Karm al-Mufti, Jerusalem," in *George Antonius Collection,* Middle East Centre Archive, St Antony's College, Oxford University (hereafter *Antonius Collection*); *Palestine Royal Commission Report 1937,* 102–3.

147. This point was agreed on early in the revolt during a meeting of prominent activists in Nablus, including Akram Zuʿaytir, who recorded its proceedings. Zuʿaytir 1992, 61.

148. Abu Gharbiyya 1993, 89.

149. "Munawarat Khaddaʿa," *Filastin* 20, no. 105–3296 (July 23, 1936): 1 and 8.

150. "La Nurid Istidʿaʿ al-Lajna al-Malakiyya," *Filastin* 20, no. 70–3261 (May 25, 1936): 10. Also see Musa ʿAlami's memorandum for the commission, which was signed by senior Arab civil servants in Jerusalem; in addition to condemning the government's policy in Palestine, the memo also explained the desperate sense of frustration among Palestinians. See Wasserstein 1977; Furlonge 1969, 109–10.

151. Kousa 1936, 11.

152. H. F. Khalidi 1949, 230.

153. Darwaza 1993, 31.

154. Ibid.

155. "La Nurid Istidʿaʿ al-Lajna al-Malakiyya," 10.

156. "Al-Siyasa al-ʿUlya wa-l-Lajna al-Malakiyya," *Filastin* 20, no. 66–3257 (May 16, 1936): 1 and 8; "Mufawadat al-Lajna al-ʿUlya wa-l-Mandub al-Sami," *Filastin* 20, no. 67–3258 (May 17, 1936): 5; "Rad al-Lajna al-ʿArabiyya al-ʿUlya ʿala Khitab Wazir al-Mustaʿmarat," *Filastin* 20, no. 91–3282 (June 28, 1936): 5.

157. Darwaza 1993, 150.

158. "Muqabalat Ghair Rasmiyya li-l-Lajna al-Malakiyya," *Filastin* 20, no. 190–3381 (November 13, 1936): 8.

159. "Antonius Letter to Rogers, 15 December 1936; Written from Institute of Current World Affairs Letterhead, from Karm Al-Mufti, Jerusalem." in *George Antonius Collection.*

160. Qaddoura 1993, 37.

161. "Jarida Ingliziyya wa-l-Lajna al-Malakiyya," *Filastin* 20, no. 191–3382 (November 11, 1936): 8.

162. "Hakim Nablus Yadʿu li-Qubul al-Lajna al-Malakiyya," *Filastin* 20, no. 74–3265 (June 11, 1936): 5; "Diʿaya li-Qubul al-Lajna al-Malakiyya," *Filastin* 20, no. 91–3282 (June 28, 1936): 4. The villagers from Nablus responded by telling the high commissioner that they knew the colonial secretary already sided with the Zionists and that they knew exactly what they could expect from a Royal Commission (nothing). "Jawab al-Qarawyyin ʿala Manashir al-Hukuma," *Filastin* 20, no. 95–3286 (July 2, 1936): 4.

163. B. N. al-Hout 1986, 467. See the account of the Arab Hashemite regime's collusion with the Zionists to partition Palestine, and Great Britain's support of the project in Shlaim 1988.

164. Zuʿaytir and al-Hout 1984, 462.

165. Abu Gharbiyya 1993, 90; "Wadsworth Report to Secretary of State, 12 June 1937" (NARA 867n.00/488, RG 59, M1037). On the Arab leaders' pressure on the AHC to end the boycott, see Zuʿaytir 1992, 247–48; Husseini 2020, 4; al-ʿOmar 1999, 27.

166. H. F. Khalidi 1949, 231.

167. Porath 1981, 214; Zuʿaytir 1992, 239.

168. Darwaza 1949, 153–54.

169. Zuʿaytir 1992, 247–49; al-ʿOmar 1999, 27. The king of Saudi Arabia opposed Zionism, but was completely dependent on the British, and therefore did their bidding in encouraging Palestinian cooperation with the Royal Commission. Zahlan 2009, 21.

170. E. F. Thompson 2015. For accounts of feminist movements in the interwar Middle East, see Badran 1995; Fleischmann 2003; Weber 2008; and summarized in Matera and Kent 2017, 91–93.

171. al-Kayyali 1988, 391.

172. Palestine Royal Commission Minutes of Evidence Heard at Public Session 1937, 292.

173. "Tawjih al-Raʾi al-ʿAm," al-Difaʿ 3, no. 775 (January 4, 1937): 2; "Fi Bayan al-Wazir, al-Ingliz Yaghushuna Anfusuhum la al-ʿArab," Filastin 20, no. 86–3277 (June 23, 1936): 1; "Shahadat al-ʿArab Amam al-Lajna al-Malakiyya," Filastin 20, no. 236–3427 (January 12, 1937): 1; Matthews 2006. Literacy in Palestine was limited, especially among women, but increased throughout the mandate period. See R. Khalidi 2006, 14–15, 24.

174. al-Kayyali 1988, 405.

175. Pedersen 2015, 92. On the limitations of the petition system at the League of Nations, see Wheatley 2017, 783–786.

176. Robson 2017; Sinanoglou 2009; Dubnov and Robson 2019; Pedersen 2015, 376.

177. For an interesting account of how the partition idea evolved, see Dubnov 2019.

178. This included "willfully incarcerat[ing] innocent persons . . . brute repression . . . [and] outlawing the entire Arab Palestinian political establishment." M. K. Kelly 2017, 104.

179. al-Shuqayri 1969, 159.

180. Palestine Royal Commission Minutes 1937, 305–6.

181. Zuʿaytir 1992, 264.

182. "Hadith li-Samahat al-Mufti al-Akbar," Filastin 20, no. 204–3395 (November 28, 1936): 1 and 6.

183. Even if the challenge was counter-hegemonic, it was not a totally radical one, remaining anchored by a political vision bound by the nation-state form as it did.

## Chapter 3: The Humanitarian Politics of Jewish Suffering

1. Zuʿaytir, 272.

2. Ibid.

3. Yale, "Reflections on Syrian Nationalism."

4. Hansard Parliamentary Debates, 20 July 1937, "Palestine," Vol. 106, cols. 599–665, https://api.parliament.uk/historic-hansard/lords/1937/jul/20/palestine.

5. David Kennedy 2002.

6. Weeramantry and Berman argue that all international legal documents aim at managing international order through balancing three elements: the international community, power centers, and "those viewed as not full participants in the community of sovereigns." Weeramantry and Berman 1999. Early histories of human rights usually pointed to the Holocaust as an originary spark for the development of the human rights system. Lauren 2000, 145, 182; Falk 2000, 58; Bradley 2015, 528–51.

7. Hudson 1944, 278.

8. "Charter of the United Nations, June 26, 1945" 1950.

9. Wilke 2009, 181–201.

10. Albert Hourani made strong arguments for the recuperation of European democracy in which Jews could be safe and protected. A. Hourani 1946.

11. The full text was published, with no mention of authorship, as *The Future of Palestine, Prepared by the Arab Office, London* (Geneva, 1947). According to Walid Khalidi, it was probably written by Albert Hourani. W. Khalidi 2005, 76.

12. On humanitarianism as a structure of feeling, see Redfield and Bornstein 2010, 17. Humanitarianism was a "structure of feeling" already prominent in political discourse before the end of the Cold War, which is when some scholars and others date the rise of humanitarianism's diplomatic centrality. Didier Fassin states that humanitarianism was part of a new moral economy that "came into being during the last decades of the twentieth century" and played a historically unprecedented role in international politics from the 1990s. In Michelle Tusan's review of recent studies of humanitarianism, she notes the discrepancies in the periodization of humanitarianism. Many scholars date the rise of humanitarian intervention much earlier, from the sixteenth century to the late eighteenth century. Koskenniemi 2012; Fassin 2012a, 7; Tusan 2015.

13. Redfield and Bornstein 2010, 17.

14. Ricks 2009, 45.

15. "Al-Nas al-Harfi al-Kamil li-Rad al-Lajna al-ʿArabiyya al-ʿUlya," *Filastin*, 29, no. 242–6192 (December 12, 1945): 1 and 4.

16. al-Shuqayri 1969, 263; Wilson 1979, 73.

17. Furlonge 1969, 112, 144; W. Khalidi 2005, 72.

18. ʿAlami was the son of a former mayor of Jerusalem, part of the Palestinian elite, and a midlevel functionary in the legal department of the British mandatory administration. A. Hourani 1988, 23–24; C. Hourani 2012, 67; al-Shuqayri 1969, 263.

19. B. N. al-Hout 1986, 551.

20. Qasimiyya 2002, 76–77.

21. "Daʿwit al-ʿArab ila Muqataʿat Lajnat al-Tahqiq," *Filastin*, 29, no. 231-6181 (November 29, 1945): 1.

22. "Rad al-Jamiʿa al-ʿArabiyya ʿala Bayan Yuhaqiq Raghabat ʿArab Filastin," *Filastin* 29, no. 231–6181 (November 29, 1945): 1.

23. Hurewitz 1950, 237.

24. al-ʿOmar 1999, 264; "Al-Lajna allati Tuqarrir Masir Filastin," *Filastin* 29, no. 221–6171 (November 15, 1945): 5; "Lajnat Tahqiq li-Filastin," *Filastin* 29, no. 225–6175 (November 22, 1945): 3; "Lajnat Filastin al-Jadida Muhawalat Tahdid Waqt ʿAmaliha," *Filastin* 29, no. 225–6175 (November 22, 1945): 4; "Lajnat Tahqiq fi Mushkilat Filastin wa-ʿAdad Aʿdaʾiha," *Filastin* 29, no. 229–6179 (November 27, 1945): 1; "Lajnat Tahqiq li-Filastin Tataʿllaf min 10 Aʿdaʾ," *Filastin* 29, no. 230–6180 (November 28, 1945): 1; "Lajnat al-Tahqiq al-Mushtaraka li-Qadiyat Filastin," *Filastin* 29, no. 231–6181 (November 29, 1945): 1; "Lajnat al-Tahqiq wa-Idhaʿit Asmaʾ Aʿdaʾiha," *Filastin* 29, no. 237–6187 (December 6, 1945): 1; "Lajnat al-Tahqiq al-Mushtaraka li-Qadiyat Filastin: Dhikr Asmaʾ Baʿd al-Murashahin al-Ingliz li-ʿUdwyatiha," *Filastin* 29, no. 236–6186 (December 6, 1945): 3.

25. "Jacob Rosenheim, Letter to James McDonald, 28 February 1946," in *William Linn Westermann Papers*, Columbia University Library, box 2/L.

26. "Ishaʿat Kadhiba," *Filastin* 29, no. 250–6200 (December 21, 1945). "Nafi Taʾlif Lajna li-l-Taʿawun maʿ Lajnat al-Tahqiq," 1946, in *Spears Collection*, box 4/3, 1946; "Arab Office, London, to Arab Office, Jerusalem," *Spears Collection* box 4/3; "Report on Anglo-American Committee Sittings in London," 1946, in *Spears Collection* box 4/3.

27. "Arabs Not Bound by Inquiry Findings," article from *Palestine Post*, reprinted in *Arab Office Newsletter*, no. 35 5/2 (1946): 6.

28. Ibid., 77.

29. Reid 1981, 303; Qasimiyya 2002, 286–88.

30. A. Hourani 1993, 27–56.

31. Bayly 2016, 437; Beinin 2019; Hanssen 2016, 71.

32. Gallagher 1996, 27–56; Sayigh 2015.

33. Also to be included in this list of educated liberals is Nejla Abu ʿIzzeddin. She received a PhD from the University of Chicago in 1934, was part of the Arab Office preparing the Palestinian case in Washington DC, and went on to teach and write books on Arab history. Thanks are due to Ellen Fleischman for insights into Abu ʿIzzeddin's role in the Arab Office.

34. Beinin 2019. Al-Shuqayri's tone prompted a rebuke from Singleton. Hanssen 2016, 85.

35. Harry S. Truman, "Statement by the President on the Problem of Jewish Refugees in Europe," November 13, 1945, Harry S. Truman 1945–1953 Public Papers, Harry S. Truman Presidential Library and Museum (hereafter *Truman Papers*), Confidential Files, re. Palestine, 1944–1946.

36. "Testimony of Azzam Pasha before the Anglo-American Committee of Inquiry," March 2, 1946, *Lamont Microfilm*, Reel 9; Levenberg 1991, 620. Richard

Crossman was impressed by Azzam Pasha when he spoke before the Anglo-American Committee of Inquiry on March 2, 1946. He recorded in his diary that he had no doubt that Azzam Pasha had spoken "for the whole Arab world as he conveyed the Arab moral case against the Jews." Crossman described Azzam's argument as one that, if accepted, "cut away at a single stroke the whole Jewish case." Azzam spoke of "brothers" and "cousins" who had become transformed into Zionists. American committee member William Philips was similarly if grudgingly impressed by Azzam Pasha's argument as stating a case that "one could not completely ignore." Louis 1984, 145; Phillips 1952, 119.

37. "Hawadith wa-Akhbar, Jamal al-Husayni wa-Lajnat al-Tahqiq," *Filastin*, 29, no. 258–6208 (December 30, 1945): 3; "Telegram to Secretary of State," 2 March 1946, in *Sir Alan Cunningham Collection*, Middle East Centre Archive, St Antony's College, Oxford University (hereafter *Cunningham Collection*), box 1/1.

38. Azzam Pasha's position may itself have been influenced by former British MP and founder of the Committee for Arab Affairs, Sir Edward Spears, who wrote a letter to the Iraqi legation encouraging the heads of Arab delegations to the UN to not "lose an unique opportunity of putting forward the Arab point of view on Palestine." "Letter to Colonel Wadi, Iraqi Legation, London," 14 January 1946, in *Sir Edward Spears Collection*, Middle East Centre Archive, St Antony's College, Oxford University (hereafter *Spears Collection*), box 4/3.

39. Wilson 1979, 76.

40. Crossman 1947, 139; William Phillips, *William Phillips Diaries, 1917–1947*, March 12, 1946, Houghton Library, Harvard College Library, box 19/5. At least his agreement to talk to the Anglo-American Committee helped secure al-Husayni's release from Rhodesia, where the British had exiled him throughout most of World War II in an attempt to stifle his nationalist activism. Whatever his possible inclinations or delectations, he was "received happily by the crowds" on his to return to Palestine. "Telegram from Cunningham to Secretary of State," 2 March 1946, in *Cunningham Collection*, box 1/1; Nachmani 1987, 86; Qasimiyya 2002, 285.

41. McDonald et al. 2014, 147. On Hajj Amin's efforts to strengthen the Palestinians' international position against the British by seeking Nazi support, just as he sought help in the Allied world, see Pappé 2010, loc. 5954, 6382, 6599, 6953–6984.

42. This local urban elite dated back to pre-Ottoman times. Pappé 2010, loc. 146.

43. One would not categorize Jamal's uncle as a liberal. Haj Amin Muhammad al-Husayni has been reviled by Zionists for seeking political assistance from the Germans before and during WWII, an episode "manipulated by Israeli historiography to Nazify the Palestinian movement as a whole," Ibid., loc. 7209.

44. Ibid., loc. 4866, 5031.

45. Ibid., loc. 5024.

46. Levenberg 1991, 620.

47. There are many accounts of this committee and its genesis. The most recent monograph is Judis 2014. Most accounts in English focus on the Zionists' interactions with the committee. See, for example, M. J. Cohen 1979; M. J. Cohen 1987a, 1987b; Podet 1986; Radosh and Radosh 2009; Shai Tamari 2008. Also see Hurewitz 1950. Several articles attend more to the Palestinian and Arab perspectives, including Beinin 2019; W. Khalidi 1986; W. Khalidi 2005; Louis 1984; Qaddoura 1993. Memoirs of Westerners who worked on the committee include Crum 1947; Crossman 1947; Edwardes 1946; Phillips 1952; Wilson 1979.

48. W. Khalidi 2005, 70; "Al-Lajna allati Tuqarrir Masir Filastin," 5.

49. Truman, "Statement by the President on the Problem of Jewish Refugees in Europe."

50. Nachmani 1987, 71.

51. "A Scholar and a Diplomat; Harold Beeley," *New York Times*, April 10, 1958.

52. For bibliographic notes on the commissioners, see Crossman 1947, 23–24; Wilson 1979, 70–71.

53. The personal papers and memoirs exist for about half of this all-male cast, and they give a consistent sense of what issues concerned the Westerners, their ideals, and their assessments of their committee work, as well as some insights into their colorful personalities and personal ambitions. With a heavy focus on the Zionists and their concerns, they offer extremely minimal information about the Palestinian and Arab contributions to the committee's deliberations. For that perspective, Arabic newspapers and the memoirs and diaries of some of the participants and their contemporaries provide a sense of the Palestinians' ideas and actions in this period. Their pamphlets, the memos and reports that they submitted to the committee, and the testimonials they presented give the clearest indication of what Palestinian representatives were trying to achieve and the values that spurred those aims.

54. Ahmad al-Shuqayri, "Testimony to the Committee," March 25, 1946, *Lamont Microfilm*, Reel 10.

55. al-Shuqayri, "Testimony."

56. Arab leaders had plenty of experience with constitutionalism and representative democracy from their time in the Ottoman Parliament, so "Wilson's principle of government by consent was therefore received not as a foreign innovation, but rather as a familiar and accepted principle." Thompson 2013, 134. In his analysis of elections in the late Ottoman period in what would become Palestine, Rashid Khalidi notes that "parts of the Middle East enjoyed elements of democracy, including freedom of speech and assembly, a free press, and hotly contested elections, as far back as the late Ottoman period" while recognizing the limitations on democratic freedoms. R. Khalidi 1984, 461. Gerber and Büssow discuss how municipal elections were contested by Jewish, Christian, and Muslim members. Gerber 1985; Büssow 2011.

57. al-Shuqayri, "Testimony."

58. McDonald et al., 2014, 20.

59. Frank Aydelotte, "Palestine Diary, 1945–46," April 16, 1946, in *Frank Aydelotte Papers, 1905–1956*, Friends Historical Library, Swarthmore College (hereafter *Aydelotte Papers*); "'Arabi Yantaqid A'da' Lajnat al-Tahqiq al-Amrikiyya wa-Yubriq li-l-Ra'is Truman," *Filastin* 29, no. 244–6194 December 14, 1945): 3. Loy Henderson opposed McDonald's appointment because he was "extremely active in the cause of the Zionists." McDonald et al. 2014, 21.

60. McDonald et al. 2007.

61. E. M. Wilson 1979, 70, 78; Gendzier 2015, 41.

62. Crossman 1947, 139.

63. For a summary of the committee members' positions, see Beinin 2019.

64. "Albert Hourani, Memo," 24 November 1945, Israel State Archives, Collection פ (peh) (hereafter *ISA*), box 338/15.

65. Three new measures in this white paper included reduced immigration quotas for Jews arriving in Palestine, restrictions on settlement and land sales to Jews, and constitutional measures that would lead to a single binational state under Arab majority rule with provisions to protect the rights of the Jewish minority. The Palestinian Arab Higher Committee rejected the white paper at the time because it fell short of Arab demands, offered the Arabs eventual independence in only vague terms, and maintained the mandate as the framework of British governance. See the pamphlet, *Reply of the Arab Higher Committee for Palestine to the White Paper Issued by the British Government on May 17, 1939*, Library of Congress (Washington, DC), https://www.loc.gov/resource/amedeltaher.2017498677. On the white paper in the British imperial context, see Apter 2008.

66. In what appears to be "A Draft for a Section of the Arab Office Report to the AACI," titled "5. The form of a Palestinian State," and "6. The Jews in a Palestinian State," the principle of equal citizenship "irrespective of race or religion" and full citizenship for Jews in the proposed future Palestinian state was reiterated. *ISA*, box 328/11. The Arab national leadership and Arab League had proposed allowing Jewish citizenship to those Jews resident in Palestine by 1936. Achcar 2009.

67. Kochavi 2001, 105; Louis 1984, 392–93; Miller 2008; M. J. Cohen 1982a, 1982b; Clifford 1978, 118; Wilson 1979; Judis 2014; Williams 1971.

68. Louis 1984; Judis 2014.

69. On Zionist pressure groups, see Wilson 1979, 31; McKinzie 1975; M. J. Cohen 1982a, 49. On US interests in Middle East oil, see Gendzier 2015; and Labell 2011.

70. Louis 1984, 13; Kochavi 2001, 105; "'The Palestine Report' Address given at Chatham House," 5 July 1946, in *Richard Crossman Collection*, Middle East Centre Archives, St Antony's College, Oxford University (hereafter *Crossman Collection*), box 1/1.

71. Louis 1984, 388. Also see McKinzie 1975; Judis 2014, 203.

72. G. D. Cohen 2006, 134.

73. Louis 1984, 388. Also see McKinzie 1975; "Letter to Prime Minister Attlee Concerning the Need for Resettlement of Jewish Refugees in Palestine," August 31, 1945, in *Truman Papers*, https://www.trumanlibrary.gov/library/public-papers/188/letter-prime-minister-attlee-concerning-need-resettlement-jewish-refugees.

74. "Message to the King of Saudi Arabia Concerning Palestine," October 28, 1946, in *Truman Papers*, https://www.trumanlibrary.org/publicpapers/index.php?pid=1787&st=humanitarian&str=Jews.

75. "Press Release Message to His Majesty King Ibn Saud," October 28 1946, in *David K. Niles Papers*, Harry S. Truman Library and Museum (hereafter *Niles Papers*), box 162/4. In his statement to the United Jewish Appeal delegation, Truman asserted that the needs of Jewish sufferers must be met. "Feb 25, 1946," in *Niles Papers*, box 29/Israel file, 1946, January–June.

76. Wilson 1979, 57; McKinzie 1975.

77. "Niles to Political Action Committee for Palestine," May 31, 1946, in *Niles Papers*, box 28/Displaced Persons and Immigration File 1945–June 1947.

78. Louis 1984, 420.

79. G. D. Cohen 2014, 193, 201.

80. Quoted in Ron Leir, "He Was a Beacon of Light to the World," *The Observer Online*, November 17, 2015. Similar views were expressed in the testimony of Reinhold Niebuhr and David Ben-Gurion. Hertzberg 1970, 94.

81. McDonald et al. 2014, 125.

82. Litvak and Webman 2009, 36–37.

83. Kochavi 2001, 106.

84. Louis 1984, 389, f.n.14.

85. "Record of a Meeting between High Commissioner [Alan Cunningham] and the Arab Higher Committee," 5 January 1946, in *Cunningham Collection*, box 5/1.

86. Telegram to Arab states, in Hall to Cunningham, Jan. 3, 1946; cited in M. J. Cohen 1982a, 98.

87. McDonald et al. 2014, 53.

88. Hourani and Morrison 1946, 5; Miller 2008, 479.

89. Shibli 1946, 10. An article in *Filastin* asked why Western states did not accommodate the Jews if they were so concerned for their well-being. "Shahadat Aynishtayn wa-Haq Amam Lajnat al-Tahqiq," *Filastin* 29, no. 267–6218 (January 13, 1946): 1 and 4.

90. Shibli 1946.

91. Davidson 2001, 210, fn. 159.

92. "Translation of Testimony of Ibn Saud to AACI, 16 April 1946," in *Spears Collection*, box 4/3.

93. "Memorandum of the Institute of Arab American Affairs, on the Recommendations of the Anglo-American Committee of Inquiry" (New York: Institute of Arab American Affairs, August 1946).

94. Litvak and Webman 2009, 48.

95. Ibid., 48.

96. "Testimony of Fadil Jamali to the Anglo-American Committee of Inquiry, Mena House, Cairo," March 5, 1946, in *Joseph C. Hutcheson Papers*, Tarlton Law Library, University of Texas, Austin (hereafter *Hutcheson Papers*), box L6/12. The written submission of the Arab League made the same point. "Memorandum of Secretariat General of the Arab League to the Anglo-American Committee of Inquiry," March 1, 1946, in *Hutcheson Papers*, box L6/2.

97. The Transjordan statement to the committee asserted that a return for Jews to their homes in a democratically transformed Europe would be the best solution. If that was not possible, they should be permitted to go to countries other than Palestine, which would not be adversely affected by their immigration. *Government of Trans-Jordan, Memorandum to the Anglo-American Committee of Inquiry*, March 19, 1946 (*Lamont Microfilm*, Reel 5).

98. Wilson 1979, 65.

99. "Al-Wufud al-ʿArabiyya Tudhish Lajnat al-Tahqiq bi-ʿArdiha al-Mantiqi li-Qadiyat Filastin," *Filastin* 29, no. 284-6234 (February 2, 1946): 1.

100. "Shahadat Aynishtayn wa-Haq Amam Lajnat al-Tahqiq," 1 and 4; W. Khalidi 1986, 108–9.

101. "Message to the King of Saudi Arabia Concerning Palestine," *Truman Papers*.

102. It might be contended that the Jewish refugees would not have wanted to seek refuge in Arab countries at this time. Tensions had grown between Jewish communities in some Arab countries and reached the point of violent crisis in Iraq and elsewhere. But, according to historian Orit Bashkin, some Jewish refugees had fled to Baghdad. Jewish Iraqi intellectuals were anti-Zionist, and the pro-Palestinian stance of Iraqi Jews was confirmed during testimony to the Anglo-American Committee. Bashkin 2012, 34–36, 103–7, 117–20, 186.

103. Ben-Gurion saw the opening of other countries to Jews as a danger to Zionism. Cherni 2004, 62; Hacohen 1991, 253–54; Achcar 2009, 16.

104. Davidson 2001, 168. Also see Achcar 2009, 47.

105. Gildersleeve 1947, ii.

106. "Testimony of Fadil Jamali" in *Hutcheson Papers*; Yusuf Yassin, *Saudi Legation to British-American Commission* (Hollis, *Lamont Microfilm*, Reel 5, n.d.); *Government of Trans-Jordan, Memorandum* (*Lamont Microfilm*).

107. See, for example, Fayiz Sayigh, "Note on the Palestine Problem: Submitted to the Anglo-American Inquiry Committee, Prepared on Behalf of the National Party. Beirut, March 19, 1946," in *Hutcheson Papers*, box L6/3, 7. For more on Sayegh's arguments to this committee and other international forums, see Allen 2019.

108. Omar Hassan Sidki Dajany, "Testimony to Anglo-American Committee of Inquiry," in *Hutcheson Papers*, box L6/2.

109. See examples of public compassion for the Jews from the 1930s and 1940s in Achcar 2009, 30, 47, 164; and Gershoni and Jankowski 2010, 162–65.

110. Compassion for the "victims of Nazis" was again expressed in the memorandum of the Institute of Arab American Affairs. "Memorandum of the Institute of Arab American Affairs," 9–10.

111. Hitti 1946.

112. Ibid.

113. "Opinion Poll," in *Niles Papers*, box 28/Displaced Persons and Immigration File 1945–June 1947.

114. "Frank Aydelotte to Earl Harrison (Citizens Committee on Displaced Persons)," February 10, 1947, in *Aydelotte Papers*, Series 9, RG 6, box 134. Also see W. Khalidi 1986, 108–9.

115. In his memoir, William Phillips reasserted the "great importance" that the committee report placed on the problem of displaced persons. He also noted that subsequent discussion mostly ignored the report's suggestion that if victor nations could help find homes "for these helpless sufferers from the war, the pressure on Palestine as place of refuge for the Jews would be lessened." Phillips 1952, 294.

116. "Phillip Hitti to Senator H. Alexander Smith," August 4 and 18, 1958, in *Phillip Khuri Hitti Papers*, University of Minnesota, College of Liberal Arts, Immigration History Research Center (hereafter *Hitti Papers*), box 11/13.

117. "Frank Aydelotte to Earl Harrison" in *Aydelotte Papers*.

118. Hitti 1946.

119. "Richard Crossman, Letter to Wife," 12 (March 1946?), in *Crossman Collection*, box 1/2; "Richard Crossman, Letter to Wife," n.d., probably March 23, 1946, in *Crossman Collection*, box 1/2.

120. McDonald et al. 2014, 50.

121. Aydelotte, "Palestine Diary" March 23, 1946.

122. "Richard Crossman, Letter to Wife," 12 (March 1946?), in *Crossman Collection*.

123. "Richard Crossman, Letter to Wife," n.d. in *Crossman Collection*.

124. Beeley 1977.

125. "Notes on Palestine Report of Anglo-American Committee," n.d., probably May 8, 1946, in *Crossman Collection*, box 1/1. Among those who Crossman dismissed as "charming degenerates" were some of the people who had been rejecting the British mandate since the Balfour Declaration was issued in 1917 appropriating Palestine in order to give it away to the Zionists. See Allen 2017a.

126. Joseph Hutcheson, "Restraint: The Price of Freedom, Speech given by Hutcheson to the Ann Arbor Law School, April 28, 1950," in *Hutcheson Papers*, box L21/11; Honeyman 2007, 135.

127. See Aydelotte's diary for his impression of the committee's legalistic methods. Aydelotte recognized their report to be an exercise in presenting "an objective statement

of the facts." Aydelotte, "Palestine Diary," April 2, 1946. Richard Crossman, "Letter to Attlee," May 7, 1946, in *Crossman Collection*, box 1/1. Also Crossman 1947, 7.

128. On liberal legalism, see Hoffmann 2016, 12.

129. "Memorandum of Secretariat General of the Arab League," in *Hutcheson Papers*.

130. Ibid.

131. Ibid.

132. Jamal al-Husayni, speaking in the name of the Arab Higher Council, said: "The Arabs have refused the Balfour Declaration from the beginning. . . . The Balfour Declaration, before anything, contradicts the Natural Rights of the Arabs and therefore it is invalid." Qasimiyya 1974, 286.

133. Sayigh, "Note on the Palestine Problem."

134. Ricks 2009, 45 (fn. 88). In their response to the committee report, the Institute of Arab American Affairs expressed support for the first recommendation "based on the provision of the UN charter calling for 'universal respect for, and observance of, human rights and fundamental freedoms for all without distinction." They objected to the other recommendations that contravened this. "Memorandum of the Institute of Arab American Affairs," 11.

135. *The Future of Palestine*, 16; Tawfiq Salih al-Husayni, "Fi Yowm Tasrih Balfur al-Mash'um: Bayan al-Hizb al-'Arabi al-Filastini ila al-Umma al-Karima," *Filastin* 29, no. 210–6160 (November 2, 1945): 2; Jamal Husseini, "'The Arab Case,' Memo Submitted to the Committee on Behalf of the Arabs of Palestine," March 12, 1946, in *Hutcheson Papers*, box L6/2. Handwritten notes on the final page of the memo, apparently by Hutcheson, read: "The point he makes well is that the Arabs [illegible word] are not immigrants but native born and these native born are to be subjected to the domination of the immigrants who will be allowed in against the will of the native born owners of the land."

136. On the testimony of Palestinian lawyer Henry Cattan, presenting March 23, 1946 on behalf of the Arab Higher Committee, see McDonald et al. 2014, 179, fn 128.

137. W. Khalidi 2005, 73. Al-Shuqayri later defended Arabs in land cases as a means of opposing Zionist takeover of the country. Reid 1981, 306.

138. al-Shuqayri, "Testimony."

139. See Sayigh, "Note on the Palestine Problem."

140. Not all Arab presenters expressed such faith in the committee or the international legal community. The Muslim Brothers in Haifa rejected any attempt to make Arabs and Muslims think they could realize their national goals through the Security Council or the UN, "since it has been revealed from the many attempts that this International Organisation is nothing but a mere cloak of the greediness of the big imperialist states." "Decisions from the Conference of the Muslim Brothers in Haifa, 27 October 1947," in B. N. al-Hout 1986, 794.

141. C. Hourani 2012, 60.

142. See *The Future of Palestine*, Appendix C, 116.

143. A. Hourani 2005, 81. Also see *The Future of Palestine*, 70.

144. The proposal is spelled out in *The Future of Palestine*, 78–89. Many of these same principles were repeated in a US Department of State proposal for Palestine's future, dated June 4, 1947. A "common Palestinian citizenship" and shared governance of the country feature prominently in the plan. Josh Ruebner, "A Forgotten US Vision for a Single Democratic State in Palestine," *The Electronic Intifada*, March 3, 2017, https://electronicintifada.net/blogs/josh-ruebner/forgotten-us-vision-single-democratic-state-palestine. For the entire memorandum, which also includes details about what a UN trustee's proposed responsibilities in Palestine would be; details about how a constitution would be drawn up; and how immigration should be handled, see *Foreign Relations of the United States, 1947, The Near East and Africa*, Vol. V, Office of the Historian, 1947, https://history.state.gov/historicaldocuments/frus1947v05/d772.

145. *The Future of Palestine*, Appendix A.

146. Wilson 1979, 84–85; Crossman 1947, 140.

147. For examples of Arab representatives expressing their sympathy with Jewish suffering, see Albert Hourani's testimony, in which he said he felt "deeply and personally . . . [the] suffering of the Jew." A. Hourani 2005, 89. Also see Achcar 2009, 30, 47. The US Department of State Palestine desk officer and US secretary for the committee recorded impressions of the rigid, unimaginative Arabs. See Wilson 1979, 76.

148. Richard Crossman deemed Arab nationalism to be "much more intransigent than Zionism," but then again, they "never expected the Arab to be other than an Arab, and [they] took for granted that his point of view would be quite different from ours." Crossman 1947, 73. "Of these three, Hitti was by all odds the best. The other two rather seemed to weaken their case by over-statement." McDonald et al. 2014, 36.

149. Crossman 1947, 133.

150. Aydelotte, "Palestine Diary," March 8, 1946.

151. See, for example, "The Palestine Question: Is There an Answer? A Radio Discussion with William E. Hocking, Arthur P. Scott and Carl H. Voss. October 28, 1945," in *Hitti Papers*, box 12/8.

152. McDonald et al. 2014, 68.

153. Crossman 1947, 134; Louis 1984, 413.

154. Wilson 1979, 76. Other Arab witnesses were also asked in some detail if there were any circumstances in which Jewish refugees could be let in to Palestine. The consistent response was that the political situation could not allow it, that Europe and America should take in refugees, and that it was a matter for the UN to sort out according to agreed international principles. "Public Hearing 1 February 1946," in *Hutcheson*

*Papers,* box L12/6. McDonald recorded this as "intransigence" and advertised it as such in his public talks after the Anglo-American Report was issued. McDonald, "Address at the Conference of the American Christian Palestine Committee," *McDonald Papers,* box 23/6, 237.

155. Committee member Aydelotte agreed. "Frank Aydelotte to Earl Harrison," in *Aydelotte Papers;* "Aydelotte Letter to Clara," December 2, 1946, in *Aydelotte Papers,* Series 9, RG 6, box 134.

156. *The Future of Palestine,* 85.

157. "Public Hearing 1 February 1946," in *Hutcheson Papers.*

158. A. Hourani 2005, 85; *The Future of Palestine,* 85.

159. Wilson 1979, 80.

160. A. Hourani, "Testimony to the Committee," March 25, 1946, *Lamont Microfilm,* Reel 10.

161. Mehta 1999, 47–48. For another analysis of these issues, see Allen 2017b.

162. Zelden 1997, 905.

163. Joseph C. Hutcheson, "Palestine, Anglo-American Problem Child," in *Hutcheson Papers,* box L6/18.

164. Joseph C. Hutcheson, "Racialism, Nativism, Xenophobia, the Little Foxes That Spoil the Vines of Europe and the Middle East, December 16, 1946, Speech Manuscript, Delivered to the Houston Committee on Foreign Relations," in *Hutcheson Papers,* box 6/19; Hutcheson, "Palestine, Anglo-American Problem Child," in *Hutcheson Papers.*

165. Hutcheson, "Palestine, Anglo-American Problem Child," in *Hutcheson Papers.*

166. Hutcheson, "Racialism," in *Hutcheson Papers.*

167. Osiel 1997, 68; Shklar 1984, 7–44, 236–44.

168. Mehta 1997.

169. On the humanitarian structure of feeling, see Redfield and Bornstein 2010, 17. On humanitarianism's periodization, see Fassin 2012a, 7; Rodogno 2016a.

170. Tusan 2015, 96. According to Moyn, contra Koskenniemi, American international legal thinking has consistently been underwritten by a moralism and universalism. Moyn 2013.

171. Fassin 2012a, 274.

172. *The Future of Palestine* 70; A. Hourani 1946.

173. al-Shuqayri, "Testimony."

174. Compare, for example, Elizabeth Povinelli's discussion of the limits of liberalism, in which she contrasts moral sensibility and liberal rationality as stances that are ostensibly opposite, or claimed to be so. What this Palestinian case reveals is that liberalism entails a moral sensibility itself. Povinelli 2002, 10.

175. Nelson 2004, 220.

176. McDonald et al. 2014, 206.

177. "Hutcheson Letter to US Committee Members, in Response to Questions Posed by Mishmar Hasher Hatzair Daily," April 29, 1947, in *Aydelotte Papers,* Series 9, RG 6, box 133.

178. Wilson 1979, 80.

179. Earl G. Harrison, "Report, Earl G. Harrison's 'Mission to Europe to Inquire into the Condition and Needs of Those among the Displaced Persons in the Liberated Countries of Western Europe and in the SHAEF Area of Germany—with Particular Reference to the Jewish Refugees—Who May Possibly Be Stateless or Nonrepatriable,'" in *World War II: Holocaust, The Extermination of European Jews* (Dwight D. Eisenhower's Pre-Presidential Papers, box 116, Truman Harry S. (4); NAID #12007695), https://www.eisenhowerlibrary.gov/research/online-documents/world-war-ii-holocaust-extermination-european-jews.

180. "Joseph Hutcheson to Palmer (Brother)," 16 January 1946, in *Hutcheson Papers* L14/9.

181. Crossman 1947, 133.

182. There were large increases in the rate of Jewish immigration, especially in 1933–1936 and onward. See Mccarthy 1990, 34–36; Abu-Lughod 1971, 153; Ruedy 1971, 124. In 1948, before the war, Arabs were 1.4 million out of a population of 2 million in mandate Palestine, constituting a majority in fifteen of sixteen subdistricts, owning nearly 90 percent of the country's privately owned land. R. Khalidi 2006, 1.

183. "Purely Tentative Thoughts on Our Terms of Reference," No Attribution, Undated. Probably written by Hutcheson, in *Hutcheson Papers*, box L7/4.

184. Hourani and Maugham 1946, 5.

185. Hutcheson's insistence on balance between the Zionists and Palestinians also ignored the obligations of both humanitarianism and justice that would have required all countries, especially in Europe (and the United States), to open their borders and actively seek to repatriate Jewish and other refugees.

186. "Crossman Address to Chatham House, 5 July 1946," in *Crossman Collection,* box 1/1; McDonald et al. 2014, 197, 201, 211, 215, 216.

187. "Anglo-American Committee of Inquiry," Avalon Project, Yale University, https://avalon.law.yale.edu/subject_menus/angtoc.asp.

188. For a more complete chronicling, see Ghandour 2010, 123–65; R. Khalidi 2006; Huneidi 2001.

189. Albert Hourani, "Jew and Arab, Letter to Editor," *The Times*, London, July 30, 1946, 5.

190. On the link between ethics and self-regard, see Anderson, quoted in Keane 2015, 135. On the British self-portrayal of their supposed balanced approach, see R. Khalidi 2006, 31.

191. Blanshard 1970, 322.

192. Ibid., 325.

193. Hutcheson, "Restraint: The Price of Freedom," in *Hutcheson Papers*. US President Roosevelt remarked on Hutcheson's "progressive and liberal tendencies." Another observer described Hutcheson as a "true nineteenth century Liberal," who believed "implicitly in the importance of the individual and individual rights." Zelden 1997, 910.

194. Hutcheson, "Restraint: The Price of Freedom," in *Hutcheson Papers*.

195. Goda 2015, 220.

196. Zelden 1997, 906; McDonald et al. 2014, 206.

197. Zelden 1997, 910–11, 913.

198. Louis 1984, 402.

199. Crossman 1947, 39; Crum 1947.

200. See Frank Aydelotte, "Letter to Buxton," December 17, 1948, "Letter to Buxton," June 16, 1947, and "Letter to Hutcheson," May 14, 1946, in *Aydelotte Papers*, Series 9 RG 6, box 134.

201. Aydelotte "Letter to Hutcheson," May 14, 1946, in *Aydelotte Papers*.

202. "Joseph Hutcheson Letter to Bentov," 29 April 1947, in *Aydelotte Papers*, Series 9 RG 6, box 134.

203. Frank Aydelotte, "Letter to Hutcheson," October 15, 1947, and "Letter to Hutcheson," November 11, 1947, in *Aydelotte Papers*, Series 9, RG 6, box 134; Joseph Hutcheson, "Letter to Aydelotte," November 8, 1947, in *Aydelotte Papers*, Series 9, RG 6, box 134.

204. McDonald et al. 2014, 206.

205. Hanssen 2016, 90.

206. Frank Buxton, "Letter to Aydelotte," June 16, 1947, in *Aydelotte Papers*, Series 9, RG 6, box 134.

207. Frank Aydelotte, "Letter to Hutcheson," September 17, 1947, in *Aydelotte Papers*, Series 9, RG 6, box 134.

208. Shklar 1984, 237.

209. Povinelli 2002, 17.

210. Roders 2004, 204.

211. Ricks 2009, 312–315.

212. A. Hourani 1988; Alami 1949.

213. C. Hourani 2012, 66.

214. Alami 1949.

215. C. Hourani 2012, 60.

216. Louis 1984, 390.

217. Zerilli 2015.

218. al-Shuqayri, "Testimony."

219. Hutcheson, "Letter to brother Allen," March 6, 1946, in *Hutcheson Papers*, L14.

220. Bob 2009; also see Allen 2009a; Sontag 2003.

221. Alan Cunningham "Letter to G. H. Hall," April 5, 1946, in *Cunningham Collection*, box 5/2.

222. Hurewitz 1950, 237.

223. Italics in original booklet. Sayigh, "Note on the Palestine Problem," in *Hutcheson Papers*.

224. Judis 2014, 275; Louis 1984, 391; Rabbi Wise, "Letter to David Niles," October 24, 1946, in *Niles Papers,* box 27/Correspondence File 1945–1981; "Wallace R. Deuel, Chicago Daily News Foreign Service, " February 26, 1947, in *Niles Papers,* box 27/Correspondence File 1945–1981; "Truman Statement," February 26, 1947, in *Niles Papers,* box 28/Displaced Persons and Immigration File 1945–June 1947; M. J. Cohen 1979; Wilson 1979, 58.

225. Berlant 2005, 47.

226. Crossman 1947, 119.

227. al-Shuqayri 1969, 265.

228. Aydelotte wrote in his diary that he had not realized how much it was getting on his nerves to hear people speaking Arabic and Hebrew, "but the French sounded lovely." Aydelotte, "Palestine Diary, 1945–46," April 2, 1946, in *Aydelotte Papers*.

229. The Anglo-American Committee of Inquiry Report is available here: http://avalon.law.yale.edu/20th_century/angcov.asp.

230. Judis 2010, 220.

231. *Lausanne Conference on near Eastern Affairs 1922–1923: Records of Proceedings and Draft Terms of Peace* (London: HMSO, 1923); Yildirim 2006.

232. Aydelotte, "Palestine Diary, 1945–46," April 6, 1946, in *Aydelotte Papers*; Frank Aydelotte, "Letter to Benjamin Carson, Editor of the US Patriotic Educator," September 18, 1946, in *Aydelotte Papers*, Series 9, RG 6, box 134.

233. McDonald et al. 2014, 227.

234. Darwaza 1993, 562; al-ʿOmar 1999, 262–64.

235. Judis 2010, 220.

236. "Memorandum of the Institute of Arab American Affairs," 7.

237. The committee also contributed to the authorization of the recently formed Arab League. In providing them a venue in which to appear, they became international representatives of many who had never been given the chance to vote for them as such.

## Chapter 4: Third World Solidarity at the General Assembly

1. "Address to U.N.S.C.O.P. 16 (17?) July 1947," in *Cunningham Collection,* box 5/1. In February 1947, the British had announced that they were submitting the Palestine question to the UN General Assembly. Ben-Dror 2014, 19.

2. UNGA 1947, A/307.

3. On Zionist lobbying of UNSCOP, see Ben-Dror 2014. On the UNSCOP report partition recommendations, see Imseis 2019, 53; Kattan 2009, 147–52.

4. Historian William Roger Louis suggests that the momentary emotions provoked in UNSCOP

members by their touring of displaced persons camps and the turning back of the boat, *Exodus*, to Germany also helps explain the outcome. Louis 1984, 470–71.

5. Imseis 2019, 44.

6. The number of refugees is debated, with some estimates putting it as high as 960,000. Takkenberg 1998, 18–19.

7. On the war, see Morris 2001, 37.

8. Robinson 2013. For more on Palestinian citizens of Israel, see Dallasheh 2016; Tatour 2016.

9. I. Feldman 2012, 390; Imseis 2019, 106.

10. Descendants of the first wave of Palestinians refugees and those made refugees in subsequent violent expulsions are included in this figure. UNRWA 2019.

11. UNSC 1967a, S/RES/242. For an assessment of the political and legal effects of UN SCR 242, see Dajani 2007/2008.

12. UNGA 1969b, A/PV.1755.

13. Jarring 1999.

14. Normand and Zaidi 2008, 292.

15. Prashad 2007, 14. On the African Group's anti-apartheid efforts at the UN, see Irwin 2012. For an analysis of the Special Committee on Decolonisation, see Mittelman 1976.

16. On the African states' role in the human rights agenda, see Eckel 2010, 129; Burke 2010, 69.

17. Normand and Zaidi 2008, 136.

18. Mazower 2012, 196–97, 200, 212.

19. Mazower 2004.

20. Normand and Zaidi 2008, 113–14, 131–35; Moyn 2012, 61,181, 183.

21. Normand and Zaidi 2008, 110.

22. Merry and Coutin, 2014; T. Kelly 2012a, 134–53.

23. For an initial statement of some of these arguments, see Allen 2016.

24. Fischbach 2019, 3, 16.

25. Research on the imbrication of international law and empire is vast and growing. Key texts include Anghie 2005, Bedjaoui 1979, Craven 2012, Gathii 2007, and Koskenniemi 2002. For a scholarly contextualization and review of this work, see Pitts 2015.

26. By "hegemonic contestation," Koskenniemi means "the process by which international actors routinely challenge each other by invoking legal rules and principles on which they have projected meanings that support their preferences and counteract those of their opponents. . . . To think of this struggle as hegemonic is to understand that the objective of the contestants is to make their partial view of that meaning appear

as the total view, their preference seem like the universal preference." Koskenniemi 2004, 199. See also, Bourdieu 1986.

27. For a comparative answer to that question, see Pahuja 2011.

28. The General Assembly announced this Special Committee in Resolution 2443 (XXIII) titled, "Respect for and implementation of human rights in occupied territories," which was adopted at its 1748th plenary meeting in December 1968. It is now called the Special Committee to Investigate Israeli Practices Affecting the Human Rights of the Palestinian People and Other Arabs of the Occupied Territories. See UNGA 1968a, A/RES/2443 (XXIII). In its first report, the Special Committee defined these rights as those that the Security Council referred to as "essential and inalienable" in its Resolution 237. See UNGA 1970a, A/8089, paras. 36–38; UNSC 1967b, S/RES/237. These are defined in the Geneva Convention relative to the Treatment of Prisoners of War, of 12 August 1949; the Geneva Convention relative to the Protection of Civilian Persons in Time of War, of 12 August 1949; and the Hague Conventions of 1899 and 1907 respecting the Laws and Customs of War on Land. As additional allegations came to light, the Special Committee included as relevant the Hague Convention for the Protection of Cultural Property in the Event of Armed Conflict (May 14, 1954) and the Hague Conventions of 1899 and 1907 respecting the Laws and Customs of War on Land. See UNGA 1973a, A/9148. The Special Committee reports annually on all Israeli-occupied territories and continues to monitor Israeli settlement activity in the occupied Syrian Golan.

29. In rebutting the Israeli representative's argument that the Special Committee was a tool of Arab propaganda, the chair of the committee pointed out: "The verbatim record of the twenty-third session of the General Assembly (1748th plenary meeting) showed that resolution 2443 (XXIII) establishing the Special Committee had been adopted by 60 votes to 22 with 37 abstentions, even securing a two-thirds majority, which was impressive evidence of the importance attached to it. Even if those who had abstained had joined those voting against the resolution, it would still have been adopted." UNGA 1970b, A/SPC/SR.744, para. 8.

30. In periods of intensified crisis, such as during the first intifada, reports were sometimes quite long; the 1988 UNSCIIP Report was 143 pages. In 1993, the 25th report of UNSCIIP stretched to 212 pages. UNGA 1988a, A/43/691; UNGA 1993, A/48/557.

31. UNGA 1989a, A/SPC/44/SR.23, para. 80.

32. Rajagopal 2000, para. 529.

33. Pahuja 2011, 34, 37.

34. As one of many examples, Libya's delegation described "the racist objective of the Zionist leaders, namely, to make Palestine as Jewish as England was English." UNGA 1970c, A/SPC/SR.746, para. 31. On the criminalization of political speech about Israel and Palestine solidarity in the United States, see "Trump's Anti-Palestinian Agenda Comes Home," *Palestine Legal*, December 11, 2019, https://palestinelegal.org/news

/2019/12/11/trumps-anti-palestinian-agenda-comes-home; and in the UK, see "Boris Johnson to Pass Law Banning Anti-Israel Boycott, Official Says," *The Independent*, December 16, 2019, https://www.independent.co.uk/news/uk/politics/boris-johnson-bds-law-israel-boycott-divestment-sanctions-palestine-a9248801.html. Also see Gould 2018.

35. For a distinct critique of international legal discourse as a belief system, which focuses on the ways international lawyers build their arguments, see d'Aspremont 2018.

36. The chair of the Special Committee argued that the violation of "several thousands of innocent persons living under military occupation" was believed by the committee to be "and should be the concern of the entire membership of the United Nations." The discussion went on: "If the investigation that the Special Committee had conducted and the recommendations it had submitted led to the creation of effective machinery for the proper enforcement and observance of the third and fourth Geneva Conventions, the United Nations would have contributed to mitigating the agony of human conflict and would have written a new chapter into the history of human rights and human relations." UNGA 1970b, A/SPC/SR.744, paras. 10, 23.

37. Ibid., para. 10.

38. For diverse analyses of the UN's relationship to Palestine and the Arab world more broadly, see Makdisi and Prashad 2017.

39. Such inscriptions have happened in what international relations scholar Jack Donnelly has categorized as declaratory, promotional, and implementational regimes. Donnelly 1986, 599, 602.

40. Stultz 1991, 1; Thörn 2009; Weissbrodt and Mahoney 1986; Dugard 2018.

41. UNGA 1974b, A/RES/3236, in which it recognized the inalienable national rights of the Palestinian people.

42. UNGA 1975a, A/RES/3376 (XXX); UNGA "International Day of Solidarity with the Palestinian People," November 29, 2019.

43. Collins 2011, 18.

44. Chamberlin 2012; Yaqub 2018, loc. 250.

45. Matar 2018, 361.

46. Yaqub 2018, loc. 2812.

47. Khouri and Salti 2018, loc. 64, 404-407.

48. Arafat's invitation was discussed at UNGA 1975b, A/PV.2399. For one account of these resolutions and the committee's work, see the analysis on the "Right of Self-Determination of the Palestinian People," prepared for the Committee on the Exercise of the Inalienable Rights of the Palestinian People in 1979. CEIRPP 1979.

49. In another instance of equating UN recognition with political significance, historian and journalist Donald Neff looked back at Arafat's speech twenty years later, deeming "the simple presence of a Palestinian leader in the halls of the U.N. marked a watershed for the Palestinian community. The United States and Israel had opposed Arafat's

appearance, as they had for years fought against recognition of Palestinians as a separate people." Donald Neff, "PLO Chairman Yasser Arafat's First Appearance at the United Nations," *Washington Report*, November–December, 1994, https://www.wrmea.org/1994 -november-december/plo-chairman-yasser-arafat-s-first-appearance-at-the-united -nations.html.

50. S. al-Hout 2011, 127. In his speech, Arafat also stated that the Palestinian people considered his invitation to the UN to be "a victory for the world Organization as much as a victory for the cause of our people," because it "indicate[d] anew that the United Nations of today is not the United Nations of the past." UNGA 1974a, A/PV. 2282 and Corr.1.

51. UNGA 1973b, A/RES/3070, para. 2; UNGA 1974c, A/RES/3246. The UN has reaffirmed the right to resort to armed struggle for people under foreign domination in many other resolutions. See Syring and Akram 2014, para. 121, n. 37.

52. UNGA 2007c, A/62/100 Corr. 1 and Add. 1.

53. For a political critique of the UN's legitimization of the partition of historic Palestine and its reduction of the issue to one of international human rights and humanitarian law, see Imseis 2019.

54. UNGA 1975b, A/PV.2399, para. 132.

55. UNGA 1971b, A/PV.1934, para. 177.

56. UNGA 1967b, A/PV.1586, para. 98.

57. UNGA 1967a, A/PV.1558.

58. Martti Koskenniemi points to the specificity of legal contestation, "in which [e]ngaging in legal discourse, persons recognise each other as carriers of rights and duties who are entitled to benefits from or who owe obligation to each other not because of charity or interest but because such rights or duties belong to every member of the community in that position. In law, benefits and burdens that belong to particular individuals or groups are universalised by reference to membership rules. What otherwise would be a mere private violation, a wrong done to me, a violation of my interest, is transformed by law into a violation against everyone in my position, a matter of concern for the political community itself." Koskenniemi 2004, 124.

59. UNGA 1989a, A/SPC/44/SR.23, paras. 10, 12, 19.

60. Allen 2018. In addition to Western Sahara under Moroccan occupation, there are still 16 non-self-governing territories administered by Western powers. Imseis 2019, 103. While Palestine remains overtly colonized, neocolonial dependency persisted in many places, offering only what Amílcar Cabral called "flag independence." Mendy 2019.

61. Fischbach 2019, 3.

62. The revolutionary currency had more than Palestine as a gold standard. According to Khalil al-Wazir (co-founder of Fateh, a major Palestinian faction, and leader in the PLO), when the PLO gained the support of Algeria, it gave them "a revolutionary credibility that was worth more than gold and guns." Byrne 2016, 179, fns. 22, 23.

63. Also see Abou-El-Fadl 2019; K. Feldman 2015; Lubin 2014.

64. Such plaudits for "the spirit of Bandung" are not uncontested, however. For a critique of the conservative compromises of Bandung, see Prashad 2007, loc. 78-115.

65. Samour 2017, 605.

66. Eslava, Fakhri, and Nesiah 2017, 5. For a bibliography of works documenting this period's development of international law from a Third World perspective, see Özsu 2019. The nature of that international law, and how Third World activists sought to shape it in subsequent decades at the UN General Assembly and elsewhere, is a question that scholars have recently started to take up. Just as international law had been a powerful tool in enabling and justifying European and North American imperial capture of non-whites, those fighting to free themselves from it looked to international legal mechanisms and institutions to undo their subjugation. The question of whether human rights were integral to self-determination struggles after World War II preoccupies much of this scholarship and has emerged in a context of renewed critique of the eurocentricity of international law. Beyond the diplomatic successes or political failures of Third World efforts to put human rights into anticolonial service, however, few ask about the broader reasons for and consequences of such a human rights and UN strategy for the people pursuing it. On international law's facilitation of colonialism, see Anghie 2005; Kauanui 2008. The centrality of human rights in decolonization in the historiography of human rights is addressed by Hoffmann and Assy 2019 and Özsu 2019. On the role of human rights in decolonization, see Afshari 2007; Burke 2006, 947; Burke 2010; Irwin 2012; Jensen 2016; Muschik 2018; Normand and Zaidi 2008; Moyn 2012. The extensive literature that critiques the eurocentric nature of international law (and the histories it has hitherto told about itself) includes Anghie 2005; Gathii 1998; Eslava and Pahuja 2012. On Algerians' successful mobilization of world and French public opinion through the UN, see Connelly 2002. On the waxing and waning confidence in the UN as an effective anti-apartheid tool, see Irwin 2012. On African-Americans' early belief in the UN as a resource for fighting white supremacy, see C. Anderson 2003.

67. Samour 2017, 610.

68. Vitalis 2013; Özsu 2017, 307.

69. UNGA 1989a, A/SPC/44/SR.23, para. 14.

70. See the statement of the representative of Ceylon and chair of the Special Committee, UNGA 1971g A/SPC/SR.799, para. 5. Also see the Syrian delegate's insistence "that those humanitarian aspects were only a reflection of the underlying drama, which was essentially political," regardless of how the chairman of the Special Committee framed their work in his letter of transmittal to the secretary-general that "consciously sought to separate the humanitarian aspects of the problem . . . from the political issues involved." UNGA 1971f, A/SPC/SR.798, para. 6.

71. UNGA 1970f, A/SPC/SR.749, para. 38.

72. On the concept of being a "problem of and for humanity," see Watenpaugh 2015.

73. UNGA 1971e, A/PV.1999, para. 37.

74. On the ways that the UN's technical approaches gloss social complexity, see Merry and Coutin 2013 and T. Kelly 2012a.

75. Some UN members cited these countries' lack of diplomatic relations with Israel—prompted by the 1967 war and Israel's violation of Resolution 242—as reducing the committee's credibility. On Yugoslavia's severing of diplomatic relations with Israel, see Abadi 1996.

76. Batovic 2010; Abadi 1996. Senegal was elected first chair of the UN Committee on the Exercise of the Inalienable Rights of the Palestinian People, which was founded in 1975 by Resolution 3376 of the United Nations General Assembly (and Yugoslavia was a member). UNGA 1975a A/RES/3376 (XXX). Somalia was sometimes a member of this Committee.

77. Kodikara 1992, 129.

78. Nissanka 1984.

79. UNGA 1970a, A/8089.

80. Ibid., para. 19.

81. See comment by Israeli representatives at the Special Political Committee, UNGA 1970e, A/SPC/SR.748, para. 29.

82. UNGA 1970a, A/8089, para. 146.

83. Ibid., paras. 67, 150–151.

84. UNGA 1970i, A/PV.1931, paras. 49, 64.

85. In addition to the discussion at the UNGA plenary, the Special Committee was also discussed that year—and in very similar terms—at the Commission on Human Rights. UNGA 1971a, E/4949 (SUPP)-E/CN.4/1068, paras. 151–174.

86. UNGA 1970i, A/PV.1931, para. 86.

87. UNGA 1970d, A/SPC/SR.747, para. 5. His delegation endorsed the findings and recommendations of the Special Committee, which were corroborated by numerous reports published in the press or disseminated by impartial international bodies. Asserting the committee's objectivity again, the delegate from Poland, Mikucku, "said that he wished to congratulate the Special Committee for its thorough examination of the evidence and its objective approach to its task. The Special Committee had acted with complete objectivity and impartiality and had scrupulously applied the recognized legal norms and procedures. Thus it had honourably discharged the task assigned to it by the General Assembly in resolution 2443 (XXIII)." UNGA 1970e, A/SPC/SR.748, para. 5.

88. See UN Special Political Committee meetings held between December 7 and 11, 1970, at UNGA 1970g, A/SPC/SR.751.

89. Lori Allen, "'Behind the Scenes': A Novice Spelunker in the Archives." *Comparatives Studies in Society and History*, 2017. cssh.lsa.umich.edu/2017/04/15/lori-allen-behind-the-scenes/.

90. Stoler 2009, 59, 68.

91. UNGA 1970e, A/SPC/SR.748, para. 1.

92. Ibid., para. 15.

93. UNGA 1971c, A/PV.1951, para. 176.

94. UNGA 1970b, A/SPC/SR.744, para. 11.

95. UNGA 1971g, A/SPC/SR.799, para. 51.

96. Ibid., para. 54.

97. See, for example, the Israeli representative's questions about the date of a supplementary report's transmittal and adoption: "Past, present and conjectures about the future did not, of course, trouble the Special Committee, especially as it considered past, present, and future, as well as fact and fable, to be interchangeable." Ibid., para. 11.

98. For more on Fayez Sayegh at the UN, see Allen 2019.

99. UNGA 1970f, A/SPC/SR.749, para. 56.

100. UNGA 1970i, A/PV.1931. The resolution mentioned was passed as Resolution 2727. It called on Israel to implement the Special Committee's recommendations "and to comply with its obligations under the Geneva Convention relative to the Protection of Civilian Persons in Time of War . . . the Universal Declaration of Human Rights and the relevant resolutions adopted by the various international organizations." UNGA 1970h, A/RES/2727(XXV).

101. UNGA 1970e, A/SPC/SR.748, para. 5.

102. UNGA 1968b, A/PV/1749.

103. UNGA 1970d, A/SPC/SR.747, para. 36.

104. Ibid., para. 23; UNGA 1970f, A/SPC/SR.749, para. 4.

105. UNGA 1970c, A/SPC/SR.746, para. 18. The Special Political Committee had agreed during its 435th meeting to authorize a Palestinian delegation "to address the Committee and to make such statements as they might deem necessary, without such authorization implying recognition of the organization concerned." UNGA 1971d, A/SPC/SR.782, para. 1.

106. Imseis argues that Palestine has been "a prominent part of the development of observer status in the practice of the Secretary-General and the Assembly, and in this way helped advance the principle of universality within the Organization both for itself and as a pioneer for other subaltern groups." He also concludes his historical study of the role of international law in Palestine with the suggestion that the "festering case" of Palestine in the UN "remains a litmus test for the credibility of international law and the international system as a whole." Imseis 2019, 194, 209.

107. See, for example, the six draft resolutions that were voted on and adopted in 1985, UNGA 1985, A/SPC/41/L.20-26.

108. UNGA 1969b, A/PV.1775, para. 4.

109. UNSCIIP also often issues periodic reports in between the annual reports.

110. Confidential UN Records of Testimony, 1970. (On file with author.)

111. Mallard and McGoey 2018; Allen 2009a; Fassin 2008.

112. On the hailing of subjects, see Althusser 1971. For one example of the Special Committee's reliance on local legal expertise, see its 1988 report, UNGA 1988b, A/43/694, para. 254.

113. Confidential UN Records of Testimony, 1974. (On file with author.)

114. Ibid.

115. See the petition from detainees being held at the Israeli prison called Ansar 3, included in the 1988 report, UNGA 1988b, A/43/694.

116. Confidential UN Records of Testimony, 1976. (On file with author.)

117. UNGA 1970a, A/8089, para. 55.

118. Ibid, para. 80. For more on the torture of Palestinian prisoners in this period, see al-Haq 1983; al-Haq 1984.

119. Greenspan 1972, para. 377.

120. Confidential UN Records of Testimony, 1989. (On file with author.)

121. Ibid.

122. Ibid.

123. Ibid.

124. Confidential UN Records of Testimony, 1979. (On file with author.)

125. Confidential UN Records of Testimony, 1970.

126. Confidential UN Records of Testimony, 1980. (On file with author.)

127. Confidential UN Records of Testimony, 1970.

128. Ibid.

129. Confidential UN Records of Testimony, 1988. (On file with author.)

130. Confidential UN Records of Testimony, 1975. (On file with author.)

131. Ibid.

132. Confidential UN Records of Testimony, 1979.

133. Confidential UN Records of Testimony, 1974.

134. Pahuja 2011, 178.

135. UNGA 1967b, A/PV.1586. For similar expressions of anxiety, see the contribution of Magalhaes Pinto, UNGA 1969b, A/PV.1755.

136. For a comparative analysis of UN networks that become their own raison d'etre, see Riles 2000. And for an analysis of how human rights proceduralism overshadows substance at the UN, see T. Kelly 2009.

137. UNGA 1969a, A/PV.1753.

138. Andrew Killgore, "In Memoriam: 25 Years After His Death, Dr. Fayez Sayegh's Towering Legacy Lives On," *Washington Report*, 2005, https://www.wrmea.org/005 -december/in-memoriam-25-years-after-his-death-dr.-fayez-sayeghs-towering -legacy-lives-on.html.

139. See Lear 2008, Redfield 2013, and especially Parla 2019.

140. Parla 2019, 177.

141. Allen 2013.

142. Confidential UN Records of Testimony, 1979.

143. UNGA 1989b, A/44/PV.78; also see UNGA 1977, Resolution 32/130.

144. The issue of Israel's discriminatory treatment of Palestinian citizens did occasionally arise, as in the Egyptian delegation's rebuttal of Israel's claims that the Special Committee was biased in its remit: "The investigation applies to the Arab territories under Israeli occupation; it is not an investigation of Israel or of what is happening in Israel. I would say that what is happening in Israel—its policies of racial discrimination and oppression indeed needs investigation; but that is not at issue today. At issue today is the investigation of Israeli practices violating the human rights of the inhabitants of the occupied Arab territories." UNGA 1971h, A/PV.2027, para 47.

145. UNGA 1991, A/SPC/46/SP.28, para. 9.

146. Ibid., para.5.

147. On the human rights industry in Palestine, see Allen 2009a; Allen 2013; Hanafi and Tabar 2006.

148. UNGA 1991, A/SPC/46/SP.28, para. 6.

149. This is similar to how anthropologist Ayşe Parla describes the functioning of hope in other contexts. Parla 2019, 65, 177.

## Chapter 5: The Silences of Democratic Listening

1. Mouin Rabbani predicted that "future historians are likely to consider it Oslo's last gasp." Rabbani 2001.

2. *Report of the Sharm el-Sheikh Fact-Finding Committee* [hereafter Mitchell Report]. Full text of the report completed on April 30, 2001 and published on May 20, 2001. For a political science analysis of the committee's work, see Deane 2009.

3. "NSU Third Submission of the Palestine Liberation Organization to the Sharm El-Sheikh Fact-Finding Committee" (document on file with the author, April 3, 2001).

4. Mitchell Report.

5. Slotta 2015, 132.

6. This is akin to the "balanced objectivity" of Western journalists that Amahl Bishara has analyzed. In the context she describes, the ideology of balance upholds the notion that opposing perspectives can and should always be presented equally, which leads to misrepresentations in journalistic texts and reinforces inequalities in institutional practices. It can encourage journalists to portray the Israeli-Palestinian conflict as balanced between two equal parties, obscuring the basic fact of Israel's military occupation. Bishara 2013.

7. Mitchell Report.

8. Rudman 2010, 10, 12.

9. Discussion with George Mitchell, November 2, 2015.

10. Mitchell 2011.

11. Slotta 2015, 132, 135. Ivison 2002, 90. On the significance of communication in a community and how the membership in a stable community spontaneously produces ease of communication, see Parekh 2000, 42, 156. For discussions on the value of speaking and being listened to, see Tully 1995, 132.

12. This was *New York Times* reporter Deborah Sontag's near poetic fulmination of applause for the Mitchell Committee's balanced report. After its release in May 2001, she wrote: "If common sense could end the Israeli-Palestinian conflict, the report released last week . . . might make a difference. . . . It apportions responsibility to both the Israelis and the Palestinians with a studied neutrality that infuriated some on both sides. . . . Its clearheaded, outsiders' assessment of a dizzyingly blood-soaked dispute reads like a triumph of evenhandedness over passion." Deborah Sontag, "A New Mideast Balance Sheet: The Mitchell Report Offers No Easy Way Out," *New York Times*, May 7, 2001, https://www.nytimes.com/2001/05/07/world/a-new-mideast-balance-sheet-the-mitchell-report-offers-no-easy-way-out.html.

13. Bishara 2013.

14. On narrative hegemony, see Said 1984. For accounts of the peace process, see Ehud Barak's version of this story in Benny Morris, "Camp David and After: An Exchange (1. An Interview with Ehud Barak)." *New York Review of Books*, 2002, https://www.nybooks.com/articles/2002/06/13/camp-david-and-after-an-exchange-1-an-interview-wi/. For a refutation of this canard and a description of Palestinian negotiation positions, see Robert Malley and Hussein Agha, "Camp David and After: An Exchange (2. A Reply to Ehud Barak)," *New York Review of Books*, 2002, https://www.nybooks.com/articles/2002/06/13/camp-david-and-after-an-exchange-2-a-reply-to-ehud/. A critical scholarly account can be found in Anziska 2018, 147.

15. On liberalism's listening subject, see Englund 2018; O'Rourke 2001.

16. Prominent just war theories are found in Walzer 2015 and Elshtain 1992. For analyses of the Responsibility to Protect doctrine, see Çubukçu 2013; Falk, Juergensmeyer, and Popovski 2012. On the process that led to the definition of "aggression" by the UN General Assembly in 1974, see International Law Commission 2015. For an analysis of the definition of acceptable targets of violence in international humanitarian law, see Kinsella 2011.

17. See "Allowing the Use of Live Ammunition against Stone-Throwers in East Jerusalem Will Have Lethal Consequences," B'Tselem, 2015, https://www.btselem.org/press_releases/20150917_allowing_use_of_live_fire_in_east_jerusalem. See "Open-Fire Policy," B'Tselem, 2017, https://www.btselem.org/firearms.

18. On the normalization of violence, see Allen 2008.

19. Declaration of Principles in M. Bassiouni 2005.

20. Names of interviewees are pseudonyms.

21. Palestinian refugees are "the largest and the longest-standing case of displaced persons in the world today." Al-Azza and al-Orzza 2013–2015.

22. Shlaim 1994.

23. Interview by Rudiger Gobel, "'The Peace Process Is A Charade': Interview with Nassar Ibrahim and Dr. Mahir Al-Tahir, Members of the Executive Committee of the Popular Front for the Liberation of Palestine (PFLP)," 1998, http://apa.online.free.fr/imprimersans.php3?id_article=727&nom_site=Agence Presse Associative (APA)&url_site=http://apa.online.free.fr.

24. Orient House was the PLO headquarters in Jerusalem.

25. Said 2001.

26. "The Taba Negotiations" 2002, 79.

27. Oxfam, *20 Facts: 20 Years Since the Oslo Accords*. 2013. https://issuu.com/oxfamopti/docs/oslo_20_factsheet_-_final; "Settlements," B'Tselem, 2019, https://www.btselem.org/settlements.

28. Mill 1991; R. Wilson 2017.

29. Stephen Zunes, "Is Mitchell Up to the Task?," *HuffPost*, 2011, https://www.huffpost.com/entry/is-mitchell-up-to-the-tas_b_160398?guccounter=1.

30. Ibid.

31. For a description of the Middle East Investment Initiative, which is headed by one of the committee's American staff, Jim Pickup, see James Militzer, "Peace Through Finance?: How the Middle East Investment Initiative Uses Financial Tools to Help a Troubled Region," *NextBillion* (blog), 2015, https://nextbillion.net/peace-through-finance/.

32. Rudman 2010.

33. Slotta 2015, 133, 144.

34. Robert Malley and Hussein Agha, "Camp David: A Tragedy of Errors," *The Guardian*, July 20, 2001.

35. Names of those quoted without surnames are pseudonyms.

36. "Israeli Settlers Chop Down Some 1,155 Palestinian Olive Trees in 'Awarta," al-Haq, 2013, http://www.alhaq.org/documentation/weekly-focuses/724-israeli-setters-chop-down-some-1155-palestinian-olive-trees-in-awarta; "Settlers Uproot and Steal 150 Olive Tree Saplings from Village," al-Haq, 2012, http://www.alhaq.org/documentation/weekly-focuses/533-settlers-uproot-and-steal-150-olive-tree-saplings-from-village; "Some 1,000 Olive Trees Uprooted to Build Bypass Road on 'Azzun Village Land," B'Tselem, 2017, https://www.btselem.org/20170205_nabi_elyas_bypass_road_land_confiscation.

37. *Olive Trees: More Than Just a Tree in Palestine*, Miftah (November 21, 2012). http://www.miftah.org/Doc/Factsheets/Miftah/English/factsheet-OliveTrees.pdf.

38. See the report by the Inter-Parliamentary Union—an organization of national parliaments that seeks to build "global democracy through political dialogue and concrete

action"—which describes the breaches of international law in Barghouti's trial. Simon Fore-man, *Human Rights of Parliamentarians: The Trial of Mr. Marwan Barghouti—Palestine,* Inter-Parliamentary Union. http://archive.ipu.org/hr-e/174/report.htm.

39. There is no explicit prohibition that makes armed struggle for self-determination illegal. Norman 2010, 71. Barghouti has called for civil and armed resistance throughout his time in Israeli prison. See, for example, "Jailed Palestinian Leader Barghouti Urges Resistance," *BBC News,* March 27, 2012, https://www.bbc.com/news/world-middle-east-17522781; Daoud Kuttab, "Jailed Palestinian Leader Calls for Armed Resistance," *Al-Monitor,* November 24, 2014, https://www.al-monitor.com/pulse/originals/2014/11/marwan-barghouti-calls-armed-resistance-against-israel.html#ixzz4xgKuUmua. It is a widely shared contention among Palestinians living in the occupied territory that armed resistance to occupation is their right. See, for example, Hani al-Masri's editorial "about the right of the Palestinian people to resist the occupation by all means. This is the right which all religions, and all international law and agreements have agreed upon." Hani al-Masri, "Marra Ukhra Hawla al-'Amaliyyat al-Istishhadiyya," *Al-Ayyam,* June 23, 2002.

40. For a useful troubling of this binary analytic, see Koskenniemi 2003.

41. Allen 2013.

42. Watson 2000.

43. "About Us," NAD, https://www.nad.ps/en/about-us.

44. "'A Review of the Negotiations Support Project for the Negotiations Affairs Department of the PLO/Palestinian Authority.' Submitted to the Department for International Development, 3 November 2004" (document on file with the author, 2004).

45. Ibid.

46. These were people who had the competence required to conduct the research and provide the policy arguments on a range of central issues, including those related to borders, Jerusalem, water, settlements, security, and refugees. Adam Smith International (ASI) is a self-described "independent international development consultancy." It was co-founded in 1992 by Peter Young, considered a "rising star at the free-market think tank the Adam Smith Institute." For a damning critique of the ASI, see Provost, Dodwell, and Scrivener 2006.

47. Dajani 2007.

48. Mitchell Report.

49. The committee was also introduced to Israeli victims, including people injured in suicide bombings.

50. "A Crisis of Faith: Second Submission of the Palestine Liberation Organization to the Sharm El Sheikh Fact-Finding Committee" (document on file with the author, December 30, 2000), 3.

51. Ibid., 6–7.

52. Ibid., 3.

53. Dajani 2007, 65.

54. Dajani makes a similar point in his discussion of UN Security Council Resolution 242 when he notes that Security Council "recommendations may help to reduce the political costs, domestically and internationally, of reaching a deal." Dajani 2007/2008.

55. "Statistics on Settlements and Settler Population," B'Tselem, http://www.btselem.org/settlements/statistics.

56. Dajani 2007, 124.

57. Dajani 2007/2008.

58. d'Aspremont 2018, 11.

59. Koskenniemi 1990, 5.

60. Ibid., 6.

61. UN Security Council resolutions listed in the Palestinian submissions to the Mitchell Committee include UNSCR 1322 (2000), which "calls upon Israel, the occupying Power, to abide scrupulously by its legal obligations and its responsibilities under the Fourth Geneva Convention relative to the Protection of Civilian Persons in Time of War of 12 August 1949," and a number of others: SCR 1073 (1996); SCR 672 (1990); SCR 478 (1980); SCR 476 (1980); SCR 338 (1973); and SCR 242 (1967). For a statement on the applicability of international humanitarian law and Israel's human rights obligations in the Occupied Palestinian Territory, see the report of the Secretary-General in UNHRC 2017, A/HRC/34/38.

62. d'Aspremont 2018, 8.

63. The notion of self-referentiality in international law that d'Aspremont puts forward is more specifically focused on the way that international legal discourse explains the formation and functioning of fundamental doctrines "by fundamental doctrines themselves." d'Aspremont 2018, 6, 4.

64. Mitchell Report.

65. Mitchell Report.

66. Mitchell 2011.

67. Mitchell called on the international community to encourage "both sides to look past their historic grievances toward a negotiation that deals with the realities of the situation today." Mitchell 2015, 313, also 316.

68. League of Nations 1937a, 16.

69. Rabbani 2001.

70. Israel Radio quoted Foreign Minister Shimon Peres as saying that the report was balanced and fair. Sontag, "A New Mideast Balance Sheet." "Official Response by the PLO to the Mitchell Report," *Al-Bab.com* (document on file with the author, n.d.), last modified June 18, 2009.

71. Zunes, "Is Mitchell Up to the Task?"

72. Discussion with diplomat, December 20, 2017.

73. Sontag "A New Mideast Balance Sheet." For an insightful analysis of the ideology of "balanced objectivity" in US news media practices in Palestine, see Bishara 2013.

## Chapter 6: The Shift to Crime and Punishment

1. In February 2009, UN Secretary General Ban Ki-moon commissioned a UN Board of Inquiry, but it was limited to investigating attacks on UN buildings and personnel. Ed Pilkington and Rory McCarthy, "UN Report Accuses Israeli Military of Negligence in Gaza War," *The Guardian*, May 5, 2009.

2. Marín 2017.

3. I. Hurd 2017, 133.

4. Otto 2016, 303.

5. Allen 2009a; Khalili 2009.

6. Engle, Miller, and Davis 2016. As the Goldstone report explained, "Criminal proceedings and sanctions have a deterrent function and offer a measure of justice for the victims of violations. The international community increasingly looks to criminal justice as an effective mechanism of accountability and justice in the face of abuse and impunity. The Mission regards the rules and definitions of international criminal law as crucial to the fulfilment of its mandate to look at all violations of IHL and IHRL by all parties to the conflict." UNHRC 2009, A/HRC/12/48, para. 286. (Hereafter Goldstone Report).

7. UNGA, Public Hearings, June 29, 2009.

8. The Palestinian Authority foreign ministry welcomed the ICC prosecutor's announcement on December 20, 2019, that she would launch a full ICC investigation into alleged war crimes, ten years after representatives of the Palestinian government signed an agreement to submit the occupied Palestinian territory to the jurisdiction of the ICC. The PA as well as Palestinian commentators stated that the decision was long overdue. See al-Jazeera and News Agencies, "ICC Wants to Prove Alleged War Crimes in Palestinian Territories," *al-Jazeera*, December 20, 2019, https://www.aljazeera.com/news/2019/12/icc-investigate-alleged-war-crimes-palestinian-territories-191220143949348.html; Ramzy Baroud, "Justice at Last? 'Panic' in Israel as the ICC Takes 'Momentous Step' in the Right Direction," *Palestine Chronicle*, January 8, 2020, https://www.palestinechronicle.com/justice-at-last-panic-in-israel-as-the-icc-takes-momentous-step-in-the-right-direction/; "After Five Years the Prosecutor of the International Criminal Court Finally Advances the Situation of Palestine from Preliminary Examination to the Pre-Trial Chamber for Questions on Territorial Jurisdiction," *al-Haq*, December 20, 2019, http://www.alhaq.org/advocacy/16323.html.

9. "Israel Obstructs UN Fact-Finding Mission to Jenin Refugee Camp—End Israel's Impunity!," Badil, 2002. http://www.badil.org/en/publication/press-releases/16-2002/311-press248-02.html.

10. Shafiq al-Masri, "Ma Hasal fi Jenin Jarimat Ibada wa-min Salahiyat Mahkamat al-Jaza' al-Dawliyya al-Da'ima al-Nazar fiha," *al-Intiqad*, 2002, https://archive .alahednews.com.lb/alahed.org/archive/2002/1005/palestine/doc8.htm.

11. Ibid.; "Israel/OT: Statement to the United Nations about the Fact-Finding Team to Inquire into the Events in Jenin," Amnesty International, 2002, https://www .amnesty.org.uk/press-releases/israelot-statement-united-nations-about-fact-finding -team-inquire-events-jenin.

12. UNSC 2002, S/RES/1405.

13. UNSC 2002, S/2002/504. When the fact-finding mission to Jenin was canceled, the UN General Assembly requested a report on Jenin from the secretary-general. It was compiled based on publicly available information and submissions from UN member states, observer missions, and NGOs without any visit to Jenin. The permanent representative of Israel refused a request for information from the under-secretary-general for political affairs. UNGA 2002, A/ES-10/186.

14. "Israel/OT," Amnesty International.

15. This was the description of Javier Zuniga, Amnesty International's director of regional strategy, who entered Jenin refugee camp on April 17, 2002. "Israel/OT," Amnesty International.

16. Human Rights Watch 2002.

17. Charmaine Seitz, "Investigating Jenin: The Jenin Refugee Camp's Jagged Concrete Hillside of Homes-Turned-into-Graves Has yet to Yield All Its Secrets," *The Nation*, May 1, 2002, https://www.thenation.com/article/investigating-jenin/.

18. Ibid.

19. "Israel/Occupied Territories: Jenin War Crimes Investigation Needed," Human Rights Watch, May 2, 2002. https://www.hrw.org/news/2002/05/02/israel/occupied -territories-jenin-war-crimes-investigation-needed.

20. An EU report to the UN noted that the Israeli military prohibited entry to Jenin camp for twelve consecutive days. UNGA 2002, A/ES-10/186. Israel declared six West Bank towns "closed military areas" and made them inaccessible to the press. UNCHR 2002, E/CN.4/2002/184.

21. A commission investigating events in the Syrian civil war adopted a working definition of "massacre" as "an intentional mass killing of civilians not directly participating in hostilities, or hors de combat fighters, by organized armed forces or groups in a single incident, in violation of international human rights or humanitarian law." UNHRC 2013, A/HRC/22/59.

22. No Lebanese murderer has been convicted for his crimes. Historian Seth Anziska has found diplomatic correspondence proving that US officials "effectively gave Israel cover to let the Phalange fighters remain in the camps" and carry out the butchery that many had predicted and some knew to be already under way. Seth Anziska, "A

Preventable Massacre," *New York Times*, September 16, 2012, http://www.nytimes.com /2012/09/17/opinion/a-preventable-massacre.html.

23. For a brief recounting of his exploits, see Baroud 2014; Ahmad Dhiyab, "al-Aham min Wafat Sharon," *al-Raya*, January 14, 2014, http://www.raya.com/news/pages /fb534715-8478-466a-a18a-87292cd80c97.

24. Former Palestinian Authority minister Ghassan Khatib referred to him as a war criminal. ABC, "Former Israeli Leader Ariel Sharon Dead, Aged 85, After Eight Years in Coma." ABC News, January 11, 2014, https://www.abc.net.au/news/2014-01-11/former -israeli-prime-minister-sharon-dead/5195912. Edward Said referred to him as a "paunchy old war criminal" in an essay titled "Double Standards" that was circulated to the al-Awda email list, October 13, 2000. Upon Sharon's death, Palestinian leaders declared him a war criminal who should have faced trial. Marc Abizeid, "Ariel Sharon, the 'Butcher of Beirut,' Is Dead," *al-Akhbar*, January 11, 2014, http://english.al-akhbar.com/node/18196. Sharon held the position of prime minister for five years.

25. Matt Rees, "Streets Red With Blood: The U.S. Realizes It Must Try Again to Stop Palestinians and Israelis from Killing One Another. Will Hope Triumph over History?," *Time*, March 18, 2002, http://content.time.com/time/magazine /article/0,9171,1002012,00.html.

26. Interview by Hafez al-Merazi with Mohammad al-Sayyid Sa'id, Osama abu Ersheid, and Hani Magali, "Jenin. Matha Hadatha fiha?," *al-Jazeera*, May 10, 2002.

27. ʿEzzat Assaʿdani, "Tahqiq al-Sabt, al-Shahida Bint al-Shahida Bint al-Shahid," *Ahram*, May 12, 2002, http://www.ahram.org.eg/Archive/2002/5/12/INVE1.HTM.

28. A few years later, another fact-finding commission was scuppered by Israeli noncooperation. On July 6, 2006, the UN Human Rights Council adopted Resolution S-1/1 calling for an investigative commission to the Gaza Strip after the commencement of "Operation Summer Rains" by the Israeli military in order to report on human rights violations committed through this "operation." Because the government of Israel would not cooperate with this commission, John Dugard, "the Special Rapporteur on the human rights situation in the Palestinian territories occupied since 1967," could not carry out this fact-finding exercise. UNGA 2007, A/HRC/5/11.

29. B'Tselem, *Operation Defensive Shield: Soldiers' Testimonies, Palestinian Testimonies.* March 21, 2002. https://www.btselem.org/download/200207_defensive_shield_eng.pdf.

30. "Israel and the Occupied Territories: Shielded from Scrutiny: IDF Violations in Jenin and Nablus," Amnesty International, November 4, 2002. https://www.amnesty .org/en/documents/MDE15/143/2002/en/.

31. UNRWA, *Profile: Jenin Camp Jenin Governorate*, March 2015, https://www .unrwa.org/sites/default/files/jenin_refugee_camp.pdf.

32. United Nations Office for the Coordination of Humanitarian Affairs (OCHA), "UNDAC/OCHA Mission Report Occupied Palestinian Territory 20 Apr 2002– 10 May 2002," ReliefWeb, May 10, 2002, https://reliefweb.int/report/occupied-palestin

ian-territory/undacocha-mission-report-occupied-palestinian-territory-20-apr; Human Rights Watch 2002.

33. Discussion with a woman in the Jenin Refugee Camp, July 17, 2002; Allen 2009a.

34. Baroud 2003, 22, 32.

35. "Ma'rakat Mukhayam Jenin. Al-Hakaya la-Zalat Hadira," *al-Quds*, April 2, 2016, http://www.alquds.com/articles/14595953703576079000/.

36. Mohammed Bakri, "The Hunting of 'Jenin Jenin': A Never-Ending Story," *Ha'aretz*, December 7, 2016, https://www.haaretz.com/opinion/.premium -the-hunting-of-jenin-jenin-a-never-ending-story-1.5469938.

37. Ibid.

38. Al-Mezan, "Bayanat Sahafiyya Hawla Lajnat al-Umam al-Muttahida li-Taqassi al-Haqa'iq fi Jenin." April 29, 2002, http://www.mezan.org/post/1160/جينن+في+الحقائق +لتقصي+المتحدة+الأمم+لجنة+حول.

39. Tabar 2012.

40. Tabar 2007, 16.

41. Whether the Gaza Strip remains occupied territory has been a matter of contention, but many international legal experts and documents assert that, given Israel's effective control over the area, it is still occupied. As Lisa Hajjar has summarized the issue, "'Occupation' is a legal designation of an international nature. Israel's occupation of Gaza continues to the present day because (a) Israel continues to exercise 'effective control' over this area, (b) the conflict that produced the occupation has not ended, and (c) an occupying state cannot unilaterally (and without international/diplomatic agreement) transform the international status of occupied territory except, perhaps, if that unilateral action terminates all manner of effective control." Lisa Hajjar, "Is Gaza Still Occupied and Why Does It Matter?," *Jadaliyya*, July 14, 2014, https://www.jadaliyya.com/Details /27557/Is-Gaza-Still-Occupied-and-Why-Does-It-Matter. The Israeli human rights NGO B'Tselem notes that the "broad scope of Israeli control in the Gaza Strip, which exists despite the lack of a physical presence of IDF soldiers in the territory, creates a reasonable basis for the assumption that this control amounts to 'effective control,' such that the laws of occupation continue to apply." "The Gaza Strip—Israel's Obligations under International Law," B'Tselem, January 1, 2017, https://www.btselem.org/gaza_strip/israels_obligations. Also see UNHRC 2007, A/ HRC/9/26, 5; Gross 2017.

42. UNHRC 2007, A/HRC/9/26. Also see UNHRC 2007, A/HRC/4/17.

43. For more on the refusal of the Government of Israel to cooperate with the mission, see UNHRC 2007, A/HRC/5/20.

44. Tutu and Chinkin 2008.

45. UNHRC 2007, A/HRC/9/26, 4.

46. Redfield 2006, 5.

47. UNHRC 2007, A/HRC/9/26, 4, 21–22.

48. Ibid., 21.

49. Chinkin 2010.

50. Tutu 2008.

51. Interview with Christine Chinkin, London, April 25, 2018.

52. Ibid.

53. "The Gaza Strip." November 11, 2017, B'Tselem, https://www.btselem.org/gaza_strip. For a thorough account of Israel's policies and "the horror that has been inflicted on Gaza," see Finkelstein 2018.

54. "Israel/Gaza: Operation 'Cast Lead'—22 Days of Death and Destruction. Facts and Figures." Amnesty International, July 2, 2009, https://www.amnesty.org/en/documents/mde15; PCHR. *Targeted Civilians: A PCHR Report on the Israeli Military Offensive against the Gaza Strip (27 December 2008–18 January 2009),*" https://pchrgaza.org/files/Reports/English/pdf_spec/gaza%20war%20report.pdf; Palestine Centre for Human Rights (PCHR), "PCHR Expresses Grave Concern Regarding Credibility of Investigations Carried Out in Response to Recommendations of the Goldstone Report—Occupied Palestinian Territory." ReliefWeb, February 5, 2010, https://reliefweb.int/report/occupied-palestinian-territory/pchr-expresses-grave-concern-regarding-credibility.

55. Badil, Adalah, al-Haq, Arab Association for Human Rights. "Gross Human Rights Violations and War Crimes in the Occupied Gaza Strip," 2009, http://www.badil.org/phocadownloadpap/legal-advocacy/un-human-rights council/HRC Special session 9_Badil, Adalah, Al Haq et al_joint written statement (January 2009).pdf.

56. Goldstone Report, para. 155.

57. Goldstone Report, e.g. paras. 25, 422, 538. The report also suggests that Palestinian armed groups may have committed crimes against humanity. Goldstone Report, para. 108.

58. Richard Falk, "The Palestinians Are Winning the Legitimacy War: Will It Matter?," *Countercurrents*, April 5, 2010, https://www.countercurrents.org/falk050410.htm.

59. ʿIsam ʿAbdel-Rahman, "Al-Khabir al-Qanuni al-Doktur ʿAbdallah al-Ashʿal: Taqrir 'Goldstone' Yuʾakkid Irtikab al-Kayan al-Sahyuni Jaraʾim Harb wa-Ahamiyatahu fi Matlab Muhakamat al-Masʾulin al-Sahayna," *Filastin al-Muslima*, November 2009. Richard Falk, former UN special rapporteur on Palestine, surmised that "this particular report touched the raw nerve of global moral and political consciousness." Falk 2012, 8.

60. Stauffer 2015, 1.

61. UNHRC 2009a.

62. Discussion with Christine Chinkin, London, April 25, 2018.

63. Expressing pride in having contributed to this development in international law, she continued: "Women, peace, and security in front of [the] security council, international criminal tribunals on sexual violence—that's an achievement." Chinkin and Gearty 2014.

64. Çubukçu, 2018, 71.

65. Chinkin discussion 2018.

66. Stauffer 2015, 1, 5.

67. Among the signatories were Desmond Tutu, Mary Robinson, Justice Richard Goldstone, and other heads of UN commissions of inquiry. In addition to Goldstone, two of the other members of the commission he would lead, Hina Jilani and Desmond Travers, were also signatories.

68. "OPT/Gaza: World's Leading Investigators Call for War Crimes Inquiry – Open Letter," Amnesty International, March 16, 2009, https://reliefweb.int/report /occupied-palestinian-territory/optgaza-worlds-leading-investigators-call-war-crimes -inquiry.

69. "Quda wa-Mudda'un Dawliyyun Yad'un li-Tahqiq Dawli Hawla al-Intihakat Khilal Harb Ghazza," *al-Ayyam*, March 16, 2009, 1.

70. Falk 2012, 9.

71. Hanan Chehata, "Exclusive MEMO Interview with Colonel Desmond Travers—Co-Author of the UN's Goldstone Report," *Live Leak*, https://www .liveleak.com/view?i=1fa_1265705780.

72. PCHR 2010.

73. "NSU Memo Re: 'The Goldstone Report': Potential Palestinian Criminal Liability—The Palestine Papers—Aljazeera Investigations," *al-Jazeera*, October 18, 2009, http://transparency.aljazeera.net/en/projects/thepalestinepapers/2012 1821121343903.html.

74. Ken Silverstein, "Six Questions for Desmond Travers on the Goldstone Report," *Harper's*, October 29, 2009, https://harpers.org/blog/2009/10/six-questions -for-desmond-travers-on-the-goldstone-report/.

75. "Al-Masjid al-Aqsa wa-Goldstone wa-l-Asirat . . . Intisar Mantiq al-Sumud," *Filastin al-Muslima*, November 2009, 3.

76. Lu'ai 'Ammar, "Ahali al-Dahaya Yastankirun Qarar 'Abbas: Limadha Ba'a Dima'ana wa Ashla'ana bi-Hathihi al-Suhula," *Filastin al-Muslima*, November 2009, 44–45.

77. Hasan al-Batal, "Lajnat Goldstone, Qa'idat Bayanat li-Jara'im al-Harb," *al-Ayyam*, April 1, 2009, 1.

78. "Haykal: Qarar 'Abbas laysa bi-Yadih," *Filastin al-Muslima*, November 2009, 9.

79. See Quigley 2010.

80. Roy 2016.

81. UNHRC, Public Hearings, Morning Session, June 29, 2009.

82. Ibid.

83. Rory McCarthy, "UN Find Challenges Israeli Version of Attack on Civilian Building in Gaza War," *The Guardian*, February 1, 2010, https://www .theguardian.com/world/2010/feb/01/gaza-war-report-accuses-israel; UNHRC 2009d.

84. Ibid.

85. "Did Israel Whitewash a Massacre in Jabaliya?," *Ma'an*, January 6, 2010, (in Arabic) http://www.maannews.net/eng/ViewDetails.aspx?ID=252123 ; UNHRC 2009a.

86. The mission heard five eyewitnesses who had been in the al-Maqadma Mosque at the time it was struck. They heard testimony from relatives of those who were killed in the attack and received their sworn and signed statements testifying to the facts they witnessed. The report addressed the destruction of this mosque in many sections of its analysis. See Goldstone Report, e.g., p. 105, 142, 157, 233–237.

87. UNHRC 2009a.

88. Ibid.

89. Kinsella 2017, 206.

90. His mother, wife, and four-year-old daughter were also wounded. UNHRC 2009b.

91. Brunnegger and Faulk 2016, 2.

92. UNHRC 2009a.

93. R. Kennedy 2014, 66.

94. On CEDAW, see UN Women 2016. On the UN world conferences on women, see "World Conferences on Women," UN Women, https://www.unwomen.org/en /how-we-work/intergovernmental-support/world-conferences-on-women. On Resolution 1325, see UN Women 2015.

95. UNHRC 2009a.

96. Ibid.

97. Edmund Sanders, "U.N. Fact-Finding Commission Faces Skepticism in Gaza," *Los Angeles Times*, June 29, 2009, https://www.latimes.com/archives/la-xpm-2009 -jun-29-fg-gaza-un-hearing29-story.html.

98. Hasan al-Batal, "Goldstone, al-Fas Birra's!," *al-Ayyam*, September 20, 2009, 1; 'Abdel Majid Sweilim, "Taqrir Goldstone: Limadha la Nata'alam min Tajarubina?," *al-Ayyam*, September 24, 2009, 1.

99. Alan M. Dershowitz, "Goldstone Needs To Do Teshuvah," *The Forward*, April 4, 2011, https://forward.com/opinion/136716/goldstone-needs-to-do-teshuvah/. Jameel Serhan of the Palestinian Independent Commission for Human Rights in Gaza said the report was very important because it confirmed that the Israeli occupation had committed war crimes. Fayez Abi-Oun, "Ghazza: al-Hay'a al-Mustaqilla Tutalib al-Umam al-Mutahida bi-Mutaba'at Tanfidh Tawsiyat Taqrir Goldstone," *al-Ayyam*, September 30, 2009.

100. "Taqrir Goldstone Yatahim Isra'il wa-'Hamas' bi-Irtikab 'Jara'im Harb' Khilal al-Harb 'ala Ghazza," *al-Ayyam*, September 16, 2009, 1.

101. Ibrahim al-Madhun, "Wa-li-l-Jina'iyya al-Dawliyya Ahkam wa-A'raf," *al-Resala*, April 2, 2015, https://bit.ly/2Y00A65.

102. "Gaza Government Sends Goldstone Updates to UN," *Ma'an*, March 16, 2011, (in Arabic) http://www.maannews.com/Content.aspx?id=368776.

103. Report on file with author, n.d. For more on economic conditions in Gaza as a result of the siege in the period before the Goldstone Mission, see Oxfam International, *Breaking the Impasse: Ending the Humanitarian Stranglehold on Palestine*. November 2007, https://oxfamilibrary.openrepository.com/bitstream/handle/10546/1140 98/bn-breaking-the-impasse-palestine-101207-en.pdf?sequence=1&isAllowed=y. For up-to-date information, see "Gaza Strip," OCHA, accessed January 5, 2020, https://www .ochaopt.org/location/gaza-strip.

104. "Hamas Clears Itself of UN War Crimes Charges," *al-Arabiyya*, January 27, 2010, https://www.alarabiya.net/articles/2010/01/27/98609.html.

105. Musa Abu Marzuq, vice president to Hamas's political office, said in an interview that the Goldstone report found Hamas innocent of all accusations leveled against it by Israel. Musa abu-Marzuq, "Hamas la Tas'a li-Iqamat Imara Islamiyya wa-la Tas'a li-Nizam Siyasi Mutakamil," *al-Mushahid al-Siyasi*, n.d., http://www.almushahid assiyasi.com/ar/4/7704. Examples of NGO responses are: "Palestinian Authority: Hamas Fails to Mount Credible Investigations into Gaza Conflict Violations," Amnesty International, February 19, 2010, https://www.amnesty.org/en/documents /MDE21/001/2010/en, 5; also see "Gaza: Hamas Report Whitewashes War Crimes," Human Rights Watch, January 28, 2010, https://www.hrw.org/news/2010/01 /28/gaza-hamas-report-whitewashes-war-crimes; "PCHR Expresses Grave Concern," PCHR. For an analysis of how the Hamas government's engagement with the Goldstone report was a performance of internationally legitimate statehood acting in accordance with international legal norms, see Allen 2013, 177–84.

106. Shuki Sadeh, "Peres: Goldstone Is a Small Man out to Hurt Israel," *Haaretz*, January 1, 2009, https://www.haaretz.com/1.5056729. Goldstone's "blood libel" left a "diabolical legacy," according to a Hudson Institute researcher. Anne Bayefsky, "The United Nations and the Goldstone Report," Hudson Institute, April 5, 2011, https://www.hudson.org/research/7896-the-united-nations-and-the-goldstone-report. It was also reported on in the right-wing Jerusalem post by Tovah Lazaroff, "UN Report a 21st Century Blood Libel, Scholar Says in Geneva," *Jerusalem Post*, September 30, 2009, https://www.jpost.com/Israel/UN-report-a-21st-century-blood-libel-scholar-says-in -Geneva.

107. Bin Dur-Yemini, "Goldstone 'Mujrim' Yakhtabi' Tahta Mazallit Huquq al-Insan," *al-Ayyam*, (Translated from *Maariv*), September 26, 2009, 15. For further summary of Israeli reactions to the report, see "The Goldstone Report: Excerpts

and Responses," *Journal for Palestine Studies* 39, no. 2 (2010), https://www.palestine
-studies.org/jps/fulltext/42268.

108. A. Talhami, "Sa uress: al-Jadal Mustamir fi Sha n al-Rad ʿala Taqrir Goldstone wa-Tawaqu at bi-an Tuwafiq Israe il "ala Tashkil' Lajnat Fahs," *al-Hayat*, January 30, 2010, https://www.sauress.com/alhayat/103058.

109. Jimmy Leas and Noura Erakat, "Delusional Self-Defense, Delusional Con-
gressional Vote," *HuffPost*, March 18, 2010, https://www.huffpost.com/entry/delusional
-self-defense-d_b_351680. The US ambassador to the UN, Susan Rice, reportedly confirmed that the US was working to render the Goldstone report ineffective. "Wikiliks
Yakshif al-Dughutat allati Tumarisuha Washinton li-Salih Isra il," *Arabs 48*, April 12,
2011, https://bit.ly/3e35gxR.

110. Perugini and Gordon 2016.

111. For a summary of this backlash, see Finkelstein 2010, 137–41. For Goldstone's
explanation of his Zionism, see his interview with Bill Moyers. Moyers 2009.

112. Goldstone 2013, 48.

113. Moyers 2009.

114. "Panel on Goldstone Report," *UN in the Middle East Research Initiative*
(American University in Beirut, Issam Fares Institute, June 7, 2010), http://dr.aub
.edu.lb/mod/data/view.php?d=3&rid=1599&filter=1.

115. Rif at Murra, "Itisa al-Mutalaba al-Sahyuniyya bi-Itmam Amaliyat al-
Tabadul, Mu aliqun Sahaiyna 'Safqit al-Sharit' Nasr li-Hamas," *Filastin al-Muslima*,
November 2009, 30–31.

116. Richard Goldstone, "Reconsidering the Goldstone Report on Israel and
War Crimes," *Washington Post*, April 1, 2011, https://www.washingtonpost.com/opin
ions/reconsidering-the-goldstone-report-on-israel-and-war-crimes/2011/04/01
/AFg111JC_story.html?noredirect=on; Conal Urquhart, "Judge Goldstone Expresses
Regrets about His Report into Gaza War," *The Guardian*, April 3, 2011, https://www.the
guardian.com/world/2011/apr/03/goldstone-regrets-report-into-gaza-war.

117. Hina Jilani, Christine Chinkin, and Desmond Travers, "Goldstone Report: Statement Issued by Members of UN Mission on Gaza War," *The Guardian*,
April 14, 2011, http://www.theguardian.com/commentisfree/2on/apr/i4/goldstone-report
-statement-un-gaza.

118. John Dugard stated, "it seems clear that Goldstone wrote his op-ed under du-
ress," in Dugard 2013–2014, 23.

119. Moyers 2009.

120. "Is the Goldstone Report Dead, High Commissioner?" Badil, February 4, 2011, http://www.badil.org/phocadownloadpap/legal-advocacy/un-human
-rights-council/pal-isr-joint-open-letter-to-unhchr-4feb-2011.pdf.

121. See the jointly issued statement "Victims' Rights Must Be Upheld" in A/HRC/S-12/NGO/4, October 14, 2009. http://www.badil.org/phoca

downloadpap/legal-advocacy/un-human-rights-council/hrc-session12-victims
-right-must-be-upheld-joint statement.pdf; "More than One Year after 'Operation Cast
Lead': Distressing Lack of Accountability and Justice for the Victims of the Conflict,"
Badil, 2010, http://www.badil.org/phocadownloadpap/legal-advocacy/un-human
-rights-council/joint written statement to the 13 session_hrc_feb 10.pdf; "Joint
Statement -BADIL and Habitat International Coalition," *Badil and Habitat International Coalition*, 2009, http://www.badil.org/phocadownloadpap/legal
-advocacy/un-human-rights-council/hrc-hic-badil goldstone ltr_29 sept 09.pdf;
"The Deadline for Justice Is Long Overdue," Badil, November 2010, 370–71,
http://www.badil.org/en/legal-advocacy/un-submissions/special-procedures.html.

   122. Goldstone Report, p. 370–371.

   123. "Panel on Goldstone Report."

## Conclusion: Toward an Anthropology of International Law, and Next Time and Again for Palestine

   1. Farge 2004, 12.

   2. Farge 2004, 96.

   3. The full quote is: "To articulate the past historically does not mean to recognize
it 'the way it really was' (Ranke). It means to seize hold of a memory as it flashes up at
a moment of danger. And this must be done alongside the attempt 'to wrest tradition
away from a conformism that is about to overpower it.'" Benjamin 1974.

   4. Rajagopal 2003. For analyses of subaltern studies' contributions and limitations, see the forum in *American Historical Review*, December 1994, https://doi.org/10
.1086/ahr/99.5.iv; Chalcraft 2008; Brennan 2014.

   5. For a broadened notion of the subaltern, see P. Thomas 2018; Allen 2019.

   6. This assertion of novelty would be undermined if we took colonial law to be a
kind of international law. Early examples of anthropology's analysis of law and colonialism are Cohn 1996b; Starr and Collier 1989.

   7. Important contributions include Clarke, Knottnerus, and de Volder 2016; El-
tringham 2013; Elander 2018; Goodale and Merry 2007; T. Kelly 2012b; R. Wilson 2001;
R. Wilson 2005. For overviews of anthropology's approaches to international law, see
Goodale 2017; Merry 2006.

   8. For examples of how groups of people influence the operations of international
legal concepts and institutions, see Allen 2013; Cabot 2013; Ticktin 2006.

   9. Terdiman 1987, 808.

   10. See Erakat 2019, loc. 199-249; Duncan Kennedy 2008; Moore 1973; Moore 2015;
Okafor 2016; Valverde 2003.

   11. Horwitz 1977, 566.

   12. In his summary of this debate, Bourdieu describes legal formalists as those who
"insist upon the absolute autonomy of legal thought and action . . . [that] results in the

establishment of a specific mode of theoretical thinking, entirely freed of any social determination." He dubs the realists to have an "instrumentalist point of view [that] tends to conceive law and jurisprudence as direct reflections of existing social power relations, in which economic determinations and, in particular, the interests of dominant groups are expressed." Bourdieu 1986, 814.

13. Moore 1973, 720.

14. Also see how legal anthropologist Tobias Kelly has expressed a similar idea: "One of the most interesting ways of doing the anthropology of law is not to focus too much on the law . . . Legality, in all its complexity and ambiguity, comes and goes, shimmering and haunting in the background, sticking and then disappearing, for good or bad." T. Kelly 2017.

15. Bourdieu 1986, 844.

16. Ibid., 817. For an application of Bourdieu's concepts to international criminal law and a review of its influence in legal sociology, see Mégret 2016. For an interesting discussion of the ramifications of Bourdieu's theory in international legal theory, see Özsu 2014.

17. Bell 2014.

18. Mégret 2016, paras. 5, 17. Also see Dezalay and Garth 1996.

19. Bourdieu 1986, 828.

20. Stoler 2009, 196.

21. Bourdieu 1986, 817.

22. Fassin 2012b, 7.

23. On law and international law as ideology, see Duncan Kennedy 1982; Krever 2013; Marks 2000.

24. Cf. Monique Nuijten's understanding of state bureaucracy as a "hope-generating machine." Nuijten 2003, 175.

25. The United States tops the list of governments undermining international law's principles, having had an ambivalent attitude toward liberal internationalism throughout the UN's history. That ambivalence has morphed into an all-out assault under the Trump regime. See Rebecca Gordon, "Why Are We Above International Law?," *The Nation*, March 26, 2019, https://www.thenation.com/article/archive/rebecca-gordon-international-criminal-court-john-bolton/; "Afghan Conflict: US Sanctions 'Kangaroo' ICC Over War Crimes Probe," *BBC*, June 12, 2020, https://www.bbc.co.uk/news/world-us-canada-53012783. In contrast, former legal advisor to the US State Department Harold Hongju Koh insists that Trump's challenges to international law have been thwarted by "transnational processes." For a summary, see Jeffrey Toobin, "Harold Koh's Verdict on Trump vs. International Law," *The New Yorker*, December 20, 2018, https://www.newyorker.com/news/daily-comment/harold-kohs-verdict-on-donald-trump-vs-international-law. For debates about attacks on international law from the left, see Marks 2007; Miéville 2005.

26. See Richard Falk, "Why the United Nations Matters (Even for the Palestinians)," *Foreign Policy Journal*, January 19, 2018, https://www.foreignpolicyjournal.com/2018/01/19/why-the-united-nations-matters-even-for-the-palestinians/. Former UN special rapporteur on Palestine John Dugard holds that "in the long run the UN, with the support of European states, will not be able to resist action based on international law" against Israel's violations. Dugard 2018, loc. 5070. Raja Shehada also seems to hold out hope: "There still may come a day when international law can again serve as an arbiter in resolving conflicts. One hopes this is the case, because of its effect not only on the Middle East but on the rest of the world as well." Raja Shehadeh, "State of Exception," *The Nation*, July 1, 2019, https://www.thenation.com/article/archive/noura-erakat-justice-for-some-book-review/. For a somewhat ambivalent stance toward international law, see Bisharat et al. 2018. Many have provided international legal analyses of the occupation and Israel's actions in Palestine more broadly. See, for example, Tilley 2012. Some argue that the longstanding approach to rendering the conflict in terms of humanitarian law is not only too narrow, but has contributed to the justification and maintenance of Israel's settler-colonial project. See Erakat 2017; Li 2011; and contributors to Barclay and Qaddumi 2011. Ardi Imseis, whose work analyzes similar issues to those addressed in this book, has also observed in Palestinian history a continuity of "the subaltern belief in the liberal rights-based global order." He expresses some kind of wonder at the phenomenon, while criticizing the false hope enflamed by international legal mechanisms: "The UN has unduly raised expectations of what application of that humanitarian normative paradigm can reasonably achieve." His dissertation provides a damning account of how "international rule by law" has constrained Palestine and Palestinians within a condition of "international legal subalternity," a structural condition "that inheres in the international legal and institutional order itself . . . [and] pits hegemonic and counter-hegemonic uses of law against one another." There is, still, a curious silence with regard to whether and how international law can be redeemed in and for Palestine. Imseis 2019, 114, 208. On the possibilities of counterhegemonic law more generally, see Eslava 2015, 273; Rajagopal 2006; Santos and Garavito 2005.

27. "Speech by Yasser Arafat," *Al-Bab*, accessed September 4, 2019, https://al-bab.com/albab-orig/albab/arab/docs/pal/arafat_gun_and_olive_branch.htm.

28. Allen 2002; Allen 2006; William Dalrymple, "Palestine: A Culture under Fire," *The Guardian*, October 2, 2002, https://www.theguardian.com/artanddesign/2002/oct/02/art.artsfeatures; Laïdi-Hanieh 2014.

29. According to Brian Klug's reading of a June 1920 analysis of the Balfour Declaration by Ahad Ha'am (Asher Ginzberg), this influential figure of cultural Zionism suggested that the time for a binational solution had come. Klug 2017. Also on binationalism in the 1940s, see Beinin 1990. On Arab-American activists' pursuit of the binational idea, see Bawardi 2014, 168, 175–176, 215, 234, 264–265.

30. For an overview of 1960s transnationalisms, see Khalili 2009, 11–40. On more recent solidarity trends, see Colla 2005, 338–64. On pan-Islamism in Palestine, see Matthews 2003. On Islamic charitable giving in Palestine and elsewhere, Benthall and Bellion-Jourdan 2003.

31. Barghouti was foundational in establishing the BDS movement for Palestinian rights. Quoted in Chalcraft 2019, 287–310, 295.

32. As legal scholar Ardi Imseis has likewise observed, the central importance of both international law and the unique role of the UN as guarantor of that law in helping forge a peaceful resolution to the question of Palestine has by now become a common article of faith within the international system, the original sin of partition notwithstanding. Nowhere has this faith been more reverent than among the Palestinian people themselves. Imseis 2019, 110.

33. B. al-Hout 1986, 794.

34. In Tomeh's critique of the "questionable ways and means by which the 'Palestine Question' was suppressed," he records the immediate and telling reaction of the Arab delegations of Egypt, Iraq, Lebanon, Syria, Saudi Arabia, and Yemen. They wrote a letter requesting an item be put on the agenda regarding Palestine that "aimed at a consideration of the Palestine Question as a whole; its roots, its origin, and the principal and derivative questions that arose from it." For Tomeh and others, to dilute the Palestinian-specific political nature of "the Palestine question" to a broadly regional conflict by naming it, merely, the "situation in the Middle East" or "questions concerning the Middle East" was unacceptable. To reduce its political valence even further by categorizing it as a humanitarian topic called "assistance to Palestine refugees" was a disaster. Even when a UN General Assembly resolution reaffirmed "the inalienable rights of the people of Palestine," the fact that it did not come under an agenda item titled "the Palestine question" led to the formation of a committee in 1970 to re-inscribe the "Palestine question" on the agenda. Tomeh 1974.

35. For more on the ways that Palestinians have seen the human rights system as a way to prove their humanity, see Allen 2013.

36. Clifford Soloway, "Beyond Negotiations: International Law and BDS," *Palestine Square*, March 27, 2019, https://palestinesquare.com/2019/03/27/beyond-negotiations-international-law-and-bds/.

37. Allen 2013; "Hamas Signs Palestinian Application for ICC Membership," *Palestine Chronicle*, August 23, 2014, http://www.palestinechronicle.com/hamas-signs-palestinian-application-for-icc-membership/.

38. Sultany has deftly and clearly enumerated the limits of a legal and human rights approach. The term "disenchantment" is his. Sultany 2011.

39. Erakat 2019, loc. 79.

40. Perhaps in this case the lack of broader political thinking around international law was a result of the leadership's only vague belief or cynical approach to international

law. Legal advisor to the Palestinian negotiators Raja Shehadeh found there to be "little interest" among the PLO leadership in his legal cautions during negotiations in the 1990s. This was the same leadership that "continued to ignore the legal dimensions of the occupation" as heads of the Palestinian Authority. Shehadeh, "State of Exception." Also see Erakat 2019, loc. 3245. But the NSU's commitment to a legal approach was incontrovertible.

41. Sultany 2011.

42. Mills 2018, emphasis added.

43. E. P. Thompson 1975, 267; Andrew I. Killgore, "25 Years After His Death, Dr. Fayez Sayegh's Towering Legacy Lives on," Washington Report on Middle East Affairs, January 25, 2010, www.washingtonreport.me/2005-december/in-memoriam-25-years-after-his-death-dr.-fayez-sayeghs-towering-legacy-lives-on.html. For interesting discussions of Thompson's perplexing declaration about law, see Peluso 2017, Cole 2001.

# References

Archival Collections

George Antonius Collection. Middle East Centre Archive, St Antony's College, Oxford University.

Frank Aydelotte Papers. Friends Historical Library, Swarthmore College.

Howard W. Bliss Collection. American University of Beirut.

British National Archives.

Central Zionist Archives (CZA), Jerusalem, Israel.

Richard Crossman Collection. Middle East Centre Archive, St Antony's College, Oxford University.

Sir Alan Cunningham Collection. Middle East Centre Archive, St Antony's College, Oxford University.

Joseph C. Hutcheson Papers. Tarlton Law Library. University of Texas, Austin.

Phillip Khuri Hitti Papers. University of Minnesota, College of Liberal Arts, Immigration History Research Center.

India Office Records. British Library, London.

Israel State Archives. Jerusalem.

King-Crane Commission Digital Collection. Oberlin College Archives. http://www2.oberlin.edu/library/digital/king-crane/.

Albert Howe Lybyer Papers. University of Illinois Archives.

David K. Niles Papers. Harry S. Truman Library and Museum.

William Phillips. Diaries, 1917–1947. Houghton Library, Harvard College Library.

*Reports of the Anglo-American Committee of Inquiry, Confidential Files, Re. Palestine, 1944–1946.* INDEX Film A 685. Lamont Library Microfilm, Harvard University.

Sir Edward Spears Collection. Middle East Centre Archive, St Antony's College, Oxford University.

Khalil A. and Eva Marshall Totah Papers. Haverford College Quaker and Special Collections.

Harry S. Truman Public Papers. Harry S. Truman Library and Museum.

William Linn Westermann Papers. Columbia University Archives, New York.

William Yale Papers. Boston University.

William Yale Papers. Yale University Library, New Haven, Connecticut.

## Arabic Newspapers

*Al-ʿAsima*

*Al-Difaʿ*

*Filastin*

*Al-Jazeera.net*

*Lisan al-Hal*

*Al-Manar*

*Al-Muqattam*

## Other Sources

Abadi, Jacob. 1996. "Israel and the Balkan States." *Middle Eastern Studies* 32 (4): 299–300.

Abboushi, W. F. 1977. "The Road to Rebellion Arab Palestine in the 1930's." *Journal of Palestine Studies* 6 (3): 23–46.

Abou-El-Fadl, Reem. 2019. "Building Egypt's Afro-Asian Hub: Infrastructures of Solidarity and the 1957 Cairo Conference." *Journal of World History* 30 (1–2): 157–92.

Abu Gharbiyya, Bahjat. 1993. *Fi Khidamm al-Nidal al-Filastini: Mudhakkirat al-Munadil Bahjat Abu Gharbiyya, 1916–1949.* Beirut: Institute for Palestine Studies.

Abu-Lughod, Janet L. 1971. "The Demographic Transformation of Palestine." In *The Transformation of Palestine: Essays on the Origin and Development of the Arab-Israeli Conflict*, edited by Ibrahim Abu-Lughod, 139–64. Evanston, IL: Northwestern University Press.

Abu-Manneh, Butrus. 1999. "The Late 19th-Century Sanjak of Jerusalem." In *The Israel/Palestine Question: A Reader*, edited by Ilan Pappé, 41–52. London: Routledge.

Abu-Rabiʾ, Ibrahim M. 2004. *Contemporary Arab Thought: Studies in Post-1967 Arab Intellectual History.* London: Pluto Press.

Achcar, Gilbert. 2009. *The Arabs and the Holocaust.* Translated by G. M. Goshgarian. New York: Metropolitan Books—Henry Holt and Company.

Afshari, Reza. 2007. "On Historiography of Human Rights: Reflections on Paul Gordon Lauren's the Evolution of International Human Rights: Visions Seen." *Human Rights Quarterly* 29 (1): 1–67.

Agrama, Hussein Ali. 2010. "Secularism, Sovereignty, Indeterminacy: Is Egypt a Secular or a Religious State?" *Comparative Studies in Society and History* 52 (3): 495–523.

Akram, Susan. 2017. "In-Depth: Thirteen Years Later, The ICJ Advisory Opinion on the Wall." *Palestine Square.* https://palestinesquare.com/2017/09/11/in-depth-thirteen-years-later-the-icj-advisory-opinion-on-the-wall/.

Alami, Musa. 1949. "The Lesson of Palestine." *Middle East Journal* 3(4): 373–405.

Allegra. 2015. "The Limits of Truth Telling: Victim-Centrism in Canada's Truth and Reconciliation Commission on Indian Residential Schools #TransitionalJustice." *Allegra.* http://allegralaboratory.net/the-limits-of-truth-telling-victim-centrism-in-canadas-truth-and-reconciliation-commission-on-indian-residential-schools-transitionaljustice/.

Allen, Lori. 2002. "There Are Many Reasons Why." *Middle East Report* (223). https://merip.org/2002/06/there-are-many-reasons-why/.

———. 2006. "The Polyvalent Politics of Martyr Commemorations in the Palestinian." *History and Memory* 18 (2): 107–38.

———. 2008. "Getting by the Occupation: How Violence Became Normal during the Second Palestinian Intifada." *Cultural Anthropology* 23 (3): 453–87.

———. 2009a. "Martyr Bodies in the Media: Human Rights, Aesthetics, and the Politics of Immediation in the Palestinian Intifada." *American Ethnologist* 36 (1): 161–180.

———. 2009b. "Mothers of Martyrs and Suicide Bombers: The Gender of Ethical Discourse in the Second Palestinian Intifada." *History and Memory* 17 (1): 32–61.

———. 2013. *The Rise and Fall of Human Rights: Cynicism and Politics in Occupied Palestine.* Stanford: Stanford University Press.

———. 2016. "UN Commissions in Palestine: Fact-Finding or Feeling With?" In *Land of Blue Helmets: The United Nations in the Arab World,* edited by Vijay Prashad and Karim Makdisi, 58–73. Berkeley: University of California Press.

———. 2017a. "A Century of Refusal: Palestinian Opposition to the Balfour Declaration." *Middle East Report Online,* November 17: https://merip.org/2017/11/a-century-of-refusal/

———. 2017b. "Determining Emotions and the Burden of Proof in Investigative Commissions to Palestine." *Comparative Studies in Society and History* 59 (2): 385–414.

———. 2018. "What's in a Link? Transnational Solidarities across Palestine and Their Intersectional Possibilities." *South Atlantic Quarterly* 117 (1): 111–33.

———. 2019. "Subaltern Critique and the History of Palestine." In *A Time For Critique,* edited by Didier Fassin and Bernard Harcourt, 153–73. New York: Columbia University Press.

———. Forthcoming. "Human Rights, Indigenous and Imperial." In *The Global Middle East,* edited by Asef Bayat and Linda Harrera. Berkeley: University of California Press.

Althusser, Louis. 1971. *Lenin and Philosophy and Other Essays.* Translated by Ben Brewster. London: New Left Books.

Ambrosius, Lloyd E. 2006. "Woodrow Wilson, Alliances, and the League of Nations." *The Journal of the Gilded Age and Progressive Era* 5 (2): 139–65.

Anders, Gerhard. 2014. "Transitional Justice, States of Emergency and Business as Usual in Sierra Leone." *Development and Change* 45 (3): 524–42.

Anderson, Carol. 2003. *Eyes Off the Prize: The United Nations and the African American Struggle for Human Rights, 1944–1955.* Cambridge: Cambridge University Press.

Anderson, Charles W. 2013. *From Petition to Confrontation: The Palestinian National Movement and the Rise of Mass Politics, 1929–1939.* PhD diss. New York: Department of Middle Eastern and Islamic Studies and Department of History, New York University.

———. 2018. "The British Mandate and the Crisis of Palestinian Landlessness, 1929–1936." *Middle Eastern Studies* 54 (2): 171–215.

Anderson, Mark. 2019. *From Boas to Black Power: Racism, Liberalism, and American Anthropology.* Stanford: Stanford University Press.

Anghie, Antony. 1993. "The Heart of My Home: Colonialism, Environmental Damage, and the Nauru Case." *Harvard International Law Journal* 34 (2): 445–506.

———. 2002. "Cultural Difference and International Law: The League of Nations and Its Two Visions of the Nation-State." *International Center for Comparative Law and Politics Review* 5 (2): 4–13.

———. 2005. *Imperialism, Sovereignty and the Making of International Law.* Cambridge: Cambridge University Press.

———. 2006a. "The Evolution of International Law: Colonial and Postcolonial Realities." *Third World Quarterly* 27 (5): 739–53.

———. 2006b. "Nationalism, Development and the Postcolonial State: The Legacies of the League of Nations." *Texas International Law Journal* 41 (3): 447–64.

Anghie, Antony, and Bhupinder S. Chimni. 2004. "Third World Approaches to International Law and Individual Responsibility in Internal Conflict." In *The Methods of International Law,* edited by Steven R. Ratner and Anne-Marie Slaughter, 185–210. Washington, DC: American Society of International Law.

"Anglo-American Committee of Inquiry." n.d. Avalon Project, Yale Law School. Accessed July 9, 2019. https://avalon.law.yale.edu/subject_menus/angtoc.asp.

Ansell, Aaron. 2015. "Democracy as the Negation of Discourse: Liberalism, Clientelism, and Agency in Brazil." *American Ethnologist* 42 (4): 688–702.

Antonius, George. 2010. *The Arab Awakening: The Story of the Arab National Movement.* London and New York: Routledge.

Anziska, Seth. 2018. *Preventing Palestine: A Political History from Camp David to Oslo.* Princeton, NJ: Princeton University Press.

Apter, Lauren Elise. 2008. "Disorderly Decolonization: The White Paper of 1939 and the End of British Rule in Palestine." PhD diss., University of Texas at Austin.

Arab Office. 1947. *The Future of Palestine*. London. Geneva.

Arsan, Andrew. 2012. "'This Age Is the Age of Associations': Committees, Petitions, and the Roots of Interwar Middle Eastern Internationalism." *Journal of Global History* 7 (2): 166–88.

Asad, Talal. 1979. "Anthropology and the Analysis of Ideology." *Man, New Series* 14 (4): 607–27.

———. 1993. *Genealogies of Religion: Discipline and Reasons of Power in Christianity and Islam*. Baltimore: John Hopkins University Press.

———. 2003. *Formations of the Secular: Christianity, Islam, Modernity*. Stanford: Stanford University Press.

———. 2015. "Thinking About Tradition, Religion, and Politics in Egypt Today." *Critical Inquiry* 42 (1): 166–214.

Ashforth, Adam. 1990a. *The Politics of Official Discourse in Twentieth-Century South Africa*. Oxford: Clarendon Press.

———. 1990b. "Reckoning Schemes of Legitimation: On Commissions of Inquiry as Power/Knowledge Forms." *Journal of Historical Sociology* 3 (1): 1–22.

Atrash, Mahmud. 2015. *Tariq al-Kifah fi Filastin wa-l-Mashriq al-'Arabi: Mudhakkirat al-Qa'id Ashuyu'i Mahmud al-Atrash al-Maghribi (1903–1939)*. Edited by Mahir Sharif. 1st ed. Beirut: Institute of Palestine Studies.

Ayalon, Ami. 2004. *Reading Palestine: Printing and Literacy, 1900–1948*. Austin: University of Texas Press.

———. 2008. "Private Publishing in the Nahda." *International Journal of Middle East Studies* 40 (4): 561–77.

Aydin, Cemil. 2015. "Globalizing the Intellectual History of the Idea of the 'Muslim World.'" In *Global Intellectual History*, edited by Samuel Moyn and Andrew Sartori, 159–186. New York: Columbia University Press.

———. 2017. *The Idea of the Muslim World: A Global Intellectual History*. Cambridge, MA: Harvard University Press.

al-Azza, Nidal and Amaya al-Orzza. 2013–2015. *Survey of Palestinian Refugees and Internally Displaced Persons*, Vol. VIII. Bethlehem: Badil Resource Center.

Badil, Adalah, and al-Haq. 2009. *Gross Human Rights Violations and War Crimes in the Occupied Gaza Strip*. https://www.un.org/unispal/document/auto-insert -184207/.

Badran, Margot. 1995. *Feminists, Islam, and Nation: Gender and the Making of Modern Egypt*. Princeton, NJ: Princeton University Press.

Baker, Ray Stannard. 1922. *Woodrow Wilson and World Settlement*. New York: Country Life Press.

Banko, Lauren. 2016. *The Invention of Palestinian Citizenship, 1918–1947*. Edinburgh: Edinburgh University Press.

Barclay, Ahmad, and Dena Qaddumi. 2011. "Roundtable on Occupation Law: Part of the Conflict or the Solution? (Part III)." *Jadaliyya*, September 22. https://www .jadaliyya.com/Details/24428/Roundtable-on-Occupation-Law-Part-of-the -Conflict-or-the-Solution-Part-III-Ahmed-Barclay-and-Dena-Qaddumi.

Baroud, Ramzy, ed. 2003. *Searching Jenin: Eyewitness Accounts of the Israeli Invasion*. Seattle: Cune Press.

———. 2014. "The Whitewashing of Ariel Sharon." *The Palestine Chronicle*, January 13. http://www.palestinechronicle.com/the-whitewashing-of-ariel-sharon/.

Bashkin, Orit. 2012. *New Babylonians: A History of Jews in Modern Iraq*. Stanford, CA: Stanford University Press.

Bassiouni, Cherif. 1997. "From Versailles to Rwanda in Seventy-Five Years: The Need to Establish a Permanent International Criminal Court." *Harvard Human Rights Journal* 11 (67). https://works.bepress.com/m-bassiouni/34/.

Bassiouni, Mahmoud, ed. 2005. *Documents on the Arab–Israeli Conflict: The Palestin-ians and the Israeli–Palestinian Peace Process*. Vol. 2. Ardsley, N.Y.: Transnational Publishers.

Batovic, Ante. 2010. "Nonaligned Yugoslavia and the Relations with the Pal-estine Liberation Organisation." Presented at the 11th Mediterranean Research Meeting at the European University Institute, Florence, Italy. https://doi.org/10.7916/D8W66SG7.

Bawalsa, Nadim. 2010. "Sakakini Defrocked." *Jerusalem Quarterly* (42): 5–25.

Bawardi, Hani. 2014. *The Making of Arab Americans: From Syrian Nationalism to U.S. Citizenship*. Austin: University of Texas Press.

Bayly, Christopher A. 2012. *Recovering Liberties: Indian Thought in the Age of Liberalism and Empire*. Cambridge: Cambridge University Press.

———. 2016. "Indian and Arabic Thought in the Liberal Age." In *Arabic Thought Beyond the Liberal Age: Towards an Intellectual History of the Nahda*, edited by Jens Hanssen and Max Weiss, 437. Cambridge: Cambridge University Press.

Bedjaoui, Mohammed. 1979. *Towards a New International Order*. New York: Holmes & Meier.

Beeley, Sir Harold. 1977. "Palestine- Interview with Sir Harold Beeley, Foreign Office and British Secretary to Anglo-American Committee." Imperial War Museum. https://www.iwm.org.uk/collections/item/object/1060005495.

Beinin, Joel. 1990. *Was the Red Flag Flying There?: Marxist Politics and the Arab-Israeli Conflict in Egypt and Israel, 1948–1965*. Berkeley: University of California Press.

———. 2019. "Arab Liberal Intellectuals and the Partition of Palestine." In *Partitions: A Transnational History of 20th Century Territorial Separatism*, edited by Arie Dub-nov and Laura Robson, 184–205. Stanford, CA: Stanford University Press.

Bell, Duncan. 2011. "Empire and Imperialism." In *The Cambridge History of Political Thought*, edited by Gregory Claeys and Stedman Jones, 864–92. Cambridge: Cambridge University Press.

———. 2014. "What Is Liberalism?" *Political Theory* 42 (6): 682–715.

———. 2016. *Reordering the World: Essays on Liberalism and Empire*. Princeton, NJ: Princeton University Press.

Ben-Dror, Elad. 2014. "The Success of the Zionist Strategy Vis-à-Vis UNSCOP." *Israel Affairs* 20 (1): 19–39.

Benjamin, Walter. 1974. "On the Concept of History." Edited by Dennis Redmond. *Gesammelten Schriften* I (2). https://www.marxists.org/reference/archive/benjamin/1940/history.htm.

Benthall, Jonathan, and Jérôme Bellion-Jourdan. 2003. *The Charitable Crescent: Politics of Aid in the Muslim World*. London: I.B. Tauris.

Benton, Lauren. 2002. *Law and Colonial Cultures: Legal Regimes in World History, 1400–1900*. Cambridge: Cambridge University Press.

———. 2012. "Introduction" *American Historical Review* 117 (4): 1092–1172.

Benton, Lauren, and Adam Clulow. 2017. "Empires and Protection: Making Interpolity Law in the Early Modern World." *Journal of Global History* 12 (1): 74–92.

Benton, Lauren, and Lisa Ford. *Rage for Order: The British Empire and the Origins of International Law, 1800-1850*. Boston: Harvard University Press, 2016.

Bentwich, Norman, and Helen Bentwich. 1965. *Mandate Memories: 1919–1948*. New York: Schocken Books.

Berlant, Lauren. 2005. "The Epistemology of State Emotion." In *Dissent in Dangerous Times*, edited by Austin Sarat, 46–78. Ann Arbor: University of Michigan Press.

Berman, Nathaniel. 1993. "'But the Alternative Is Despair': European Nationalism and the Modernist Renewal of International Law." *Harvard Law Review* 106 (8). https://doi.org/10.2307/1341788.

———. 2013. "Modernism, Nationalism, and the Rhetoric of Reconstruction." *Yale Journal of Law & the Humanities* 4 (2): 351–80.

Binder, Leonard. 1988. *Islamic Liberalism: A Critique of Development Ideologies*. Chicago: University of Chicago Press.

Bishara, Amahl. 2013. *Back Stories: U.S. News Production and Palestinian Politics*. Stanford, CA: Stanford University Press.

Bisharat, George, Jeff Handmaker, Ghada Karmi, and Alaa Tartir. 2018. "Mobilizing International Law in the Palestinian Struggle for Justice." *Global Jurist* 18: 1–6.

Blanshard, Frances. 1970. *Frank Aydelotte of Swarthmore*. Middletown, CT: Wesleyan University Press.

Block, Fred, and Margaret Somers. 2003. "In the Shadow of Speenhamland: Social Policy and the Old Poor Law." *Politics and Society* 31 (2): 1–41.

Bob, Clifford. 2009. "Merchants of Morality." *Foreign Policy* 129. https://foreignpolicy.com/2009/11/13/merchants-of-morality/.

Bourdieu, Pierre. 1986. "The Force of Law: Toward a Sociology of the Juridical Field." *Hastings Law Journal* 38 (5): 814–53.

———. 2013. *Outline of a Theory of Practice*. Translated by Richard Nice. New York: Cambridge University Press.

Boyer, Dominic, and Alexei Yurchak. 2010. "American Stiob: Or, What Late-Socialist Aesthetics of Parody Reveal about Contemporary Political Culture in the West." *Cultural Anthropology* 25 (2): 179–221.

Boyle, Susan Silsby. 2001. *Betrayal of Palestine: The Story of George Antonius*. New York: Westview Press.

Bradley, Mark Philip. 2015. "Making Peace as a Project of Moral Reconstruction." In *The Cambridge History of the Second World War*, edited by Michael Geyer and J. Adam Tooze, 528–51. Cambridge: Cambridge University Press.

Brennan, Timothy. 2014. "Subaltern Stakes." *New Left Review* 89: 67–87.

Brubaker, Rogers. 2015. *Grounds for Difference*. Cambridge, MA: Harvard University Press.

Brunnegger, Sandra, and Karen Ann Faulk, eds. 2016. *A Sense of Justice: Legal Knowledge and Lived Experience in Latin America*. Stanford: Stanford University Press.

Buchan, Russell. 2017. "Quo Vadis? Commissions of Inquiry and Their Implications for the Coherence of International Law." In *Commissions of Inquiry: Problems and Prospects*, edited by Christian Henderson, 257–284. Oxford: Hart Publishing.

Burgis, Michelle L. 2009. "A Discourse of Distinction? Palestinians, International Law, and the Promise of Humanitarianism." *Palestine Yearbook of International Law Online* 15 (1): 41–66.

Burke, Roland. 2006. "'The Compelling Dialogue of Freedom': Human Rights at the Bandung Conference." *Human Rights Quarterly* 28 (4): 947–65

———. 2010. *Decolonization and the Evolution of International Human Rights*. Philadelphia: University of Pennsylvania Press.

Büssow, Johann. 2011. *Hamidian Palestine: Politics and Society in the District of Jerusalem, 1872–1908*. Leiden & Boston: Brill. https://doi.org/10.1163/ej.9789004205697.i-620.

Byrne, Jeffrey James. 2016. *Mecca of Revolution: Algeria, Decolonization, and the Third World Order*. Oxford: Oxford University Press.

Cabot, Heath. 2013. "The Social Aesthetics of Eligibility: NGO Aid and Indeterminacy in the Greek Asylum Process." *American Ethnologist* 40 (3): 452–66.

Campos, Michelle. 2011. *Ottoman Brothers: Muslims, Christians, and Jews in Early Twentieth-Century Palestine*. Stanford, CA: Stanford University Press.

Carr, E. H. 1936. "Public Opinion As a Safeguard of Peace." *International Affairs* 15 (6): 846–62.

Chakrabarty, Dipesh. 2000. *Provincializing Europe: Postcolonial Thought and Historical Difference*. Princeton, NJ: Princeton University Press.

Chalcraft, John. 2008. "Question: What Are the Fruitful New Directions in Subaltern Studies, and How Can Those Working in Middle East Studies Most Productively Engage With Them? Pensée 1: Of Horses and Ponies." *International Journal of Middle East Studies* 40 (3): 376–78.

———. 2019. "The Boycott, Divestment, Sanctions (BDS) Movement and Radical Democracy." In *Boycotts Past and Present: From the American Revolution to the Campaign to Boycott Israel*, 287–310. London: Palgrave Macmillan.

Chamberlin, Paul Thomas. 2012. *The Global Offensive: The United States, the Palestine Liberation Organization, and the Making of the Post–Cold War Order*. Oxford: Oxford University Press.

"Charter of the United Nations, June 26, 1945." 1950. Avalon Project, Yale Law School. Washington, DC: Government Printing Office. https://avalon.law.yale.edu/20th_century/unchart.asp.

Chatterjee, Partha. 1993. *Nationalist Thought and the Colonial World: A Derivative Discourse*. Minneapolis: University of Minnesota Press.

———. 2011. "The Curious Career of Liberalism in India." *Modern Intellectual History* 8 (3): 687–96.

Cherni, Nabil. 2004. *Visions of the Wretched: Homage to Frantz Fanon*. Tunis: Manouba Faculty of Letters, Arts and Humanities.

Chimni, Bhupinder S. 2017. *International Law and World Order: A Critique of Contemporary Approaches*. 2nd ed. Cambridge: Cambridge University Press.

Chinkin, Christine M. 2010. "U.N. Human Rights Council Fact-Finding Missions: Lessons from Gaza." In *Looking to the Future: Essays on International Law in Honor of W. Michael Reisman*, edited by Mahnoush H. Arsanjani, Jacob Cogan, Robert Sloane, and Siegfried Wiessner, 475–98. Leiden, Netherlands: Martinus Nijhoff.

Chinkin, Christine M., and Conor Gearty. 2014. "Gearty Grilling: Christine Chinkin on Violence against Women and Fact-Finding in Gaza—YouTube." London School of Economics and Political Science (LSE). https://www.youtube.com/watch?v=xqmjQeHX33g.

Chinkin, Christine M., and Mary Kaldor. 2017. *International Law and New Wars*. Cambridge: Cambridge University Press.

Chua, Beng-Huat. 1979. "Democracy as Textual Accomplishment." *The Sociological Quarterly* 20 (4): 541–49.

Clarke, Kamari Maxine. 2009. *Fictions of Justice: The International Criminal Court and the Challenges of Legal Pluralism in Sub-Saharan Africa*. Cambridge: Cambridge University Press.

Clarke, Kamari Maxine, and Mark Goodale, eds. 2014. *Mirrors of Justice: Law and Power in the Post–Cold War Era*. Cambridge: Cambridge University Press.

Clarke, Kamari Maxine, Abel S. Knottnerus, and Eefje de Volder, eds. 2016. *Africa and the ICC: Perceptions of Justice*. Cambridge: Cambridge University Press.

Clifford, Clark M. 1978. "Factors Influencing President Truman's Decision to Support Partition and Recognize the State of Israel." In *The Palestine Question in American History*, edited by Clark M. Clifford, Eugene V. Rostow, and Barbara W. Tuchman, 24–45. New York: Arno Press.

Clokie, Hugh McDowall, and J. William Robinson. 1937. *Royal Commissions of Inquiry: The Significance of Investigations in British Politics*. Stanford, CA: Stanford University Press.

Clor, Harry M. 2010. "Woodrow Wilson." In *American Political Thought: The Philosophic Dimension of American Statesmanship*, edited by Morton J. Frisch and Richard G. Stevens, 192–218. New York: Transaction Publishers.

Cohen, G. Daniel. 2006. "The Politics of Recognition: Jewish Refugees in Relief Policies and Human Rights Debates, 1945–1950." *Immigrants & Minorities* 24 (2): 125–43.

———. 2014. "Elusive Neutrality: Christian Humanitarianism and the Question of Palestine, 1948–1967." *Humanity* 5 (2): 183–210.

Cohen, Michael J. 1979. "The Genesis of the Anglo-American Committee on Palestine, November 1945: A Case Study in the Assertion of American Hegemony." *The Historical Journal* 22, (1): 185–207.

———. 1982a. *Palestine and the Great Powers: 1945–1948*. Princeton, NJ: Princeton University Press.

———. 1982b. "Truman and Palestine, 1945–1948: Revisionism, Politics and Diplomacy." *Modern Judaism* 2 (1): 1–22.

———, ed. 1987. *The Rise of Israel: The Anglo-American Committee on Palestine, 1945–1946*. New York: Garland Publishing.

Cohn, Bernard S. 1987 *An Anthropologist Among the Historians and Other Essays*. Oxford: Oxford University Press.

———. 1996a. *Colonialism and Its Forms of Knowledge: The British in India*. Edited by Sherry B. Ortner, Nicholas B. Dirks, and Geoff Eley. Princeton, NJ: Princeton University Press.

———. 1996b. "Law and the Colonial State in India." In *Colonialism and Its Forms of Knowledge: The British in India*, 57–75. Princeton, NJ: Princeton University Press.

Cole, Daniel. 2001. "'An Unqualified Human Good': E.P. Thompson and the Rule of Law." *Journal of Law and Society* 28 (2): 177–203.

Coleman, Enid Gabriella, and Alex Golub. 2008. "Hacker Practice: Moral Genres and the Cultural Articulation of Liberalism." *Anthropological Theory* 8 (3): 255–77.

Colla, Elliott. 2005. "Sentimentality and Redemption: The Rhetoric of Egyptian Pop Culture Intifada Solidarity." In *Palestine, Israel, and the Politics of Popular Culture*, edited by Rebecca L. Stein and Ted Swedenburg, 338–64. Durham & London: Duke University Press.

Collins, John. 2011. *Global Palestine*. London: C. Hurst & Co. Ltd.

Comaroff, Jean, and John L. Comaroff. 1997. *Of Revelation and Revolution: The Dialectics of Modernity on a South African Frontier*. Vol. 1. Chicago: University of Chicago Press.

———. 2006. "Law and Disorder in the Postcolony: An Introduction." In *Law and Disorder in the Postcolony*, edited by Jean Comaroff and John L. Comaroff, 1–56. Chicago: University of Chicago Press.

Comaroff, John L. 2006. "Symposium Introduction: Colonialism, Culture, and the Law: A Foreword." *Law & Social Inquiry* 26 (2): 305–14.

Connelly, Matthew. 2002. *A Diplomatic Revolution: Algeria's Fight for Independence and the Origins of the Post-Cold War Era*. Oxford: Oxford University Press.

Coupland, Reginald. 1933. "The British Empire and the World Crisis." Empire Club of Canada Speeches. http://speeches.empireclub.org/results?q=Coupland&st=kw.

Covenant of the League of Nations. n.d. Avalon Project, Yale Law School. http://avalon.law.yale.edu/20th_century/leagcov.asp.

Cowan, Jane K. 2014. "Justice and the League of Nations Minority Regime." In *Mirrors of Justice: Law and Power in the Post-Cold War Era*, edited by Kamari Maxine Clarke and Mark Goodale, 270–90. Cambridge: Cambridge University Press.

———. 2015. "The Universal Periodic Review as a Public Audit Ritual: An Anthropological Perspective on Emerging Practices in the Global Governance of Human Rights." In *Human Rights and the Universal Periodic Review: Rituals and Ritualism*, edited by Hilary Charlesworth and Emma Larking, 42–62. Cambridge: Cambridge University Press.

Cowan, Jane, and Julie Billaud. 2015. "Between Learning and Schooling: The Politics of Human Rights Monitoring at the Universal Periodic Review." *Third World Quarterly* 36 (6): 1175–90.

Craven, Matthew. 2012. "Colonialism and Domination." In *Oxford Handbook of the History of International Law*, edited by Bardo Fassbender and Anne Peters, 862–889. Oxford: Oxford University Press.

Crossman, Richard. 1947. *Palestine Mission: A Personal Record*. London: Hamish Hamilton.

Crum, Bartley. 1947. *Behind the Silken Curtain, A Personal Account of Anglo-American Diplomacy in Palestine and the Middle East*. New York: Simon and Schuster.

Çubukçu, Ayça. 2013. "The Responsibility to Protect: Libya and the Problem of Transnational Solidarity." *Journal of Human Rights* 12 (1): 40–58.

———. 2018. *For the Love of Humanity: The World Tribunal on Iraq*. Philadelphia: University of Pennsylvania Press.

d'Aspremont, Jean. 2018. *International Law as a Belief System*. Cambridge: Cambridge University Press.

Dajani, Omar. 2007. "Shadow or Shade? The Roles of International Law in Palestinian-Israeli Peace Talks." *Yale Journal of International Law* 32 (1): 61–124.

———. 2007/2008. "Forty Years without Resolve: Tracing the Influence of Security Council Resolution 242 on the Middle East Peace Process." *Journal of Palestine Studies* 37 (1): 24–38.

———. 2011. "'No Security without Law': Prospects for Implementing a Rights-Based Approach in Palestinian–Israeli Security Negotiations." In *International Law and the Israeli-Palestinian Conflict: A Rights-Based Approach to Middle East Peace*, edited by Susan Akram, Michael Dumper, Michael Lynk, and Iain Scobbie, 184–206. New York: Routledge.

Dalacoura, Katarina. 1998. *Islam, Liberalism, and Human Rights*. London: I. B. Tauris.

Dallasheh, Leena. 2016. "Persevering through Colonial Transition: Nazareth's Palestinian Residents after 1948." *Journal of Palestine Studies* 45 (2): 8–23.

Darcy, Shane. 2017. "Laying the Foundations: Commissions of Inquiry and the Development of International Law." In *Commissions of Inquiry, Problems and Prospects*, edited by Christian Henderson, 231–256. Oxford: Hart Publishing.

Darwaza, Mohammad ʿIzzat. 1949. *Hawl al-Haraka al-ʿArabiyya al-Haditha*. Vol. 1. Beirut-Sidon: Manshurat al-Maktaba al-ʿAsriyya.

———. 1993. *Mudhakkirat Mohammad ʿIzzat Darwaza: Sijil Hafel: Masirat al-Haraka al-ʿArabiyya wa-l-Qadiyya al-Falastiniyya Khilal Qarn min al-Zaman, 1887–1984*. 1st ed. Beirut: Dar al-Gharb al-Islami.

Davidson, Lawrence. 2001. *America's Palestine: Popular and Official Perceptions from Balfour to Israeli Statehood*. Gainsville: University Press of Florida.

Davison, Roderic H. 1968. "Representation in the Government of the Ottoman Empire." In *Beginnings of Modernization in the Middle East: The Nineteenth Century*, edited by William R. Polk and Richard L. Chambers, 93–108. Chicago: University of Chicago Press.

Deane, Shelley. 2009. "Instituting Peace: Third Party Principles and the Mitchell Effect." *Journal of Intervention and Statebuilding* 3 (1): 65–91.

Dembour, Marie-Bénédicte, and Tobias Kelly, eds. 2007. *Paths to International Justice: Social and Legal Perspectives*. Cambridge: Cambridge University Press.

Dezalay, Yves, and Bryant G. Garth, eds. 1996. *Dealing in Virtue: International Commercial Arbitration and the Construction of a Transnational Legal Order*. Chicago: University of Chicago Press.

Di-Capua, Yoav. 2018. *No Exit: Arab Existentialism, Jean-Paul Sartre, and Decolonization*. Chicago: University of Chicago Press.

Dominian, Leon. 1917. *The Frontiers of Language and Nationality in Europe*. New York: American Geographical Society of New York by H. Holt and Company. https://archive.org/stream/frontierslanguaoounkngoog#page/n16/mode/2up.

Donnelly, Jack. 1986. "International Human Rights: A Regime Analysis." *International Organization* 40 (3): 599–642.

Drayton, Richard. 2011. "Where Does the World Historian Write From? Objectivity, Moral Conscience and the Past and Present of Imperialism." *Journal of Contemporary History* 46 (3): 671–85.

Dubnov, Arie, and Laura Robson, eds. 2019. *Partitions: A Transnational History of Twentieth-Century Territorial Separatism.* Stanford, CA: Stanford University Press.

Dubnov, Arie. 2019. "The Architect of Two Partitions or a Federalist Daydreamer? The Curious Case of Reginald Coupland." In *Partitions: A Transnational History of Twentieth-Century Territorial Separatism,* edited by Arie M. Dubnov and Laura Robson, 56–84. Stanford, CA: Stanford University Press.

Dugard, John. 2013–2014. "Lifting the Guise of Occupation and Recourse to Action before the ICJ and ICC." *Palestine Yearbook of International Law* 17 (1): 9–27.

———. 2018. *Confronting Apartheid: A Personal History of South Africa, Namibia and Palestine.* Auckland Park: Jacana Media.

Dunoff, Jeffrey L., and Mark A. Pollack, eds. 2013. *Interdisciplinary Perspectives on International Law and International Relations: The State of the Art.* Cambridge: Cambridge University Press.

Durkheim, Émile. 1995. *The Elementary Forms of Religious Life.* Edited by Karen Fields. New York: Free Press.

Duve, Thomas. 2017. "Global Legal History: A Methodological Approach." *Oxford Handbooks Online* 1. https://doi.org/10.1093/oxfordhb/9780199935352.013.25.

"East Africa: The Royal Commission." 1955. *The Round Table* 45 (180): 419–24.

Eckel, Jan. 2010. "Human Rights and Decolonization: New Perspectives and Open Questions." *Humanity: An International Journal of Human Rights, Humanitarianism, and Development* 1 (1): 111–35.

Edwardes, O. S. 1946. *Palestine: Land of Broken Promise, a Statement of the Facts Concerning Palestine and an Examination of the Anglo-American Commission.* London: Dorothy Crisp.

Edwards, Brent Hayes. 2003. *The Practice of Diaspora: Literature, Translation, and the Rise of Black Internationalism.* Cambridge MA: Harvard University Press.

el-Awaisi, Abd al-Fattah M. 1998. *The Muslim Brothers and the Palestine Question, 1928–1947.* London and New York: Tauris Academic Studies.

Elander, Maria. 2018. *Figuring Victims in International Criminal Justice: The Case of the Khmer Rouge Tribunal.* London: Routledge.

Elshakry, Marwa. 2013. *Reading Darwin in Arabic, 1860–1950.* Chicago: University of Chicago Press.

Elshtain, Jean Bethke. 1992. *Just War Theory.* New York: New York University Press.

Eltringham, Nigel. 2013. "'Illuminating the Broader Context': Anthropological and Historical Knowledge at the International Criminal Tribunal for Rwanda." *Journal of the Royal Anthropological Institute* 19 (2): 338–55.

"Emir Faisal's Talks with French Under-Secretary of Foreign Affairs Jean Gout." 1919. In *Syrian History*. National Archives of Great Britain. http://syrianhistory.com /en/photos/4669?tag=Jean+Gout.

Engle, Karen, Zinaida Miller, and D. M. Davis. 2016. "Introduction." In *Anti-Impunity and the Human Rights Agenda*, edited by Karen Engle, Zinaida Miller, and D. M. Davis, 1–12. Cambridge: Cambridge University Press.

Englund, Harri. 2018. "The Front Line of Free Speech: Beyond Parrhêsia in Finland's Migrant Debate." *American Ethnologist* 45 (1): 100–111.

Erakat, Noura. 2011. "Roundtable on Occupation Law: Part of the Conflict or the Solution?" *Jadaliyya*. http://www.jadaliyya.com/Details/24430/Roundtable-on -Occupation-Law-Part-of-the-Conflict-or-the-Solution-Part-I-Noura-Erakat.

———. 2017. "Taking the Land without the People: The 1967 Story as Told by the Law." *Journal of Palestine Studies* 47 (1): 18–38.

———. 2019. *Justice for Some: Law in the Question of Palestine*. Stanford, CA: Stanford University Press.

Eslava, Luis. 2015. *Local Space, Global Life: The Everyday Operation of International Law and Development*. Cambridge: Cambridge University Press.

Eslava, Luis, Michael Fakhri, and Vasuki Nesiah. 2017. "The Spirit of Bandung." In *Bandung, Global History, and International Law: Critical Pasts and Pending Futures*, edited by Luis Eslava, Michael Fakhri, and Vasuki Nesiah, 3–32. Cambridge: Cambridge University Press.

Eslava, Luis, and Sundhya Pahuja. 2012. "Beyond the (Post)Colonial: TWAIL and the Everyday Life of International Law." *Journal of Law and Politics in Africa, Asia and Latin America* 45 (2): 195–221.

Fabian, Johannes. 2002. *Time and the Other: How Anthropology Makes Its Object*. New York: Columbia University Press.

Falk, Richard. 2000. *Human Rights Horizons: The Pursuit of Justice in a Globalizing World*. New York: Routledge.

———. 2006. "International Law and the Future." *Third World Quarterly* 27 (5): 727–737.

———. 2012. "The Goldstone Report: Neither Implemented Nor Ignored." *Palestine Yearbook of International Law Online* 16 (1): 5–23.

———. 2014. *Palestine: The Legitimacy of Hope*. Charlottesville, VA: Just World Books.

Falk, Richard, Mark Juergensmeyer, and Vesselin Popovski, eds. 2012. *Legality and Legitimacy in Global Affairs*. Oxford: Oxford University Press.

Farge, Arlette. 2004. *The Allure of the Archives*. New Haven, CT: Yale University Press.

Fassbender, Bardo, and Anne Peters, eds. 2012. *Oxford Handbook of the History of International Law*. Oxford: Oxford University Press.

Fassin, Didier. 2008. "The Humanitarian Politics of Testimony: Subjectification through Trauma in the Israeli-Palestinian Conflict." *Cultural Anthropology* 23 (3): 531–58.

———. 2012a. *Humanitarian Reason: A Moral History of the Present*. Berkeley: University of California Press.

———. 2012b. "Introduction: Towards a Critical Moral Anthropology." In *A Companion to Moral Anthropology*, edited by Didier Fassin, 1–18. Chichester, UK: Wiley-Blackwell.

Fawaz, Leila Tarazi. 1994. *An Occasion for War: Civil Conflict in Lebanon and Damascus in 1860*. Berkeley: University of California Press.

Feldman, Ilana. 2010. "Ad Hoc Humanity: Peacekeeping and the Limits of International Community in Gaza." *American Anthropologist* 112 (3): 416–29.

———. 2012. "The Challenge of Categories: UNRWA and the Definition of a 'Palestine Refugee.'" *Journal of Refugee Studies* 25 (3): 387–406.

———. 2018. *Life Lived in Relief: Humanitarian Predicaments and Palestinian Refugee Politics*. Oakland: University of California Press.

Feldman, Keith. 2015. *A Shadow over Palestine: The Imperial Life of Race in America*. Minneapolis: University of Minnesota Press.

Finkelstein, Norman. 2010. *"This Time We Went Too Far": Truth and Consequences of the Gaza Invasion*. New York: OR Books.

———. 2018. *Gaza: An Inquest into Its Martyrdom*. Berkeley: University of California Press.

Fischbach, Michael. 2019. *Black Power and Palestine: Transnational Countries of Color*. Stanford, CA: Stanford University Press.

Fitzmaurice, Andrew. 2012. "Liberalism and Empire in Nineteenth-Century International Law." *American Historical Review* 117 (1): 122–40.

Fleischmann, Ellen. 2003. *The Nation and Its "New" Women: The Palestinian Women's Movement, 1920–1948*. Berkeley, Los Angeles, London: University of California Press.

Franck, Thomas M. 1990. *The Power of Legitimacy among Nations*. Oxford: Oxford University Press.

Freas, Erik. 2012. "Haj Amin al-Husayni and the Haram al-Sharif: A Pan-Islamic or Palestinian Nationalist Cause?" *British Journal of Middle Eastern Studies* 39 (1): 19–51.

Furlonge, Geoffrey Warren. 1969. *Palestine Is My Country: The Story of Musa Alami*. London: John Murray.

Gallagher, Nancy Elizabeth, ed. 1996. *Approaches to the History of the Middle East: Interviews with Leading Middle East Historians*. Reading, UK: Ithaca Press.

Gathii, James T. 1998. "International Law and Eurocentricity." *European Journal of International Law* 9 (1): 184–211.

———. 2007. "Imperialism, Colonialism and International Law." *Buffalo Law Review* 54 (4): 1013–1066.

Gelvin, James. 1994. "The Social Origins of Popular Nationalism in Syria: Evidence for a New Framework." *International Journal of Middle East Studies* 26 (4): 645–61.

―――. 1998. *Divided Loyalties: Nationalism and Mass Politics in Syria at the Close of Empire*. Berkeley: University of California Press.

―――. 1999. "Modernity and Its Discontents: On the Durability of Nationalism in the Arab Middle East." *Nations and Nationalism* 5 (1): 71–89.

―――. 2003. "The Ironic Legacy of the King-Crane Commission." In *The Middle East and the United State: A Historical and Political Reassessment*, edited by David W. Lesch, 2nd ed., 13–29. Oxford: Westview Press.

Gendzier, Irene L. 2015. *Dying to Forget: Oil, Power, Palestine, and the Foundations of U.S. Policy in the Middle East*. New York: Columbia University Press.

Gerber, Haim. 1985. *Ottoman Rule in Jerusalem, 1890–1914*. Berlin: K. Schwarz.

Gershoni, Israel. 1986. "The Muslim Brothers and the Arab Revolt in Palestine, 1936–39." *Middle Eastern Studies* 22 (3): 367–97.

―――. 2016. "The Demise of 'the Liberal Age'? ʿAbbas Mahmud al-ʿAqqad and Egyptian Responses to Fascism During World War II." In *Arabic Thought beyond the Liberal Age: Towards an Intellectual History of the Nahda*, edited by Jens Hanssen and Max Weiss, 298–322. Cambridge: Cambridge University Press.

Gershoni, Israel, and James P. Jankowski. 2010. *Confronting Fascism in Egypt: Dictatorship versus Democracy in the 1930s*. Stanford, CA: Stanford University Press.

Ghandour, Zeina. 2010. *A Discourse on Domination in Mandate Palestine: Imperialism, Property and Insurgency*. London: Routledge.

Gibbons, Herbert Adams. 1919. "Zionism and the World Peace." *Century Magazine* 92: 370–78.

Gildersleeve, Virginia C. 1947. "Foreword." In *Papers on Palestine II: A Collection of Articles by Leading Authorities Dealing with the Palestine Problem, Pamphlet Number 5*, i–ii. New York: Institute of Arab American Affairs.

Goda, Norman J. W. 2015. "James G. McDonald and the Fate of Holocaust Survivors." United States Holocaust Memorial Museum Monna and Otto Weinmann Annual Lecture, June 11. genocidewatch.net/wp-content/uploads/.../Holocaust-Museum-summer-calendar.pdf.

Goebel, Michael. 2017. *Anti-Imperial Metropolis: Interwar Paris and the Seeds of Third World Nationalism*. Cambridge: Cambridge University Press.

Goldstein, Judith, Miles Kahler, Robert O. Keohane, and Anne-Marie Slaughter. 2000. "Introduction: Legalization and World Politics." *International Organization* 54 (3): 385–99.

"The Goldstone Report: Excerpts and Responses." 2010. *Journal of Palestine Studies* 39 (2). https://www.palestine-studies.org/jps/fulltext/42268.

Goldstone, Richard. 2013. "Quality Control in International Fact-Finding Outside Criminal Justice for Core International Crimes." In *Quality Control in Fact-Finding*, edited by Morten Bergsmo, 35–53. Florence: Torkel Opsahl Academic EPublisher.

Goodale, Mark. 2017. *Anthropology and Law: A Critical Introduction*. New York: New York University Press.

Goodale, Mark, and Sally Engle Merry, eds. 2007. *The Practice of Human Rights: Tracking Law between the Global and the Local*. Cambridge: Cambridge University Press.

Gordon, Neve, and Nicola Perugini. 2016. "The Politics of Human Shielding: On the Resignification of Space and the Constitution of Civilians as Shields in Liberal Wars." *Environment and Planning D: Society and Space* 34 (1): 168–87.

Gorman, Daniel. 2012. *The Emergence of International Society in the 1920s*. Cambridge: Cambridge University Press.

Goswami, Manu. 2012. "Imaginary Futures and Colonial Internationalisms." *American Historical Review* 117 (5): 1461–1485.

Gould, Rebecca Ruth. 2018. "Legal Form and Legal Legitimacy: The IHRA Definition of Antisemitism as a Case Study in Censored Speech." *Law, Culture and the Humanities*. https://doi.org/10.1177/1743872118780660.

Grabill, Joseph L. 1971. *Protestant Diplomacy and the Near East: Missionary Influence on American Policy, 1810–1927*. Minneapolis: University of Minnesota Press.

Grandin, Greg. 2005. "The Instruction of Great Catastrophe: Truth Commissions, National History, and State Formation in Argentina, Chile, and Guatemala." *American Historical Review* 110 (1): 46–67.

Grandin, Greg, and Thomas Miller Klubock. 2007. "Editors' Introduction." *Radical History Review* 2007 (97): 1–10.

Gray, John. 1995. *Liberalism*. 2nd ed. Minneapolis: University of Minnesota Press.

Green, Penny, Thomas MacManus, and Alicia de la Cour Venning. 2018. "Genocide Achieved, Genocide Continues: Myanmar's Annihilation of the Rohingya." London: International State Crime Initiative. http://statecrime.org/state-crime -research/genocide-achieved-genocide-continues-myanmars-annihilation-of-the -rohingya-isci-report/.

Greenspan, Morris. 1972. "Human Rights in the Territories Occupied by Israel." *Santa Clara Law Review* 12 (2). https://digitalcommons.law.scu.edu/lawreview/vol12 /iss2/7/.

Gross, Aeyal. 2017. *The Writing on the Wall: Rethinking the International Law of Occupation*. Cambridge: Cambridge University Press.

Grossi, Ken, Maren Milligan, and Ted Waddelow. 2011. "Restoring Lost Voices of Self-Determination." Oberlin College, King-Crane Commission Digital Collection. http://www2.oberlin.edu/library/digital/king-crane/intro.html.

Grossman, Claudio. 2001. "Awas Tingni v. Nicaragua: A Landmark Case for the Inter-American System." *Human Rights Brief* 8 (3): 1–4.

Grote, Rainer, Tilmann J. Röder, and Ali M. El-Haj. 2016. *Constitutionalism, Human Rights, and Islam after the Arab Spring*. Oxford: Oxford University Press.

Habermas, Jürgen. 1984. *Theory of Communicative Action, Volume One: Reason and the Rationalization of Society*. Translated by Thomas A. McCarthy. Boston: Beacon Press.

Hacohen, Dvorah. 1991. "Ben-Gurion and the Second World War: Plans for Mass Immigration to Palestine." In *Studies in Contemporary Jewry: Jews and Messianism in the Modern Era, Metaphor and Meaning*, edited by Jonathan Frankel, vol. VII, 247–68. New York and Oxford: Oxford University Press.

Hadley, Elaine. 2010. *Living Liberalism: Practical Citizenship in Mid-Victorian Britain*. Chicago: University of Chicago Press.

Hajjar, Lisa. 2017. "Lawfare and Armed Conflicts: A Comparative Analysis of Israeli and U.S. Targeted Killing Policies and Legal Challenges against Them." In *Life in the Age of Drone Warfare*, edited by Lisa Parks and Caren Kaplan, 59–88. Durham, NC: Duke University Press.

———. 2018. "In Defense of Lawfare: The Value of Litigation in Challenging Torture." In *Confronting Torture: Essays on the Ethics, Legality, History, and Psychology of Torture Today*, edited by Scott A. Anderson and Martha Craven Nussbaum, 294–319. Chicago: University of Chicago Press.

Halabi, Awad. 2012. "Liminal Loyalties: Ottomanism and Palestinian Responses to the Turkish War of Independence, 1919–22." *Journal of Palestine Studies* 41 (3): 19–37.

Hall, Stuart. 1996. "The Problem of Ideology: Marxism Without Guarantees." In *Stuart Hall: Critical Dialogues in Cultural Studies*, edited by David Morley and Kuan-Hsing Chen, 25–46. New York: Routledge.

Hamada, Husein ʿOmar. 1983. *Mohammad ʿIzzat Darwaza: Safahat min Hayatuhu wa-Jihaduhu wa-Muʾalafatuhu*. Beirut: al-Itihad al-ʿAm li-l-Kuttab wa-l-Sahafiyin al-Filastiniyn, al-Amana al-ʿAmma.

Hanafi, Sari, and Linda Tabar. 2006. *The Emergence of a Palestinian Globalized Elite: Donors, International Organizations and Local NGOs*. Jerusalem: Muwatin, the Palestinian Institute for the Study of Democracy, Institute of Jerusalem Studies.

Hanssen, Jens. 2016. "Albert's World: Historicism, Liberal Imperialism and the Struggle for Palestine, 1936-48." In *Arabic Thought Beyond the Liberal Age: Towards an Intellectual History of the Nahda*, edited by Jens Hanssen and Max Weiss, 62–92. Cambridge: Cambridge University Press.

Hanssen, Jens, and Max Weiss, eds. 2016a. *Arabic Thought Beyond the Liberal Age: Towards an Intellectual History of the Nahda*. Cambridge: Cambridge University Press.

———. 2016b. "Introduction, Language, Mind, Freedom and Time: The Modern Arab Intellectual Tradition in Four Words." In *Arabic Thought Beyond the Liberal Age: Towards an Intellectual History of the Nahda*, edited by Jens Hanssen and Max Weiss, 1–38. Cambridge: Cambridge University Press.

———. 2016c. "Means and Ends of the Liberal Experiment." In *Arabic Thought beyond the Liberal Age: Towards an Intellectual History of the Nahda*, edited by Jens Hanssen and Max Weiss, 167–73. Cambridge: Cambridge University Press.

———. 2018. *Arabic Thought against the Authoritarian Age: Towards an Intellectual History of the Present.* Cambridge: Cambridge University Press.

al-Haq. 1983. *In Their Own Words: Human Rights Violations in the West Bank.* Ramallah.

———. 1984. *Torture and Intimidation in the West Bank: The Case of al-Fara'a Prison.* Ramallah.

Hayner, Priscilla B. 2010. *Unspeakable Truths: Facing the Challenge of Truth Commissions.* 2nd ed. New York: Routledge.

Heaven, Corinne. 2017. "A Visible College: The Community of Fact-Finding Practice." In *Commissions of Inquiry Problems and Prospects*, edited by Christian Henderson, 337–60. Oxford: Hart Publishing.

Herberichs, Gerard. 1966. "On Theories of Public Opinion and International Organization." *Public Opinion Quarterly* 30 (4): 624–36.

Herik, Larissa van den. 2015. "Accountability Through Fact-Finding: Appraising Inquiry in the Context of Srebrenica." *Netherlands International Law Review* 62 (2): 295–311.

Hertzberg, Arthur. 1970. *The Zionist Idea: A Historical Analysis and Reader.* Westport, CT: Greenwood Press.

Hilal, 'Ali-Addin. 1998. "'Azmat al-Fikr al-Liberali fi al-Watan al-'Arabi," *'Alam Al-Fikr* 26 (3–4).

Hinton, Alexander, ed. 2010. *Transitional Justice: Global Mechanisms and Local Realities after Genocide and Mass Violence.* Newark, NJ: Rutgers University Press.

———. 2018. *The Justice Facade: Trials of Transition in Cambodia.* Oxford: Oxford University Press.

Hitti, Philip. 1946. *Professor Philip Hitti Testimony Before the Anglo-American Committee on Palestine.* Washington, DC: Arab Office.

Hodder, Jake. 2016. "Toward a Geography of Black Internationalism: Bayard Rustin, Nonviolence, and the Promise of Africa." *Annals of the American Association of Geographers* 106 (6): 1360–77.

Hoff, Joan. 2008. *A Faustian Foreign Policy from Woodrow Wilson to George W. Bush: Dreams of Perfectibility.* New York: Cambridge University Press.

Hoffmann, Florian. 2016. "International Legalism and International Politics." In *The Oxford Handbook of the Theory of International Law*, edited by Anne Orford and Florian Hoffmann, 954–84. Oxford: Oxford University Press.

Hoffmann, Florian, and Bethania Assy. 2019. "(De)Colonizing Human Rights." In *The Battle for International Law in the Decolonization Era*, edited by Jochen von Bernstorff and Phillip Dann, 198–215. Oxford: Oxford University Press.

Hofstadter, Richard. 1948. *The American Political Tradition: And the Men Who Made It.* New York: Alfred Knopf.

Honeyman, Victoria. 2007. *Richard Crossman: A Reforming Radical of the Labour Party.* London: I.B. Tauris.

Horwitz, Morton. 1977. "The Rule of Law: An Unqualified Human Good?" *Yale Law Journal* 86 (3): 561–66.

Hourani, Albert. 1946. *Is Zionism the Solution of the Jewish Problem*. London: Arab Office.

———. 1988. "Musa 'Alami and the Problem of Palestine, 1933–1949." In *Studia Palaestina—Studies in Honour of Constantine K. Zurayk*, edited by Hisham Nashabe, 23–41. Beirut: Institute for Palestine Studies.

———. 1990. "The Arab Awakening Forty Years After." In *Studies In Arab History: The Antonius Lectures 1978–1987*, edited by Derek Hopwood, 193–215. New York: Palgrave Macmillan.

———. 1993. "Patterns of the Past." In *Paths to the Middle East: Ten Scholars Look Back*, edited by Thomas Naff, 27–56. Albany: State University of New York Press.

———. 2005. "The Case against a Jewish State in Palestine: Albert Hourani's Statement to the Anglo-American Committee of Enquiry of 1946." *Journal of Palestine Studies* 35 (1): 80–90.

Hourani, Albert, and Robert Maugham. 1946. "Jewish Refugees: The Zionists and Palestine." *The Times*, London, August 10.

Hourani, Albert, and J. S. Morrison. 1946. "Palestine, Arab Opinion on Partition." *The Times*, London, July 18.

Hourani, Cecil. 2012. *An Unfinished Odyssey: Lebanon and Beyond*. Beirut: A. Antoine.

al-Hout, Bayan Nuwaihid. 1986. *Al-Qiyadat wa-l-Mu'assasat al-Siyasiyya fi Filastin, 1917–1948*. Beirut: Dar al-Huda.

al-Hout, Shafiq. 2011. *My Life in the PLO: The Inside Story of the Palestinian Struggle*. New York: Pluto Press.

Howard, Harry. 1963. *The King-Crane Commission: An American Inquiry in the Middle East*. Beirut: Khayats.

Hudson, Manley O. 1944. "The International Law of the Future." *American Journal of International Law* 38 (2): 278–81.

Hughes, Matthew. 2009. "The Banality of Brutality: British Armed Forces and the Repression of the Arab Revolt in Palestine, 1936–39." *English Historical Review* CXXIV (507): 313–54.

Human Rights Watch. 2002. *Israel, the Occupied West Bank and Gaza Strip, and the Palestinian Authority Territories-Jenin: IDF Military Operations*. Vol. 14. https://www.hrw.org/reports/2002/israel3/israel0502.pdf.

Huneidi, Sahar. 2001. *A Broken Trust: Herbert Samuel, Zionism and the Palestinians 1920–1925*. London and New York: I.B. Tauris.

Hunt, Alan. 1986. "The Theory of Critical Legal Studies." *Oxford Journal of Legal Studies* 6 (1): 1–45.

Hurd, Elizabeth Shakman. 2015. *Beyond Religious Freedom: The New Global Politics of Religion*. Princeton, NJ: Princeton University Press.

Hurd, Ian. 2017. *How to Do Things with International Law*. Princeton, NJ: Princeton University Press.

Hurewitz, J. C. 1950. *The Struggle for Palestine*. New York: Norton.

Husseini, Rafiq, ed. 2020. *Exiled from Jerusalem: The Diaries of Hussein Fakhri al-Khalidi*. London: I.B. Tauris.

Imseis, Ardi. 2019. *The United Nations and the Question of Palestine: A Study in International Legal Subalternity*. PhD diss., University of Cambridge, Politics and International Studies. https://www.repository.cam.ac.uk/handle/1810/290775.

International Court of Justice. n.d. "Legal Consequences of the Construction of a Wall in the Occupied Palestinian Territory, Overview of the Case." Accessed November 26, 2018. https://www.icj-cij.org/en/case/131.

International Criminal Court. n.d. "Statement of ICC Prosecutor." Accessed August 12, 2020. https://www.icc-cpi.int/Pages/item.aspx?name=20191220-otp-statement -palestine.

International Law Commission. 2015. "Summaries of the Work of the International Law Commission, Question of Defining Aggression." Last updated July 15. http://legal.un.org/ilc/summaries/7_5.shtml.

Irwin, Ryan. 2012. *Gordian Knot: Apartheid and the Unmaking of the Liberal World Order*. Oxford: Oxford University Press.

Isa, Felipe Gomez. 2017. "The Decision by the Inter-American Court of Human Rights on the Awas Tingni vs. Nicaragua Case (2001): The Implementation Gap." *Age of Human Rights Journal* (8): 67–91.

Ivison, Duncan. 2002. *Postcolonial Liberalism*. Cambridge: Cambridge University Press.

Jackson, Simon, and Alanna O'Malley, eds. 2018. *The Institution of International Order: From the League of Nations to the United Nations*. New York: Routledge.

Jankowski, James. 1980. "Egyptian Responses to the Palestine Problem in the Interwar Period." *International Journal of Middle East Studies* 12 (1): 1–38.

Jarring, Gunnar. 1999. "Interview with Gunnar Jarring by Jean Krasno." *Yale-UN Oral History Project*, November 7. http://dag.un.org/handle/11176/89611.

Jawhariyyeh, Wasif. 2014. *The Storyteller of Jerusalem: The Life and Times of Wasif Jawhariyyeh, 1904–1948*. Edited by Salim Tamari and Issam Nassar. Northampton MA: Interlink Publishing Group.

Jeffries, Joseph Mary Nagle. 2017. *Palestine: The Reality: The Inside Story of the Balfour Declaration 1917–1938*. Northampton, MA: Olive Branch Press.

Jensen, Steven L.B. 2016. *The Making of International Human Rights: The 1960s, Decolonization and the Reconstruction of Global Values*. Cambridge: Cambridge University Press.

John, Robert, and Sami Hadawi. 1970. *The Palestine Diary: 1914–1945*. New York: New World Press.

Jouannet, Emmanuelle Tourme. 2015. *A Short Introduction to International Law*. Cambridge: Cambridge University Press.

Joyce, Daniel. 2016. "Liberal Internationalism." In *The Oxford Handbook of the Theory of International Law*, edited by Anne Orford and Florian Hoffman, 471–87. Oxford: Oxford University Press.

Judis, John B. 2014. *Genesis: Truman, American Jews, and the Origins of the Arab/Israeli Conflict*. New York: Farrar, Straus and Giroux.

Kahn, Noor. 2011. *Egyptian-Indian Nationalist Collaboration and the British Empire*. New York: Palgrave Macmillan.

Kanafani, Ghassan. 1972. "The 1936–39 Revolt in Palestine Publication." New York: Committee for a Democratic Palestine. https://www.marxists.org/archive/kanafani /1972/revolt.htm.

Kattan, Victor. 2009. *From Coexistence to Conquest: International Law and the Origins of the Arab-Israeli Conflict, 1891–1949*. London: Pluto Press.

Katz, Ethan B., Lisa Moses Leff, and Maud S. Mandel, eds. 2017. *Colonialism and the Jews*. Bloomington: Indiana University Press.

Kauanui, J. Kehaulani. 2008. *Hawaiian Blood: Colonialism and the Politics of Sovereignty and Indigeneity*. Durham, NC: Duke University Press.

Kayali, Hasan. 2008. "Liberal Practices in the Transformation from Empire to Nation-State: The Rump Ottoman Empire, 1918–1923." In *Liberal Thought in the Eastern Mediterranean: Late 19th Century until the 1960s*, edited by Christoph Schumann, 175–94. Leiden, Netherlands: Brill.

Kayaoğlu, Turan. 2010. *Legal Imperialism: Sovereignty and Extraterritoriality in Japan, the Ottoman Empire, and China*. Cambridge: Cambridge University Press.

al-Kayyali, Abdel Wahhab. 1988. *Watha'iq al-Muqawama al-Filastiniyya al-'Arabiyya did al-Ihtilal al-Britani wa-l-Sahyuniyya (1939–1918)*. 2nd ed. Beirut: Institute of Palestine Studies.

Keane, Webb. 2015. "Varieties of Ethical Stance." In *Four Lectures on Ethics: Anthropological Perspectives*, edited by Michael Lambek, Veena Das, Didier Fassin, and Webb Keane. Chicago: HAU Books.

Keller, Matthew R. 2014. "When Is the State's Gaze Focused? British Royal Commissions and the Bureaucratization of Conflict." *Journal of Historical Sociology* 27 (2): 204–35.

Kelly, Matthew Kraig. 2017. *The Crime of Nationalism: Britain, Palestine, and Nation-Building on the Fringe of Empire*. Berkeley: University of California Press.

Kelly, Tobias. 2009. "The UN Committee Against Torture: Human Rights Monitoring and the Legal Recognition of Cruelty." *Human Rights Quarterly* 31 (3): 777–800.

———. 2011. "The Cause of Human Rights: Doubts about Torture, Law, and Ethics at the United Nations." *Journal of the Royal Anthropological Institute* 17 (4): 728–44.

———. 2012a. "Politics of Shame: The Bureaucratisation of International Human Rights Monitoring." In *The Gloss of Harmony: The Politics of Policy Making in International Organizations*, edited by Birgit Muller, 134–53. New York: Pluto Press.

———. 2012b. "Sympathy and Suspicion: Torture, Asylum, and Humanity." *Journal of the Royal Anthropological Institute* 18 (4): 753–68.

———. 2017. "The Future of Anthropology of Law." *Political and Legal Anthropology Review*, February 10. https://polarjournal.org/2017/02/10/emergent-conversations-part-6/.

———. 2018. "Beyond Ethics: Conscience, Pacifism, and the Political in Wartime Britain." *HAU: Journal of Ethnographic Theory* 8 (1–2): 114–28.

Kennedy, David. 1987. "The Move to Institutions." *Cardozo Law Review* 8 (5): 841–988.

———. 2002. "The Twentieth-Century Discipline of International Law in the United States." In *Looking Back at Law's Century*, edited by Austin Sarat, Bryant G. Garth, and Robert A. Kagan, 386—483. Ithaca, NY: Cornell University Press.

Kennedy, Duncan. 1982. "Antonio Gramsci and the Legal System." *ALSA Forum* 6 (1): 32–37.

———. 2008. "A Left Phenomenological Alternative to the Hart/Kelsen Theory." In *Legal Reasoning: Collected Essays*, 153–74. Aurora: The Davies Group.

Kennedy, Roseanne. 2014. "Moving Testimony: Human Rights, Palestinian Memory, and the Transnational Public Sphere." In *Transnational Memory: Circulation, Articulation, Scales*, edited by Chiara De Cesari and Ann Rigney, 51–78. Berlin, Boston: de Gruyter.

Khalaf, Issa. 1997. "The Effect of Socioeconomic Change on Arab Societal Collapse in Mandate Palestine." *International Journal of Middle East Studies* 29 (1): 93–112.

Khalidi, Hussein Fakhri. 1949. *Wa-Mada ʾAhd al-Mujamalat: Mudhakkirat al-Duktur Husayn Fakhri al-Khalidi.* Vol 1. Beirut: Dar al-Shuruq.

Khalidi, Omar. 2009. "Indian Muslims and Palestinian Awqaf." *Jerusalem Quarterly* (40): 52–58.

Khalidi, Rashid. 1984. "The 1912 Election Campaign in the Cities of Bilad al-Sham." *International Journal of Middle East Studies* 16 (4): 461–74.

———. 1997. *Palestinian Identity: The Construction of Modern National Consciousness.* New York: Columbia University Press.

———. 2006. *The Iron Cage: The Story of the Palestinian Struggle for Statehood.* Boston: Beacon Press.

———. 2013. *Brokers of Deceit: How the US Has Undermined Peace in the Middle East.* Boston: Beacon Press.

Khalidi, Walid. 1986. "The Arab Perspective." In *The End of the Palestine Mandate*, edited by William Roger Louis and Robert W. Stookey, 104–136. Austin: University of Texas Press.

———. 2005. "On Albert Hourani, the Arab Office, and the Anglo-American Committee of 1946." *Journal of Palestine Studies* 35 (1): 60–79.

Khalil, Osamah F. 2016. *America's Dream Palace: Middle East Expertise and the Rise of the National Security State.* Cambridge, MA: Harvard University Press.

Khalili, Laleh. 2009. *Heroes and Martyrs of Palestine: The Politics of National Commemoration*. Cambridge: Cambridge University Press.

Khouri, Kristine, and Rasha Salti. 2018. *Past Disquiet: Artists, International Solidarity, and Museums-in-Exile*. Warsaw: Museum of Modern Art in Warsaw.

Khoury, Philip S. 1985. "Divided Loyalties? Syria and the Question of Palestine, 1919–39." *Middle Eastern Studies* (21): 324–48.

Khuri-Makdisi, Ilham. 2013. *The Eastern Mediterranean and the Making of Global Radicalism, 1860–1914*. Berkeley, Los Angeles, London: University of California Press.

"The King-Crane Commission Report: Syria." 1919. Hellenic Resources Institute. http://www.hri.org/docs/king-crane/syria.html#statement.

Kinsella, Helen. 2011. *The Image before the Weapon: A Critical History of the Distinction between Combatant and Civilian*. New York: Cornell University Press.

———. 2017. "Superfluous Injury and Unnecessary Suffering: National Liberation and the Laws of War." In *International Origins of Social and Political Theory (Political Power and Social Theory, Volume 32)*, edited by Tarak Barkawi and George Lawson, 205–31. Bingley, UK: Emerald Publishing.

Kirkbride, Sir Alec Seath. 1987. "'. . . Until You Are Dead,' (Palestine, 1937)." In *From Haven to Conquest: Readings in Zionism and the Palestine Problem until 1948*, edited by Walid Khalidi, 2nd ed. Washington, DC: Institute of Palestine Studies.

Klug, Brian. 2017. "In Their Own Words: Three British Jewish Reactions to the Balfour Declaration." Talk presented at the Balfour Declaration: One Hundred Years in History and Memory, Princeton University, Princeton, NJ. May 8.

Knock, Thomas J. 1995. *To End All Wars: Woodrow Wilson and the Quest for a New World Order*. Princeton, NJ: Princeton University Press.

Knox, Robert. 2013. "Civilizing Interventions? Race, War and International Law." *Cambridge Review of International Affairs* 26 (1): 111–32.

———. 2016. "Marxist Approaches to International Law." In *The Oxford Handbook of the Theory of International Law*, edited by Anne Orford and Florian Hoffmann, 1:306–26. Oxford: Oxford University Press.

Kochavi, Arieh J. 2001. *Post-Holocaust Politics: Britain, the United States and Jewish Refugees, 1945–1948*. Chapel Hill and London: University of North Carolina Press.

Kodikara, Shelton U. 1992. *Foreign Policy of Sri Lanka: A Third World Perspective*. Delhi: Chanakya Publications.

Koskenniemi, Martti. 1989. *From Apology to Utopia: The Structure of International Legal Argument*. Helsinki: Finnish Lawyers' Publishing.

———. 1990. "The Politics of International Law." *European Journal of International Law* 1 (1): 4–32.

———. 2002. *The Gentle Civilizer of Nations: The Rise and Fall of International Law, 1870–1960*. Cambridge: Cambridge University Press.

———. 2003. "What Is International Law For?" In *International Law*, edited by Malcolm Evans, 4th ed., 89–114. Oxford: Oxford University Press.

———. 2004. "International Law and Hegemony: A Reconfiguration." *Cambridge Review of International Affairs* 17 (2): 197–218.

———. 2012. "Humanity's Law by Ruti G. Teitel." *Ethics & International Affairs* 26 (3). https://www.ethicsandinternationalaffairs.org/2012/humanitys-law-by-ruti-g -teitel/.

———. 2016. "Expanding Histories of International Law." *American Journal of Legal History* 56 (1): 104–12.

Krämer, Gudrun. 2011. *A History of Palestine: From the Ottoman Conquest to the Founding of the State of Israel*. Princeton, NJ: Princeton University Press.

Krever, Tor. 2013. "International Criminal Law: An Ideology Critique." *Leiden Journal of International Law* 26 (3): 701–23.

———. 2014. "Dispensing Global Justice." *New Left Review* (85): 67–97.

Krige, Sue. 1997. "Segregation, Science and Commissions of Enquiry: The Contestation over Native Education Policy in South Africa, 1930–36." *Journal of Southern African Studies* 23 (3): 491–506.

Labelle, Maurice Jr. 2011. "'The Only Thorn': Early Saudi-American Relations and the Question of Palestine, 1945–1949." *Diplomatic History* 35 (2): 257–81.

Laïdi-Hanieh, Adila. 2014. "Grievability as Political Claim Making: The 100 Shaheed-100 Lives Exhibition." *Arab Studies Journal* 22 (1): 46–73.

Lauren, Paul Gordon. 2000. *The Evolution of International Human Rights: Visions Seen*. Philadelphia: University of Pennsylvania Press.

Lauriat, Barbara. 2010. "'The Examination of Everything'—Royal Commissions in British Legal History." *Statute Law Review* 31 (1): 24–46.

*Lausanne Conference on near Eastern Affairs 1922–1923: Records of Proceedings and Draft Terms of Peace*. 1923. London: HMSO.

League of Nations. 1937a. Permanent Mandates Commission, Minutes of the Thirty-Second (Extraordinary) Session, Held at Geneva from July 30 to August 18. Geneva.

———. 1937b. "Petition from Mme. Zlikha Shihabi and Others, on Behalf of the Arab Women Committee of Jerusalem, Forwarded on December 22nd, 1936, by the United Kingdom Government, with Its Observations." Permanent Mandates Commission, Minutes of the Thirty-Second (Extraordinary) Session, Held at Geneva from July 30 to August 18. Geneva.

League of Nations Covenant, Article 15. n.d. Avalon Project, Yale Law School. http://avalon.law.yale.edu/20th_century/leagcov.asp#art15.

League of Nations Covenant, Article 22. n.d. Avalon Project, Yale Law School. http://avalon.law.yale.edu/20th_century/leagcov.asp#art22.

Lear, Jonathan. 2008. *Radical Hope: Ethics in the Face of Cultural Devastation*. Cambridge and London: Harvard University Press.

Lesch, Ann Mosely. 1979. *Arab Politics in Palestine, 1917–1939: The Frustration of a Nationalist Movement*. Ithaca and London: Cornell University Press.

Levenberg, Haim. 1991. "Bevin's Disillusionment: The London Conference, Autumn 1946." *Middle Eastern Studies* 27 (4): 615–30.

Levinson, Sanford. 1983. "Escaping Liberalism: Easier Said Than Done. Review of The Politics of Law: A Progressive Critique by David Kairys." *Harvard Law Review* 96 (6): 1466–88.

Li, Darryl. 2011. "Occupation Law and the One-State Reality." *Jadaliyya*, August 2.

———. 2020. *The Universal Enemy: Jihad, Empire, and the Challenge of Solidarity*. Stanford, CA: Stanford University Press.

Litvak, Meir, and Esther Webman. 2009. *From Empathy to Denial: Arab Responses to the Holocaust*. New York: Columbia University Press.

Loades, David. 1997. *Power in Tudor England*. New York: St. Martin's Press.

Lockman, Zachary. 1996. *Comrades and Enemies: Arab and Jewish Workers in Palestine, 1906–1948*. Berkeley and Los Angeles: University of California Press.

Loevy, Karin. 2016. "Reinventing a Region (1915–22): Visions of the Middle East in Legal and Diplomatic Texts Leading to the Palestine Mandate." *Israel Law Review* 49 (3): 309–37.

Lorca, Arnulf Becker. 2011. "Sovereignty beyond the West: The End of Classical International Law." *Journal of the History of International Law* 13 (1): 7–73.

———. 2014. *Mestizo International Law*. Cambridge: Cambridge University Press.

Louis, William Roger. 1984. *The British Empire in the Middle East, 1945–1951: Arab Nationalism, the United States, and Postwar Imperialism*. Oxford: Clarendon Press.

Lubin, Alex. 2014. *Geographies of Liberation: The Making of an Afro-Arab Political Imaginary*. Chapel Hill, NC: University of North Carolina Press.

Magliveras, Konstantin. 1991. "The Withdrawal From the League of Nations Revisited." *Penn State International Law Review* 10 (1): 25–71.

Mahmood, Saba. 1996. "Interview with Talal Asad: Modern Power and the Reconfiguration of Religious Traditions." *SEHR: Contested Polities* 5 (1). https://web.stanford .edu/group/SHR/5-1/text/asad.html.

———. 2012. *Politics of Piety: The Islamic Revival and the Feminist Subject*. Princeton, NJ: Princeton University Press.

Mahmud, Lilith. 2016. "We Have Never Been Liberal: Occidentalist Myths and the Impending Fascist Apocalypse." *Hot Spots, Cultural Anthropology*. https://culanth .org/fieldsights/981-we-have-never-been-liberal-occidentalist-myths-and-the -impending-fascist-apocalypse.

Makalani, Minkah. 2011. *In the Cause of Freedom: Radical Black Internationalism from Harlem to London, 1917–1939*. Chapel Hill: University of North Carolina Press.

Makdisi, Karim, and Vijay Prashad. 2017. "Introduction." In *Land of Blue Helmets: The United Nations and the Arab World*, edited by Karim Makdisi and Vijay Prashad, 1–4. Berkeley: University of California Press.

Makdisi, Usama. 2002a. "After 1860: Debating Religion, Reform, and Nationalism in the Ottoman Empire." *International Journal of Middle East Studies* 34 (4): 601–17.

———. 2002b. "Ottoman Orientalism." *American Historical Review* (17): 768–796.

———. 2008a. *Artillery of Heaven: American Missionaries and the Failed Conversion of the Middle East*. Edited by Mark Philip Bradley and Paul A. Kramer. Ithaca and London: Cornell University Press.

———. 2008b. "The Question of American Liberalism and the Origins of the American Board Mission to the Levant and Its Historiography." In *Liberal Thought in the Eastern Mediterranean: Late 19th Century Until the 1960s*, edited by Christoph Schumann, 15–28. Leiden, Netherlands: Brill.

———. 2010. *Faith Misplaced: The Broken Promise of U.S.-Arab Relations: 1820–2001*. New York: Public Affairs/Perseus Books.

Mallard, Grégoire, and Linsey McGoey. 2018. "Strategic Ignorance and Global Governance: An Ecumenical Approach to Epistemologies of Global Power." *British Journal of Sociology* 69 (4): 884–909.

Mamdani, Mahmood. 2001. *When Victims Become Killers: Colonialism, Nativism, and the Genocide in Rwanda*. Princeton, NJ: Princeton University Press.

Manela, Erez. 2007. *The Wilsonian Moment: Self-Determination and the International Origins of Anticolonial Nationalism*. Oxford: Oxford University Press.

Mantena, Karuna. 2007. "The Crisis of Liberal Imperialism." In *Victorian Visions of Global Order*, edited by Duncan Bell, 113–35. Cambridge: Cambridge University Press.

———. 2009. *Alibis of Empire: Henry Maine and the Ends of Liberal Imperialism*. Princeton, NJ: Princeton University Press.

Maogoto, Jackson Nyamunya. 2014. "The 1919 Paris Peace Conference and the Allied Commission: Challenging Sovereignty Through Supranational Criminal Jurisdiction." In *Historical Origins of International Criminal Law*, edited by Morten Bergsmo, Cheah Wui Ling, and Yi Ping, vol. 1, 171–193. Brussels: Torkel Opsahl Academic EPublisher.

Maoz, Asher. 2000. "Historical Adjudication: Courts of Law, Commissions of Inquiry, and 'Historical Truth.'" *Law and History Review* 18 (3): 559–606.

Marín, Alejandro Pozo. 2017. *The Moral Relativism of Subordinating Civilians to Terrorists: MSF Reflections after a Tragic Year of Hospital Bombings*. Barcelona. https://arhp.msf.es/attacks-against-medical-mission/moral-relativism-subordinating-civilians-terrorists.

Marks, Susan. 2000. *The Riddle of All Constitutions: International Law, Democracy, and the Critique of Ideology*. Oxford: Oxford University Press.

————. 2007. "International Judicial Activism and the Commodity-Form Theory of International Law." *European Journal of International Law* 18 (1): 199–211.

————. 2009. "Introduction." In *International Law on the Left: Re-Examining Marxist Legacies*, edited by Susan Marks, 1–29. Cambridge: Cambridge University Press.

Matar, Dina. 2018. "Comparative Studies of South Asia, Africa and the Middle East." *Comparative Studies of South Asia, Africa and the Middle East* 38 (2): 354–64.

Matera, Marc, and Susan Kingsley Kent. 2017. *The Global 1930s: The International Decade*. London and New York: Routledge.

Mattar, Philip. 1988. "The Mufti of Jerusalem and the Politics of Palestine." *Middle East Journal* 42 (2): 227–40.

————. 2005. *Encyclopedia of the Palestinians*. New York: Facts on File.

Matthews, Weldon C. 2003. "Pan-Islam or Arab Nationalism? The Meaning of the 1931 Jerusalem Islamic Congress Reconsidered." *International Journal of Middle East Studies* 35 (1): 1–22.

————. 2006. *Confronting an Empire, Constructing a Nation: Arab Nationalists and Popular Politics in Mandate Palestine*. London and New York: I.B. Tauris.

Mayer, Ann Elizabeth. 2013. *Islam and Human Rights: Tradition and Politics*. 5th ed. New York: Routledge.

Mayer, Thomas. 1983. *Egypt and the Palestine Question, 1936–1945*. Berlin: Klaus Schwarz Verlag.

Mazower, Mark. 1997. "Minorities and the League of Nations in Interwar Europe." *Daedalus* 126 (2): 47–63.

————. 2000. *Dark Continent: Europe's Twentieth Century*. New York: Vintage Books.

————. 2004. "The Strange Triumph of Human Rights, 1933–1950." *Historical Journal* 47 (2): 379–98.

————. 2012. *Governing the World: The History of an Idea, 1815 to the Present*. New York: Penguin Books.

Mazzarella, William. 2017. *The Mana of Mass Society*. Chicago and London: University of Chicago Press.

McAlister, Melani. 2005. *Epic Encounters: Culture, Media, and U.S. Interests in the Middle East since 1945*. Berkeley, Los Angeles, and London: University of California Press.

McCarthy, Justin. 1990. *The Population of Palestine*. New York: Columbia University Press.

McDonald, James G., Richard Breitman, Barbara McDonald Stewart, and Severin Hochberg, eds. 2007. *Advocate for the Doomed: The Diaries and Papers of James G. McDonald, 1932–1935*. Bloomington: Indiana University Press.

McDonald, James G., Norman J. W. Goda, Barbara McDonald Stewart, Severin Hochberg, and Richard Breitman. 2014. *To the Gates of Jerusalem: The Diaries and Papers of James G. McDonald, 1945–1947*. Bloomington: Indiana University Press.

McKinzie, Richard D. 1975. "Evan M. Wilson Oral History Interview." *Truman Library*. Washington, DC, July 18. https://www.trumanlibrary.org/oralhist/wilsonem.htm.

Mearsheimer, John J., and Stephen M. Walt. 2006. "The Israel Lobby and U.S. Foreign Policy." *Middle East Policy* 13 (3): 29–87.

Mégret, Frédéric. 2016. "International Criminal Justice as a Juridical Field." *Champ Pénal/Penal Field* XIII (13). https://doi.org/10.4000/champpenal.9284.

Mehta, Uday Singh. 1997. "Liberal Strategies of Exclusion." In *Tensions of Empire: Colonial Cultures in a Bourgeois World*, edited by Frederick Cooper and Ann Laura Stoler, 59–76. Berkeley: University of California Press.

———. 1999. *Liberalism and Empire: A Study in Nineteenth-Century British Liberal Thought*. Chicago: University of Chicago Press.

Meiu, George Paul. 2015. "Colonialism and Sexuality." In *The International Encyclopedia of Human Sexuality*, edited by Patricia Whelehan and Anne Bolin, vol. 1, 1–3. Malden, Oxford: John Wiley & Sons.

Mendy, Peter Karibe. 2019. *Amilcar Cabral: Nationalist and Pan-Africanist Revolutionary*. Athens: Ohio University Press.

Merry, Sally Engle. 2006. "Anthropology and International Law." *Annual Review of Anthropology* 35 (1): 99–116.

Merry, Sally Engle, and Susan Bibler Coutin. 2014. "Technologies of Truth in the Anthropology of Conflict: AES/APLA Presidential Address, 2013." *American Ethnologist* 41 (1): 1–16.

Miéville, China. 2005 *Between Equal Rights: A Marxist Theory of International Law*. Leiden, Netherlands, and Boston: Brill.

Mill, John Stuart. 1991. "On Liberty." In *On Liberty and Other Essays*, edited by John Gray, 1–128. Oxford: Oxford University Press, first published 1859.

Millen-Penn, Ken. 1995. "Democratic Control, Public Opinion, and League Diplomacy." *World Affairs* 157 (4): 207–18.

Miller, Rory. 2008. "'The Rhetoric of Reaction': British Arabists, Jewish Refugees and the Palestine Question." *Israel Affairs* 14 (3): 467–85.

Mills, Charles. 2017. *Black Rights/Right Wrongs: The Critique of Racial Liberalism*. Oxford: Oxford University Press.

———. 2018. *Liberalism and Racial Justice*. Simpson Center for the Humanities, Katz Distinguished Lecture in the Humanities, University of Washington, Kane Hall, May 29. YouTube video, https://www.youtube.com/watch?v=n7KVrx42aqI.

Mitchell, George J. 2011. "Interview with George Mitchell (6) by Andrea L'Hommedieu." George J. Mitchell Oral History Project, Bowdoin College. https://digitalcommons.bowdoin.edu/mitchelloralhistory/67/.

————. 2015. *The Negotiator: A Memoir*. New York: Simon & Schuster Paperbacks.

Mittelman, James. 1976. "Collective Decolonisation and the U.N. Committee of 24." *Journal of Modern African Studies* 14 (1): 41–64.

Molchadsky, Nadav Gadi. 2015. "History in the Public Courtroom: Commissions of Inquiry and Struggles over the History and Memory of Israeli Traumas." PhD diss., University of California, Los Angeles. https://escholarship.org/uc/item /3vf2g7r0.

Mongia, Radhika V. 2004. "Impartial Regimes of Truth: Indentured Indian Labour and the Status of the Inquiry." *Cultural Studies* 18 (5): 749–68.

Moore, Sally Falk. 1973. "Law and Social Change: The Semi-Autonomous Social Field as an Appropriate Subject of Study." *Law & Society Review* 7 (4): 719–46.

————. 2015. "An Unusual Career: Considering Political/Legal Orders and Unofficial Parallel Realities." *Annual Review of Law and Social Science* 11 (1): 1–14.

Morris, Benny. 2001. "Revisiting the Palestinian Exodus of 1948." In *The War for Palestine: Rewriting the History of 1948*, edited by Eugene L. Rogan and Avi Shlaim, 37–59. Cambridge: Cambridge University Press.

Moustafa, Tamir. 2018. *Constituting Religion: Islam, Liberal Rights, and the Malaysian State*. Cambridge: Cambridge University Press.

Moyers, Bill. 2009. "Transcripts with Richard Goldstone." *Bill Moyers Journal*, October 23. http://www.pbs.org/moyers/journal/10232009/transcript1.html.

Moyn, Samuel. 2012. *The Last Utopia: Human Rights in History*. Cambridge, MA: Harvard University Press.

————. 2013. "The International Law That Is America: Reflections on the Last Chapter of the Gentle Civilizer of Nations." *Faculty Scholarship Series* 27 (2): 399–415.

Mufti, Aamir R. 2015. "Talal Asad on 'Violence, Law, and Humanitarianism': A Response." *Critical Inquiry*. https://criticalinquiry.uchicago.edu/talal_asad_on _violence_law_and_humanitarianism_a_response/.

Muschik, Eva-Maria. 2018. "Managing the World: The United Nations, Decolonization, and the Strange Triumph of State Sovereignty in the 1950s and 1960s." *Journal of Global History* 13 (1): 121–44.

Mutua, Makau W. 2000. "What Is TWAIL?" American Society of International Law, Proceedings of the 94th Annual Meeting.

Nachmani, Amikam. 1987. *Great Power Discord in Palestine: The Anglo-American Committee of Inquiry into the Problems of European Jewry and Palestine, 1945–1946*. London and Totowa, N.J.: Frank Cass.

Nafi, Basheer M. 1998. *Arabism, Islamism and the Palestine Question, 1908–1941: A Political History*. Ithaca, NY: Ithaca Press.

Naqqara, Hanna Dib. 2011. *Mudhakkirat Muhami Filastini: Hanna Dib Naqqara, Muhami al-Ard wa-Sha`b*. Edited by `Atallah Sa`id Qubti. 2nd ed. Beirut: Institute of Palestine Studies.

Nelson, Deborah. 2004. "Suffering and Thinking: The Scandal of Tone in Hannah Arendt's Eichmann in Jerusalem." In *Compassion: The Culture and Politics of an Emotion*, edited by Lauren Gail Berlant, 219–44. New York and London: Routledge.

Newton, Francis E. 1987. "Searchlight on Palestine, 1936–1938." In *From Haven to Conquest: Readings in Zionism and the Palestine Problem until 1948*, 2nd ed. Washington,
DC: Institute of Palestine Studies.

Niezen, Ronald. 2013. *Truth and Indignation: Canada's Truth and Reconciliation Commission on Indian Residential Schools*. Toronto: University of Toronto Press.

Niezen, Ronald, and Maria Sapignoli, eds. 2017. *Palaces of Hope: The Anthropology of
Global Organizations*. Cambridge: Cambridge University Press.

Nissanka, H. S. S. 1984. *Sri Lanka's Foreign Policy: A Study in Non-Alignment*. New
Delhi: Vikas Publishing House.

Noelle-Neumann, Elisabeth. 1979. "Public Opinion and the Classical Tradition: A Re
Evaluation." *Public Opinion Quarterly* 43 (2): 143–56.

Norman, Julie M. 2010. *The Second Palestinian Intifada: Civil Resistance*. New York:
Routledge.

Normand, Robert, and Sarah Zaidi. 2008. *Human Rights at the UN: The Political History of Universal Justice*. Bloomington: Indiana University Press.

Norris, Jacob. 2008. "Repression and Rebellion: Britain's Response to the Arab Revolt
in Palestine of 1936–39." *Journal of Imperial and Commonwealth History* 36 (1):
25–45.

———. 2013. *Land of Progress: Palestine in the Age of Colonial Development, 1905–1948*.
Oxford: Oxford University Press.

Nouwen, Sarah, and Michael Becker. n.d. "International Commissions of Inquiry:
What Difference Do They Make? Taking an Empirical Approach." *European
Journal of International Law*. https://doi.org/https://doi.org/10.17863/CAM
.38690.

Nuijten, Monique. 2003. *Power, Community and the State: The Political Anthropology of
Organisation in Mexico*. London: Pluto Press.

O'Rourke, Kevin. 2001. *John Stuart Mill and Freedom of Expression: The Genesis of a
Theory*. London and New York: Routledge.

Oh, Irene. 2007. *The Rights of God: Islam, Human Rights, and Comparative Ethics*.
Washington DC: Georgetown University Press.

Okafor, Obiora. 2016. "Praxis and the International (Human Rights) Law Scholar:
Toward the Intensification of TWAILian Dramaturgy." *Articles & Book Chapters*
2644. https://digitalcommons.osgoode.yorku.ca/scholarly_works/2644.

al-ʿOmar, ʿAbdel Karim, ed. 1999. *Mudhakkirat al-Haj Amin Muhammad al-Husayni*.
Damascus: al-Ahli li-l-Tibaʿa wa-l-Nashr.

Omar, Hussein. 2019. "The Arab Spring of 1919." *London Review of Books*, April 4.
https://www.lrb.co.uk/blog/2019/april/the-arab-spring-of-1919.

Osiel, Mark. 1997. *Mass Atrocity, Collective Memory, and the Law*. New Brunswick and London: Transaction Publishers.

Otto, Dianne. 1996. "Subalternity and International Law: The Problems of Global Community and the Incommensurability of Difference." *Social & Legal Studies* 5 (3): 337–64.

———. 2016. "Impunity in a Different Register: People's Tribunals and Questions of Judgment, Law, and Responsibility." In *Anti-Impunity and the Human Rights Agenda*, edited by Karen Engle, Zinaida Miller, and D. M. Davis, 291–328. Cambridge: Cambridge University Press.

Özsu, Umut. 2009. "De-Territorializing and Re-Territorializing Lotus: Sovereignty and Systematicity as Dialectical Nation-Building in Early Republican Turkey." *Leiden Journal of International Law* 22 (1): 29–49.

———. 2014. "International Legal Fields." *Humanity: An International Journal of Human Rights, Humanitarianism, and Development* 5 (2): 277–92.

———. 2016a. "The Ottoman Empire, the Origins of Extraterritoriality, and International Legal Theory." In *The Oxford Handbook of the Theory of International Law*, edited by Anne Orford and Florian Hoffmann, vol. 1, 123–37. Oxford: Oxford University Press.

———. 2016b. "Ottoman International Law?" *Journal of the Ottoman and Turkish Studies Association* 3 (2): 369–76.

———. 2017. "'Let Us First of All Have Unity Among Us': Bandung, International Law, and the Empty Politics of Solidarity." In *Bandung, Global History, and International Law*, edited by Luis Eslava, Michael Fakhri, and Vasuki Nesiah, 293–308. Cambridge: Cambridge University Press.

———. 2019. "Determining New Selves: Mohammed Bedjaoui on Algeria, Western Sahara, and Post-Classical International Law." In *The Battle for International Law in the Decolonization Era*, edited by Jochen von Bernstorff and Philipp Dann, 341–57. Oxford: Oxford University Press.

Pahuja, Sundhya. 2011. *Decolonising International Law: Development, Economic Growth and the Politics of Universality*. Cambridge: Cambridge University Press.

Palabiyik, Mustafa Serdar. 2014. "The Emergence of the Idea of 'International Law' in the Ottoman Empire before the Treaty of Paris (1856)." *Middle Eastern Studies* 50 (2): 233–51.

*Palestine Royal Commission Report*. 1937. Colonial Offices.

*Palestine Royal Commission Minutes of Evidence Heard at Public Session*. 1937. London: His Majesty's Stationery Office.

Pappé, Ilan. 2010. *The Rise and Fall of a Palestinian Dynasty: The Husaynis, 1700–1948*. Berkeley: University of California Press.

Parekh, Bhikhu. 2000. *Rethinking Multiculturalism: Cultural Diversity and Political Theory*. Cambridge, MA: Harvard University Press.

Parla, Ayşe. 2019. *Precarious Hope: Migration and the Limits of Belonging in Turkey.* Stanford, CA: Stanford University Press.

Parsons, Laila. 2015. "Rebels without Borders: Southern Syria and Palestine, 1919–1936." In *The Routledge Handbook of the History of the Middle East Mandates*, edited by Cyrus Schayegh and Andrew Arsan, 395–408. London and New York: Routledge.

Patrick, Andrew. 2011. "Reading the King-Crane Commission of 1919: Discourses of Race, Modernity, and Self-Determination in Competing American Visions for the Post-Ottoman Middle East." PhD diss., University of Manchester.

———. 2015. *America's Forgotten Middle East Initiative: The King-Crane Commission of 1919.* New York: I.B.Tauris.

Pedersen, Susan. 2006. "The Meaning of the Mandates System an Argument." *Geschichte Und Gesellschaft* 32 (4): 560–82.

———. 2007. "Back to the League of Nations." *American Historical Review* 112 (4): 1091–1117.

———. 2010. "Getting Out of Iraq—in 1932: The League of Nations and the Road to Normative Statehood." *American Historical Review* 115 (4): 975–1000.

———. 2015. *The Guardians: The League of Nations and the Crisis of Empire.* New York: Oxford University Press.

Pels, Peter. 1997. "The Anthropology of Colonialism: Culture, History, and the Emergence of Western Governmentality." *Annual Review of Anthropology* 26: 163–83.

Peluso, Nancy Lee. 2017. "Whigs and Hunters: The Origins of the Black Act, by E.P. Thompson." *Journal of Peasant Studies* 44 (1): 309–21.

Perugini, Nicola, and Neve Gordon. 2016. "The Threat of Human Rights." *OpenGlobalRights*, February 23. https://www.openglobalrights.org/threat-of-human-rights/.

Phillips, William. 1952. *Ventures in Diplomacy.* London: John Murray.

Pirie, Fernanda. 2013. *The Anthropology of Law.* Oxford: Oxford University Press.

Pitts, Jennifer. 2000. "Empire and Democracy: Tocqueville and the Algeria Question." *Journal of Political Philosophy* 8 (3): 295–318.

———. 2005. *A Turn to Empire: The Rise of Imperial Liberalism in Britain and France.* Princeton, NJ: Princeton University Press.

———. 2010. "Political Theory of Empire and Imperialism." *Annual Review of Political Science* 13 (1): 211–235.

———. 2012. "Empire and Legal Universalisms in the Eighteenth Century." *American Historical Review* 117 (1): 92–121.

———. 2015. "The Critical History of International Law." *Political Theory* 43 (4): 541–52.

———. 2017. "International Relations and the Critical History of International Law." *International Relations* 31 (3): 282–98.

———. 2018. *Boundaries of the International, Law and Empire.* Cambridge, MA, and London: Harvard University Press.

Podet, Allen Howard. 1986. *The Success and Failure of the Anglo-American Committee of Inquiry, 1945–1946 : Last Chance in Palestine*. Vol. 3. Lewiston, N.Y.: E. Mellen Press.

Porath, Yehoshua. 1974. *The Emergence of the Palestinian-Arab National Movement, 1918–1929*. London: Frank Cass.

———. 1981. *The Palestine Arab National Movement: From Riots to Rebellion, 1929–1939*. Vol. 2. London: Frank Cass.

Povinelli, Elizabeth A. 2002. *The Cunning of Recognition: Indigenous Alterities and the Making of Australian Multiculturalism*. Durham, NC, and London: Duke University Press.

———. 2011. *Economies of Abandonment: Social Belonging and Endurance in Late Liberalism*. Durham, NC: Duke University Press.

Prashad, Vijay. 2007. *The Darker Nations: A People's History of the Third World*. New York: The New Press.

Provence, Michael. 2017. *The Last Ottoman Generation and the Making of the Modern Middle East*. Cambridge: Cambridge University Press.

Provost, Claire, Aisha Dodwell, and Alex Scrivener. 2006. "The Privatisation of UK Aid." London. https://slidelegend.com/the-privatisation-of-uk-aid-global-justice-now_59d154861723ddd66a026e13.html.

Qaddoura, Jamal Muhammad. 1993. *Al-Qadiyya al-Filastiniyya wa-Lijan al-Tahqiq, 1937–1947*. Sidi Bel Abbas: Dar al-Hmar li-l-Tiba'a wa-l-Nashr.

Qasimiyya, Khairiya, ed. 1974. *'Awni 'Abd al-Hadi: Awraq Khassa*. Beirut: Palestinian Liberation Organization.

———, ed. 2002. *Mudhakkirat 'Awni 'Abd al-Hadi*. Beirut: Centre for Arab Unity Studies.

Quigley, John. 2010. "The International Criminal Court and the Gaza War." *Palestine Yearbook of International Law Online* 16 (1): 25–54.

Rabbani, Mouin. 2001. "The Mitchell Report: Oslo's Last Gasp?" *Middle East Research and Information Project*, June 1. https://merip.org/2001/06/the-mitchell-report/.

———. 2015. "Expert Q&A: Palestine Accedes to the ICC." *Institute for Middle East Understanding*, January 14. https://imeu.org/article/expert-qa-palestine-accedes-to-the-icc.

Radosh, Allis, and Ronald Radosh. 2009. *A Safe Haven: Harry S. Truman and the Founding of Israel*. New York: Harper Collins Publishers.

Rahman, Shafiur. 2018. "What Will the UN Fact-Finding Mission's Report Mean for Rohingya?" *The Diplomat*, August. https://thediplomat.com/2018/08/what-will-the-un-fact-finding-missions-report-mean-for-rohingya/.

Rajagopal, Balakrishnan. 2000. "From Resistance to Renewal: The Third World, Social Movements, and the Expansion of International Institutions." *Harvard International Law Journal* 41 (2): 529–78.

———. 2003. *International Law from Below: Development, Social Movements, and Third World Resistance*. Cambridge: Cambridge University Press.

———. 2006. "Counter-Hegemonic International Law: Rethinking Human Rights and Development as a Third World Strategy." *Third World Quarterly* 27 (5): 767–83.

Rasulov, Akbar. 2014. "CLS and Marxism: A History of an Affair." *Transnational Legal Theory* 5 (4): 622–639. https://papers.ssrn.com/sol3/papers.cfm?abstract_id =2633885.

Redfield, Peter. 2006. "A Less Modest Witness." *American Ethnologist* 33 (1): 3–26.

———. 2013. *Life in Crisis: The Ethical Journey of Doctors without Borders*. Berkeley and Los Angeles: University of California Press.

Redfield, Peter, and Erica Bornstein. 2010. "An Introduction to the Anthropology of Humanitarianism." In *Forces of Compassion: Humanitarianism between Ethics and Politics*, edited by Erica Bornstein and Peter Redfield, 3–30. Santa Fe, NM: School for Advanced Research Press.

Reid, Donald M. 1981. *Lawyers and Politics in the Arab World, 1880–1960*. Minneapolis: Bibliotheca Islamica.

Reimer, Michael. 2006. "The King-Crane Commission at the Juncture of Politics and Historiography." *Critique: Critical Middle Eastern Studies* 15 (2): 129–50.

"Report of the Royal Commission on the South African War." 1903. *British Medical Journal* 2 (2226): 484–87.

Ricks, Thomas M. 2009. *Turbulent Times in Palestine: The Diaries of Khalil Totah, 1886–1955*. Jerusalem: Institute for Palestine Studies.

Riles, Annelise. 2000. *The Network Inside Out*. Ann Arbor: University of Michigan Press.

Robinson, Shira. 2013. *Citizen Strangers: Palestinians and the Birth of Israel's Liberal Settler State*. Stanford, CA: Stanford University Press.

Robson, Laura. 2017. *States of Separation: Transfer, Partition, and the Making of the Modern Middle East*. Oakland: University of California Press.

Rodenhäuser, Tilman. 2013. "Progressive Development of International Human Rights Law: The Reports of the Independent International Commission of Inquiry on the Syrian Arab Republic." *EJIL: Talk!*, https://www.ejiltalk.org/progressive -development-of-international-human-rights-law-the-reports-of-the-independent -international-commission-of-inquiry-on-the-syrian-arab-republic/.

Roders, Daniel T. 2004. "The Traditions of Liberalism in Questions of Tradition." In *Questions of Tradition*, edited by Mark Phillips and Gordon Schochet, 203–32. Toronto: University of Toronto Press.

Rodogno, Davide. 2016a. "Humanitarian Intervention in the Nineteenth Century." In *The Oxford Handbook of the Responsibility to Protect*, edited by Alex J. Bellamy and Tim Dunne. Oxford: Oxford University Press. https://doi.org/10.1093/oxfordhb /9780198753841.013.2.

———. 2016b. "The Ottoman Empire, the Issue of Interventions upon Grounds of Humanity, and Western European Legal Scholars during the Nineteenth Century." *Journal of the History of International Law* 18 (1): 5–41.

Roy, Sara. 2016. *The Gaza Strip: The Political Economy of De-Development*. 3rd ed. Washington DC: Institute for Palestine Studies.

"Royal Commission," 1936. *UK Parliament*, HC Deb (May 26) vol. 312, c1848W.

Rudman, Warren. 2010. "Interview with Warren Rudman by Brien Williams." *George J. Mitchell Oral History Project*, no. Paper 33 (June 2). https://digitalcommons .bowdoin.edu/mitchelloralhistory/33.

Ruedy, John. 1971. "Dynamics of Land Alienation (in Palestine)." In *The Transformation of Palestine: Essays on the Origin and Development of the Arab-Israeli Conflict*, edited by Ibrahim Abu-Lughod, 119–38. Evanston, IL: Northwestern University Press.

Sachedina, Abdulaziz Abdulhussein. 2009. *Islam and the Challenge of Human Rights*. Oxford: Oxford University Press.

Said, Edward. 1979. *Orientalism*. New York: Random House.

———. 1984. "Permission to Narrate." *Journal of Palestine Studies* 13 (3): 27–48.

———. 2001. "The Desertions of Arafat." *New Left Review* 11: 27–33.

Sakakini, Khalil. 1955. *Katha Ana ya Dunya: Yowmiyat Khalil Sakakini*. Edited by Hala Sakakini. Jerusalem: al-Matbaʿa al-Tijariyya.

———. 2004. *Yowmiyat Khalil al-Sakakini: Yowmiyat, Rasaʾil, Taʾamulat. Al-Kitab al-Thalith: Ikhtibar al-Intidab wa-Masʾilat al-Huwiyya, 1919–1922*. Edited by Akram Musallim. Vol. 3. Ramallah and Jerusalem: Khalil Sakakini Cultural Centre and Institute of Jerusalem Studies.

Samour, Nahed. 2017. "Palestine at Bandung." In *Bandung, Global History, and International Law*, edited by Luis Eslava, Michael Fakhri, and Vasuki Nesiah, 595–615. Cambridge: Cambridge University Press.

Santos, Boaventura de Sousa, and César A. Rodríguez Garavito, eds. 2005. *Law and Globalization from Below: Towards a Cosmopolitan Legality*. Cambridge: Cambridge University Press.

Sartori, Andrew. 2006. "The British Empire and Its Liberal Mission." *Journal of Modern History* 78 (3): 623–42.

———. 2014. *Liberalism in Empire: An Alternative History*. Oakland: University of California Press.

———. 2017. "Review Article: C. A. Bayly and the Question of Indian Political Thought." *Modern Asian Studies* 51 (3): 867–77.

Satia, Priya. 2006. "The Defense of Inhumanity: Air Control and the British Idea of Arabia." *American Historical Review* 111 (1): 16–51.

———. 2014. "Drones: A History from the British Middle East." *Humanity: An International Journal of Human Rights, Humanitarianism, and Development* 5 (1): 1–31.

Sayegh, Fayez. 2013. "Zionist Colonialism in Palestine (1965)." *Settler Colonial Studies* 2 (1): 206–25.

Sayigh, Rosemary, ed. 2015. *Yusif Sayigh: Arab Economist and Palestinian Patriot: A Fractured Life Story*. Cairo: American University in Cairo Press.

Schielke, Samuli. 2010. "Being Good in Ramadan: Ambivalence, Fragmentation, and the Moral Self in the Lives of Young Egyptians." In *Islam, Politics, Anthropology*, edited by Filippo Osella and Benjamin F. Soares, 23–38. West Sussex, UK: Wiley-Blackwell.

———. 2014. "Review of Questioning Secularism: Islam, Sovereignty, and the Rule of Law in Modern Egypt." *PoLAR Online* 37 (2): 402–4.

Schiller, Naomi. 2013. "Reckoning with Press Freedom: Community Media, Liberalism, and the Processual State in Caracas, Venezuela." *American Ethnologist* 40 (3): 540–54.

———. 2015. "Anthropology of Liberalism." *The International Encyclopedia of the Social and Behavioral Sciences,* 2nd ed. Dominic Boyer and Ulf Hannerz, anthropology section co-editors. London: Reed Elsevier, 2015.

Schlag, Pierre. 1998. *The Enchantment of Reason*. Durham, NC: Duke University Press.

Schumann, Christoph. 2008. "Introduction." In *Liberal Thought in the Eastern Mediterranean: Late 19th Century until the 1960s*, edited by Christoph Schumann, 1–14. Leiden, Netherlands: Brill.

Scott, David. 1999. *Refashioning Futures: Criticism after Postcoloniality*. Princeton, NJ: Princeton University Press.

Segev, Tom. 2000. *One Palestine, Complete: Jews and Arabs under the Mandate*. Translated by Haim Watzman. New York: Metropolitan Books.

Seikaly, Sherene. 2016. *Men of Capital: Scarcity and Economy in Mandate Palestine*. Stanford, CA: Stanford University Press.

Sewell, William H. Jr. 1996. "Historical Events as Transformations of Structures: Inventing Revolution at the Bastille." *Theory and Society* 25 (6): 841–81.

Sfard, Michael. 2018. *The Wall and the Gate: Israel, Palestine, and the Legal Battle for Human Rights*. New York: Metropolitan Books.

Shamir, Ronen, and Daphna Hacker. 2001. "Colonialism's Civilizing Mission: The Case of the Indian Hemp Drug Commission." *Law & Social Inquiry* 26 (2): 435–61.

Sharm El-Sheikh Fact-Finding Committee Report. 2001. US Department of State Archive. https://2001-2009.state.gov/p/nea/rls/rpt/3060.htm.

Shenhav, Yehouda A., and Nadav Gabay. 2001. "Managing Political Conflicts: The Sociology of State Commissions of Inquiry in Israel." *Israel Studies* 6 (1): 126–56.

Shibli, Jabir. 1946. *The Palestine Reality*. Pamphlet N. New York: Institute of Arab American Affairs.

Shklar, Judith N. 1984. *Ordinary Vices*. Cambridge and London: Belknap Press of Harvard University Press.

Shlaim, Avi. 1988. *Collusion across the Jordan: King Abdullah, the Zionist Movement, and the Partition of Palestine*. Clarendon: Columbia University Press.

———. 1994. "The Oslo Accord." *Journal of Palestine Studies* 23 (3): 24–40.

———. 1995. "The Debate About 1948." *International Journal of Middle East Studies* 27 (3): 287–304.

———. 2010. *Israel and Palestine: Reappraisals, Revisions, Refutations*. New York: Verso.

———. 2017. "Perfidious Albion and Israel-Palestine." *Al Jazeera*, January 19.

Shubayb, Samih. 2001. *Al-Sahafa al-Filastiniyya al-Maqru'a fi al-Shatat*. Ramallah: Muwatin: The Palestinian Organization for the Study of Democracy.

al-Shuqayri, Ahmad. 1969. *Arba'un 'Aman fi al-Haya al-'Arabia wa-l-Dawliyya*. Beirut: Dar al-Nahar li-l-Nashr.

Sikkink, Kathryn. 2011. *The Justice Cascade: How Human Rights Prosecutions Are Changing World Politics*. New York: W. W. Norton & Company.

Simon, Jonathan. 2005. "Parrhesiastic Accountability: Investigatory Commissions and Executive Power in an Age of Terror." *Yale Law Journal* 114 (6): 1419–55.

Simson, H. J. 1937. *British Rule, and Rebellion*. Edinburgh and London: William Blackwood & Sons.

Sinanoglou, Penny. 2009. "British Plans for the Partition of Palestine, 1929–1938." *Historical Journal* 52 (1): 131–52.

Sitze, Adam. 2013. *The Impossible Machine: A Genealogy of South Africa's Truth and Reconciliation Commission*. Ann Arbor: University of Michigan Press.

Slotta, James. 2015. "Phatic Rituals of the Liberal Democratic Polity: Hearing Voices in the Hearings of the Royal Commission on Aboriginal Peoples." *Comparative Studies in Society and History* 57 (1): 130–60.

Sluga, Glenda. 2013. *Internationalism in the Age of Nationalism*. Philadelphia: University of Pennsylvania Press.

Sluga, Glenda, and Patricia Clavin, eds. 2017. *Internationalisms: A Twentieth-Century History*. Cambridge: Cambridge University Press.

Smith, Leonard V. 2018. *Sovereignty at the Paris Peace Conference of 1919*. Oxford: Oxford University Press.

Smith, Neil. 2003. *American Empire: Roosevelt's Geographer and the Prelude to Globalization*. Berkeley: University of California Press.

Sontag, Susan. 2003. *Regarding the Pain of Others*. New York: Farrar, Straus and Giroux.

Stanton, Andrea L. 2013. *"This Is Jerusalem Calling": State Radio in Mandate Palestine*. Austin: University of Texas Press.

Starr, June, and Jane Fishburne Collier, eds. 1989. *History and Power in the Study of Law: New Directions in Legal Anthropology*. Ithaca, NY: Cornell University Press.

Stauffer, Jill. 2015. *Ethical Loneliness: The Injustice of Not Being Heard*. New York: Columbia University Press.

Stocking, George W. 1991. *Victorian Anthropology*. New York: Free Press.

Stoler, Ann Laura. 1995. *Race and the Education of Desire: Foucault's History of Sexuality and the Colonial Order of Things*. Durham, NC: Duke University Press.

———. 2009. *Along the Archival Grain: Epistemic Anxieties and Colonial Common Sense*. Princeton, NJ: Princeton University Press.

———. 2010. *Carnal Knowledge and Imperial Power: Race and the Intimate in Colonial Rule*. Berkeley: California University Press.

Stultz, Newell. 1991. "Evolution of the United Nations Anti-Apartheid Regime." *Human Rights Quarterly* 13 (1): 1–23.

Sultany, Nimer. 2011. "Roundtable on Occupation Law: Part of the Conflict or the Solution? (Part V)." *Jadaliyya*, September 22.

Swedenburg, Ted. 1995. *Memories of Revolt: The 1936–1939 Rebellion and the Palestinian National Past*. Minneapolis: University of Minnesota Press.

Sylvest, Casper. 2008. "'Our Passion for Legality': International Law and Imperialism in Late Nineteenth-Century Britain." *Review of International Studies* 34 (3): 403–23.

———. 2009. *British Liberal Internationalism, 1880–1930: Making Progress?* Manchester, UK: Manchester University Press.

———. 2013. "Legal Evolution and the Redemption of International Law." In *British Liberal Internationalism, 1880–1930*, 61–91. Manchester, UK: Manchester University Press.

Syring, Tom, and Susan Akram, eds. 2014. *Still Waiting for Tomorrow: The Law and Politics of Unresolved Refugee Crises*. Newcastle, UK: Cambridge Scholars Publishing.

"The Taba Negotiations (January 2001)." 2002. *Journal of Palestine Studies* 31 (3): 79–89.

Tabar, Linda. 2007. "Memory, Agency, Counter-Narrative: Testimonies from Jenin Refugee Camp." *Critical Arts* 21 (1): 6–31.

———. 2012. "The 'Urban Redesign' of Jenin Refugee Camp: Humanitarian Intervention and Rational Violence." *Journal of Palestine Studies* 41 (2): 44–61.

Takkenberg, Alex. 1998. *The Status of Palestinian Refugees in International Law*. New York: Clarendon Press.

Tamari, Salim. 2011. *Year of the Locust: A Soldier's Diary and the Erasure of Palestine's Ottoman Past*. Berkeley: University of California Press.

———. 2017. *The Great War and the Remaking of Palestine*. Oakland: University of California Press.

Tamari, Shai. 2008. "Conflict over Palestine: Zionism and the Anglo-American Commission of Inquiry, 1945–1947." MA thesis, University of North Carolina at Chapel Hill.

Tams, Christian J. 2006. "League of Nations." *Max Planck Encyclopedia of Public International Law*. Oxford: Oxford University Press. https://doi.org/10.1093/law:epil/9780199231690/e519.

Tatour, Lana. 2016. "Domination and Resistance in Liberal Settler Colonialism: Palestinians in Israel between the Homeland and the Transnational." PhD diss., University of Warwick.

Tell, Tariq. "Husayn-McMahon Correspondence." In *International Encyclopedia of the First World War*, edited by Ute Daniel, Peter Gatrell, Oliver Janz, Heather Jones, Jennifer Keene, Alan Kramer, and Bill Nasson. Last updated February 27, 2017. https://encyclopedia.1914-1918-online.net/article/husayn-mcmahon _correspondence.

Terdiman, Richard. 1987. "Translator's Introduction: The Force of Law: Toward a Sociology of the Juridical Field." *Hastings Law Journal* 38 (5): 805–13.

Thomas, Greg. 2007. *The Sexual Demon of Colonial Power: Pan-African Embodiment and Erotic Schemes of Empire*. Bloomington: Indiana University Press.

Thomas, Martin. 2005. *The French Empire Between the Wars: Imperialism, Politics and Society*. Manchester, UK: Manchester University Press.

Thomas, Peter. 2018. "Refiguring the Subaltern." *Political Theory* 46 (6): 861–84.

Thompson, Edward Palmer. 1975. *Whigs and Hunters: The Origin of the Black Act*. New York: Pantheon Books.

Thompson, Elizabeth F. 2009. "Justice Interrupted: Historical Perspectives on Promoting Democracy in the Middle East." United States Institute of Peace, Special Report 225. Washington DC. https://www.usip.org/publications/2009/06/justice -interrupted-historical-perspectives-promoting-democracy-middle-east.

———. 2013. *Justice Interrupted: The Struggle for Constitutional Government in the Middle East*. Boston: Harvard University Press.

———. 2015. "Rashid Rida and the 1920 Syrian-Arab Constitution: How the French Mandate Undermined Islamic Liberalism." In *The Routledge Handbook of the History of the Middle East Mandates*, edited by Cyrus Schayegh and Andrew Arsan, 244–57. New York: Routledge.

Thörn, Håkan. 2009. "The Meaning(s) of Solidarity: Narratives of Anti-Apartheid Activism." *Journal of Southern African Studies* 35 (2): 417–36.

Throntveit, Trygve. 2011. "What Was Wilson Thinking? A Review of the Literature on Wilson and World Politics." *White House Studies* 10 (4): 460–74.

Ticktin, Miriam. 2006. "Where Ethics and Politics Meet: The Violence of Humanitarianism in France." *American Ethnologist* 33 (1): 33–49.

Tilley, Virginia. 2012. *Beyond Occupation: Apartheid, Colonialism and International Law in the Occupied Palestinian Territories*. New York: Pluto Press.

Tomeh, George. 1974. "When the UN Dropped the Palestinian Question." *Journal of Palestine Studies* 4 (1): 15–30.

Tonkin, Hannah, and Dapo Akande. 2011. "International Commissions of Inquiry: A New Form of Adjudication?" *EJIL: Talk*. https://www.ejiltalk.org/international -commissions-of-inquiry-a-new-form-of-adjudication/.

Tooze, Adam. 2014. *The Deluge: The Great War and the Remaking of Global Order, 1916–1931.* London: Penguin.

Toynbee, Arnold J. 1936. *Survey of International Affairs, 1935.* London: Oxford University Press.

Tress, Madeleine. 1988. "The Role of the Peasantry in the Palestine Revolt, 1936–1939." *Peasant Studies* 15 (3): 161–90.

Trouillot, Michel-Rolph. 1995. *Silencing the Past: Power and the Production of History.* Boston: Beacon Press.

Tully, James. 1995. *Strange Multiplicity: Constitutionalism in an Age of Diversity.* Cambridge: Cambridge University Press.

Tusan, Michelle. 2014. "'Crimes against Humanity': Human Rights, the British Empire, and the Origins of the Response to the Armenian Genocide." *American Historical Review* 119 (1): 47–77.

———. 2015. "Humanitarianism, Genocide and Liberalism." *Journal of Genocide Research* 17 (1): 83–105.

Tutu, Archbishop Desmond. 2008. "Statement by Archbishop Desmond Tutu, Leader of the High Level Fact-Finding Mission into events at Beit Hanoun on 8 November 2006." https://www2.ohchr.org/english/bodies/hrcouncil/docs/Statement_by_Archbishop_Desmond_Tutu.pdf.

Tutu, Archbishop Desmond, and Christine Chinkin. 2008. "Human Rights Council Fact-Finding Mission into Events in Beit Hanoun—Press Conference (Excerpts)." In *Human Rights Council Fact-Finding Mission into Events in Beit Hanoun.* Gaza City. https://unispal.un.org/DPA/DPR/unispal.nsf/0/98977AD154087BEC85257460006F143D.

United Nations Committee on the Exercise of the Inalienable Rights of the Palestinian People (CEIRPP). 1979. "The Right of Self-Determination of the Palestinian People, Question of Palestine." [ST/SG/SER.F/3]. https://www.un.org/unispal/document/auto-insert-196558/.

United Nations General Assembly (UNGA). 1947. *Special Committee on Palestine, Report of the First Committee.* Second Session, 70th Meeting, A/307. May 13. https://unispal.un.org/DPA/DPR/unispal.nsf/0/06F1E89B3B48291B802564B40049CC67.

———. 1967a. "Fifth Emergency Special Assembly." 1558th Plenary Meeting, A/PV.1558. July 21.

———. 1967b. "Twenty-Second, Official Records." 1586th Plenary Meeting, A/PV.1586. October 11.

———. 1968a. "2443 (XXIII) Respect for and Implementation of Human Rights in the Occupied Territories." A/RES/2443 (XXIII). December 19.

———. 1968b. "Twenty-Third Session, Official Records." 1749th Plenary Meeting, A/PV/1749. December 19.

———. 1969a. "Twenty-Fourth Session, Official Records." 1753rd Plenary Meeting, A/PV.1753. September 16.

———. 1969b. "Twenty-Fourth Session, Official Records." 1755th Plenary Meeting A/PV.1755. September 18.

———. 1969c. "Twenty-Fourth Session, Official Records." 1775th Plenary Meeting A/PV.1775. October 2.

———. 1970a. "Report of the Special Committee to Investigate Israeli Practices Affecting the Human Rights of the Population of the Occupied Territories." 25th Session, A/8089. October 5.

———. 1970b. "Report of the Special Committee to Investigate Israeli Practices Affecting the Human Rights of the Population of the Occupied Territories." Special Political Committee, 25th Session, 744th Meeting, A/SPC/SR.744. December 7.

———. 1970c. "Report of the Special Committee to Investigate Israeli Practices Affecting the Human Rights of the Population of the Occupied Territories (continued)." Special Political Committee, 25th Session, 746th Meeting, A/SPC/SR.746. December 8.

———. 1970d. "Report of the Special Committee to Investigate Israeli Practices Affecting the Human Rights of the Population of the Occupied Territories (continued)." Special Political Committee, 25th Session, 747th Meeting, A/SPC/SR.747. December 9.

———. 1970e. "Report of the Special Committee to Investigate Israeli Practices Affecting the Human Rights of the Population of the Occupied Territories (continued)." Special Political Committee, 25th Session, 748th Meeting, A/SPC/SR.748. December 10.

———. 1970f. "Report of the Special Committee to Investigate Israeli Practices Affecting the Human Rights of the Population of the Occupied Territories (continued)." Special Political Committee, 25th Session, 749th Meeting, A/SPC/SR.749. December 10.

———. 1970g. "Report of the Special Committee to Investigate Israeli Practices Affecting the Human Rights of the Population of the Occupied Territories (continued)." Special Political Committee, 25th Session, 751th Meeting, A/SPC/SR.751. December 11.

———. 1970h. "Resolution 2727, Report of the Special Committee to Investigate Israeli Practices Affecting the Human Rights of the Population of the Occupied Territories." 25th Session, A/RES/2727(XXV). December 15.

———. 1970i. "Twenty-Fifth Session, Official Records." 1931st Plenary Meeting, A/PV.1931. December 15.

———. 1971a. "Commission on Human Rights: Report on 27th Session Supplement No. 4, E/4949 (SUPP)-E/CN.4/1068." Economic and Social Council, February 22.

———. 1971b. "Twenty-Sixth Session, Official Records." 1934th Plenary Meeting, A/PV.1934. September 21.

———. 1971c. "Twenty-Sixth Session, Official Records." 1951st Plenary Meeting, A/PV.1951. October 4.

———. 1971d. "Twenty-Sixth Session Official Records." Special Political Committee, 26th Session, 782nd Meeting, A/SPC/SR.782. November 18.

———. 1971e. "Twenty-Sixth Session, Official Records." 1999th Plenary Meeting, A/PV.1999. December 3.

———. 1971f. "Twenty-Sixth Session Official Records." Special Political Committee, 26th Session, A/SPC/SR.798. December 13.

———. 1971g. "Twenty-Sixth Session Official Records." Special Political Committee, 26th Session, 799th Meeting, A/SPC/SR.799. December 14.

———. 1971h. "Twenty-Sixth Session, Official Records." 2027th Plenary Meeting, A/PV.2027. December 20.

———. 1973a. "Report of the Special Committee to Investigate Israeli Practices Affecting the Human Rights of the Population of the Occupied Territories." 28th Session, A/9148. October 25.

———. 1973b. "Resolution 3070 (XXVIII), Importance of the Universal Realization of the Right of Peoples to Self-Determination and of the Speedy Granting of Independence to Colonial Countries and Peoples for the Effective Guarantee and Observance of Human Rights." 28th Session, A/RES/3070. November 30.

———. 1974a. "Twenty-Ninth Session, Official Records." 2282nd Plenary Meeting, A/PV. 2282 and Corr.1. November 13.

———. 1974b. "Resolution 3236 (XXIX), Question of Palestine." 29th Session, A/RES/3236. November 22.

———. 1974c. "Resolution 3246 (XXIX), Importance of the Universal Realization of the Right of Peoples to Self-Determination and of the Speedy Granting of Independence to Colonial Countries and Peoples for the Effective Guarantee and Observance of Human Rights." 2393rd Plenary Meeting, A/RES/3246 (XXIX). November 29.

———. 1975a. "Question of Palestine." 2399th Plenary Meeting, A/RES/3376 (XXX). November 10.

———. 1975b. "Thirtieth Session, Official Records." 2399th Plenary Meeting, A/PV.2399. November 10.

———. 1977. "Resolution 32/130, Alternative Approaches and Ways and Means within the United Nations System for Improving the Effective Enjoyment of Human Rights and Fundamental Freedoms." 32nd Session, A/RES/32/130. December 16.

———. 1988a. "Report of the Secretary-General [on the Convening of an International Peace Conference on the Middle East]." 43rd Session, A/43/691. September 30.

———. 1988b. "Report of the Special Committee to Investigate Israeli Practices Affecting the Human Rights of the Population of the Occupied Territories." 43rd Session, A/43/694. October 24.

———. 1989a. "Report of the Special Committee to Investigate Israeli Practices Affecting the Human Rights of the Population of the Occupied Territories (continued)." Special Political Committee, 44th Session, 23rd Meeting, A/SPC/44/SR.23. November 21.

———. 1989b. "Provisional Verbatim Record of the Seventy Eight Meeting." 44th Session of the General Assembly, A/44/PV.78. December 21.

———. 1991. "Report of the Special Committee to Investigate Israeli Practices Affecting the Human Rights of the Palestinian People and Other Arabs of the Occupied Territories." 28th Meeting. A/SPC/46/SP.28. November 26.

———. 1993. "Report of the Special Committee to Investigate Israeli Practices Affecting the Human Rights of the Population of the Occupied Territories." 48th Session, A/48/557. November 1.

———. 2002. "Report of the Secretary-General Prepared Pursuant to General Assembly Resolution ES-10/10, Agenda Item 5: Illegal Israeli Actions in Occupied East Jerusalem and the Rest of the Occupied Palestinian Territory." 10th Emergency Special Session, A/ES-10/186. July 30.

———. 2007a. "Item 2 of the Provisional Agenda, Implementation of General Assembly Resolution 60/251 of 15 March 2006 Entitled 'Human Rights Council.'" 4th Session, A/HRC/4/17. January 29.

———. 2007b. "Agenda Item 2, Implementation of General Assembly Resolution 60/251 of 15 March 2006 Entitled 'Human Rights Council.'" 5th Session, A/HRC/5/11. June 8.

———. 2007c. "Question of Palestine." 62nd Session, A/62/100 Corr. 1 and Add. 1. June 15.

———. 2007d. "Agenda Item 2, Implementation of General Assembly Resolution 60/251 of 15 March 2006 Entitled 'Human Rights Council.'" 5th Session, A/HRC/5/20. June 18.

———. 2008. "Agenda Item 7, Human Rights Situation in Palestine and Other Occupied Arab Territories." 9th Session, A/HRC/9/26. September 1.

———. 2009. "Agenda Item 7, Report of the United Nations Fact-Finding Mission on the Gaza Conflict." 12th Session, A/HRC/12/48. September 25.

———. 2013. "Report of the Independent International Commission of Inquiry on the Syrian Arab Republic." 22nd Session, A/HRC/22/59. February 5.

United Nations Human Rights Council. 2002. "Commission on Human Rights, Agenda Item 4, Report of the United Nations High Commissioner for Human Rights and Follow-up to the World Conference on Human Rights." 58th Session, E/CN.4/2002/184. April 24.

————. 2009a. "United Nations Fact Finding Mission on the Gaza Conflict, Public Hearings—Gaza City, Morning Session." June 28. https://www.un.org/webcast /unhrc/archive.asp?go=041. Unofficial transcript.

————. 2009b. "United Nations Fact-Finding Mission on the Gaza Conflict, Public Hearings—Gaza City, Morning Session." June 29. http://oldltd.mithyalabs.com /doc/082548/.

————. 2009c. "United Nations Fact-Finding Mission on the Gaza Conflict, Public Hearings—Gaza City, Morning Session." June 29. http://oldltd.mithyalabs.com /doc/808cab/.

————. 2009d. "United Nations Fact-Finding Mission on the Gaza Conflict, Public Hearings—Gaza City, Afternoon Session." June 29. https://www.ohchr.org /Documents/HRBodies/HRCouncil/SpecialSession/Session9/Transcript 29062009PM.doc

————. 2017. "Report of the Secretary-General: Human Rights Situation in the Occupied Palestinian Territory, including East Jerusalem." 34th Session, A/ HRC/34/38. April 13.

————. 2018. "Statement by UN High Commissioner for Human Rights Zeid Ra'ad Al Hussein," May 18. https://www.ohchr.org/EN/HRBodies/HRC/Pages/News Detail.aspx?NewsID=23100&LangID=E.

————. n.d. "International Commissions of Inquiry, Commissions on Human Rights, Fact-Finding Missions and other Investigations." Accessed January 10, 2020. https://www.ohchr.org/EN/HRBodies/HRC/Pages/COIs.aspx.

————. n.d. "The United Nations Commission of Inquiry on the 2018 Protests in the Occupied Palestinian Territory." Accessed January 4, 2020. https://www.ohchr .org/EN/HRBodies/HRC/CoIOPT/Pages/OPT.aspx

United Nations Human Rights Office of the High Commissioner (OHCHR). 2008. "UN Expert Praises Nicaragua for Formally Confirming Land Ownership for Indigenous Group." OHCHR. December 17.

————. 2018. "Report of Independent International Fact-Finding Mission on Myanmar." 39th Session, A/HRC/39/64. September 12.

————. n.d. "International Day of Solidarity with the Palestinian People, 29 November." United Nations. Accessed September 2, 2019. https://www.un.org/en /observances/international-day-of-solidarity-with-the-palestinian-people.

United Nations Relief and Works Agency (UNRWA). 2019. "UNRWA in Figures 2018–2019." March 8.

————. n.d. "Where We Work, Lebanon." Accessed November 16, 2018. https://www .unrwa.org/where-we-work/lebanon.

United Nations Security Council (UNSC). 1967a. "Resolution 242." S/RES/242. November 22. http://www.un.org/en/ga/search/view_doc.asp?symbol=S/RES /242%281967%29.

———. 1967b. "Resolution 237 (1967)." S/RES/237. June 16.

———. 2000. "Resolution 1322 (2000)." S/RES/1322. October 7.

———. 2002a. "Resolution 1405 (2002)." 4516th Meeting, S/RES/1405. April 19.

———. 2002b. "Jenin Refugee Camp Fact-Finding Team: Letter from the Secretary-General to the President of the Security Council." S/2002/504. May 1 https://relief web.int/report/israel/jenin-refugee-camp-fact-finding-team-letter-secretary -general-president-security.

UN Women. 2015. "The Story of Resolution 1325 | Women, Peace and Security," https://www.youtube.com/watch?v=mZH5hIOyU4Y.

———. 2016. "UN Women Releases CEDAW for Youth." December 19. https:// www.unwomen.org/en/news/stories/2016/12/un-women-releases-cedaw-for -youth.

Valverde, Mariana. 2003. "'Which Side Are You On?' Uses of the Everyday in Socio-legal Scholarship." *Political and Legal Anthropology Review* 26 (1): 86–98.

Verdery, Richard N. 1971. "Arab 'Disturbances' and the Commissions of Inquiry." In *The Transformation of Palestine: Essays on the Origin and Development of the Arab-Israeli Conflict*, edited by Ibrahim A. Abu-Lughod and Arnold Toynbee, 275–304. Evanston, IL: Northwestern University Press.

Vitalis, Robert. 2013. "The Midnight Ride of Kwame Nkrumah and Other Fables of Bandung (Ban-Doong)." *Humanity: An International Journal of Human Rights, Humanitarianism, and Development* 4 (2): 261–88.

Walzer, Michael. 2015. *Just and Unjust Wars: A Moral Argument with Historical Illustrations*. 5th ed. New York: Basic Books.

Wambaugh, Sarah. 1933. *Plebiscites Since the World War: With a Collection of Official Documents*. Washington: Carnegie Endowment for International Peace.

Waqayyan, Khalifah. 2012. *Al-Qadiyya al-ʿArabiyya fi Ashiʿr al-Kuwayti*. 2nd ed. Kuwait: Khalifah ʿAbdallah al-Waqayyan.

Wasserstein, Bernard. 1977. "'Clipping the Claws of the Colonisers': Arab Officials in the Government of Palestine, 1917–48." *Middle Eastern Studies* 13 (2): 171–94.

Watenpaugh, Keith David. 2006. *Being Modern in the Middle East: Revolution, Nationalism, Colonialism, and the Arab Middle Class*. Princeton, NJ, and Oxford: Princeton University Press.

———. 2015. *Bread from Stones: The Middle East and the Making of Modern Humanitarianism*. Oakland: University of California Press.

Watson, Geoffrey. 2000. *The Oslo Accords: International Law and the Israeli–Palestinian Peace Agreements*. Oxford: Oxford University Press.

Weber, Charlotte. 2008. "Between Nationalism and Feminism: The Eastern Women's Congresses of 1930 and 1932." *Journal of Middle East Women's Studies* 4 (1): 83–106.

Weeramantry, Christopher, and Nathaniel Berman. 1999. "The Grotius Lecture Series." *American University International Law Review* 14 (6): 1515–69.

Weissbrodt, David, and Georgina Mahoney. 1986. "International Legal Action Against Apartheid." *Law and Inequality* 4: 485–508.

Wells, John H.G. 1936. *The Shape of Things to Come: The Ultimate Revolution*. New York: Macmillan.

Wertheim, Stephen. 2012. "The League of Nations: A Retreat from International Law?" *Journal of Global History* 7 (2): 210–32.

Wheatley, Natasha. 2015. "Mandatory Interpretation: Legal Hermeneutics and the New International Order in Arab and Jewish Petitions to the League of Nations." *Past & Present* 227 (1): 205–48.

———. 2017. "New Subjects in International Law and Order." In *Internationalisms: A Twentieth-Century History*, edited by Glenda Sluga and Patricia Clavin, 265–86. Cambridge: Cambridge University Press.

Wildangel, Rene. 2004. "The Emergence of the Public: Arab Palestinian Media in British Mandate Palestine 1929–1945." In *History of Printing and Publishing in the Languages and Countries of the Middle East*, edited by Philip Sadgrove. Oxford: Oxford University Press.

Wilder, Gary. 2005. *The French Imperial Nation-State: Negritude and Colonial Humanism between the Two World Wars*. Chicago: University of Chicago Press.

Wilke, Christiane. 2009. "Reconsecrating the Temple of Justice: Invocations of Civilization and Humanity in the Nuremberg Justice Case." *Canadian Journal of Law and Society* 24: 181–201.

Williams, Francis. 1971. "Prime Minister Attlee on President Truman's Palestine Policy, 1945–1946." In *From Haven to Conquest: Readings in Zionism and the Palestine Problem until 1948*, edited by Walid Khalidi. Beirut: Institute for Palestine Studies.

Wilson, Evan M. 1979. *Decision on Palestine: How the U.S. Came to Recognize Israel*. Stanford, CA: Hoover Institution Press.

Wilson, Richard. 2001. *The Politics of Truth and Reconciliation in South Africa: Legitimizing the Post-Apartheid State*. Cambridge: Cambridge University Press.

———. 2005. "Judging History: The Historical Record of the International Criminal Tribunal for the Former Yugoslavia." *Human Rights Quarterly* 27 (3): 908–42.

———. 2011. *Writing History in International Criminal Trials*. Cambridge: Cambridge University Press.

———. 2017. *Incitement on Trial: Prosecuting International Speech Crimes*. Cambridge: Cambridge University Press.

Wilson, Woodrow. 1918a. "President Wilson's Address to Congress, Analyzing German and Austrian Peace Utterances," *World War I Document Archive*. https://wwi.lib.byu.edu/index.php/President_Wilson's_Address_to_Congress,_Analyzing_German_and_Austrian_Peace_Utterances.

———. 1918b. "President Woodrow Wilson's Fourteen Points." Avalon Project, Yale Law School. http://avalon.law.yale.edu/20th_century/wilson14.asp.

Wyrtzen, Jonathan. 2016. *Making Morocco: Colonial Intervention and the Politics of Identity.* Ithaca, NY, and London: Cornell University Press.

Yaqub, Nadia. 2018. *Palestinian Cinema in the Days of Revolution.* Austin: University of Texas.

Yazbak, Mahmoud. 2000. "From Poverty to Revolt: Economic Factors in the Outbreak of the 1936 Rebellion in Palestine." *Middle Eastern Studies* 36 (3): 93–113.

Yildirim, Onur. 2006. *Diplomacy and Displacement: Reconsidering the Turco-Greek Exchange of Populations, 1922–1934.* London: Routledge.

Zahlan, Rosemarie Said. 2009. *Palestine and the Gulf States: The Presence at the Table.* New York: Routledge.

Zelden, Charles L. 1997. "The Judge Intuitive: The Life and Judicial Philosophy of Joseph C. Hutcheson, Jr." *South Texas Law Review* 39: 905–17.

Zerilli, Linda M. G. 2015. "Feminist Critiques of Liberalism." In *The Cambridge Companion to Liberalism*, edited by Steven Wall, 355–80. Cambridge: Cambridge University Press.

Zuʿaytir, Akram. 1992. *Al-Haraka al-Wataniyya al-Filastiniyya, 1935–1939: Yowmiyat Akram Zuʿaytir.* Beirut: Institute of Palestine Studies.

Zuʿaytir, Akram, and Bayan Nuwaihid al-Hout. 1984. *Wathaʾiq al-Haraka al-Wataniyya al-Filastiniyya, 1918–1939. Min Awraq Akram Zuʿaytir.* Beirut: Institute of Palestine Studies.

# Index

Istiqlal (Independence) Party [Palestine British mandate], 94
Italy: Abyssinia Crisis (1936) of, 73, 76–78, 79; annexation of Ethiopia by, 73; Arabic newspapers on Libyans' struggle against, 75

Jabalya refugee camp (Gaza Strip), 229
Jacobson, Eddie, 114
Jagland, Thorbjoern, 189
Jamali, Fadel, 119, 120
Japan, 73
Jarring, Gunnar, 146
Jawhariyyeh, Wasif, 88, 90–91
Jenin (West Bank): Israeli shelling of, 210, 213, 214; Jenin refugee camp destroyed, 215, 218–19; witnessing and testimonies on shelling of, 217–21
*Jenin, Jenin* (documentary), 220
"Jeningrad" (poetry and music), 219
Jerusalem: Arab control established in 636 CE over, 127; Jordanian UN delegate condemning Israel occupation of, 161; military occupation of east, 10, 21, 145; Sharon's visit to Haram Al-Sharif (Al-Aqsa Mosque compound) in, 185–87, 189, 191, 192–93
Jewish immigration: British mandate policies encouraging, 135; comparing Armenian refugee immigration to, 122; increasing rates (1933–1936) and onward of, 296n182; 100,000 certificates issued by AACI for, 134–35, 142; Palestine pressured by AACI to allow, 117; Passfield White Paper (1930) on limiting, 282n141; Phillip Hitti on discourse linking Jewish state to, 121–25. *See also* Jewish refugees
Jewish minorities (Palestine): Arab Office proposals to AACI including full citizenship of, 114, 129–30,

133–34, 140, 294n144; Arab petitions (1919) on rights and protections of, 52–54; King-Crane Commission (1919) concerns rights of, 57–61, 68; Syrian-Arab constitution (1920) protection of, 63
Jewish national home: Balfour Declaration's recommendation of, 50–51, 68, 127–28; establishment of Israel (1948) as a, 10; Hussein–McMahon correspondence (1915–1916) on, 65; League of Nations' charter committing to a, 2; opposition of King-Crane Commission's Arab representation to, 43, 50–52; Phillip Hitti on discourse linking Jewish refugees to, 121–25; Yale's recommendation (1919) on creating, 60–61. *See also* Israel
Jewish people: AACI tasked with examining position in Europe of the, 112; IAAA on politicization of suffering by the, 118; Lloyd George's comparison of Arabs (1919) and, 56; Palestinian distinction between Zionists and indigenous, 51–52; refusing suffering as political currency of the, 116–19; as 31 percent of Palestine (1946) population, 135; Truman's sympathy toward, 115–16. *See also* suffering
Jewish refugees: AACI criticism of Hourani's lack of sympathy to, 131–32; appeal of the humanitarian crisis of the, 140–43; injustice of causing suffering to alleviate suffering of, 141; Palestinian Arabs on sharing humanitarian relief for, 119–25, 130, 131–32, 294n154; Transjordan statement on return to Europe by the, 291n97; Western hypocrisy regarding universal problem of, 117, 118–19, 122–23. *See also* Jewish immigration

Made in United States
Orlando, FL
26 September 2024

51975057R00259